Blue Revolution

Blue Revolution
Integrated Land and Water Resource Management

SECOND EDITION

Ian R Calder

London • Sterling, VA

Second edition first published by Earthscan
in the UK and the USA in 2005
Reprinted 2006
First edition 1999

ISBN-10: 1 84407 239 8 Paperback

ISBN-13: 978 1 84407 239 2 Paperback

Typesetting by MapSet Ltd, Gateshead, UK
Printed and bound in the UK by Bath Press
Cover design by Yvonne Booth

For a full list of publications please contact:

Earthscan
8–12 Camden High Street
London, NW1 0JH, UK
Tel: +44 (0)20 7387 8558
Fax: +44 (0)20 7387 8998
Email: earthinfo@earthscan.co.uk
Web: **www.earthscan.co.uk**

A catalogue record for this book is available from the British Library

Library of Congress Cataloging-in-Publication Data

Calder, Ian R.
  Blue revolution : integrated land and water resources management / by Ian R.
  Calder.— 2nd ed.
       p. cm.
  Includes bibliographical references and index.
  ISBN 1-84407-239-8
    1. Integrated water development. 2. Land use—Environmental aspects. I. Title.
  TC405.C14 2005
  333.91—dc22

                                                                        2005003796

Earthscan is an imprint of James & James (Science Publishers) Ltd and publishes in
association with the International Institute for Environment and Development.

This book is printed on elemental chlorine free paper

Contents

Boxes, Tables, Figures and Plates

BOXES

TABLES

FIGURES

PLATES

Note: Sources for boxes, tables, figures and plates are given immediately below the material. Where no source is attributed the material was supplied by the author for this publication.

Acronyms and Abbreviations

AMP	asset management planning
BEA	Bureau of Economic Analysis (USA)
CAE	Chinese Academy of Engineering
CAQDAS	computer-assisted qualitative data analysis software
CAMS	catchment abstraction management strategies
CARE	conservation, amenity, recreation and environment
CCICED	China Council for International Cooperation on Environment and Development
CDM	Clean Development Mechanism
CG	consultative group
CGIAR	Consultative Group on International Agriculture Research
CIFOR	Center for International Forestry Research
CLUWRR	Centre for Land Use and Water Resources Research
CMP	Catchment Management Plan (of NRA, UK)
COM	Council of Ministers
CPSS	collaborative planning support system
CRP	Conservation Reserve Program
CSIRO	Commonwealth Scientific and Industrial Research Organization (Australia)
CUSW	Cebu Uniting for Sustainable Water
DETR	Department of Environment, Transport and the Regions (UK)
DFID	Department for International Development (formerly ODA) (UK)
DGIS	Netherlands Government Directorate General for International Cooperation
DPJ	Democratic Party of Japan
DSS	decision support system
DTI	Department of Trade and Industry (UK)
DWAF	Department of Water Affairs and Forestry (South Africa)
EA	Environment Agency (UK)
EEA	European Environment Agency
EEB	European Environmental Bureau
EPA	Environmental Protection Agency (USA)
ETFRN	European Tropical Forest Research Network
FAO	Food and Agriculture Organization (United Nations)

FRP	Forestry Research Programme (DFID)
GARNET	Global Applied Research Network
GCM	global circulation model
GDP	gross domestic product
GHG	greenhouse gas
GIS	geographic information system
GLASOD	Global Assessment of Soil Degradation Project
GMES	Global Monitoring for Environment and Security
GNP	gross national product
GTZ	Deutsche Gessellschaft für Technische Zusammenarbeit (Germany)
GUI	graphical user interface
GWP	Global Water Partnership
HDI	human development index
HIPC	heavily indebted poor countries
HIV/AIDS	human immunodeficiency virus/acquired immunodeficiency syndrome
HR	Hydraulics Research
HYLUC	hydrological land use change model
IAHS	International Association for Hydrological Science
IAWQ	International Association of Water Quality
ICID	International Commission on Irrigation and Drainage
ICOLD	International Commission on Large Dams
ICRAF	International Centre for Research in Agroforestry
ICRISAT	International Crops Research Institute for the Semi Arid Tropics
ICWE	International Conference on Water and the Environment
IEESA	Integrated Economic and Environmental Satellite Account
IET	international emissions trading
IFAD	International Fund for Agricultural Development
IFPRI	International Food Policy Research Institute
IH	Institute of Hydrology
IHP	International Hydrology Programme
IIED	International Institute for Environment and Development
IIMI	International Irrigation Management Institute
IK	indigenous knowledge
ILWRM	integrated land and water resource management
IPPC	Intergovernmental Panel on Climate Change
IPTRID	International Program on Technology Research in Irrigation and Drainage
IRC	International Water and Sanitation Centre
IUCN	International Union for Conservation of Nature
IWMI	International Water Management Institute
IWRM	integrated water resource management
JASS	*Journal of Artificial Societies and Social Simulation*
LAI	Leaf Area Index
LEAP	local environment agency plan

LUC	land use change model
LUWRR	land use and water resources research
MDG	millennium development goals
MES	markets for environmental services
MRC	Mekong River Commission (Vietnam)
NFPP	Natural Forest Protection Programme (China)
NGO	non-governmental organization
NORAD	Norwegian Agency for International Development
NRA	National Rivers Authority
NRBAP	Nile River Basin Action Plan
NWA	National Water Act (RSA)
ODA	Overseas Development Administration (now DFID)
ODI	Overseas Development Institute
OECD	Organisation for Economic Co-operation and Development
OFWAT	Office of Water Services
PARIS21	Partnership in Statistics for Development in the 21st Century
PES	payments for environmental services
PPF	production possibility frontier
PSM	problem structuring method
RSA	Republic of South Africa
RSPB	Royal Society for the Protection of Birds (UK)
RUPES	rewarding the upland poor for environmental services
SAC	structural adjustment credit
SAL	structural adjustment loan
SAP	Structural Adjustment Programme
SDR	sediment delivery ratio
SEI	Stockholm Environment Institute (Sweden)
SFA	State Forestry Administration (China)
SFRA	stream flow reduction activity
SHE	Système Hydrologique Européen
SHETRAN	Système Hydrologique Européen Transport
SIWI	Stockholm International Water Institute (Sweden)
SLCP	Sloping Land Conversion Programme (China)
SOAS	School of Oriental and African Studies, University of London (UK)
SRES	Special Report on Emission Scenarios
SSSI	site of special scientific interest
SWIM	System-Wide Initiative on Water Management
TAC	Technical Advisory Committee
TECCONILE	Technical Cooperation Committee for the Promotion of the Development and Environmental Protection of the Nile Basin
THED	Theory of Himalayan Environmental Degradation
TWE	transferable water entitlement
UNCED	United Nations Conference on the Environment and Development

UNDP	United Nations Development Programme
UNEP	United Nations Environment Programme
UNESCO	United Nations Educational, Scientific and Cultural Organization
UNFCCC	United Nations Framework Convention on Climate Change
UNIDO	United Nations Industrial Development Organization
USDA	US Department of Agriculture
USFS	United States Forest Service
USLE	Universal Soil Loss Equation
VKI	Water Quality Institute (Denmark)
WAG	Water Use and Growth (Model)
WATSAN	Water and Sanitation
WB	World Bank
WBCSD	World Business Council for Sustainable Development
WCD	World Commission on Dams
WEDC	Water Engineering and Development Centre
WFD	Water Framework Directive
WHO	World Health Organization
WRC(SA)	Water Research Commission (South Africa)
WRINCLE	Water Resources: INfluence of CLimate change in Europe project
WRSRL	Water Resource Systems Research Laboratory
WSSCC	Water Supply and Sanitation Collaborative Council
WTP	willingness to pay
WWC	World Water Council
WWF	World Wide Fund For Nature
ZINWA	Zimbabwe National Water Authority

Preface

The modern history of water resource and catchment management can be traced from its origins in the achievements of the 19th century engineers whose great civil engineering feats provided wholesome water to the world's growing and industrializing cities. Probably no other single factor contributed as much to the improved quality of life, and life expectancy, of city dwellers as this gift of safe water and the provision of water-based sanitation systems which then became possible. In those days the surface water catchments, or gathering grounds, were managed to assure the pristine quality of the water. Human occupation was regarded with distrust: it was at best a necessary evil, which had to be contained as far as possible. The success of the engineering approach was not just limited to water supply. The engineer had the ability to 'tame the river'. Through impoundments, barrages and sluices, river flow from catchments could be regulated to reduce floods and to provide more water during times of drought. The Tennessee Valley Authority, which was established in 1933 to control the Tennessee River, a tributary of the Ohio in the USA, perhaps best exemplifies this approach.

More recently the ethos of catchment and water resource management has shifted away from the tightly focused engineering viewpoint. At the same time our perceptions of what we mean by a catchment have subtly changed. Originally 'catchment' may have meant just the headwaters where impoundments had been built to capture water for supply, irrigation and hydroelectricity purposes. Now catchments are regarded more as the hydrological units which occupy the whole land surface of the globe. As demands on water increase this has to be the case, for upland headwater catchments can no longer meet our needs. The need to recycle water, together with the need to exploit groundwater, means that more and more we regard every part of the land surface of the globe as part of a catchment which can either supply water or receive our waste water. With this new perception people and the environment can no longer be ignored, and both the human and environmental dimensions are achieving much greater prominence in catchment and water resource management. Indeed, in the preface to the first edition of this book, it was stated that the balance had shifted to such an extent that although 'watershed' appeared in the title of one development project initiated in India in 1997 (the Karnataka Watersheds Development Project, funded by the Department for International Development (DFID)) virtually no reference was made to water in the original project document. More recently the same type of development project implemented in Andra Pradesh, Madhya Pradesh and Orissa has been termed a 'rural livelihood project'. Whatever the name, there are great dangers in moving the balance too far and implementing these projects without a proper understanding of the water resource constraints – a particular issue that has been updated in this new edition of *Blue Revolution*.

But this book does not aim to be prescriptive about how the balance should be obtained nor on how water resource management should be carried out. Its purpose is to discuss the issues and to provide new information on land use and water interactions and the policy instruments and management tools that are now becoming available so that those who are involved in and affected by what is now being termed integrated land and water resource management (ILWRM) can make the best decisions.

The perception of ILWRM that is outlined here is inevitably influenced by the background of the author, whose experience lies in research in the physical sciences, management of water resources in a developing country (Malawi) and through acting as the hydrological adviser to a national overseas development organization (ODA, now DFID). The country case studies of the revolution in the way land and water are managed are those that the author knows best; omission of studies does not imply that equally or more important developments may not be taking place in other countries. The perceptions and world-views of economists, ecologists and sociologists, although of course equally valid, are probably not adequately represented here. Clearly for this holistic or systemic approach to land and water resource management to succeed, these views must be integrated and properly balanced. Other components also need to be included. In the first edition of *Blue Revolution* the need was expressed for the incorporation of water and sanitation (WATSAN) components within ILWRM. This has subsequently become even more pressing with the large-scale implementation of piped water and sanitation schemes in many countries of the developing world to meet the Millennium Development Goals (MDGs). Without taking proper account of the water resource constraints and the economic (not just capital but maintenance) and environmental costs associated with these schemes we may be building up long term problems of river pollution and environmental damage similar to those brought about in the developed world at the time of the industrial revolution, problems that we are only now starting to address.

For the future the key questions of climate change and meeting the food needs of the world's growing population are challenges for the blue revolution.

It could be argued that in paleo-climates in the past, with higher CO_2 levels, when the climate and ocean energy transfer systems were in overdrive, transferring heat energy from the equator to the poles, there were no deserts and fewer of the cold tundra regions we have now. Overall, this scenario might well have suited us better, in terms of living conditions and potential food production, than our present climate. No one likes change or unpredictability, and too rapid a change, making adaptation difficult, is clearly not what we want. But given the choice of global warming or cooling, surely the former is better than the latter?

Although the human race appears capable of almost unlimited ingenuity when faced with new challenges, the Malthusian concerns of meeting the food needs of a growing world population cannot easily be dismissed. Malin Falkenmark has raised these sometimes unpopular questions and has suggested what may be an equally unpopular solution: that ultimately we will need to consider enlarging the rain-fed agricultural areas of the world by moving into the rangelands or the forests.

Acknowledgements

The author wishes to acknowledge all those who have contributed and are contributing to the blue revolution. The ideas presented in this book have arisen from many sources and many disciplines and apologies are given to those whose citations may have inadvertently been omitted. One of the first applications of the term 'blue revolution' known to the author was by Tony Milburn, executive director of the International Association of Water Quality (IAWQ), at the Stockholm Water Symposium in 1996 (Milburn, 1997). At that time it had connotations of increased production; in the context of this book it is intended to indicate the new holistic approach to water management.

The role of the South African government not only in developing an integrated approach to water management as elucidated in the new Water Bill but in fostering a truly participative approach among stakeholders is acknowledged and endorsed.

Particular thanks are given to those who have contributed through discussion and the provision of material to the various case studies that are presented here.

Introduction:
The Revolution

A revolution in the way land and water are managed is under way. There are new appreciations of how land use impacts on water resources and a new recognition that some present land-use systems are unsustainable, so that in the medium to long term, water resources will be irreversibly degraded. There is a new willingness to reconsider land-use and water-resource issues in the light of the ideals and concepts identified at the United Nations Conference on the Environment and Development (UNCED) and in later UN conferences which have sought a more people-focused equity and poverty alleviation agenda, whilst placing this within the context of economic development and good governance. Together with this new understanding of the land use/water resource system and the new development ideals, new tools and methodologies are being developed to assist the development and execution of water resource management strategies.

Whereas the green revolution provided the means for the developing world to feed itself, the blue revolution addresses much wider issues. These concern both our own generation and future generations as they relate to the long-term sustainability of the water resource as it affects not only food production, but also the basic human needs for drinking water and sanitation, for ecology and the environment, and for our modern industries and power generation. The green revolution was a technological revolution driven by advances in plant breeding, pest control and the application of fertilizers, its outcome being much greater farm productivity. The blue revolution, although supported by technological advances, is more a philosophical revolution in the way in which we respect the world's environment and one of its most precious assets, water. The outcome of this revolution will be plans and strategies, and new designs for land use and all water-related developments.

No attempt is made here to engender another environmental scare story. It is not claimed that without the blue revolution the world will be doomed within 50 years by entering an ice age or encountering global meltdown or a catastrophic population or resources crisis. The gloomy predictions based on the carrying capacity of world populations in relation to water resources (Falkenmark, 1989) hopefully will not come to fruition. Overstating the dangers may be counter-productive in terms of focusing necessary support. Policymakers and the public are not unaware of the vested interests of environmental scientists and environmental institutions in furthering crisis scenarios. But the words of Tony Allan (Allan, 2004) that 'pessimists are wrong but useful; optimists are right but dangerous' remind us that even though the pessimists may sometimes be overstating the case, they nevertheless have a very important function in helping to mobilize the necessary remedial actions. The need for the Revolution is urgent nonetheless. Not in 50 years, but now, there are examples of essentially irreversible environmental degradation, the catastrophic degradation of the Aral Sea and its surroundings being perhaps the most publicized (see UN Department for Policy Coordination and Sustainable Development, 1997). More are in the making, which, without urgent action, will also lead to irreversible decline. Even more are the examples of unsustainable, inequitable and uneconomic land use and water resource systems that need to be addressed.

This book describes the progress of the blue revolution. It outlines some of the new understanding of how land use influences hydrological processes and water resources; it describes the new ideals; it provides examples of case studies where the blue revolution is being applied or needs to be applied and the new methodologies that are being developed to advance it.

The book focuses on the new understanding of the interrelationships between land use and water resources, and these are explored in the context of whether much of the widely disseminated folklore and 'mother statements', so often inextricably linked with issues of land use, are based on myth or reality. These myths are so often promulgated by both the media and, perhaps more seriously, by national and international environmental and water-related organizations, that they have permeated and affected land use and water resource planning at the very highest levels.

For two reasons the focus is on the role of forests. This is because forests have very different hydrological properties compared with other land uses. They are often a major land use in upland, mountainous areas, which in many countries are the wetter sites for replenishing surface water resources. A new approach to estimating the relationship between land use and evaporation and hence on the quantity of water available for runoff or recharge, based on the 'limits' concept, is reviewed.

The new revolutionary ideals arising from the combination of the UNCED and Structural Adjustment Programme (SAP) principles and the new awareness of the need for sustainability, the implications of which are only slowly being appreciated, are outlined.

The perverse outcomes of many present land- and water-related policies and the conflicts between land use and water resources in Africa, Asia and Australia underline the need and urgency for the new approach.

The blue revolution needs to recognize that conflicts can arise between the different sectors which may be trying to further different ideals, that environmental objectives including conservation, amenity and recreation may be at variance with economic development (which may include big infrastructure water transfer and dam programmes) and may be at variance again with social, human development and equity goals. Negotiation will be required to find solutions. But we are not dealing with what economists call a 'zero-sum game' situation where if one party in the negotiations wins the other loses by the same amount, we are dealing with a situation where all parties hold broadly similar values. At the most basic level we all strive for a secure future, both financially and in a deeper spiritual or well-being sense, for ourselves and our dependants. There are solutions that need to be and can be found which collectively benefit all of us. For conflict resolution, in real world situations where there are many actors with ill-defined objectives, an optimal solution may be neither necessary nor achievable. Using Herbert Simon's (Simon, 1969) concept of 'satisficing', finding a satisfactory solution to all parties, whilst recognizing there may be more than one solution, is perhaps the approach the Revolution should adopt.

New methods for linking land-use hydrological models with economics and ecology through decision support systems, together with new tools and equity-focused policy instruments, are outlined and proposed as a framework for the future integrated management of land and water developments at the catchment scale.

Chapter 1

New Understanding:
Land Use and Water Interactions

The relationship between land use and water is of interest worldwide. In many developing countries changes in land use are rapidly taking place and the largest change in terms of land area, and arguably also in terms of water resource impacts, arises from afforestation and deforestation activities. Whilst demands for agricultural land and firewood place increasing pressure on the dwindling indigenous forest resource, demands for timber and pulp are leading to increasing areas undergoing commercial afforestation with fast-growing monocultures of often exotic tree species. Agricultural demands for irrigation water compete with those of urban conurbations and industry for water supply. Hydroelectricity, often erroneously thought to have a neutral effect on water resources because evaporation from reservoirs is not taken into account, is another big user of water in many developing countries, particularly those in southern Africa. For example, the flow over the Victoria Falls is approximately equal to the flow from the Kariba dam downstream; all the additional flow into Lake Kariba from the northern-flowing rivers from Zimbabwe and the southern-flowing rivers from Zambia can be considered as lost to evaporation. Expanding industry, increasing urban populations without adequate sewage treatment facilities and greater intensification of agriculture, whilst not significantly affecting the quantity of the resource, all pose problems for its quality.

Land-use change not only affects the water resource but may also have long-term effects on the land resource. Removal of natural vegetation, overgrazing, poor irrigation and land management methodologies, overexploitation of vegetative cover for domestic use and industrial pollution have all been recognized as causes of soil degradation. Soil degradation may in turn affect the quantity and quality of water as it infiltrates and moves through the soil profile, and thus alter the hydrological response of catchments and the hydrological cycle.

These are the problems faced by many developing countries when trying to maintain their water and land resources. New approaches to integrated water resource management are being developed. The concepts of demand management and valuing the resource in economic terms, which allow competition between higher-value uses such as industry and water supply to urban conurbations, as opposed to low-value usage such as irrigation, are becoming increasingly accepted.

Knowledge of how land use interacts with the hydrological cycle in relation to evaporation, erosion, land degradation, runoff and infiltration has been built on studies in many parts of the world. These studies use a variety of techniques, ranging from geographically large experiments on complete river catchment areas to detailed examination of the physical and physiological processes operating within the water cycle.

EVAPORATION FROM DIFFERENT VEGETATION TYPES

Although the physics and the physiology of the evaporation process have been the subject of extensive research programmes, and detailed and sophisticated evaporation models have resulted, the outcome of this research exercise has not always been of direct benefit to integrated water resource management (IWRM). This is because sophisticated evaporation models usually require detailed knowledge of soil and crop parameters and detailed meteorological data which may not be generally available.

Recent advances in our understanding of the differences in evaporation from different vegetation types are reviewed here to provide the basis for the development of an alternative approach to estimating evaporation, outlined in Chapter 3, using the 'limits' concept.

Rainfall over the land surface provides the input for recharging the soil with water, replenishing groundwater reservoirs and providing runoff in streams and rivers. Some of this rainfall will evaporate into the atmosphere before it can reach either watercourses or groundwater. This evaporation occurs via three pathways: interception, transpiration and evaporation from bare soil (Figure 1.1). Interception is that proportion of the rainfall held on vegetation surfaces and re-evaporated before it reaches the ground. The water that is drawn up through plant roots and evaporated from the leaves through the stomata (the small pores in the leaf surface) is known as transpiration. The comparative importance of these different pathways is related primarily to the type of vegetation, soil conditions and the climate.

Principal Reasons for Differences in Evaporation Between Short and Tall Crops

Forests usually evaporate more water than shorter vegetation or annual crops for two reasons: forests are tall and forest trees generally have deeper root systems (Figure 1.2). In wet climates, where the surfaces of vegetation remain wet for long periods, interception from forests is higher than that from shorter crops because the very rough surfaces of forests assist the aerodynamic transport of water vapour into the atmosphere. This is analogous to the 'clothes

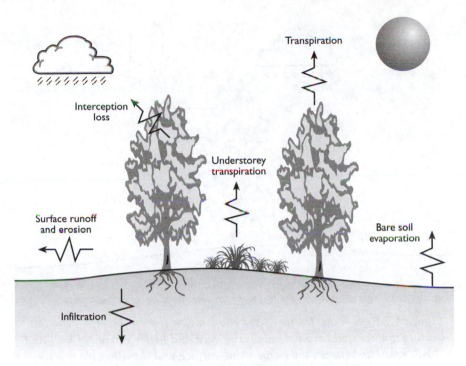

Figure 1.1 *Principal evaporation pathways*

line' effect: wet clothes pegged out on a line will dry quicker than those laid out flat on the ground. Not only does the increased aerodynamic transport increase the rate at which evaporated water molecules leave the surface by reducing the aerodynamic resistance, but it also increases the rate at which heat can be supplied by the atmosphere to the cooler vegetation surface to support the evaporation process. This source of energy, known as advection, is of such significance that annual evaporation rates from forests in wet climates can exceed those that could be sustained by direct radiation from the sun by a factor of two. The difference between the evaporative requirement and the radiant supply is accounted for by the advected energy drawn from the air mass as it moves over the forest.

In drier climates, because forest trees generally have much deeper root systems than short vegetation or agricultural crops, they are able to tap and transpire more soil water during dry periods, and this also leads to higher evaporation rates overall (Figure 1.3).

Although knowledge of these mechanisms can give a general indication of how the water use of forests may differ from that of other vegetation types, quantifying this difference is still very difficult. This is because there is no simple 'evaporation meter' that can be used to measure the evaporation from the different vegetation types. Also, our knowledge of the complex physical and physiological processes which control evaporation from different vegetation types is still far from complete.

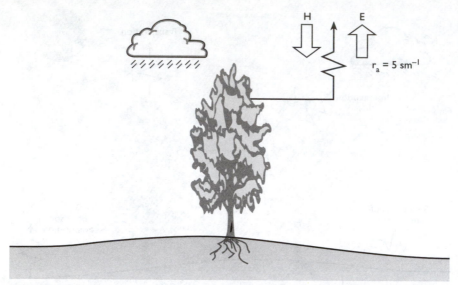

Note: H, E and r_a refer to sensible heat, latent heat and aerodynamic resistance respectively.

Figure 1.2 *Reason one for increased evaporation from forest: trees are tall, leading to increased aerodynamic turbulence and better mixing of heat and water vapour between the evaporating surface and the atmosphere – the clothes line effect – which can lead to evaporative rates from wet forest exceeding those from short vegetation by a factor of ten*

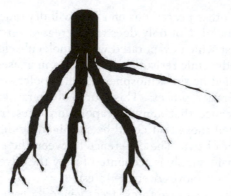

Figure 1.3 *Reason two for increased evaporation from forest: trees have deeper roots than short crops and keep transpiring longer during the dry season*

Measurement Methods

There are a number of approaches possible for measuring evaporation from vegetation (Figure 1.4):

1 Water taken up by roots and transpired through the leaves of plants can be inferred by measuring changes in soil moisture over a period of time.

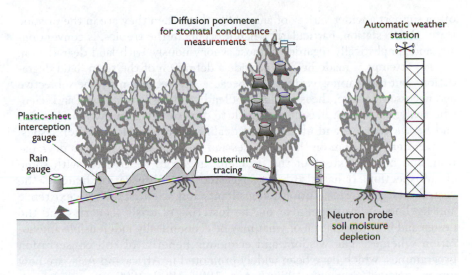

Figure 1.4 *Experimental techniques for measuring evaporation*

2   Measurements of the rates of sap flow in the plants themselves can be obtained using tracer methods that use either heat or isotopes of water as the tracer.
3   Measurements of the behaviour of stomata in the leaves, when coupled with information about leaf area and the climatic conditions, can also be used to calculate transpiration rates.
4   Micro-meteorological measurements of fluxes of heat, water vapour and momentum above vegetation surfaces can be used to calculate rates of evaporation. Eddy covariance methods which correlate temperature and humidity differences within eddies with their direction of movement are now being commonly used within the standardized FLUXNET scheme of international observation stations (see Kabat et al, 2004).

Interception, which is determined by the physical rather than the physiological properties of vegetation, is usually measured as the difference in rainfall recorded above and beneath the forest canopy.

LAND DEGRADATION

The term 'land degradation', like the term 'desertification', has no universally accepted definition. The dictionary describes degradation as a loss of strength, efficacy or value; the wearing away of higher lands. Inevitably the recognition of degradation is subjective. The farmer will recognize degradation where crops can no longer be grown. Nevertheless, it is possible that this 'degraded' land might be providing a more valuable water crop. 'Degradation' of soils and slopes in the mountains, whether occurring naturally or being accelerated by human activities, may be the reason for the fertility of soils in the alluvial plains in the valleys. Paradoxically, 'degraded' and polluted watercourses may often support a wider variety of animal life than when they are in the pristine state. Deforestation, particularly when it occurs in the tropics, is conventionally and simplistically regarded, almost synonymously, with land degradation.

No attempt is made here to provide a definition of the term 'land degradation', but the warning is given that because any definition will be subjective and necessarily vague, the issue does not lend itself easily to rational and scientific analysis. Often it becomes difficult to discern between myth and reality and between cause and effect when dealing with land degradation issues. Conventional wisdom on the processes and mechanisms leading to degradation, and on the extent of the problem, needs to be treated with some circumspection. It has also been suggested that obfuscation benefits the vested interests of institutions, consultants and scientists whose existence and livelihoods are dependent on the fostering of crisis scenarios and the design and implementation of what may be economically indefensible amelioration schemes. The wisdom and economic benefits of soil conservation programmes, which have been widely promoted in Africa and Asia, are now under question (Stocking, 1996; Enters, 1998, 1999, 2000; see also section on Erosion by Water on page 15).

Nevertheless land degradation, in its many guises, is a major issue in land and water resource management, and it is urgent that the cause and processes responsible be understood and the extent of the problem properly assessed (Stocking and Murnaghan, 2001), so that it can be addressed within the context of integrated land and water resource management (ILWRM).

Causes of Land Degradation

As the term land degradation does not lend itself to a simple definition which is generally accepted, it is perhaps not surprising that its fundamental causes also remain obscure and the subject of debate.

Within the developed and industrialized world there can be little doubt that technological advances without adequate controls are a major cause. Here the finger points to industrialization with its consequent pollution and to intensive agricultural practices using either agrochemicals in excess or poorly managed irrigation schemes.

In the developing world the causes are much less clear and perhaps lie more in the realm of socio-economics and sociology rather than technology. Indeed the cause–effect relationships involving degradation have been questioned in both Asia and Africa.

Asia and the Theory of Himalayan Environmental Degradation

The 'Theory of Himalayan Environmental Degradation' (THED), summarized from Ives and Messerli (1989) and Ives (2005) postulates that:

1 Following the introduction of the modern health care, medicine and malaria suppression in the Terai region of Nepal after 1950, an unprece-

dented wave of population growth occurred which does not yet appear to have peaked.

2   This veritable population explosion, with an overall doubling period of about 27 years, is augmented by uncounted and uncontrolled illegal immigration from India into the Nepalese Terai.... This has led to rapidly increasing demands for fuelwood, construction timber and fodder.

3   The next step in what has been described as a vicious circle, is that the needs of the burgeoning subsistence population has led to massive deforestation, amounting to a loss of half the forest reserves of Nepal within a 30-year period (1950–1980).

4   The deforestation, which includes the cutting of agricultural terraces on steeper and more marginal mountain slopes, has led to a catastrophic increase in soil erosion and loss of productive land through accelerated landslide incidence, and to the disruption of the normal hydrological cycle.

5   This situation, in turn, has led to increased runoff during the summer monsoon and increases in disastrous flooding and massive siltation in the plains, resulting in lower water levels and the drying up of springs and wells during the dry season. Related ills are: rapid siltation of reservoirs, abrupt changes in the courses of rivers, the spread of barren sand and gravel across rich agricultural land on the plains, and increased incidence of disease in downstream areas.

6   The increased sediment load of the rivers emanating from the Himalayan system is extending the Ganges and Brahmaputra delta and causing islands to form in the Bay of Bengal. Among the evidence cited are extensive plumes of sediment that can be seen on LANDSAT imagery to extend several hundred kilometres into the bay.

7   The continued loss of agricultural land in the mountains leads to another round of deforestation to enable the construction of more terraces on which to grow subsistence crops. Yet, as the labour of walking greater distances from the village to fuelwood supplies increases with the receding forest perimeter, a critical threshold is reached whereby the available human energy (principally female) becomes progressively overtaxed and an increasing quantity of animal dung is used for fuel.

8   Consequently, another vicious circle is linked to the first one: terraced soils are deprived of natural fertilizer – the animal dung now being used for fuel – thus depriving the agricultural terraces, in many instances, of their only source of fertilizer. This lowers crop yields. Also, the ensuing weakened soil structure further augments the incidence of landslides. Even more trees are cut on more marginal and steeper slopes to make room for more agricultural terraces to feed the ever-growing subsistence population.

Ives and Messerli conclude that:

> *The Theory of Himalayan Environmental Degradation is not a valid entity and must be broken down into its component parts*

and each part must be evaluated on its own merits. Thus the major linkage, population growth and deforestation in the mountains leading to massive damage on the plains, is not accepted. We favour the more cautious approach based upon acknowledgment that the long-term geophysical processes are more than adequate to account for the on-going formation of the plains as the continuously rising mountains are progressively eroded. We would argue, for instance, that appropriate forest establishment in the mountains is vital, but only for the well-being of the mountain environments and the mountain peoples dependent upon those environments. If reforestation in the mountains is conceived as a palliative for the problems of the plains, it is likely that vast resources will be expended to reap only disappointment. Moreover, this conception may divert attention away from the necessity of water resources management and adaptations to the natural environment of the plains.

THED asserts that anthropogenic (caused by human action) or accelerated erosion is a serious problem in the steep-sloped and fragile natural environments of the Himalayan region. THED suggests that this land degradation is driven by population growth, increased numbers of livestock and ineffective local agricultural techniques. It identifies extension of cultivation onto steeper slopes, clearance of forest, overgrazing and unsustainable gathering of fuelwood and fodder as the major land management practices that have caused accelerated erosion and increased sedimentation of river beds and serious floods downstream (including, in India, the Kosi, Brahmaputra, Sutlej, Beas and Ganges, and in China the Yangtze, Red, Nu, Salween and Mekong Rivers).

Developed during the 1970s, THED became the dominant narrative (or 'sanctioned discourse', see Chapter 5) which was accepted and promoted in varying degrees by most environmental and forestry-related organizations and funding institutions. It was thought to apply over the whole Himalayan region including in India, the Kosi, Brahmaputra, Sutlej, Beas, and Ganges River Basins and in China, the Yangtze, Red, Nu, Salween and Mekong Rivers (Blaikie and Muldavin, 2004).

Piers Blaikie and Joshua Muldavin (2004) commented that under the rationalist model of policymaking, the discrediting of the THED should have led, over a period of perhaps 10 or 15 years, to:

- less emphasis on expert-designed soil and water conservation and watershed management, and more tolerance for indigenous conservation of agricultural land, pastures and forests;
- at least a partial relaxation of coercive restrictions on land use and agricultural technologies such as shifting cultivation;
- an acceptance that serious flooding downstream, sedimentation of reservoirs and damage to hydroelectric plants through flooding and sediment load could not be reduced substantially through rigid and restrictive upstream land-use policies;

- a refocusing of development efforts away from narrow notions of resource conservation (important though this must continue to be) toward sustainable livelihoods for local people who rely on forests and pastures; and
- a transformation of land tenure away from state-owned regimes and restrictive leases toward a more trusting and flexible regime that grants local people the right to manage forests and pastures.

But they conclude that nothing substantial of this sort has occurred. Furthermore, resistance to pressures from international bodies and national activist groups has been the norm at all levels of government, from senior policy makers to field staff. Even today many policies, such as the Natural Forest Protection Programme and the Sloping Lands Conversion Programme that are being implemented in China, seem to be predicated on ideas underlying the THED (Chapter 5).

Africa: The Causes of Land Degradation

Increasing populations and 'population pressure' have been advanced as one of the causes of land degradation, but studies in the Machakos region of Kenya suggest that this is not always the case. Tiffen and co-authors (1994) in their book *More People, Less Erosion*, show that in the Machakos, increasing population densities in recent years have gone hand in hand with environmental recovery. But these claims have not been universally accepted. Questions have been raised whether the Machakos region is representative of agricultural intensification practices in the rest of Africa and whether it is really on a sustainable growth path.

The conventional view of rural populations always being the cause of deforestation and 'degradation' of savannah areas of Africa, and of greater populations causing increasing deforestation and 'degradation' is also questioned in the book, *Misreading the African Landscape* by Fairhead and Leach (1996). They argue that the forest 'islands' around villages in the savannah region of Guinea are not the remnants of a previous extensive forest cover degraded by an increasing rural population but the result of the rural population actually fostering these 'islands' in a landscape which would otherwise be less woody. The implication here is that population growth has resulted in greater forest cover not less.

The ownership of land, rights of land tenure and poverty have also been put forward as important factors related to degradation. The British Government's White Paper on International Development (DFID, 1997) states:

> *At the national level, there is a strong link between poverty and environmental degradation. Poor people are often the main direct human casualties of environmental degradation and mismanagement. In rural areas, competition for access to resources, especially land, often squeezes poor people into marginal, low productivity lands, where they have no alternative but to over-*

> *exploit soils and forests. In towns and cities, poor people typically have to live and work where pollution is worst and the associated health hazards are highest.*

The White Paper also makes the plea:

> *Natural resources must be managed sustainably or else contin- ued economic growth will not be possible. But some use must be accepted or development will not happen. We will help developing countries integrate environmental concerns into their decision- making by supporting their efforts to prepare plans and policies for sound management of their natural resources and national strategies for sustainable development.*

The new understanding that is emerging within the blue revolution is that neither the causes of, nor the solutions to, environmental problems are simple, nor do they rest within one sector or discipline. Solutions can only come within an integrated approach to land and water management.

Extent and Severity of Land Degradation

The Global Assessment of Soil Degradation Project (GLASOD), which was supported financially by The United Nations Environment Programme (UNEP), led to the creation of the world map of the status of human-induced soil degradation (Oldeman et al, 1991). It was a collaborative effort involving 250 soil scientists throughout the world and has been helpful in classifying degradation from a soil scientist's perspective, and illustrating the worldwide extent of the problem. The scientists were asked to categorize only soils degraded over the previous 45 years as a result of human intervention. Two categories of human-induced soil degradation processes were recognized. The first dealt with soil degradation through displacement of soil material and the second with chemical and physical soil deterioration. The processes responsi- ble for the first category, soil displacement, were recognized as water and wind erosion. Chemical and physical deterioration were considered to be brought about by loss of nutrients, salinization, acidification and pollution, and by the compaction, waterlogging and subsidence of organic soils (Table 1.1).

Of the total area affected by soil degradation (1964 million hectares), water erosion was responsible for the majority (1094 million hectares). Water erosion, which leads to rill and gully formation, is conventionally associated with the removal of vegetative cover, overgrazing and deforestation activities. Reforestation with plantation forestry is often advocated as the panacea but this may not always be a wise course of action (see also Chapter 2). Wind erosion, also associated with loss of vegetative cover, represents 28 per cent of the affected areas, whilst chemical and physical deterioration account for 12 and 4 per cent respectively. The GLASOD programme classified the degree of degradation under four degrees of severity: light, implying some

Table 1.1 *Areas and severity of human-induced soil degradation for the world*

Erosion process	Area affected by different degrees of degradation (Mha)					
	Light	Moderate	Strong	Extreme	Total	Total (%)
Water						
Loss of topsoil	301.2	454.5	161.2	3.8	920.3	
Terrain deformation	42.0	72.2	56.0	2.8	173.3	
Total	343.2	526.7	217.2	6.6	1093.7	55.7
Wind						
Loss of topsoil	230.5	213.5	9.4	0.9	454.2	
Terrain deformation	38.1	30.0	14.4	–	82.5	
Overblowing	–	10.1	0.5	1.0	11.6	
Total	268.6	253.6	24.3	1.9	548.3	27.9
Chemical						
Loss of nutrients	52.4	63.1	19.8	–	135.3	
Salinization	34.8	20.4	20.3	0.8	76.3	
Pollution	4.1	17.1	0.5	–	21.8	
Acidification	1.7	2.7	1.3	–	5.7	
Total	93.0	103.3	41.9	0.8	239.1	12.2
Physical						
Compaction	34.8	22.1	11.3	–	68.2	
Waterlogging	6.0	3.7	0.8	–	10.5	
Subsidence of organic soils	3.4	1.0	0.2	–	4.6	
Total	44.2	26.8	12.3	–	83.3	4.2
Total (Mha)	749.0	910.5	295.7	9.3	1964.4	
Total (%)	38.1	46.1	15.1	0.5	4.0	100

Source: Oldeman et al, 1991

reduction in productivity; moderate, indicating greatly reduced productivity with remedial measures which may be beyond the means of farmers in developing countries; strong, indicating soils that are no longer reclaimable at the farm level; and extreme, which indicated soils that were unable to be reclaimed and were beyond restoration.

Erosion by Water

Water is the principal agent of erosion and is responsible for 56 per cent of the world's man-induced soil degradation (Table 1.1). Water erosion occurs mainly as the result of three, sometimes interrelated, processes: sheet erosion, channel erosion and mass movement. In cold climates, erosion from water in the frozen form, which occurs when freeze–thaw cycles detach soil particles that are then carried away by rainfall or snowmelt-produced runoff, can also be significant. Erosion is a natural process, although it can be accelerated by human intervention. As described by Newson (1992a):

> *...soils are produced from a bedrock or drift mineral base by weathering and are then eroded as part of the long-term evolution of landscapes. Soil erosion only becomes a problem when its rate is accelerated above that of other landscape development processes – notably weathering – because it becomes visible; it becomes a river management problem when it constrains agricultural production and leads to river and reservoir sedimentation.*

Erosion has different impacts at different scales. At the field or hill-slope scale where 'on-site' erosion may be taking place, material will be removed, while at the larger catchment scale, 'off site' from the source of the erosion, sediments may be being deposited in the river channels, reservoirs and alluvial fans. In many catchments, only part of the material that is eroded from the slopes, the on-site erosion, is carried to the stream network. The rest may be held in temporary storage in depressions, foot slopes, small alluvial fans, behind debris, on flood plains or deposited in the beds of ephemeral channels. It is recognized that as the size of catchments increases, the number of storage opportunities for the retention of sediments also increases, and it is generally found that the sediment delivery ratio (SDR), the ratio of the on-site erosion to the amount of sediment carried by the stream, decreases markedly with catchment size (Walling, 1983). For small catchments the SDR is typically 0.1, for major catchments, 0.05 and for large river systems, 0.01.

Stocking (1996) shows how, unwittingly or deliberately, those who benefit from soil erosion crisis scenarios have very often used direct scaling, based on area, from the small erosion measurement plot to the catchment scale. In doing so, they have conveniently omitted from their calculations the eroded component that is redeposited soon after mobilization, an omission which can lead to overestimates of soil erosion by at least two orders of magnitude. Stocking also highlights other potential dangers associated with small field plot measurements of soil erosion in which, traditionally, soil and water are measured in a trough below a bounded plot with typical dimensions of 20m upslope by 3m cross slope. Together with the scaling issue already mentioned, and hence the opportunities for vastly exaggerating the magnitude of the soil erosion problem, he argues that absolute erosion rates from small plot experiments are not, on their own, very helpful for inferring impacts on plant productivity. Erosion–productivity linkages are complex. He cites as examples the fact that on a very susceptible shallow soil, 1cm of erosion may cause serious reductions in plant yields, whereas on a well-drained, high-fertility clay, productivity may be unaffected. On a duplex soil, where erosion may expose clays with greater water holding capacity, productivity may actually increase. He also describes the many experimental errors associated with small field plot measurements, stressing in particular those arising from the intrusive nature of the measurement itself, which alters the erosive and deposition processes. Although Stocking concedes that small field plot erosion studies may have value for determining parameter values for the universal soil loss equation (see below), for demonstrating the differential effects of land uses and for demonstrating the effects of planting crops in certain ways, the real value of the 'massive erosion research programmes based on small plots' that have been carried out in many developing countries must surely now be in question. Also in question are the economic justifications (Enters, 1998) for many of the major soil conservation programmes that have been advocated for averting many of these soil erosion 'crises'. The quality of, and the need for the profusion of, institutions which rely for their existence on propagating conventional amelioration and soil conservation wisdom, should also not escape scrutiny. Stocking (1996) warns that:

> *scientists are just one set of actors in the 'soil erosion game', a game in which it is advantageous a) not to admit you do not know the answer; b) to make unverifiable assumptions so that, if your answers provide bad advice, blame does not attach to the professionals; and c) to exaggerate the seriousness of the process to gain kudos, prestige, power, influence and, of course, further work.*

Sheet Erosion

Sheet erosion begins when drops of water, either raindrops or drops falling from vegetation, strike the ground and detach soil particles by splash. Depending upon the size of the drop and the velocity it has attained, the kinetic energy of the drop, which is released when it strikes the ground, may be sufficient to break the bonds between soil particles and detach them. The movement of water across the ground surface is needed to transport the particles away and complete the process. Without surface runoff the soil erosion losses from nearly level fields are small.

The size of the drop and the distance it falls are crucially important (see below and also Chapter 2). These determine the velocity and the kinetic energy that is achieved. There is also a degree of positive feedback within the process because whenever soil particles are detached, there will be an increase in any surface runoff generation as the finer particles clog soil pores and reduce infiltration.

The erosive potential of rainfall increases with increasing rainfall intensity for two reasons. First, in conditions of high rainfall intensity, infiltration rates are more likely to be exceeded and the conditions for generating surface runoff are more likely to be met. Second, as rainfall intensities increase, rain drop size also increases. Various equations have been used to describe the relationship between intensity and drop size; one of the first, and one still applicable in most rainfall conditions, is that described by Marshall and Palmer (1948). This empirical equation describes the spectrum of drop sizes that are associated with a particular rainfall intensity and how the spectra shift with changing intensity (Figure 1.5).

Conventionally, empirical methods such as the universal soil loss equation (USLE) (US Department of Agricultural Research Service, 1961; Wischmeier and Smith, 1965) have been used to estimate sheet erosion rates, at the plot scale, for different land uses. The USLE equation is cast as a simple multi-

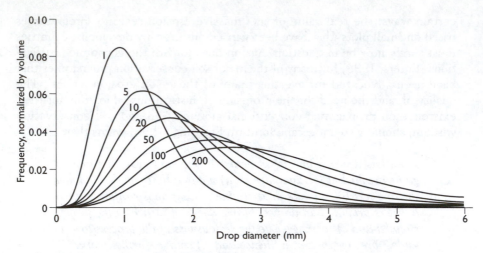

Figure 1.5 *Frequency distribution of rain drop sizes predicted by the Marshall-Palmer equation, normalized by volume (ie, normalized for equal depths of rain at each intensity), shown for rainfall intensities of 1–200mmh^{-1}*

plicative expression predicting the mass of soil removed from a unit area per annum assuming a knowledge of various causal factors:

$$A=RKLSCP$$

where A is the soil loss per unit area, (usually expressed in tons/acre), R is the rainfall erosivity factor, K is the soil erodibility factor (expressed in tons/acre), L is the field length factor, S is the field slope factor, C is the cropping-management factor normalized to a tilled area with continuous fallow, and P is the conservation practice factor normalized to straight-row farming up and down the slope.

Although the equation was originally devised and calibrated for use in the USA, it has since been used much more widely and various refinements have been introduced to extend the range of calibration (Mitchell and Bubenzer, 1980). However, it is recognized that the equation performs best for medium-textured soils on moderate slopes at the spatial scale of about 100m and time scales of a year. When used within its range of calibration, it has proved to be a valuable tool in soil conservation management and can assist in the prediction of annual soil losses under different land uses, and hence aid the selection of cropping and management options and conservation practices.

For erosion prediction over shorter timescales and under variable input conditions, more process-based models of sheet erosion (Morgan et al, 1984) have been developed which consider the soil detachment and transport processes separately. The importance of taking into account the role of vegetation canopies because they modify raindrop size and affect rainfall erosivity is discussed below and in Chapter 2.

Sheet erosion of soils can alter the hydrological functioning of catchments. Where surface infiltration rates are reduced through crusting or the total removal of the soil profile, surface runoff and the likelihood of floods will increase. Recharge to aquifers will also be reduced with concurrent reductions in flows in streams.

This is an area which would benefit from 'new understanding': the relationship between land degradation and hydrological functioning of catchments remains poorly understood and difficult to assess for particular catchments.

Channel Erosion

Channel erosion, which includes bed and bank erosion, can be a very significant process in natural alluvial channels. It can also be a factor in causing land degradation from channels created by man. These may have been created deliberately, as mechanisms for carrying, for example, drainage water from land drainage schemes and roads, or accidentally, as a result of poor land management practices. Compaction channels formed following land disturbance caused by logging, and crop harvesting in wet conditions, are particular examples. The sediment transport capacity of a channel is generally proportional to the product of the water flow and the channel slope, and inversely proportional to the bed or bank sediment size.

Channel formation following land disturbance may also lead to gully erosion. Here, waterfall erosion at the gully head, channel erosion in the gully and mass movement of material from the sides of the gully all erode the gully and drive the gully head upslope.

Mass Movement

Mass movement in the form of landslides is associated with conditions of steep topography and saturated soils and sometimes tectonic movement. Undercutting by rivers may be another factor, but of primary importance are incidences of prolonged and high-intensity rains. The role of vegetation in preventing landslides is generally thought to be positive as a result of the binding effect of roots, but these benefits are only operative over the rooting depth of the vegetation. Where deep slips occur – usually more serious and taking longer to stabilize – the presence or absence of vegetation does not seem to be a factor. Human interventions through the building of roads and irrigation canals involving the undercutting of slopes and, in the case of irrigation canals, the saturation of adjacent soils as a result of seepage, have been identified (Bruijnzeel, 1990) as causal mechanisms.

Vegetation, Forests and Erosion

The role of vegetation and particularly forests in relation to erosion is of special interest to IWRM. Conventional wisdom would have us believe that deforestation is often the cause of soil erosion and land degradation and that afforestation is the panacea. Such simplistic views are no longer acceptable. Our understanding of the relationships between forests and erosion has made considerable advances in recent years.

It is now recognized that forests can have both beneficial and adverse effects on erosion. Benefits may result from the binding effects of roots, which can prevent landslides on steep slopes, and from the generally high rates of infiltration under natural forest which tend to minimize surface run-off. Generally, the adverse effects are associated with poor management practices involving bad logging techniques which compact the soil and increase the surface flow, or drainage activities and road construction, both of which disturb the soil.

Excessive grazing by farm animals also leads to soil compaction, the removal of understorey plants and greater erosion risk.

Drop Size Modification

Forests can also influence soil erosion by altering the drop size distribution of the incident rainfall. Contrary to popular belief, forest canopies do not necessarily 'protect' the soil from raindrop impacts. In recent years there has been new understanding of the relationship between different tree species, canopies and erosion. Although not generally recognized, the potential for increased erosion from drops falling from forest canopies was demonstrated over 50 years ago by Chapman (1948). However, the importance of species in determining drop size and erosive impacts has not always been well understood. There have been claims that the drop size spectra of drops falling from vegetation are largely independent of vegetation type (Brandt, 1989). The logical consequence of this line of thought is that erosivity would be considered to be unrelated to the type of vegetation.

However, a new theory derived from observations developed from disdrometer observations of the modified drop size spectra beneath canopies of different tree species (Hall and Calder, 1993) suggests a different perspective. These measurements show a well-defined, repeatable relationship between the spectrum of drop sizes recorded beneath a particular tree species, termed the characteristic spectrum (Figure 1.6). (Here the spectra are shown as cumulative, rather than frequency spectra, to make it easier to distinguish between spectra.) This same below-canopy spectrum is obtained irrespective of the size spectra of drops incident on the canopy (Figure 1.7).

These characteristic spectra, with median-volume drop diameters of 2.2, 2.8 and 4.4mm for *Pinus caribaea*, *Eucalyptus camaldulensis* and *Tectona grandis*, respectively, can also usefully be compared (see Figure 1.8) with the spectra expected in natural rainfall as predicted by the Marshall-Palmer

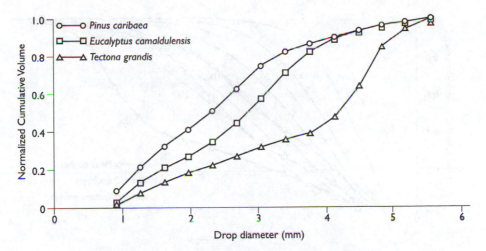

Figure 1.6 *Characteristic net rainfall drop size spectra for* Pinus caribaea, Eucalyptus camaldulensis *and* Tectona grandis

equation (the rainfall spectra are the same as those shown in Figure 1.5 but redrawn in cumulative form). Clearly the foliage of these tree species will not always reduce the drop size of the incident rainfall. For *Pinus caribaea*, a rainfall intensity exceeding 50mmh^{-1} will be required before any diminution in drop size will occur. For *Eucalyptus camaldulensis* the 'break-even' intensity is about 200mmh^{-1}, whilst for *Tectona grandis* it would be 3000mmh^{-1}, an intensity which could never be attained by natural rainfall.

If it is assumed that the height of vegetation is sufficient for all drops to have reached terminal velocity, it is possible to show the characteristic spectra

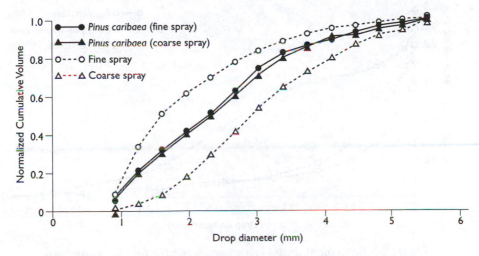

Figure 1.7 *Characteristic net rainfall drop size spectra recorded for* Pinus caribaea *when subject to fine (1.6mm median-volume drop diameter) and coarse (2.9mm median-volume drop diameter) sprays*

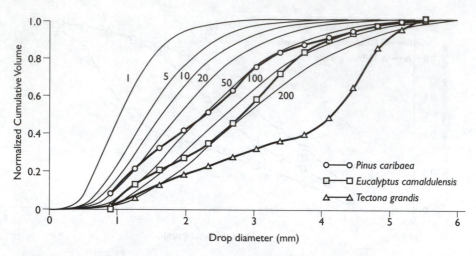

Figure 1.8 *Characteristic net rainfall drop size spectra recorded for* Pinus caribaea, Eucalyptus camaldulensis *and* Tectona grandis *and rainfall spectra predicted by the Marshall-Palmer equation for different rainfall intensities (in mmh^{-1})*

in terms of kinetic energy. In Figure 1.9 the fraction by volume of the sub-canopy drops having kinetic energies exceeding a specified value are shown. This shows how important species differences are in generating drops with different kinetic energies. Median volume drops from *Tectona grandis* will have nine times the kinetic energy of those from *Pinus caribaea*.

In summary, the new understanding arising from this work has established that:

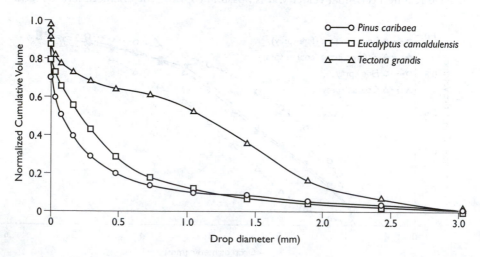

Figure 1.9 *Equivalent drop kinetic energy spectra for* Pinus caribaea, Eucalyptus camaldulensis *and* Tectona grandis *assuming all drops have reached terminal velocity*

Plate 1.1 *Splash-induced erosion under a teak forest in southern India following an understorey fire*

- Below-canopy drop size is independent of the size of raindrops falling on the top of the canopy.
- The below-canopy drop size spectrum is a 'characteristic' of the species.
- Drop size spectra vary widely between species. This can result in large differences in the potential for erosion; drops falling from *Tectona grandis* can have as much as nine times the kinetic energy of those from *Pinus caribaea*.

Splash-Induced Erosion: An Observation

Evidence for how severe splash-induced erosion beneath forest canopies can be was provided by observations beneath a teak forest in Karnataka, southern India, in 1993. During the dry season of 1993 a fire (a common occurrence in teak plantations) had removed the protective litter layer and understorey vegetation. Some regrowth of the understorey had started prior to a severe night-time storm at the outbreak of the monsoon. Major sheet erosion had clearly taken place overnight (Plate 1.1), particularly from the soil which had not been protected by regrowth (Plate 1.2).

The 'columns' of soil beneath the protective leaves of the regrowth were approximately 2.5cm high, indicating that overnight approximately this depth of soil had been removed by sheet erosion.

Observations of root exposures in other parts of the plantation indicated that erosion to a depth of 2m had occurred from the plantation since it had been planted about 80 years previously.

Plate 1.2 *Understorey regrowth protects the soil from drops
falling from the leaves of a teak forest*

These field observations lend dramatic support to the new views on erosion:

- For storms with small raindrop sizes (usually those of low intensity), individual drops tend to amalgamate on the surface of a leaf until a large drop is formed which then falls off under the influence of gravity. If the trees are tall, this large drop may reach such a velocity before it reaches the ground that it has both a higher kinetic energy and a higher potential for detaching soil particles than drops in the natural rainfall (see also Chapter 2). In low-intensity storms, therefore, forest canopies will not protect the soil and erosion may be increased.
- Conversely, for storms with the largest drop sizes, such as high-intensity convective storms common in the tropics, vegetation canopies may break up the large drops and reduce both the mean drop size and the mean kinetic energy of the incident rain. For the highest-intensity storms, it can be expected that forests will have an ameliorating effect on erosion, except for large-leafed species such as teak, which will always produce drop sizes larger than the incident rainfall (Figure 1.8) and can never exert an ameliorating effect.

Splash-induced Erosion – Studies in Japan

Splash-induced erosion beneath forest canopies has been recognized as an important issue in Japan, particularly under poorly managed Japanese cypress plantations (Plate 1.3).

Source: Japan Soil and Water Control Corporation, Tokyo, Japan

Plate 1.3 *Splash-induced erosion under Japanese cypress*

A research team led by Professor Masakazu Suzuki and Dr Kuraji Koichiro at the Laboratory of Forest Hydrology and Erosion Control Engineering of the University of Tokyo has developed disdrometers using modern laser technologies for measuring drop size distributions (Nanko et al, 2004). Concurrent observations were made with these instruments under the canopies of three different tree species and in the open for five storm events. These revealed significant differences in drop size characteristics between primary rainfall and each of the different tree species. Median volume drops were greater under the trees than in the primary rainfall, presenting the possibility of increased splash-induced erosion if the forest soils have no surface cover. The median volume drop diameters ranged from 1.33 in the open through 2.15 for *Chamaecyparis obtuse* (cypress), 2.75 for *Cryptomeria japonica* (cedar) and 2.88 for *Quercus variabilis* (beech).These results provide further information on the characteristic drop size spectrum of different species and add to those previously reported of 2.2, 2.8 and 4.4 for *Pinus caribaea*, *Eucalyptus camaldulensis* and *Tectona grandis*, respectively.

LAND USE, CLIMATE CHANGE AND WATER RESOURCES

The interactions between land use, climate change and water resources present an active area of research, but one in which there is little consensus regarding the scale of the effects. Central to the research effort is the use of global circulation models (GCM) to represent the transfer of heat, water vapour and momentum between the surface of the earth and the atmosphere. GCMs require values for the parameters relating to the surface vegetation type and the availability of water to the vegetation to allow the estimation of the heat and mass transfer terms under the atmospheric and rainfall conditions calculated by the GCM. Some of the limitations of the approach, particularly in relation to calculating the impacts of anthropogenic climate change (greenhouse effect) on water resources, have been identified by Bonell (1999). Bonell, quoting an International Hydrology Programme (IHP) expert group (Shiklomanov, 1999), recognized that, even given the same initial starting conditions, different GCMs lead to widely differing estimates of the extent of the climate change.

Nevertheless, GCMs represent the best technology available for predicting future climate change and, whilst it must be accepted that considerable uncertainty is attached to future GCM predictions, there is a need to understand how the range of climate change scenarios translates to future water resource scenarios.

Climate change scenarios derived from GCMs are now becoming available for different parts of the world, but there are methodological difficulties in using these to estimate water resource impacts. A central difficulty is that, although they are able to simulate present climate in terms of annual or seasonal averages at the continental scale, GCMs are not able to represent the smaller-scale features in time and space that are more relevant to hydrological and water resource applications. This is because GCMs generate an estimate of the average rainfall over a large (often 50x50km) grid square for the GCM time step. This spatially averaged rainfall with low intensity, essentially a 'drizzle', has to be downscaled using knowledge of the spatial/temporal properties of the local rainfall (Figure 1.10). This approach was adopted for Europe in the WRINCLE (Water Resources: INfluence of CLimate change in Europe) project led by Newcastle University (Kilsby et al, 1998).

Within this project, multi-site spatial–temporal rainfall model parameters were fitted to current climate data using a stochastic rainfall generator based on Poisson probability statistics (Figure 1.11). The calibrated model was then used with GCM outputs and an analytical hydrological model to produce discharge statistics. These outputs were then summarized for Europe in a digital atlas covering precipitation, river discharge and water resource impacts with respect to the means and absolute and relative changes from the present baseline (WRINCLE, 2004).

Recent studies of climate change impacts on water resources and water stress are provided by Arnell (2004) using the climate and socio-economic scenarios known as SRES (from the Intergovernmental Panel on Climate Change's Special Report on Emissions Scenarios, IPCC (2000)). These studies assessed the relative effect of both climate change and population growth on future global and regional water resource stresses. This was achieved by combining the SRES socio-economic scenarios with climate projections made using six GCMs driven by the SRES emissions scenarios. River runoff was simulated at a spatial resolution of 0.5x0.5° under current

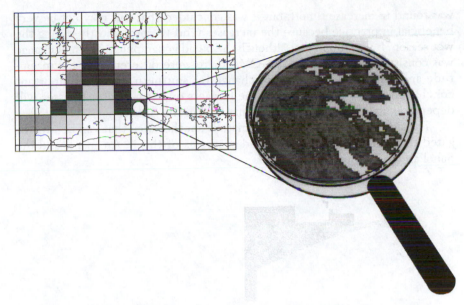

Figure 1.10 *Global circulation models produce a 'drizzle' over the grid square which needs to be downscaled to produce a more realistic distribution of rainfall in time and space*

and future climates using a macro-scale hydrological model. The results indicated increased water resources stress in those parts of the world where runoff is decreased; these included the Mediterranean region, parts of Europe, central and southern America, and southern Africa. In other water-stressed parts of the world – particularly in southern and eastern Asia – climate change

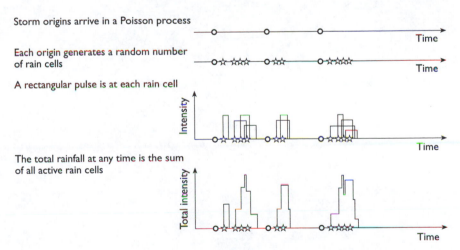

Figure 1.11 *Stochastic rainfall generator uses the generalized Neyman-Scott rectangular pulses model for downscaling GCM rainfall estimates in time and space*

was found to increase runoff, but it was concluded that this may not be very beneficial in practice because the increases tend to come mostly during the wet season. It was found that although the broad geographic pattern of change was consistent between the six GCMs, there were differences in the magnitude and also in the direction of change for southern Asia. An important conclusion of the study was that the impacts on actual water stresses will depend on how water resources are managed in the future.

The influence of land use on climate is another area that can be investigated through the use of GCMs and examples of this in Amazonia and the Sahel are given in the next chapter.

Chapter 2

Forests and Water:
Myths and Mother Statements

Much folklore and many myths remain about the role of land use and its relation to hydrology, and these hinder rational decision making. This is particularly true in relation to forestry, agroforestry and hydrology: claims by enthusiastic agroforesters and foresters are often not supportable. The perception that forests are always necessarily 'good' for the environment and water resources has, however, become so deeply ingrained in our collective psyches that it is usually accepted unthinkingly. The view is routinely reinforced by the media and is all-pervasive; it has become enshrined in some of our most influential environmental policy documents. The report by the United Nations Conference on Environment and Development (UNCED, 1992) states:

> *The impacts of loss and degradation of forests are in the form of soil erosion, loss of biological diversity, damage to wildlife habitats and degradation of watershed areas, deterioration of the quality of life and reduction of the options for development.*

These simplistic views, particularly because they imply the inevitable link between the absence of forests and 'degradation' of water resources, have created a mindset which not only links degradation with less forest but rehabilitation and conservation with more forest. This mindset has caused, and continues to cause, governments, development agencies and UN organizations to commit funds to afforestation or reforestation programmes in the mistaken belief that this is the best way to improve water resources.

Foresters have long been suspected of deliberately propagating some of these forest hydrology myths. Pereira (1989) states in relation to forests and rainfall:

> *The worldwide evidence that high hills and mountains usually have more rainfall and more natural forests than do the adjacent lowlands has historically led to confusion of cause and effect. Although the physical explanations have been known for more*

than 50 years, the idea that forests cause or attract rainfall has persisted. The myth was created more than a century ago by foresters in defence of their trees… The myth was written into the textbooks and became an article of faith for early generations of foresters.

The overwhelming hydrological evidence supports Pereira's view that forests are not generators of rainfall, yet this 'myth', like many others in forest hydrology, may contain a modicum of truth that prevents it from being totally 'laid to rest'.

Swift (1996) has argued, in relation to forests and 'desertification', that the work of E.P. Stebbing, a forester working for the Indian Forest Service in the 1930s, had great influence. Stebbing (1937) promoted the view that the Sahara was both extending and moving southwards, a process more commonly referred to now as 'desertification'. He argued that this extension was the direct result of land use practices, and refers to

… the present method of agricultural livelihood of the population living in these regions, with their unchecked action of firing the countryside annually, and methods of pasturage – all tend to assist sand penetration, drying up of water supplies and desiccation.

Reforestation was advocated as the panacea.

When scrutinized, much of the folklore and many of the 'mother statements' relating to forestry and the environment are seen to be either exaggerated or untenable. For others, we still require research to understand the full picture. Seven 'mother statements' in relation to forests, productivity and hydrology are considered:

1   Forests increase rainfall.
2   Forests increase runoff.
3   Forests regulate flows.
4   Forests reduce erosion.
5   Forests reduce floods.
6   Forests 'sterilize' water supplies and improve water quality.
7   Agroforestry systems increase productivity.

Clearly it is important to know what veracity can be attached to these statements for the proper management of water resources and land use. Many forestry projects in developing countries are supported because of assumed environmental/hydrological benefits, whilst in many cases the hydrological benefits may at best be marginal and at worst negative. The evidence for and against each of these 'mother statements' is taken in turn and appraised; the need for further research is also assessed.

FORESTS INCREASE RAINFALL?

Pereira (1989) denounced the linkage between forests and increased rainfall as a myth, yet there may be some situations in which this positive linkage cannot be totally discounted and in which the presence of forests does lead to a small increase in rainfall. However, as explained later, this small increase in rainfall input will nearly always be more than compensated for by increased evaporation, leading to an overall reduction in water resources. Theory indicates that the height of trees will slightly increase the orographic effect, which will, in turn, lead to a slight increase in the rainfall. Modelling studies using meso-scale climate models have shown that some of the intercepted water retained by forest canopies and re-evaporated will return as increased rainfall (Blyth et al, 1994), but this result, although indicating an increase in the gross rainfall above the vegetation, would suggest that the overall net rainfall reaching the ground surface would be reduced as a result of the presence of the forest.

Application of GCMs (Rowntree, 1988) indicates that vegetation changes will have a regional impact on climate. Use of these models in Amazonia shows that total removal of the Amazonian rainforest would affect rainfall patterns with reductions in the rainfall, particularly in the drier north-east of the continent, by about 0.5mm per day on average (Figure 2.1).

For the whole of the Amazon basin, rainfall would be reduced by 6 per cent (Institute of Hydrology, 1994).

The variation in the seasonal rainfall over Amazonia under a complete deforestation scenario has been reported by Werth and Avissar (2002) using the Goddard Institute for Space Studies GCM. This study shows that the largest decrease in rainfall of about 1mmd^{-1} occurs in the wet season, with essentially no change in rainfall in the dry season.

Similarly, GCM modelling studies for the Sahel (Xue, 1997) indicate that past removal of the indigenous bush vegetation will have altered the spatial distribution of rainfall in a manner that bears a close correlation with observed changes in the distribution patterns (Figures 2.2a and 2.2b). Zeng and colleagues (1999) have shown that although much of the temporal variation in rainfall over the Sahel in the past 50 years can be explained by incorporating just the atmosphere, ocean and land within a GCM, the incorporation of a vegetation component does give further improvements.

In southern India, however, studies of historical rainfall records (Meher-Homji, 1980) indicate that annual rainfall over the last 100 years has not decreased despite the large-scale conversion of the dry deciduous forest to agriculture, although there is some evidence of a decrease in the number of rain days.

The land-to-atmosphere flux changes brought about by afforestation and deforestation activities comprise one of the most commonly studied perturbations to regional and global climate.

Perhaps less well investigated are the perturbations, often considerably larger at the regional scale, brought about by increased use of irrigation. The potential for large-scale irrigation to influence regional climate has been

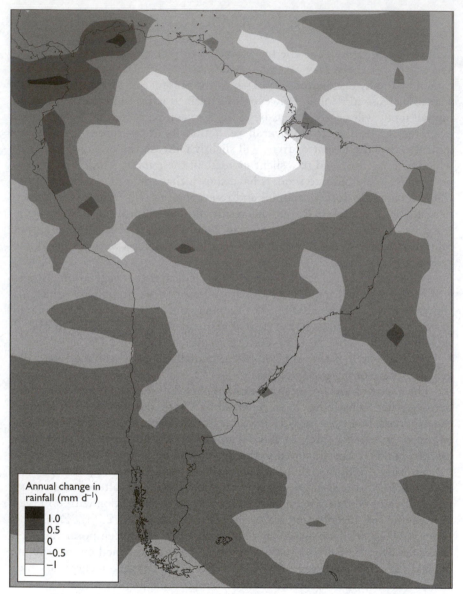

Annual change in
rainfall (mm d⁻¹)

1.0
0.5
0
−0.5
−1

Figure 2.1 *Predictions made by the Hadley Centre GCM of the spatial variation of the annual change in rainfall (mmd⁻¹) over Amazonia resulting from complete removal of the Amazon forest*

demonstrated by Geerts (2002) in Australia, where monthly mean regional temperatures were reduced by about 1K. In countries such as India and China, although deforestation has undoubtedly occurred in the past – reducing latent heat fluxes to the atmosphere and increasing river flows – the increased areas under irrigation must have more than counterbalanced the flux perturbations caused by deforestation. The increasing number of catchments approaching 'closure' (see Chapter 5) would indicate that the balance

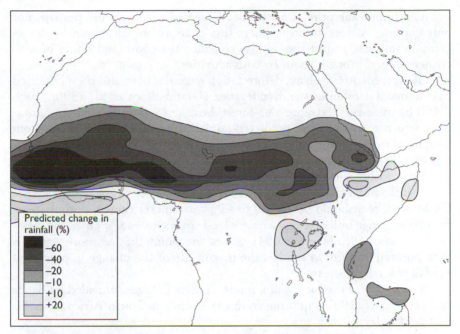

Figure 2.2a *Predicted change in rainfall for the months July to September over Central Africa as a result of the degradation of the Sahel vegetation during the last 30 years*

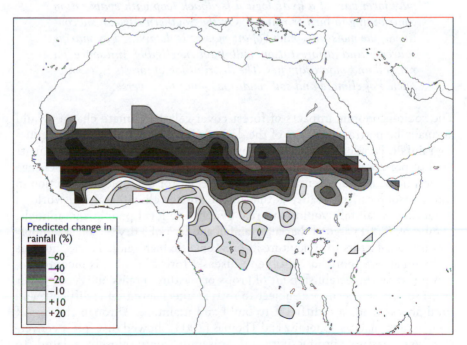

Figure 2.2b *Observed change in the rainfall pattern*

has now tipped the other way. In Asia GCM scenarios should perhaps not only consider surface-to-atmosphere flux changes brought about by deforestation in isolation but should also consider the combined effect of area changes in land brought about by both activities.

GCM scenarios involving deforestation scenarios have also been criticized by Thomas Giambelluca and colleagues (Giambelluca et al, 1996, 1999, 2000) by using very extreme 'non-forest' heat and vapour flux parameterizations which accentuate the predicted rainfall differences. They claim, from field measurements in northern Thailand, that most deforested land surfaces, especially intermediate and advanced secondary vegetation, are more similar, in terms of land–surface interaction, to the model simulation of forest than deforested land as depicted in most GCM simulations. They suggest that GCM modellers should be careful to adopt parameter values appropriate to the diverse range of forest replacement land covers instead of just using grassland scenarios. Bruijnzeel (2004) makes the point that as more detail is incorporated into GCM models the magnitude of the change in predicted rainfall generally decreases.

A summary of the biophysical forest–climate linkages, provided by Bands and colleagues (1987), quoting from experience in South Africa, remains pertinent today:

> *Forests are associated with high rainfall, cool slopes or moist areas. There is some evidence that, on a continental scale, forests may form part of a hydrological feedback loop with evaporation contributing to further rainfall. On the Southern African subcontinent, the moisture content of air masses is dominated by marine sources, and afforestation will have negligible influence on rainfall and macroclimates. The distribution of forests is a consequence of climate and soil conditions – not the reverse.*

The socio-economic impacts of forest cover-related climate change would normally be portrayed as part of the doom 'narrative' of deforestation reducing rainfall. Paradoxically, although hydrologists and global change scientists tend to portray the importance of obtaining knowledge about climate change by emphasizing the potential damaging effects, for example, a reduction in water resources, the reality is that in the wetter climates of the world, a reduction in rainfall would have real benefits to local people and animals. Sombroek (2001) argued that high rainfall and lack of a dry season are important limiting factors to agriculture in Amazonia. In high-rainfall areas, humans and animals are more susceptible to disease; forest burning is incomplete, complicating the establishment of crops or pasture; grains and many other crops such as soybeans are subject to rotting; mechanization is difficult; and rural access roads are difficult to build and maintain. Through the use of multivariate analysis, Chomitz and Thomas (2003) showed that forest conversion and pasture productivity in Amazonia were closely related to precipitation, soil quality, infrastructure and market access, proximity to past conversion and protection status. They found that high precipitation had a strong deterrent effect on agriculture and that the probability that land is claimed, used for agriculture or intensively stocked with cattle declines substantially with increasing precipitation levels, holding other factors (such as road access) constant. Proxies for land abandonment are also higher in high-rainfall areas. Together these findings suggest that the wetter Western Amazon is inhospitable to exploitation for pasture using current technologies but would, under climate change scenarios of reduced rainfall, become more productive.

Conclusions

The evidence from field measurements and modelling studies suggests that although the effects of forests on rainfall are likely to be relatively small, they cannot be totally dismissed from a water resource perspective. In high-rainfall regions of the World a reduction in rainfall may have socio-economic benefits.

Research Requirement

Further research is required to determine the magnitude of the effect, particularly at the regional scale, and to determine if other land-use changes, such as those involving irrigation, which also alter land-to-atmosphere fluxes, might be having counterbalancing effects.

FORESTS INCREASE RUNOFF?

A new understanding has been gained in recent years of evaporation from forests in dry and wet conditions based on process studies. These studies, and the vast majority of the world's catchment experiments, indicate decreased runoff from areas under forests as compared with areas under shorter crops. This knowledge has been gained from a host of different studies using a range of different techniques and methodologies. 'Natural' lysimeters have been used to measure total evaporation. Transpiration has been determined using soil moisture measurements (Bell, 1976); micro-meteorological and eddy correlation methods (Dyer, 1961); plant physiological studies and tree cutting studies (Roberts, 1977,1978); and heat, radioactive and stable isotope tracing methods (Cohen et al, 1981; Kline et al, 1970; Luvall and Murphy, 1982; Calder, 1991). Interception has been determined by a number of techniques including interception gauges (Calder and Rosier, 1976), gamma-ray and microwave attenuation methods (Olszyczka, 1979; Calder and Wright,1986; Bouten et al,1991), 'wet lysimeters' and rainfall simulators (Calder et al, 1996).

These studies indicate that in wet conditions interception losses will be higher from forests than from shorter crops primarily because of the increased atmospheric transport of water vapour from their aerodynamically rough surfaces.

In dry (drought) conditions the studies show that transpiration from forests is likely to be greater because of the generally increased rooting depth of trees compared with shorter crops and their consequent greater access to soil water.

The new understanding indicates that in both very wet and very dry climates, evaporation from forests is likely to be higher than that from shorter crops and consequently runoff will be decreased from forested areas, contrary to the widely accepted folklore.

The few exceptions (which lend some support to the folklore) are as follows:

- Cloud forests where cloud-water deposition may exceed interception losses.
- Very old forests. Langford (1976) showed that following a bushfire in a very old (200 years) mountain ash (*Eucalyptus regnans*) forest covering 48 per cent of the Maroondah catchment – one of the water supply catchments for Melbourne in Australia, runoff was reduced by 24 per cent. The reason for this reduction in flow has been attributed to the increased evaporation from the vigorous regrowth forest that had a much higher leaf-area index than the former very old ash forest.
- Observations and modelling studies of the evaporation from broadleaf forest growing on chalk soils in southern England have been interpreted as showing reduced water use compared with grassland (Harding et al, 1992). More recent research (Roberts et al, 2001) which has been carried out to investigate these results, exceptional in world terms, now suggests little difference in water use between grass and broadleaf forest. This, in itself, remains an unusual result in world terms but is believed to relate to the particular soil water retention characteristics of chalk soils which are able to retain and release large amounts of water to the roots of vegetation (both grassland and forest), allowing transpiration to proceed at close to potential rates (see also Chapter 6.) for long periods during the summer months.

Conclusions

Notwithstanding the exceptions outlined above, catchment experiments generally indicate reduced runoff from forested areas compared with those under shorter vegetation (Bosch and Hewlett, 1982).

Caveat

Information on the evaporative characteristics of different tree species/soil type combinations are still required if evaporation estimates with an uncertainty of less than 30 per cent are required. In both temperate and tropical climates evaporative differences between species and soil types are expected to vary by about this amount. For example, 30 per cent differences in the water use of the same species of eucalyptus growing on different soils have been recorded in southern India (Calder et al, 1993), whilst similar differences have been recorded between different tree species growing on the same soil type, also in India (Calder et al, 1997a).

FORESTS REGULATE FLOWS AND INCREASE DRY SEASON FLOWS?

Although it is possible, with only a few exceptions, to draw general conclusions with respect to the impacts of forests on annual flow, the same cannot be claimed for the impacts of forests on seasonal flow. Different, site-specific, often competing processes may be operating and both the direction and magnitude of the impact may be difficult to predict for a particular site.

From theoretical considerations it would be expected that:

- increased transpiration and increased dry-period transpiration will increase soil moisture deficits and reduce dry season flows;
- increased infiltration under (natural) forest will lead to higher soil water recharge and increased dry season flows; and
- for cloud forests, increased cloud-water deposition may augment dry season flows.

There are also observations (Robinson et al, 1997) which indicate that for the uplands of the UK, drainage activities associated with plantation forestry increase dry season flows both through the initial dewatering and in the longer term through alterations to the hydraulics of the drainage system. The importance of mechanical cracking associated with field drainage and its effects on drainage flows has been highlighted by Robinson et al (1985), whilst the work of Reid and Parkinson (1984) indicates that landform and soil type may sometimes be the dominant factors determining soil moisture and drainage flow response.

There are also observations from South Africa that increased dry-period transpiration is reducing low flows. Bosch (1979) has demonstrated, from catchment studies at Cathedral Peak in Natal, that pine afforestation of former grassland not only reduces annual streamflow by 440mm, but also reduces the dry season flow by 15mm. Van Lill et al (1980), reporting studies at Mokobulaan in the Transvaal, showed that afforestation of grassland with *Eucalyptus grandis* reduced annual flows by 300–380mm, with 200–260mm of the reduction occurring during the wet summer season. More recently, Scott and Smith (1997), analysing results from five of the South African catchment studies, concluded that percentage reductions in low (dry season) flow as a result of afforestation were actually greater than the reduction in annual flow. Scott and Lesch (1997) also report that on the Mokobulaan research catchments under *Eucalyptus grandis*, the streamflow completely dried up 9 years after planting; the eucalypts were clear felled at age 16 years but perennial streamflow did not return for another 5 years. They attribute this large lag time to the very deep soil moisture deficits generated by the eucalypts, which require many years of rainfall before field capacity conditions can be established and recharge of the groundwater aquifer and perennial flows can take place.

Studies in India draw similar conclusions. Sikka and colleagues (Sikka et al, 2003) investigated the impacts on both flood flows and low flows of converting natural grassland to eucalypt plantation in the Nilgiris region of south India. The detailed and long-term (1968–1992) paired-catchment experiments in the Nilgiris, in which the responses from a 'control' catchment under natural grassland were compared with those from a catchment with 59 per cent eucalypt cover (monitored over a period encompassing two rotations of the eucalypt crop), indicate very significant reductions in low flows during the dry season. Expressed in terms of a 'low flow index' (defined as the 10-day average flow which is exceeded for 95 per cent of the time of the flow record), the low flows were reduced by approximately one-half during the first rotation and by one-quarter during the second rotation of the eucalypt crop.

In Taiwan, following the clear cut of a natural hardwood forested watershed, Hsia and Koh (1982) reported increases in dry season flow of as much as 91 per cent compared with a control catchment (see the Forests Reduce Erosion? section on page 39 for details).

Bruijnzeel (1990) discussed the impacts of tropical forests on dry season flows and concludes that the infiltration properties of the forest are critical in determining how the available water is partitioned between runoff and recharge (leading to increased dry season flows).

The study carried out for the World Bank to investigate the hydrological impacts of a proposed afforestation scheme for the Panama Canal Watershed to 'improve flows and dry season flows' (Chapter 6) was not able to detect any significant trends (ie no 'signal') in time of low flow response on catchments which had experienced ~80 per cent deforestation over the past 50 years. The 'noise', the decadal variation in low flow response, was similar for both the deforested catchments and one that had retained intact forest cover. The modelling studies discussed in association with this project (Chapter 6) indicate that the interplay of soil and geological water storage factors, together with vegetation cover, may be critical in determining low flow response. On 'flashy' catchments with little groundwater storage capacity, the capacity may be filled at the end of the rainy season irrespective of the evaporative properties of the vegetation cover. The response might then be considered as geologically determined and relatively unaffected by vegetation cover. On catchments with greater groundwater storage capacity, differences in vegetation cover and evaporative response may result in differences in groundwater storage at the end of the rainy season which may result in differences in the storage 'decay' response, providing flow during the dry season. In this situation the dry season flow would be strongly determined by the vegetation cover.

Conclusions

Competing processes may result in either increased or reduced dry season flows. Effects on dry season flows are likely to be very site specific. Except for the Coalburn situation in which the increase in dry season flows was attributed to 'dewatering' of the catchment following drainage activities, the most recently published articles detailing studies of forest impacts on low flows are indicating a range of impacts from a very significant reduction of low flows from plantation forests compared with other vegetation types, to a 'no change' situation when indigenous forest is cleared (the Panama example). The geological conditions which determine groundwater storage capacity may be a critical factor in determining the range of low flow response following a change in vegetation cover. In none of the authenticated studies is there any evidence for the 'sponge effect'.

From theoretical considerations it is possible that reduced infiltration in degraded soils following forest clearing might outweigh the extra evaporation from forests, but it is becoming increasingly clear that if this situation exists it must only apply in the relatively rare situation of severe degradation – a situation that could be remedied by good land management, which would not necessarily warrant afforestation.

It cannot be assumed that afforestation will increase dry season flows; the available evidence indicates that it is more likely to reduce dry season flows.

Caveat

The complexity of the competing processes affecting dry season flows indicates that detailed, site-specific models will be required to predict impacts. In general, the role of vegetation in determining the infiltration properties of soils – as it affects the hydrological functioning of catchments through surface runoff generation, recharge, high and low flows and catchment degradation – remains poorly understood. Modelling approaches that are able to take into account vegetation and soil physical properties including the conductivity/water content properties of the soil, and possibly the spatial distribution of these properties, will be required to predict these site-specific impacts.

FORESTS REDUCE EROSION?

If foresters are under suspicion for propagating the myth that forests are the cause of high rainfall in upland areas, then there may be equal suspicions raised regarding the oft-cited universal claims of the benefits of forests in relation to reduced erosion. As with impacts on seasonal flows, the impacts on erosion are likely to be site specific, and again, many (often competing) processes are likely to be operating.

In relation to beneficial impacts, conventional theory and observations indicate that:

- the high infiltration rate in natural mixed forests reduces the incidence of surface runoff and reduces erosion transport;
- the reduced soil water pressure and the binding effect of tree roots enhance slope stability, which tends to reduce erosion; and
- on steep slopes, forestry or agroforestry may be the preferred option where conventional soil conservation techniques and bunding may be insufficient to retain mass movement of soil.

Adverse effects, often related to forest management activities, may result from:

- bad logging techniques which compact the soil and increase surface flow;
- pre-planting drainage activities which may initiate gully formation;
- the windthrow of trees and the weight of the tree crop reduces slope stability, which tends to increase erosion;
- road construction and road traffic, which can initiate landslides, gully formation and the mobilization of sediments;
- excessive grazing by farm animals, which leads to soil compaction, the removal of understorey plants and greater erosion risk; and
- splash-induced erosion from drops falling from the leaves of forest canopies.

The effects of catchment deforestation on erosion and the benefits gained by afforesting degraded and eroded catchments will be very dependent on the situation and the management methods employed.

Quoting Bruijnzeel (1990) 'In situations of high natural sediment yield as a result of steep terrain, high rainfall rates and geological factors, little, if any influence will be exerted by man'.

In the Himalayas, for example, there is evidence that a large proportion of suspended sediments in the rivers is contributed by big, deep, geologically induced landslides, which occur on any type of land cover, including forests (Galay, 1985).

Also, on drier land, in situations where overland flow is negligible, little advantage will be gained from afforestation. Versfeld (1981) has shown that at Jonkershoek in the Western Cape of South Africa, land cover has very little effect on the generation of overland flow and soil erosion. On the other hand, in more intermediate conditions of relatively low natural rates of erosion and under more stable geological conditions, human-induced effects may be considerable. In these situations, catchment degradation may well be hastened by deforestation and there may also be opportunities for reversing degradation by well-managed afforestation programmes.

In relation to conditions of steep slopes and high rainfall rates, some recently reported studies in Honduras provide unique insights into the dominant processes controlling sediment movement. These studies, conducted by Jon Hellin and Martin Haigh (2002a, b), aimed at determining the best form of erosion control. They examined the effects on moderate and steep slopes of a treatment of artificial vetiver grass barriers installed at 6-m intervals compared with control plots with no treatment. The plots were in an area of traditional maize cultivation on ground cleared from secondary forest. In most years it was found that there was no significant difference in the amount of soil eroded between control and treatment plots, nor any difference in the productivity of the plots. In dry years, maize production was higher in the control plots. This was attributed to the greater soil depth and soil water holding capacity of soil accumulated behind the barriers in the treatment plots. These studies were ongoing at the time that Hurricane Mitch passed over the experimental site, bringing the experiments to a halt, but at the same time providing the very rare opportunity to assess erosion rates for the two different treatments in very extreme rainfall conditions. Their analysis demonstrated two key points:

1   Under these extreme hurricane conditions there was no significant difference in erosion between control and treated plots – both were equally susceptible to landslides.
2   The erosion caused by landslides in just a few days during Hurricane Mitch was about 600 times the annual average rate of surface soil erosion.

This raised questions about the efficacy of traditional soil erosion control technologies when in the long-term, assuming Hurricane Mitch to have been a 1-in-200-year event, landslide erosion taking place in extreme events would far outweigh that produced from the more gradual surface erosion.

Haigh and colleagues (Haigh et al, 2004), in a paper on headwater deforestation, also report that 'Photographic records at Santa Rosa show a swarm of landslides and debris flows on the forested hills behind the research plots' which would indicate that it was not only the areas cleared for agriculture that were susceptible to landslides but also areas of natural forest. Similar observations have been made in Sarawak (Palmer, 2004, personal communication).

In an informal internet debate reported in the FAO Electronic Workshop on Land–Water Linkages in 2000 (Calder, 2000), which also discussed Hurricane Mitch, there were no clear conclusions drawn with respect to the benefits of forests on steep slopes exposed to hurricane conditions (Box 2.1) or whether afforestation was necessarily the best remedial treatment for slopes which had undergone landslides.

Lu and colleagues (2001) have reported on experiences in Taiwan; 74 per cent of the island is mountainous with steep slopes and weak geologic formations. Rainfall is high (annual average 2500mm) and the typhoon season brings torrential rainfall resulting in flooding, debris torrents and landslides. Together with problems due to flooding there are also problems in parts of the island due to seasonal water shortages. These are expected to become more severe as Taiwan's population expands from its current 590 people per square kilometre. The authors describe results from the ongoing catchment experiments and hydrological studies:

Box 2.1 Extracts from an internet debate: Forests and landslides

Ian Cherret (working on an FAO project, Honduras) on Hurricane Mitch:

Calder's comment on management activities is very relevant (that management activities associated with forestry such as cultivation, drainage, road construction and soil compaction during logging are more likely to influence flood/erosion response than the presence or absence of the forests themselves). This would be a good time to do field research in Honduras – Choluteca Basin – where first impressions are that extensive landslides did so much damage (a rough estimate of level of sediment carried by flood waters running through Tegucigalpa at their height is 15–17 per cent). The impression is also that landslides were concentrated where mature trees had been cleared (only shallow roots holding the saturated soil) or pine woods that had suffered extensive burning last May (impoverished soils). This deserves investigating. Recent research by Texas A & M on an AID-funded project in the worst hit basin suggests that soil loss through landslides is at least as important in Central America as loss through runoff and wind (Technical Bulletin No. 98-2 1998). And the key to landslide control is deep roots provided by large trees.

Our experiences do not contradict the conclusions of Calder or Chomitz (relating to the importance of management activities), but they do indicate that part of the need for further research requires unravelling relationships such as that of SOIL and vegetational cover as opposed to TREES per se.

Jim Smyle (Natural Resources Specialist, Project RUTA, Costa Rica):

The second topic (relating to lack of vegetation causing landslides) can be a bit more thorny, as it can be governed by very local factors and those factors may have little to do with vegetation. For example, the Choluteca basin had a tremendous amount of landsliding. It is also heavily deforested. It also appears to have a geology and soil type which makes it highly susceptible to landsliding. Deep-rooted trees could be the answer...though in Hawaii's unconsolidated upland soils the weight of forest on hillslopes often makes them MORE susceptible to sliding.

Ian Cherret (working on an FAO project, Honduras) on Hurricane Mitch:

In the watershed Lempira Sur in Rio Mocal, serious landslides occurred in the upper watershed on mount Celaque, the highest peak (2900m) in Honduras, at over 2000 metres! They were deforested areas though – a thousand people have had to be relocated from just one landslide. Clearly the underlying geology has something to do with the propensity to landslides. I believe that there is a need for a more scientific study looking at factors such as slope, cover, geomorphology and rainfall pattern.

Source: Calder (2000)

we recognize that forest cover has limitations in attenuating major
flood peaks and debris flows; the extent to which different forest
types can mitigate such effects is not well understood in Taiwan.

But although the potential benefits of forests on flood and debris flows have
not yet been established, the water resource downsides of forest cover are well
understood, as illustrated by the earlier results of Hsia and Koh (1982) for the
Lienhuachi paired-catchment experiment in central Taiwan. This study reported
(albeit for the relatively short period of 2 years) that, compared with a control
catchment, the water yield increases following the clear cutting of a 5.86-ha
natural hardwood forested watershed were 240mm (27 per cent) and 46mm
(91 per cent) for the 1979 wet and dry seasons, respectively, and 184mm (41
per cent) and 20mm (70 per cent) for the 1980 wet and dry seasons. The as-
yet unquantified benefits of Taiwanese forests in relation to flood and debris
flow need therefore to be carefully considered in relation to the costs of the
quantified reductions in seasonal water yield – where as much as 91 per cent
increases in dry season flow might be expected as a result of forest removal.

An interesting and alternative perspective on what are usually portrayed
as landslide 'disasters' is provided by Ives and colleagues (Ives et al, 2002).
They report instances in the Himalayan region where landslides are not always
produced by natural catastrophes. They claim that sometimes they are deliberately induced by farmers, by rerouting streams, as a means of providing
'soft run-out earth' which can be more easily worked into agricultural terrace
systems.

Together with providing important insights into erosion processes on steep
slopes and under conditions of high rainfall, the same paper on headwater deforestation by Haigh and colleagues (Haigh et al, 2004) also presents sedimentation
data for the middle Danube River Basin in Europe. This might be considered to
be representative of the 'more intermediate conditions of relatively low natural
rates of erosion and under more stable geological conditions – where man-
induced effects may be considerable'. These data relate to annual average
sediment accumulation in reservoirs fed by rivers draining 27 catchments of
different sizes and with different degrees of forest cover (Table 2.1).

Haigh and colleagues present this data graphically as sediment accumulation as a function of non-forested catchment area (Figure 2.3). The
implication of this graph is that reduced forest cover is associated with very
large and significant increases in sedimentation.

But if the same data are presented in a different form, a form in which
the effect of catchment size is removed by normalization, a rather different
conclusion can be drawn. In Figure 2.4 the sediment deposition, expressed in
units of volume of sediment per unit area of catchment, is plotted against the
fraction of the catchment area deforested. Here we see little justification for
concluding that there is a significant linkage between sediment production
and forest cover. The relationship shown in Figure 2.4 indicates essentially no
statistically significant difference in the sediment production on a per unit
area basis of catchments with different degrees of forest cover (coefficient of
determination, $R^2 = 0.09$). Reappraisal of this data, which initially appeared

Table 2.1 Summary of sedimentation data for the reservoir and headwater region of the middle Danube River Basin in Europe, Western Carpathian Mountains

Reservoir	Reservoir watershed area (km²)	Reservoir flooded area (ha)	Reservoir capacity (1000m³)	Non-forested watershed area (km²)	Average annual sediment accumulation (m³)	Average annual sediment accumulation normalized by watershed area (m³km⁻²)
1 Pl.Vozokany	20.1	17	164	18.09	7554	376
2 Vel'ky Dur	10.2	10	130	10.20	3762	369
3 Drzenice	17.5	7	98	12.25	3676	210
4 Mankovce	18.0	3	50	9.00	188	10
5 Kolinany	17.0	13	106	15.30	1474	87
6 Capor	13.1	8	128	13.10	556	42
7 Jelenec	11.1	7	174	5.55	1861	168
8 Bajtava	5.5	7	48	4.95	721	131
9 Dedinka	16.4	15	246	14.76	4326	264
10 Dubnik	12.5	14	240	12.50	2360	189
11 Mana	6.2	8	169	6.20	960	155
12 Travnica	25.3	20	288	20.24	7478	296
13 Svodin	9.8	14	221	9.80	4171	426
14 Brezolupy	24.0	7	90	9.60	3143	131
15 Nedasovce	28.0	6	60	14.00	1174	42
16 Ratka	0.8	1	17	0.48	250	313
17 Bolesov	11.1	2	26	4.44	544	49
18 Glabusovce	8.7	14	180	6.96	580	67
19 Karna	2.0	2	17	1.20	578	289
20 Kosic. Olsany	3.5	2	25	2.80	505	144
21 Pol'ov	5.1	5	75	5.10	971	190
22 Trstena pri H	8.4	2	34	5.88	864	103
23 V.Kamenica	11.4	2	32	7.98	2972	261
24 Gem.Teplica	3.7	14	257	2.22	1067	288
25 Hrusov I.	2.6	4	36	1.82	1150	442
26 Nizny Zipov	3.5	9	146	3.50	1270	363
27 Bor-Tovarne	7.5	8	203	3.75	1464	195

Source: Modified from Haigh et al (2004)

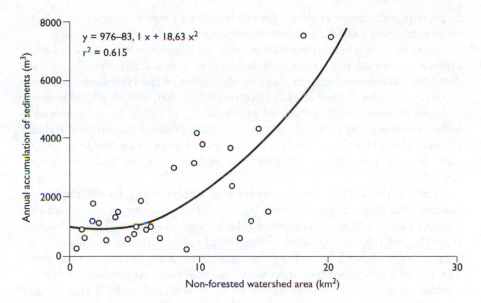

Figure 2.3 *Relationship between sediment deposition (m³) and non-forested catchment area for reservoirs in Western Carpathia, Slovakia*

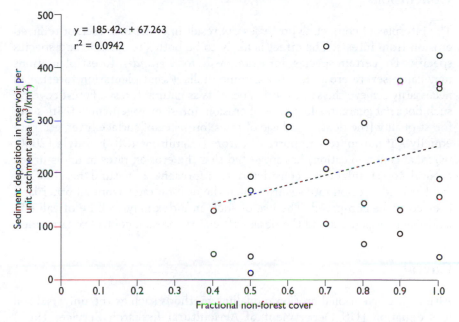

Note: Data taken from Table 2.1

Figure 2.4 *Relationship between sediment deposition, expressed in units of volume of sediment per unit area of catchment (m³km⁻²), and the fraction of the catchment area that is deforested, for reservoirs in Western Carpathia, Slovakia*

to provide such strong evidence for the benefits of forest cover in relation to erosion on these basins, on closer inspection reveals this to be an illusion.

In situations where afforestation schemes may have benefit in reducing erosion, it should not necessarily be seen as a quick panacea. In heavily degraded catchments, such as those on the slopes of the Himalayas, so much eroded material will have already been mobilized that, even if all the human-induced erosion could be stopped immediately, it would be many decades before there was any reduction in the amount of material carried by the rivers (Pearce, 1986; Hamilton, 1987). The choice of tree species will also be important in any programme designed to reduce erosion and catchment degradation.

Recent theoretical developments and observations (see Chapter 1) confirm that drop size modification by the vegetation canopies of trees can be a major factor leading to enhanced splash-induced erosion. These observations (Figure 1.6) indicate that the degree of modification is species-related, with tree species with larger leaves generally generating the largest drop sizes. The use of large-leaved tree species such as teak (*Tectona grandis*) in erosion control programmes would therefore be ill advised, especially if there is any possibility of understorey removal taking place.

Conclusions

The interplay of competing processes can result in either increased or reduced erosion from forests. The effect is likely to be both site specific and species specific. For certain species, for example *Tectona grandis*, forest plantations may cause severe erosion. It is a common fallacy that plantation forests can necessarily achieve the same erosion benefits as natural forests. Forest cover as such does not guarantee low rates of erosion; forest management activities and forest quality (the density and age of trees, presence of surface litter, etc.) are equally – if not more – important factors (Hamilton, 1987). Smyle (2000, personal communication) has suggested that the erosion rates in undisturbed natural forest might be considered to represent a 'natural baseline' or 'background' erosion rate against which the erosion rates from all other land uses could be compared. The use of such an index may well be of value in land-use management and the design of realistic erosion control programmes.

Caveat

Although conventional erosion modelling methods such as the universal soil loss equation (US Department of Agricultural Research Service, 1961) provide a practical solution to many problems associated with soil loss from agricultural lands, it may not be adequate for the prediction of erosion resulting from afforestation activities. Understanding of the erosive potential of drops falling from different tree species is not adequately appreciated; soil conservation techniques related to vegetation type, soils and slope characteristics have not yet been fully developed.

FORESTS REDUCE FLOODS?

It is a widely held view, propagated by foresters and the media, that forests are of great benefit in reducing floods. Disastrous floods in Bangladesh and northern India are almost always associated with 'deforestation of the Himalayas'; similarly, in Europe, floods are often attributed by the media to 'deforestation in the Alps'. However, hydrological studies carried out in many parts of the world – America (Hewlett and Helvey, 1970), South Africa (Hewlett and Bosch, 1984), UK (Kirby et al, 1991; Robinson and Newson, 1986; Johnson, 1995), New Zealand (Taylor and Pearce, 1982) and Asia (Bruijnzeel and Bremmer, 1989; Ives and Messerli, 1989; Hofer, 1998a, 1998b) – and involving many disciplines including hydrology, soil science and climatology, demonstrate a great complexity in the way in which the biophysical processes affecting flood response interact (Bonell, 1993): a complexity unimagined in most populist accounts of land use and flood interactions. Some recent electronic conferences have also thrown new light on the different mechanisms that may be at work and have identified areas where scientific understanding of the processes is still lacking.

In broad terms we might expect land use to affect the severity of floods in two ways: through affecting channel flow or channel form, either of which may cause rivers to overflow their banks.

The flow rate and peak flow rate in a river may be affected both by the total quantity of runoff produced during a flood event and also by alteration of the timing of the flood peak, particularly as these flood peaks arrive and are 'added together' from tributary rivers. Changes in channel form may occur as a result of alteration of the channel network through, for example, construction of drainage ditches or road drains or through 'obstruction' of the river channel by processes such as sedimentation of the channel, catastrophic landslides and through debris blocking culverts and bridges. Here, it can be seen that the forest- and land use-related processes which can affect erosion might also affect flood generation.

The complexity of land-use influences on evaporation, on surface runoff generation and on erosion, which affect channel flow and channel form, prohibits simple generalization of impacts. But the scientific evidence does allow the derivation of guiding principles which have been identified and reviewed by a number of authors (Lull and Reinhart, 1972; Hewlett, 1982; Bosch and Hewlett, 1982; Hamilton, 1987; Bruijnzeel, 1990; Swanston, 1991; Calder, 1992c, 1999, 2000; McCulloch and Robinson, 1993).

From theoretical considerations it would be expected that interception of rainfall by forests would reduce floods by removing a proportion of the storm rainfall and by allowing the build up of soil moisture deficits. These effects would be expected to be most significant for small storms and least significant for the largest storms.

The analysis carried out by Mark Robinson and Malcolm Newson on the Wye and Severn experimental catchments at Plynlimon, in central Wales, illustrates this effect. Both catchments have areas of around 10km^2; the Wye is under short moorland vegetation whilst the Severn is under commercial conifer

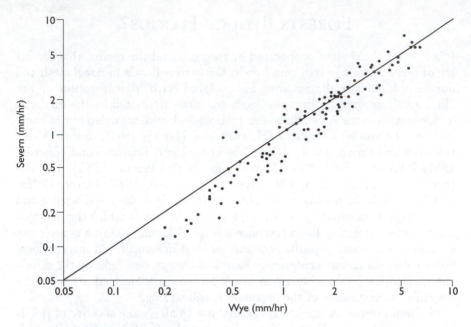

Note: Flows are expressed as hourly depths
Source: Robinson and Newson (1986)

Figure 2.5 *Comparison of peak 15-min flows for over 100 storms on the Wye (moorland) and Severn (70% forested) catchments*

forestry and has undergone site preparation activities, including the installation of drainage ditches. For the period 1975–1978 they selected over 100 rainfall events, giving peak discharges ranging over two orders of magnitude (Figure 2.5). They concluded that for small storms, peak flows were consistently greater from the moorland Wye catchment compared with the forested Severn, whereas for larger events (giving discharge peaks greater than 1mmh^{-1}) there was no systematic difference between the peaks for the two catchments.

The benefits of forestry in reducing flood peaks might therefore be most pronounced for small, frequent flood events. For the largest, more damaging but less frequent events, which are sometimes termed long return period events, the benefits are likely to be much reduced (see Box 2.2). A notional relationship of the form shown in Figure 2.6 would be expected. For certain types of commercial forests (see below) there is a debate as to whether 'factory' forests might actually increase, rather than reduce, flood peaks for the largest events.

It is important to bear in mind differences in response that might occur between natural and plantation forests. Soils under natural forests tend to be relatively porous with high infiltration rates (and consequently low rates of surface runoff) and generally exhibit low rates of erosion. This is not neces-sarily the case for plantation forests. Whereas natural forest soils may take centuries to evolve, plantation soil may still have the former essentially grass-land or agricultural soil beneath. Where no understorey of vegetation is

---

BOX 2.2 LONG RETURN PERIOD EVENTS AND PROBABILITIES

The magnitude of extreme flood and storm events has traditionally been characterized in terms of the 'return period', where the larger the flood, the longer the return period. Neither hydrologist nor the general public find this concept particularly easy to understand and a probability index is now preferred (see Institute of Civil Engineers, 2001). For a 100-year (return period) flood we would say that the odds are 100 to 1 against such a flood (or greater flood) occurring in any year (100–1 chance flood) or, alternatively, it could be expressed as a flood with a 1 per cent annual probability of occurring. Casting magnitudes in probability terms avoids the apparently nonsensical situation of a number of 100-year floods occurring within a short period of time – as has happened recently in the UK. It also avoids sending out the potentially dangerous message that once a large flood has occurred, say a 100-year flood, it will be another 100 years before another one happens.

---

maintained, or where management activities involving site preparation, cultivation, drainage, road construction and logging take place, plantation forests may have detrimental effects (Anderson et al, 1976). Forest management activities involved with drainage and planting, road construction, road use and logging may not only contribute to increases in rates of surface runoff during storm conditions but also increase the transport of sediments into watercourses. The benefits of forests, whether natural or plantation, for preventing landslips and catastrophic erosion events are likely to be site specific and possibly event specific. For example, the binding effects of roots and the generally drier conditions under forest will tend to stabilize slopes in storm conditions, whereas the windthrow of trees, when it occurs, can be particularly devastating in terms of debris transport into rivers with the added potential of not only blocking watercourses but also fouling bridges and culverts and causing added flood damage.

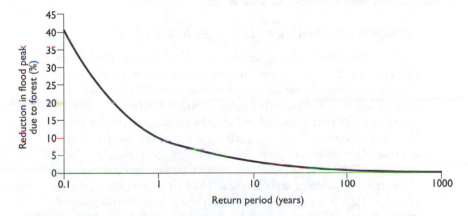

Figure 2.6 *Schematic representation of the reduction in flood peak that might be expected from an 'average' forest for floods of different magnitudes*

The scientific perception also recognizes that although the effects of land use change on floods may be detectable on small catchments, the 'signal' is likely to be weaker on large catchments. Three reasons have been suggested for this weakened signal:

1   Processes which may reduce the 'time to peak' (and thereby increase the magnitude of the peak of the flood in small catchments) may have less effect, proportionately, in large basins because the flood peaks arriving from the small catchments are not likely to arrive together, i.e. they will not be in synchrony.
2   The proportionate change in land use is likely to be higher for small catchments.
3   Storms of sufficient spatial scale to saturate large basins are likely to be of the largest magnitude, and for these extreme storm events (low probability), the effects of land use change on flood response are expected to be least pronounced.

The 'emerging consensus' of opinion from the scientific community on these issues was illustrated in an informal internet debate which was stimulated by the writings of Kaimowitz (1998), published in the influential *Polex* newsletter of the Consultative Group on International Agriculture Research (CGIAR). This newsletter was instrumental in drawing attention to the disparity between the scientific perception of the causes of floods, which had been the focus of a number of papers prepared for a wider, policymaking audience (Chomitz and Kumari, 1998; Calder, 1998a; 1999), and the public perception as reflected by national and development organizations' response strategies. The debate involved representatives of the World Bank, CGIAR, international consultants and educational and research organizations. A summary of these discussions was reported in the Food and Agriculture Organization (FAO) Electronic Workshop on Land–Water Linkages in Rural Watersheds, October 2000. Two excerpts are presented below relating to forest and sediment linkages and scale issues:

Deforestation–Sediment Linkages to Flooding

A discussion on the relationship between land use and flooding in the case of the recent disaster in Central America due to Hurricane Mitch drew on observations from China where the accumulation of sediment and other deposited material (channel aggradations) may have led to the need to raise dikes (or build the Three Gorges Dam) to maintain the same level of flood control. Observations from Honduras suggest that a rough estimate of the level of sediment carried by floodwaters running through Tegucigalpa at their height is 15–17 per cent. Participants also noted the question of how to assess the relative importance of channel aggradations due to deforestation and the problem of human encroachment in flood plains.

Scale Issues

Discussions on efforts to collect data and develop computer models of water and sediment runoff, including those undertaken by the USDA Forest Service on experimental watersheds, highlighted the problem of scale. At small scales, increased water and sediment runoff due to deforestation can be identified and incorporated into hydrological models. At larger scales, increases in flood flows are not so easily discerned or modelled. A participant noted that this may be due to the integration of the cumulative effects from an entire watershed, of which only a relatively small percentage may have been affected by deforestation. More centrally, however, participants felt that the increase in scale reduces the likelihood of coincident peaks (in flows) far downstream. This 'hydraulic attenuation' (which tends to result in decreased flood peaks but longer time based hydrographs) may mask an overall increase in flow during storm events in large basins. It was felt that more hydrologic modelling at these larger scales was necessary in order to develop some sense of the magnitude of increased runoff in relation to the size, intensity and movement of large storms. Such work would test the working hypothesis that as the size of the flood event increases, the effects of land use would become less important. Given that most of the larger flood disasters occur at such large scales, such information would be important for decision-making. (Calder, 2000)

Since the FAO electronic workshop of 2000, a number of studies reporting experiences in the UK, Europe, America and India at the small to medium catchment scale have provided further important information on the role of forests and floods.

In Chapter 5 of the UK Forestry Commission's report *Climate Change: Impacts on UK Forests*, Tom Nisbet (2002), recognizing the public perception, states, 'Forestry is viewed by many as having an important role to play in reducing flood risk'. On consideration of some of the scientific arguments reviewed in the report, he concludes that '...the scope for forests to reduce the severity of major floods that are derived from an extended period of very heavy rainfall is rather limited'. He also gives examples of circumstances in which afforestation programmes in the UK may actually have increased the flood risk:

Cultivation and drainage practices can exert a strong effect on the timing of runoff from forest catchments. Deep ploughing and intensive drainage have the greatest impact since they increase the density of water channels by 60 times or more. This can increase flood flows by up to 20–30 per cent and decrease the time to peak by about one-third for completely drained catchments. The effect is long lasting, although it declines through time with soil subsidence and the infilling of drains. Badly designed

> *drainage systems and the diversion of runoff from one catchment to another can also cause local flooding problems.* (Nisbet, 2002)

From America, Jonathan La Marche and Dennis Lettenmair (2001) have described the results obtained from comprehensive field experiments and a modelling study of the extensively logged 149-km^2 catchment of the Deschutes River, Washington, USA.

Through the use of a calibrated model they showed that at this experimental catchment scale, forest removal (without introducing any road effects) would increase the mean annual flood by about 10 per cent. For floods of greater magnitude (longer return period) the model predictions indicated a decreasing (percentage) effect. The effects of forest roads (without any forest removal), which effectively increase the density of the stream network, were predicted to increase the mean annual flood by a similar amount (~10 per cent). But, unlike the forest removal effect, the 'road' effect was shown to increase with increasing flood magnitude. While the effect of forests in flood amelioration decreases as the size of the storm event increases, the road (with associated drains) is a permanent fixture that contributes to the runoff directly as the storm input increases. It is critical to differentiate between the effects of removal of forest cover and the effects of roads used to access the forest and to help remove that cover. Timing of water runoff can change as roads and related drainage structures intercept, collect and divert water. This accelerates water delivery to the stream; more water becomes runoff, which increases the potential for runoff peaks to occur earlier, to be of greater magnitude and to recede more quickly than in watersheds without roads (Wemple et al, 1996).

This study helps disentangle the 'road' and 'forest removal' effects associated with logging. The implication is that forest clearance per se would not increase average annual size floods by much more than about 10 per cent (see Figure 2.6). For the largest, most damaging floods we would expect considerably less than a 10 per cent increase, and less again at larger spatial scales. The USDA publication *Forest Service Roads: A Synthesis of Scientific Information* (USDA Forest Service 2000), summarizing the results of a number of recent American studies on the effects of roading and timber harvest on hydrologic regimes, states that:

> *Collectively, these studies suggest that the effect of roads on basin stream flow is generally smaller than the effect of forest cutting, primarily because the area occupied by roads is much smaller than that occupied by harvest operations. Generally, hydrologic recovery after road building takes much longer than after forest harvest because roads modify physical hydrologic pathways but harvesting principally affects evapotranspiration processes.*

Sikka and colleagues (Sikka et al, 2003) have reported on the impacts on both flood flows and low flows of converting natural grassland to eucalypt plantation in the Nilgiris region of south India. Fast-growing eucalypt plantations are highly efficient in terms of plot water use efficiency (i.e. the amount of above ground biomass produced per unit of water evaporated), but have long been recognized as disproportionately large consumers of water and thus are expected to reduce catchment flows (Calder, 1996a). The studies of Sikka and colleagues confirm these expectations. The detailed and long-term (1968–1992) paired-catchment experiments in the Nilgiris, where the responses from a 'control' catchment under natural grassland were compared with those from a catchment with 59 per cent eucalypt cover monitored over a period encompassing two rotations of the eucalypt crop, show, from the point of view of hydroelectric power generators, very serious reductions in low flows during the dry season. Expressed in terms of a 'low flow index' (defined as the 10 days average flow which is exceeded for 95 per cent of the time of the flow record), the low flows were reduced by approximately one-half during the first rotation and by one-quarter during the second rotation of the eucalypt crop.

Flood flows were also reduced but, importantly, the authors conclusions from the analysis of probability plots of peak discharge from the two catchments were that the 'effect of blue gum plantation (*Eucalyptus globulus*) on peak flows becomes insignificant for the largest floods', i.e. those with a low annual probability of flooding (high return periods). Any small gains the plantations achieved through reducing peak flows were therefore obtained at the expense of very serious reductions (for hydropower generation) in low flows.

Again, Robinson and Dupeyrat (2005) from the UK have reported studies of the changing flow regime following logging on the Plynlimon experimental catchments in central Wales. They report changes in annual yield, low flows and peak flows in nested catchments at scales from about 1 to 10km^2. Although the authors were primarily investigating changes in flows following logging, whereas in India Sikka and colleagues were investigating the changes in flows as the trees grew, the conclusions drawn from both studies were similar. Robinson and Dupeyrat conclude 'somewhat surprisingly, and in marked contrast with much of the extensive literature on the subject, there was no evidence that forest felling had a significant influence on peak flows'. They did qualify this result by saying that 'it should be noted that peak flow increases have often been attributed to soil compaction and disturbance reducing infiltration. Following modern forest management guidelines, care was generally taken during the felling to reduce soil damage and hence surface runoff by the use of brash mats.' They also reported that forest cutting increased annual flows and augmented low flows, a result also consistent with the studies reported by Sikka and colleagues.

Robinson, together with European researchers (Robinson et al, 2003), investigated under the FOREX (Forestry and Extreme Flows) project, funded by the European Commission's FAIR programme, the impacts of forest on peak and low flows through analysis of data from 28 small basins across Europe. The conclusions were that:

Overall, the results from these studies conducted under realistic forest management procedures have shown that the potential for forests to reduce peak and low flows is much less than has often been widely claimed. Consequently, other than at a local scale, for the particular cases of managed plantations on poorly drained soils in NW Europe and Eucalyptus in Southern Europe, forestry appears to probably have a relatively small role to play in managing regional or large-scale flood risk or influencing drought flows across Europe.

The authors also reported that whilst the effects of forests and forest management on the extreme flows of rivers may often be thought uniquely site specific, the FOREX study found relatively consistent results between regions and sites which gave confidence to the generality of the results.

The scientific evidence for land use (particularly forest) impacts on floods has generally been derived from research directed at understanding individual processes on a small spatial scale, often at the tree or plot scale, together with research at the experimental catchment scale (as described above). Because of the complexity of the interacting processes which will be affected by land use change, the net effect, or 'integrated effect', becomes increasingly difficult to predict at increasing spatial scales. All the more important then are the results from studies that have investigated impacts at large basin scales.

Arguably the most important and illuminating in this respect are the University of Berne, Institute of Geography's detailed and comprehensive studies (Hofer, 1998a, 1998b) of the flood regime of the Ganga–Brahmaputra–Meghna river system. Based on detailed analysis of the hydrological records of the past 40 years, Hofer states '...it can be inferred that floods are a normal process in the Ganga–Brahmaputra–Meghna lowlands. Neither the frequency nor the magnitude of flooding has increased over the last few decades. Consequently there is no reason to believe that floods in the lowlands have intensified as a result of human impact in the highlands'.

Earlier, Marston and colleagues (Marston et al, 1996) had arrived at a similar conclusion, but working at a smaller spatial scale. They recognized that 'monsoon season floods in the central Nepal Himalaya have been difficult to predict with any precision, reliability or accuracy'. Using field data at 22 stream crossings, together with drainage basin morphometric data and forest cover data to determine the dominant controls on bank-full discharge from monsoon storms, they claimed that 'results demonstrate that 82 per cent of the variation in bank-full discharge can be explained as a function of drainage area alone; forest cover did not add explanatory power'.

Conclusions

For the largest, most damaging flood events there is little scientific evidence to support anecdotal reports of deforestation being the cause. As the severity of the flood increases the benefits of having forest cover appears to be reduced. The high infiltration rates under natural forests serve to reduce surface runoff and flood response. Field studies generally indicate that it is often the management activities associated with forestry – cultivation, drainage, road construction (Jones and Grant, 1996) and soil compaction during logging – which are more likely to influence flood response than the presence or absence of the forests themselves.

Caveat

Carefully conducted, controlled catchment experiments with different climates, soils and species will be required to resolve this issue, but species impacts are probably not as significant as often portrayed. Management activities are most likely to be paramount. There remains a need to better understand the interrelationship between different hydrological functions that are impacted by land use change, such as that among sediment, the build-up of river channels and flood heights. As the linkages between the impacts of forest and non-forest cover (such as roads) become better identified, the alternatives for minimizing associated flood risk will become clearer.

FORESTS 'STERILIZE' WATER SUPPLIES AND IMPROVE WATER QUALITY?

Forests were historically the preferred land use for water supply catchments because of their perceived 'sterile' qualities associated with an absence of livestock and human activities. More recently the generally reduced fertilizer and pesticide applications to forests compared with agricultural lands have been regarded as a benefit with regard to the water quality of runoff and recharge. Reduced soil erosion from natural forests can also be regarded as a benefit.

Offsetting these benefits, management activities such as cultivation, drainage, road construction, road use and felling are all likely to increase erosion and nutrient leaching. Furthermore, deposition of most atmospheric pollutants to forests is higher because of the reduced aerodynamic resistance of forest canopies compared with those of shorter crops. In high-pollution (industrial) regions this is likely to lead to both long-term acidification of the catchment and acidification of runoff. An example in which water quality was worsened by forests is provided by recent studies at Sherwood Forest in the Midlands of England (see Chapter 6). It is believed that high atmospheric pollutant deposition, both gaseous and particulate, has lead to increased deposition of nitrates and chlorates. Beneath pine forest at Sherwood, nitrate concentrations in soil water exceed World Health Organization limits for drinking water.

Conclusions

Except in regions of high pollution, water quality is likely to be better from forested catchments. Adverse effects of forests on water quality are more likely to be related to bad management practices than the presence of the forests themselves.

Caveat

Studies may still be required to determine the magnitude of the impacts for specific sites and the means to minimize adverse impacts.

AGROFORESTRY SYSTEMS INCREASE PRODUCTIVITY?

Agriculturists have long recognized the productivity benefits that can be gained by mixing different agricultural crops. When a crop such as pigeon pea is mixed with sorghum or maize, much higher production is obtained compared with pure crops of these species which occupy the same total ground area. When productivity of the mixture is superior to that of monoculture it is regarded that the mixture is overyielding and that complementarity has occurred. The production possibility frontier (PPF) is one way in which complementarity and overyielding between crop mixtures can be illustrated (Ranganathan and de Wit, 1996). It can also serve to illustrate the neutral and underyielding situations which can occur between crops due to competition or when one crop inhibits the growth of the other through allelopathic effects (Figure 2.7).

Complementarity can occur when the crops in a mixture can together make better use of resources whose supplies are limited. When the resources that crops need for growth (water, light, nutrients and carbon dioxide) are in excess of those needs (i.e. in unlimited supply), densely planted monocultures are generally found to be the most efficient at capturing resources and will have the highest biomass production. Complementarity usually is brought about when one of three conditions is satisfied:

1   Spatial complementarity occurs when the mixture is better able to access resources (such as water, nutrients and light) than the monoculture.
2   Temporal complementarity occurs when the temporal requirements for resources are matched so that high needs in one crop are matched by low needs in the other.
3   The third case is when one of the crops is a legume and can fix nitrogen as a soil nutrient resource which can be of benefit to the other crops.

With the exception of nitrogen fixation, overyielding through complementarity can only come about through greater use of existing limited water or nutrient resources. Most commonly, in arid and semi-arid environments, water will be a resource in limited supply and for complementarity and overyielding to occur, water use by the mixture will be increased over that of monocultures and less water will be available for other downstream uses whether these be 'environmental' or for supply purposes (see Chapter 4). Within the context of integrated land and water resource management, the benefits of increased productivity need to be assessed in relation to the costs to other possible potential downstream users of the water and 'the environment' as a user, together with the extra labour costs that may be entailed in the sowing, tillage and cropping of a mixture.

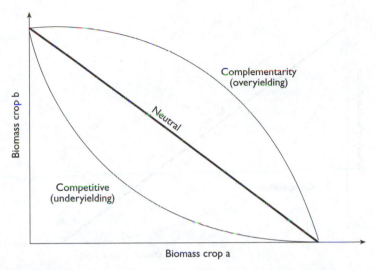

Note: The *x* and *y* axes represent biomass production by pure stands of each species and mixtures are shown on the hypotenuse. When the productivity of the mixture lies above the hypotenuse, complementarity occurs, and when it lies below, competition has reduced productivity below that which could be achieved with optimal sole stands of each species.
Source: Following Ong et al, 1996

Figure 2.7 *Production possibility frontiers (PPF) showing competition and complementarity for two hypothetical crops, a and b.*

It is thought that the increased productivity that has been recorded for mixtures of agricultural crops is largely the result of temporal complementarity, especially when one crop is an annual and the other a biennial, or as a result of nitrogen fixation by one of the crops. Mixtures with pigeon pea, grown either as an annual or biennial legume, exhibit both, and pigeon pea has been found to show complementarity with many species such as maize, sorghum, groundnut and cowpea (Ranganathan and de Wit, 1996).

Agroforestry is built on the belief that mixtures of agricultural crops and trees can also lead to increased productivity, the belief that it is possible to find overyielding mixtures of crops and trees which, when combined, would have a higher yield than when grown separately on the same land area.

A substantial agroforestry literature exists which claims that there are experimental results from agroforestry trials which support this belief. Yet these claims may be erroneous and the trials flawed. From detailed studies of resource capture for both intercropping and agroforestry systems – carried out at the International Crops Research Institute for the Semi Arid Tropics (ICRISAT) sites at Hyderabad in India and the International Centre for Research in Agroforestry (ICRAF) sites at Machakos in Kenya – Ong et al (1991 and 1996) have developed a scientific framework and process understanding which undermine many of the agroforesters' claims for increased biomass from agroforestry systems. These experimental studies suggest that with agroforestry systems, often the best that can be achieved is near to neutral productivity (Figure 2.8).

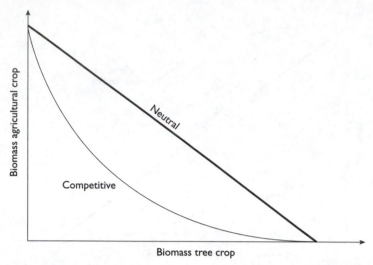

Note: Through competition for resources, particularly water, generally the best that can be achieved is the neutral condition. It is now realized that the presence of the trees will, for all known tree and agricultural crop mixtures, reduce the productivity of the agricultural crop

Figure 2.8 *Competition and complementarity relationship shown as a production possibility frontiers (PPF) for a typical agricultural crop and tree crop mixture*

By the application of rigorous scientific reasoning, Ong et al (ibid) have also identified some of the pitfalls that have trapped agroforestry researchers into thinking that complementarity and overyielding systems had been achieved. These have arisen mainly because the control plots containing the monocultures have not been under optimal conditions so that the mixture achieved a favourable bias.

One identified pitfall is that, for the convenience of statistical analysis, the same plant densities are used in both the monocultures and the mixtures, although, to achieve optimal productivity in the monoculture, higher densities would be required.

A second is that the mixture and monoculture are managed identically even though this management may result in sub-optimal productivity in the monoculture. For example, pruning, which has been used in the mixture to reduce competition from the trees and to return nutrients to the system, would not produce optimal productivity if applied to the control plot.

A third example is that plot sizes may be too small, allowing tree roots from the mixture or the monoculture tree plots to penetrate into the plots of the agricultural monoculture and reduce their yields (van Noordwijk et al, 1996). Ong (1996) has shown from studies at Machakos, Kenya, that the roots of the tree *Leucaena leucocephala* can reduce the yield of maize 5m away within 2 years of growth.

One of the fundamental differences between agroforestry systems and intercropping systems is that the tree component in an agroforestry system, after the initial establishment period, has a well developed and deep root system. Opportunities for spatial complementarity of below-ground resources are therefore limited because the tree roots tend to exploit the whole root zone. Furthermore, after the initial establishment, the tree roots are always present in the soil profile, so there are no opportunities for temporal complementarity. Although trees with nitrogen-fixing root nodules may have potential for complementarity with some agricultural crops, the competitive advantage of trees, which have 'first choice' in tapping soil water and nutrients when the agricultural crops are sown, will usually outweigh these benefits.

Spatial complementarity of above-ground resources, particularly in relation to light capture, is achievable with tree–crop mixtures. Rao et al (1990) have shown that at the ICRISAT site at Hyderabad, a mixture of *Leucaena leucocephala* and millet increased the light capture above that of a sole millet crop. However, this improved light capture did not result in increased biomass production of the mixture – the biomass produced by the trees was essentially equal to the loss in biomass yield of the crop. This lack of improvement has been explained (Cannell et al, 1998) in terms of the photosynthetic processes operating in trees (all C3 type), which are less efficient in their light-to-biomass conversion efficiencies than crops such as millet, which are of C4 type and will have much higher efficiencies. Even though greater resource capture is achieved, this does not translate into higher total productivity.

It is now becoming apparent that trees in agroforestry systems will generally lead to a reduction in biomass of the associated crop (Ong 1996) and neutral total biomass production is usually the best that can be expected.

Modelling studies by Cannell et al (1998) also support this view. Through the use of a process-based agroforestry model which takes into account competition for light and water (but not nutrients), they were able to simulate the growth of a sorghum and tree-crop mixture under different climatic conditions. Their conclusions can be summarized as follows:

- At sites with less than 800mm rainfall, maximum total site biomass production was obtained with a monoculture, without overstorey trees.
- At sites with 800–1000mm rainfall, neutral biomass production was obtained with a mixture.
- At sites with greater than 1000mm rainfall, biomass production would be increased with a mixture provided the leaf area index (LAI) of the trees was greater than 0.25 – but this increase in overall production would be at the expense of a 60 per cent reduction in sorghum grain yields.
- Any decrease in crop yields due to tree competition will automatically increase the frequency of years with poor yields and threaten food security.

Therefore, for low-rainfall sites, monocultures would clearly be the best option and even at higher-rainfall sites, to achieve higher total biomass production, it would be necessary to accept a large (60 per cent) reduction in the sorghum crop yield. Cannell et al (ibid) make the point that 'the biomass produced by the trees must be of considerable value relative to that of sorghum grain for this sacrifice in yield to be worthwhile'. They do not give examples of any tree species which would qualify on this account!

Only when soils are very low in nitrogen and the tree crop is a nitrogen fixer such as *Leucaena leucocephala* can there be potential for biomass improvement in the associated crop (ICRAF, 1994). Yet when the extra manpower requirements are taken into account in managing agroforestry systems to achieve the complementarity nitrogen fixation advantage, even considering the cost of fertilizer additions needed to achieve the same end, this benefit may not be seen as being particularly attractive to farmers.

In the more usual situation of soils which are not totally nitrogen deficient, where trees will lead to a reduction in biomass of the associated crop, the reduction in economic productivity is likely to be proportionately much greater. This is especially true for grain-producing crops or crops grown in semi-arid, marginal conditions where loss of growth and biomass could lead to total crop failure. Again, when the input costs are taken into account in mixed crop systems, which will be the same or greater than those in monocultures in terms of the cost of seed and the extra manpower requirements, this will further reduce the net production value of the mixed crop compared with monocultures.

The 'Holy Grail' of agroforestry – a tree species which has roots at a depth which can exploit deep soil resources of water and nutrients but with few roots in the surface layers to compete with shallow-rooted agricultural crops – is still being sought, but even if such a species ever were discovered, the spatial complementarity achieved would not be without costs. As for overyielding intercrops, the productivity gains would be at the expense of increased resource use and, when the resource is water, any increased productivity gains would need to be assessed in relation to the (marginal) cost of the extra water consumed.

These research findings have far-reaching implications for the practice of agroforestry. They question one of the basic precepts of agroforestry – that optimal mixtures of trees and agricultural crops will lead to an increase in productivity. The results clarify a situation which has been dogged for years by flawed experimental design, obfuscation of results and a singular lack of awareness that lateral transmission of tree roots can occur over considerable distances and can, when dealing with plot designs of small size, influence control plots. The research shows, contrary to the 'mother statements' underlying much of agroforestry practice, that there are in fact few opportunities for gains in productivity by mixing trees with agricultural crops.

Conclusions

Despite the claims made by overenthusiastic agroforesters, there is little scientific evidence to show that enhanced productivity can be achieved in agroforestry systems. Growth of the woody component will virtually always be associated with a decrease in biomass and value of the associated annual agricultural crop. Enhanced productivity from agroforestry systems must be largely regarded as a myth. The huge investment in the development and demonstration of agroforestry systems purporting to increase productivity might not have been wasted had more attention been paid by development workers to the indigenous knowledge of local people.

Caveat

Although close proximity competition from the woody component in agroforestry systems generally prevent productivity benefits, there might well be achievable synergies in agricultural crop and tree crop systems which rely on rotations or tree crop fallows. With these systems it is possible that the deep-rooted nature of most trees may, despite consuming deep soil water reserves, bring to the surface through leaf fall, nutrients which are located at depths greater than annual crops can tap. A rotation with an annual crop may then allow these nutrients to be used by the crop. The crop itself, through having a less-developed root system, will not be able to use all the rainfall, and some water will be available to recharge deeper layers in the soil that the tree crop had previously removed (see reference to sustainable management systems in India in Chapter 6).

OVERTHROWING THE 'OLD PARADIGM'

The mindset created by the old paradigm which links the absence of forests with 'degradation' of water resources, and 'more forest' with improved water resources, has not yet been destroyed. Until it is replaced it will continue to cause governments, development agencies and UN organizations to commit and waste funds on afforestation or reforestation programmes in the belief that this is the best way to improve water resources.

An example would be in Sri Lanka where in the early 1990s the UK Overseas Development Administration (ODA) initiated a large-scale forestry programme on the Mahaweli catchments based on the 'old paradigm' assumption that pine reforestation would 'regulate flows and reduce erosion' in the catchments feeding the Victoria reservoir complex. It is now realized (Calder, 1992c; Finlayson, 1998) that the pine afforestation is serving only to reduce both annual and seasonal flows. Even if planted at the highest altitudes (where there are still some remaining indigenous cloud forests at Horton Plains), recent research indicates that afforestation would give no net benefit to flows; the measured interception losses from the forest exceed the enhanced cloud-water deposition. Furthermore, the planting is generally taking place on old, degraded tea plantations, where on-site soil erosion has virtually ceased following the regrowth of grasslands. Forestry operations involved with planting and road construction will almost certainly lead to an increase in on-site erosion. Understorey fires under the pines, a common occurrence in Sri Lanka, also leave the soil exposed to splash-induced erosion from the forest canopy. The forestry project is therefore having the opposite effect to that intended. Interestingly, Stocking (1996) claims that even where there is bad on-site erosion on the Mahaweli catchment (and erosion from tobacco fields planted on steep slopes is probably the worst source of erosion on the catchment) sediments are not reaching the reservoirs. Stocking claims that the products of erosion from the slopes are being deposited on the lower slopes and floodplains, and paddy field farmers are actually benefiting from the sediment by incorporating it into their paddies.

Slowly, as the blue revolution takes hold and as UN and other development organizations become more aware of the new paradigms relating to land use and water resources (see Chomitz and Kumari, 1998), the pressure will be on national governments to adopt a more questioning attitude to the simplistic 'old paradigm' perceptions about forests and water resources.

Chapter 3

Water Resources and the Limits Concept: A Systems Approach to Estimating Evaporation

The brilliant pioneering work of Howard Penman – originally driven by the needs of the military to know about soil moisture conditions on battlefields which might prevent the movement of tanks and heavy equipment – established a sound physical climate-related basis for the estimation of evaporation from any surface. Penman's achievement was to solve the three equations which govern the exchange of energy, momentum and heat at an evaporating surface to eliminate the surface temperature term. Through the incorporation of simplifications (the 'del' approximation – see Calder, 1991) and empirical parameters which related to the properties of the evaporating surface, Penman was able to derive an equation which has been very successful for estimating the evaporation from open water bodies and short vegetation which is not subject to water stress. Monteith (1965), through the incorporation of two terms, the stomatal resistance (the resistance to water movement through stomata) and the aerodynamic resistance (the resistance to water movement from the surface into the atmosphere), provided a framework for estimating evaporation from any surface, whether covered with short or tall vegetation, and whether water limited or not. Evaporation equations based on the concept of the energy balance and the aerodynamic transport equation (Penman, 1948; Monteith, 1965) are central to most of the modern hydrological methods of estimating evaporation from different surfaces, whether these surfaces are natural vegetation, water or man-made surfaces such as those of urban areas.

These methods have been widely used in models that describe the spatial distribution of evaporation, both in GCMs and in distributed catchment models such as the Système Hydrologique Européen (SHE) (Abbott et al, 1986) and more recent developments such as Système Hydrologique Européen Transport (SHETRAN) (Ewen et al, 1999).

The obvious success of this approach in many applications has provided little incentive for innovation. Indeed so successful was Penman in promoting his original equation, which implicitly placed heavy reliance on radiation as the primary control on evaporation, that researchers who had observations which were at variance with the equation were either reluctant to publish or had difficulty in publishing their results. This situation applied to the author. For many years Penman was unable to accept the results from the Plynlimon forest lysimeter study (see Chapter 5) which indicated that annual evaporation exceeded that given by the Penman equation by 100 per cent.

Neither the physical basis nor the potential accuracy of the Penman-Monteith approach is questioned: it is its practical applicability that is questioned here. For practical applications we are virtually always limited by knowledge of the model parameters, particularly in their spatially distributed form. Furthermore, approaches using the energy balance and aerodynamic transport equations place great emphasis on the importance of these climatic 'demand-led' terms. This may be entirely appropriate in the temperate climates of the world where these evaporation equations were developed, but in many parts of the world, particularly in the very dry regions, the actual evaporation is perhaps only a small fraction of the demand and it may be more reasonable to estimate evaporation from considerations of limits on supply. In other regions different processes may be limiting or more important in controlling evaporation.

The conventional estimation of water use by different vegetation types growing in different parts of the world has required detailed and expensive programmes to measure the evaporation directly, or indirectly by measuring evaporation model parameters. An alternative, supplementary approach, however, has been proposed by Calder (1996a and 1998b) based on a knowledge of the limiting processes. This approach could be regarded as taking a more holistic or systems perspective on the processes controlling evaporation: less are we concerned with estimating evaporation as some simple or linear function of atmospheric demand; more are we willing to consider the availability of water supply and which scaling (emergent) properties of the vegetation are relevant for estimating evaporation. The manner in which vegetation is wetted is considered, as is vegetation 'size'. It has been suggested (Calder, 1998b) that the results from studies carried out in the wet and dry climates of both temperate and tropical zones can be interpreted in terms of six types of controls and limits on the evaporation process: advection, radiation, physiology, soil moisture, tree size and drop size. From knowledge of the climatic zone and the type of crop, it is claimed that 'broad-brush' estimates of water use, of sufficient accuracy for many IWRM requirements, can be obtained. Water use measurements in the different climatic zones and for different vegetation types are reviewed in the context of the limits concept below.

WET TEMPERATE CLIMATE: SHORT AND TALL CROPS

The results from studies carried out at the Plynlimon experimental catchments in central Wales, at the Balquhidder experimental catchments in central Scotland and at the Crinan Canal catchments in the west of Scotland,

Plate 3.1 *A neutron probe being used on the Plynlimon forest lysimeter*

illustrate some of the important controls on evaporation from vegetation growing in these wet temperate climates (Calder, 1986, 1990 and 1992a; Kirby et al, 1991; Johnson, 1995).

Advection Limit

The Plynlimon 'natural' plot lysimeter (Plate 3.1) contains 26 spruce trees, is hydraulically isolated by containing walls and impermeable clay subsoil, and clearly demonstrates the importance of the interception process for upland forest.

Annual forest interception losses, determined by large plastic-sheet net-rainfall gauges, were about twice those arising from transpiration as determined from the lysimeter and neutron probe measurements. The total evaporative loss, from both transpiration and interception, required a latent heat supply. This was supplied by large-scale advection and exceeded the radiant energy input to the forest (Table 3.1).

The uplands of the UK are subject to a maritime climate typified by high rainfall, a high number of rain days per year and high wind speeds. These uplands are an example of a location where large-scale advection of energy routinely occurs from moving air masses as they pass over wet forest cover. The high aerodynamic roughness of forest compared with shorter vegetation types allows the transport of heat to the forest surface from the air, and the transport of water vapour from the surface into the atmosphere, to occur at

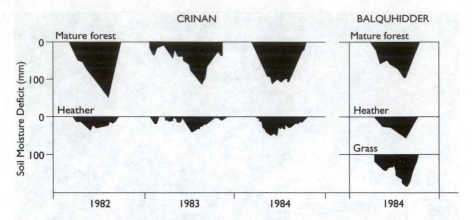

Figure 3.1 *Soil moisture deficits determined from neutron probe measurements at Crinan and Balquhidder*

rates up to ten times higher than those possible for shorter vegetation. The use of advected energy is therefore much higher for forest and is the principal reason for the much higher evaporative losses from upland forests compared with shorter vegetation types. In the UK, uplands advection can probably be regarded not only as a major source of energy for forest evaporation but as the principal limit on the evaporative process.

Radiation and Physiological Limits

Shorter vegetation is less able to draw on advective energy to augment evaporation rates. For shorter vegetation, aerodynamic roughness is lower and evaporation rates are more closely linked to the supply of radiant energy: they are radiation-limited. Stomatal controls (physiological controls on transpiration) also become more important. Soil moisture deficits recorded under heather, *Calluna vulgaris*, grass and coniferous forest at the Balquhidder and Crinan sites are shown in Figure 3.1.

Modelling studies (Calder, 1990) indicate that at these wet, upland sites with an annual rainfall in excess of 1500mm and with vegetation growing on generally deep peaty soils, soil moisture availability is not usually a limit on evaporation. The differences in the soil moisture deficits under heather and grass are principally a reflection of the increased physiological controls on transpiration imposed by heather compared with grass. The much higher deficits recorded under forest are again a demonstration of the overriding importance of interception in determining forest evaporation in these climates.

Dry Temperate Climate:
Short and Tall Crops

Physiological and Soil Moisture Limits

Measurements of the evaporative and soil moisture regime under ash and beech forest in southern England were included as part of an investigation into the hydrological impact of increased areas of broadleaf plantations (Harding et al, 1992).

At these sites evaporation was strongly influenced by physiological controls on transpiration imposed by the trees and soil moisture availability and, to a lesser extent, interception. Differences in soil moisture availability were strongly related to soil type. For ash and beech growing on soil overlying chalk, the available soil water was essentially infinite, whereas at the clay soil site, the available water to the trees was of the order of 280mm (Figure 3.2).

From measurements of stomatal conductance, Harding and colleagues concluded that the physiological controls on the transpiration from a beech forest were sufficient to reduce the total annual water use to less than that expected for grass. However, this conclusion that the water use of the forest is less than that for a short crop has recently been questioned and is the subject of current investigations that are described in Chapter 5.

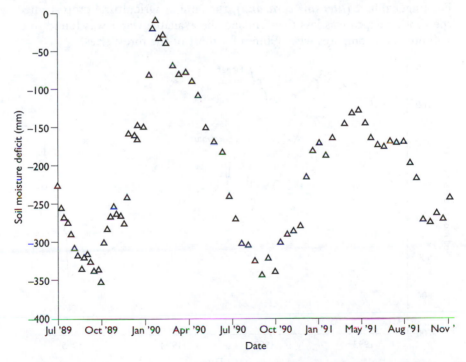

Figure 3.2 *Observations of soil moisture deficits exceeding 350mm under beech on a chalk site at Black Wood in southern England*

Radiation and Soil Moisture Controls

For grassland and other shorter crops, it is generally recognized that the major determinants of evaporation are radiation controls together with soil moisture controls. The Penman approach (Penman, 1963) – which takes account of the radiation control within the calculation of potential evaporation and accounts for soil moisture control within a 'root constant' function – has been shown to be quite adequate for calculating evaporation from short crops in generally dry, temperate conditions.

Dry Tropical Climate: Short and Tall Crops

Soil Moisture

As part of a study to investigate the hydrological impact of eucalyptus plantations in the dry zone of Karnataka in southern India, comparative studies were carried out on the evaporative characteristics and soil moisture deficits under eucalyptus plantation, indigenous forest and agricultural crops. For all of the four sites where investigations were carried out, soil moisture availability was found to be a major limit on evaporation for both agricultural crops and trees. For finger millet (*Eleusine coracana*), the annual agricultural crop studied, the rooting depth was less than 2m and the available water was found to be 160mm. This compares with 390mm for most of the forest sites.

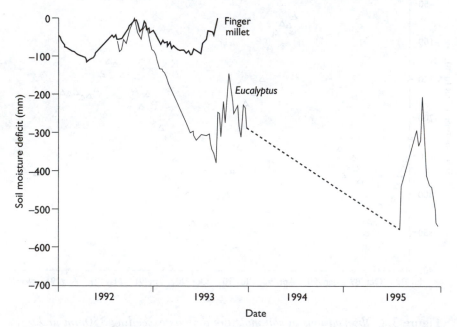

Figure 3.3 *Soil moisture deficits recorded beneath* Eucalyptus camaldulensis *and finger millet at the Hosakote site, India*

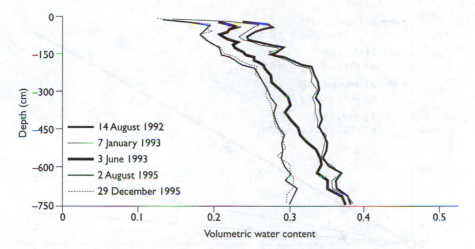

Figure 3.4 *Neutron probe observations of profile volumetric water content beneath* Eucalyptus camaldulensis *at Hosakote, India*

At one of the eucalyptus sites, the Hosakote experimental site of the Karnataka Forest Department, the roots are now known to extend to much greater depths. Recent studies using neutron probe measurements made to a depth of 8m on a 'farmer's field' experiment (Calder et al, 1997a), have shown huge differences in the soil moisture deficits recorded beneath finger millet and eucalyptus (Figure 3.3).

The results (Figure 3.4) show that not only can eucalyptus roots reach the lowest measurement depth of 8m but that they can reach this depth within 2–3 years of being planted. Together with evaporating essentially all the rainfall that enters the soil, these trees are able to extract approximately an additional 100mm of water from each metre depth of soil the roots penetrate. The concept of soil moisture availability cannot easily be applied to the eucalyptus plantations at this site.

The deep rooting behaviour of *Eucalyptus* species has also been reported in South Africa, where Dye (1996) found *Eucalyptus grandis* abstracting from a depth of 8m.

Nevertheless, for agricultural crops it is clear that reduced soil moisture availability was the principal reason why the annual evaporation from these crops was generally about half that from either plantation or indigenous forest.

Tree Size

These Indian studies also demonstrated, for the relatively young (less than seven years old) plantation trees used in the study, a linear scaling relationship between transpiration rate and basal cross-sectional area (Figure 3.5). For older plantations (greater than ten years old) where self-thinning was taking place as a result of competition, the relationship was less well defined (Calder et al, 1992).

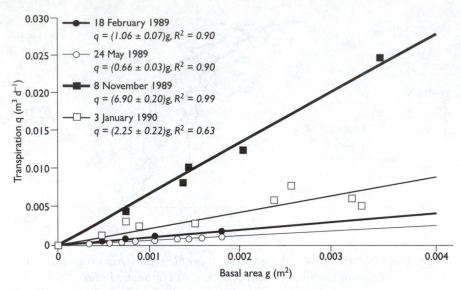

Figure 3.5 *Measured transpiration rates as a function of tree basal area at Puradal, India*

It would appear that although evaporative demand is clearly the driving mechanism for evaporation, for most of the year it is not limiting; the primary controls are soil moisture availability, and for the tree crops, an additional factor relating to tree size. At the sites in India (which experience an extended dry season) interception losses, which amount to less than 13 per cent of the annual 800mm rainfall, are not important in determining soil moisture deficits and are not a major component of the total evaporation.

The results from semi-arid Karnataka (Calder et al, 1993), which indicate that evaporation is limited principally by soil water availability and plant physiological controls, are therefore in direct contrast to the observations from the wet uplands of the UK where evaporation is principally limited by atmospheric demand through advection and radiation controls.

Wet Tropical Climate: Tall Crops

Drop Size Controls

At wetter sites in the tropics, interception is a more significant component of the annual forest evaporation. From studies carried out in rainforest in Indonesia (Calder et al, 1986) the importance of raindrop size in determining interception losses from tropical forest was first realized. Application of a stochastic interception model, which explicitly took into account drop size, was required to describe the interception process in these conditions. This model shows that up to ten times as much rain may be required to achieve the same degree of canopy wetting for tropical convective storms, which have

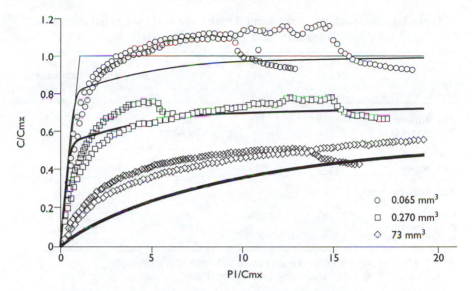

Figure 3.6 *Canopy storage measurements obtained with a rainfall simulator showing that the final degree of canopy saturation is much greater when wetted with drops of smaller size*

large drop sizes, than would be necessary for the range of smaller drop sizes usually encountered for frontal rain in the UK. There are also results from studies using rainfall simulators which show that the final degree of canopy saturation also varies with drop size, being greater for drops of smaller size (Figure 3.6).

Vegetation canopies also influence the drop size of the net rainfall: deeper layers in the canopy will be more influenced by the modified drop size spectrum falling from canopy layers above than by that of the incident rain. Studies have shown (Hall and Calder, 1993) that different vegetation canopies have very distinct canopy spectra (Figure 1.6). For canopies with a low leaf-area index, the interception characteristics would therefore be expected to be related more to the drop size of the incident rain, whereas for canopies with a higher leaf-area index, the characteristics would be less dependent on the drop size of the rainfall.

The advantages to be gained by incorporating the drop size dependence in interception models for use in tropical conditions were demonstrated by Hall et al (1996a) for a tropical forest site in Sri Lanka. The performance of the two-layer stochastic interception model (Calder, 1996b; Calder et al, 1996), which explicitly takes into account drop size, was very much better in describing the initial wetting-up phase of the storm, and hence the overall interception loss, than conventional interception models (Rutter et al, 1971). The drop size dependence of canopy wetting provides part of the reason why forest interception varies so much worldwide, and why interception losses from coniferous temperate forests are so much higher than from tropical forests (Table 3.1).

Table 3.1 *Observations of the annual water use and energy balance of wet temperate and wet tropical forests*

Site	Rain (mm)	Transpiration (mm)	Interception (mm)	Total Evaporation (mm)	Net Radiation (mm equiv.)
Wet Temperate Plynlimon, Wales 1975	2013	335	529 (26%)	864	617
Wet Tropical West Java Aug 1980–July 1981	2835	886	595 (21%)§	1481 ±12%	1543 ±10%
Wet Tropical Ducke Forest, Brazil	2593	1030	363 (14%)	1393	1514

Note: The Ducke Forest site experiences dry periods which may limit transpiration.
Source: Calder (1978), Calder et al (1986), Shuttleworth (1988)

The model shows that canopy wetting will be achieved most rapidly and maximum canopy storage will be highest, leading to high interception losses overall, when the volume of individual raindrops and drops draining from the canopy are both small. These conditions apply for coniferous forests in the low-intensity, small raindrop size climate of the uplands of the UK. In contrast, when both individual raindrop volumes and leaf drop volumes are large, canopy wetting will be achieved much more slowly, the final degree of canopy saturation will be less and interception losses are likely to be much reduced. This situation is typified by tropical rainforest experiencing high-intensity convective storms of large drop size.

Radiation Limit

The wet evergreen forests of the tropics represent another situation in which climatic demand is likely to limit forest evaporation. However, climate circulation patterns in the tropics do not favour large-scale advection of energy to support evaporation rates, and evaporation rates are likely to be closely constrained by the availability of solar radiation. Whereas in the wet, temperate, maritime climate of Plynlimon in central Wales, the energy requirements of the total evaporation far exceed the supply of radiant energy to the forest (Table 3.1), at the humid tropical forest site at Janlappa, West Java, the energy requirements of the total evaporation were, within experimental error, equal to the supply of radiant energy. At the Ducke Forest site the evaporation was less than the depth equivalent of the radiation supply, but significant dry periods were recorded at this site which may have exerted soil moisture limitations.

Data compiled by Bruijnzeel (1990) for other studies of evaporation from humid, lowland tropical rainforest show a similar picture (Table 3.2, Figure

Table 3.2 *Annual evaporation and precipitation for selected tropical lowland forests*

Site and Source of Information	Precipitation (mm.yr⁻¹)	Evaporation (mm.yr⁻¹)	Length of observations (yr)
Latin America			
Ducke Reserve, Brazil (Shuttleworth, 1988)	2468	1311	2
Ducke Reserve, Brazil (Leopoldo et al, 1982b)	2075	1675	1
Bacio Modelo, Brazil (Leopoldo et al, 1982a)	2089	1548	1
Tonka, Surinam (Poels, 1987)	2143	1630	4
Gregoire I (Roche, 1982)	3676	1528	8
Gregoire II (Roche, 1982)	3697	1437	8
Gregoire III (Roche, 1982)	3751	1444	8
Barro Colorado, Panama (Dietrich et al, 1982)	2425	1440	2
Idem	1684	886	1
Africa			
Tai I, Ivory Coast (Collinet et al, 1984)	2003	1465	1
Tai II, Ivory Coast (Collinet et al, 1984)	1986	1363	1
Banco I, Ivory Coast (Huttel, 1975)	1800	1145	3
Banco II, Ivory Coast (Huttel, 1975)	1800	1195	2
Yapo, Ivory Coast (Huttel, 1975)	1950	1425	1
Guma, Sierra Leone (Ledger, 1975)	5795	1146	3
Yangambi, Congo (Focan and Fripiat, 1953)	1860	1433	1
South-East Asia			
Sungai Tekam C, Malaya (DID, 1986)	1727	1498	6
Sungai Tekam B, Malaya (DID, 1986)	1781	1606	3
Sungai Lui, Malaya (Low and Goh, 1972; DID, 1972)	2410	1516	3
Angat, Phillipines (Baconguis, 1980)	3236	1232	6
Babinda, Queensland (Gilmour, 1977; Bonell and Gilmour, 1978)	4037	1421	6
Janlappa, Indonesia (Calder et al, 1986)	2851	1481	1

Source: Bruijnzeel (1990)

3.7). Although the supply of net radiation was not reported for these studies, it is reasonable to assume that it is in a similar range of 1500–1550mm per year. With this assumption the results show that only in dry years, or at the Guma, Sierra Leone site, which experiences a five-month dry season, was the evaporation very much less than the net radiation supply.

As humid rainforest is able to convert virtually the equivalent of all the net radiation into evaporation, it is unlikely that any other land use will be able to evaporate at a higher rate. Conversion of forest to annual crops in these areas, as well as in most other areas of the world, is likely to result in increased annual streamflows.

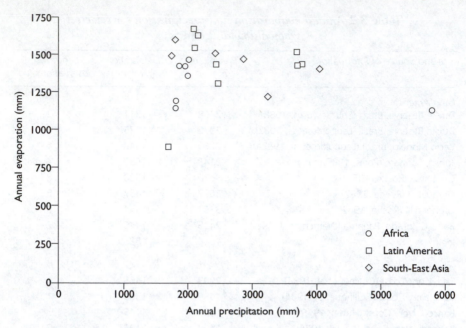

Figure 3.7 *Annual evaporation plotted against annual precipitation for tropical lowland forest*

Chapter 4

The New Ideals

This chapter traces the development of the concepts of integrated water resource management (IWRM) and later developments known as integrated land and water resource management (ILWRM), which recognize the need for the specific inclusion of issues of land use. It describes the attempts to formulate the new ideals. It outlines the new methodologies needed for meeting them, for addressing the crucial issue of balancing the needs of economic development and the environment whilst addressing equity and sustainability requirements. It outlines some of the key organizations and policy developments which have been influenced by, and are also influencing, this evolving process of improved land and water management.

United Nations organizations have played a major role in the development of these new approaches. Some 20 major UN water-related international conferences have been held in the past three decades, 13 since the Rio UNCED Earth Summit in 1992. With a more specific land and water focus, the FAO has recently carried out an initiative, 'Preparing the Next Generation of Watershed Management Programmes', which involved three regional conferences and a final conference, culminating in the 'Sassari Declaration'. There is no doubt that these UN conferences have been hugely influential in developing the IWRM and ILWRM concepts, but questions are now being raised as to whether we really need so many. The more recent conferences show a growing tendency towards producing declarations which repeat many of the formerly developed ideals. Inevitably there is also the growing tendency of 'preaching to the already converted'. Perhaps what is required in the future is less attention to the mutually reinforcing UN club of organizations and associates preaching these ideals and more attention being paid to addressing what is going wrong on the ground, why these ideals are not being met, why many land and water policies are resulting in perverse outcomes (see Chapter 5) and to finding out whether development programmes are really effective through putting in place more quantitative methods of monitoring performance.

THE ENVIRONMENT AND EARLY DEVELOPMENTS

Concern over the global implications of water problems was voiced as far back as the United Nations Conference on the Human Environment in Stockholm in 1972. The UN-sponsored Conference on Water at Mar del Plata, Argentina, in 1977 was seminal in the formation of the new approach and in promoting the importance of water and water management to world governments. A later water conference, the International Conference on Water and the Environment (ICWE) in Dublin, Ireland, in January 1992, saw the attendance of 500 participants, including government-designated experts from 100 countries and representatives of 80 international, intergovernmental and non-governmental organizations.

The water community represented at the Dublin conference saw it as an opportunity to put its views to the world leaders who would be assembled at the United Nations Conference on Environment and Development (UNCED) in Rio de Janeiro later in June 1992.

The water experts saw the emerging global water resources picture as critical. At its closing session, the Conference adopted the Dublin Statement and the Conference Report. The problems highlighted were not seen as speculative in nature, nor were they thought likely to affect our planet only in the distant future. They were perceived as 'here and now' and it was recognized that 'the future survival of many millions of people demands immediate and effective action'.

The Conference participants called for fundamental new approaches to the assessment, development and management of freshwater resources, which could only be brought about through political commitment and involvement from the highest levels of government to the smallest communities. They recognized that:

> commitment will need to be backed by substantial and immediate investments, public awareness campaigns, legislative and institutional changes, technology development, and capacity building programmes. Underlying all these must be a greater recognition of the interdependence of all peoples, and of their place in the natural world.

The Dublin Principles

The Dublin Conference Report sets out recommendations for action at local, national and international levels, based on four guiding principles.

Principle One

Fresh water is a finite and vulnerable resource, essential to sustain life, development and the environment.

Since water sustains life, effective management of water resources demands a holistic approach, linking social and economic development with protection of natural ecosystems. Effective management links land and water uses across the whole of a catchment area or ground water aquifer.

Principle Two

Water development and management should be based on a participatory approach, involving users, planners and policymakers at all levels.

The participatory approach (see Appendix 2) involves raising awareness of the importance of water among policymakers and the general public. It means that decisions are taken at the lowest appropriate level, with full public consultation and involvement of users in the planning and implementation of water projects.

Principle Three

Women play a central part in the provision, management and safeguarding of water.

This pivotal role of women as providers and users of water and guardians of the living environment has seldom been reflected in institutional arrangements for the development and management of water resources. Acceptance and implementation of this principle requires positive policies to address women's specific needs, and to equip and empower women to participate at all levels in water resources programmes, including decision-making and implementation, in ways defined by them.

Principle Four

Water has an economic value in all its competing uses and should be recognized as an economic good.

Within this principle, it is vital to recognize first the basic right of all human beings to have access to clean water and sanitation at an affordable price. Past failure to recognize the economic value of water has led to wasteful and environmentally damaging uses of the resource. Managing water as an economic good is an important way of achieving efficient and equitable use, and of encouraging conservation and protection of water resources.

ECONOMICS AND STRUCTURAL ADJUSTMENT PROGRAMMES

After the momentous events in Europe following the collapse of the Berlin Wall in 1989, many of the world's major economies, including the former Soviet Union, China, India and Egypt opted for change from a centrally planned and command economy to an economy which was more market oriented. The ideal embodied in the new economic strategy, often supported by an economic structural adjustment programme (SAP), was to increase efficiency by promoting market orientation, trade liberalization, deregulation, privatization, stakeholder participation and decentralization. (Stabilization and SAPs had come into being much earlier in the 1970s as a response by the World Bank and other international development institutions to assist developing countries with the macro-economic shocks brought about by the increase in oil prices, debt crises and world recession.)

The requirement to link SAPs with integrated water resource management is well illustrated by Zimbabwe's experiences with such a programme. In 1990, Zimbabwe, following the lead of other major economic blocs, adopted the first phase of an SAP. Here the restructuring sought to promote higher growth and to reduce poverty and unemployment by reducing fiscal and parastatal deficits, instituting prudent monetary policy, liberalizing trade policies and the foreign exchange system, carrying out domestic deregulation and by establishing a social safety net and training programmes for vulnerable groups. The focus was on the formal sector as the engine of growth. Economic SAPs are not without their opponents and even the World Bank, a major financial supporter of Zimbabwe's SAP, recognized that the performance in Zimbabwe was less than expected. Although a principal objective of the programme was to reduce poverty, it is now recognized that it was the poorest sector of the community that suffered most during the adjustment. It is also recognized that a major factor which limited the success of the first phase of the SAP in Zimbabwe was that the programme was forced through at a time when, in the early 1990s, southern Africa was suffering a severe drought. The tight interrelationship between water management and economic management is demonstrated nowhere more clearly than in southern Africa, and Zimbabwe was quick to realize that a water resource management strategy (see Chapter 5) was needed to go hand-in-hand with the SAP.

The relationship between SAPs and the natural environment is now also raising concerns, although it appears very difficult to make generalizations about the impacts of these programmes. Studies carried out by UNEP (Panayotou and Hupe, 1996) indicate that environmental impacts are very site specific and can be positive or negative.

Although there is much debate on the best mechanisms for implementing an SAP to reduce the hardships inevitably created in some sectors, there is little doubt that the principles and ideals underlying these programmes are likely to remain a basis for economic development for many countries. The recognition of the need to take into account the links between basin economics and land and water resource developments also raises questions as to how both water and land use can be valued.

The Value of Water

Enshrined in the UNCED principles is the concept that water should be recognized and treated as an economic good and economists are now able to devise methods for calculating the value of water as a commodity in its many uses. But in many non-western cultures water has value above that of a mere commodity: it has a spiritual value. To the African, water is seen as 'the giver of life'; to the Maori it is seen as an 'essential ingredient of life', 'a gift handed down by their ancestors' (see Chapter 6).

Perhaps these views should not be regarded as conflicting but as complementary if, through higher valuation, whether economic or spiritual, they result in a better appreciation of the resource and more sustainable and less wasteful usage.

The advantages to be gained by ascribing a value to water and charging users a tariff related to this value are numerous. They include:

- provision of funds for water developments;
- reducing demands on the public sector for the capital and recurrent cost of providing water;
- releasing water for higher value use and assisting the prioritization of water allocation;
- the resolution of resource conflicts between, for example, demands for water, power, fisheries and transport;
- environmental benefits, through demand management, by releasing more water for environmental usage; and
- demand management, reducing the demand for water.

Provision of funds for water developments becomes increasingly important as cheaper sources of water become used up. The World Bank (Bhatia and Falkenmark, 1992) estimated that the cost of providing water from the 'next' project was often two to three times that of providing water from the 'current' project. Although US$10 billion was being spent each year on improving water supply and sanitation in the developing world in the early 1990s, it was estimated by the World Bank that the investment would, even if costs were fixed, have to be five times this rate if reasonable water services were to be had by all by the year 2000. Cost recovery is therefore an important feature of a water pricing policy.

Reducing demands on the public sector and donor organizations as a result of cost recovery should, in theory, release funds for other forms of development. The World Bank estimated that in 1991 only 10 per cent of the cost of water projects that it funded was financed by internal cash generation.

Releasing water for higher value uses will come about if water pricing is set at such a level that it discourages lower value uses. Water pricing can therefore be an effective instrument in water allocation.

The resolution of resource conflicts may be aided by realistic resource pricing instruments. Competition between agriculture, environmental and hydroelectric requirements for water would be eased in Zimbabwe through water pricing, and agricultural demands for electric power for pumping groundwater for irrigation in India might be alleviated through realistic pricing of both water and electricity (see Chapter 6).

The environment as a valid user of water is becoming increasingly recognized. Also recognized is the increasing damage to the environment that comes through the growing supply and consumption of water. Abstractions for water supply, agriculture and industry mean less flow in rivers and the drawdown of water bodies. Lower flows in rivers also reduce the assimilative capacity and, with the discharge of pollutants, may lead to toxic conditions for wildlife and extra costs to public services for the treatment of water. Demand management, through curbing water use, may have environmental benefits. In Australia increasing charges for irrigation water is one of the instruments proposed to curb increasing salinization problems (see Chapter 6).

Arguably, within the context of IWRM, the greatest benefits to be achieved from a pricing policy for water are in relation to controlling demands for water in situations where the water resource is close to being fully exploited.

The principles of demand management and the methods that have been developed for valuing water are described below.

Demand Management

The equivalent of the Hippocratic Oath for water engineers is to promise to meet all reasonable needs for water without question by enlarging and improving supplies. (Winpenny, 1992)

In many developed countries the ethos of the water engineer was to equate efficiency with maximum use of the water resource for the users. Taken to its limit, any residual flows in rivers were seen as wastage. With this ethos, environmental and ecological considerations and downstream users, especially if they were trans-national users, were given little weight in the quest for 'development'.

This ethos still reigns in water departments in many countries in both the developed and developing world. Career development for water engineers is seen through association with large civil engineering projects – the larger being the better. It has been likened to a 'right of passage' for water engineers. But this ethos is no longer the powerful driving force it was of yesteryear. Water engineers are to some extent the victims of their own success. Most of the world's best sites for water developments have already been developed and the costs of developing the remaining sites are becoming prohibitive. Even where governments and donors are prepared to overlook the massive environmental and socio-economic costs of developing the remaining water resources, the sheer economic costs involved are usually a sufficient disincentive. Except for 'Trade for Aid' deals, international funding for large water developments is increasingly difficult to obtain. Only in the few remaining countries which have not yet fully shaken off the constraints of command economies are large water developments still going ahead, an example being China and the Three Gorges Project. In simple terms the money for large water developments is no longer available. The trend away from supply-driven large water schemes towards greater demand management was well summarized by Arthur (1997); he recognized that 'in the background of the differentiation between need and want, lies a much wider ideological conflict about the limits to growth'.

In most countries the accepted 'knee jerk' response to water supply short-ages was to augment supplies. In the short term, demand management devices such as rationing, prohibited uses, public exhortation and the use of stand-pipes or the cutting-off of supplies, are widely applied. But these non-price devices, although often effective, are both costly and inconvenient to users and do not take account of the relative value of water to different consumers.

Where water is provided to users at a price less than the supply cost, a situation common in most parts of the world except the UK, the incentive for conservation and waste reduction is absent. This negative demand manage-ment leads to the paradox that in a situation where the water resource is already under stress, the subsidy is actually encouraging users to make additional demands upon it.

The alternative approach, consistent with the concepts of IWRM, is to recognize that water resources are limited and new sources cannot be devel-oped indefinitely. Demand management in some form must ultimately be applied and the use of pricing is an instrument which can be both effective and can be defended by rational and objective arguments. If water is viewed simply as a commodity, forgetting for the moment its spiritual and aesthetic considerations in many cultures, it would be reasonable to expect that it should be priced to cover at least its cost of provision and priced so that low value uses are discouraged and supplies are available for the higher value users who are able and willing to pay for it. Clearly the strict adherence of these principles needs to be treated with some caution to ensure that, for example, the poorest sections of the community are not disadvantaged and that the application of these economic principles does not contravene the accepted spiritual and cultural beliefs associated with water. This need not necessarily be a problem. Under water subsidy conditions it is generally the richest sections of the community, which are pipeline-connected to the supply, whether for irrigation water or domestic purposes, that receive the greatest benefits in receiving water below the provision costs. It is the poor urban dweller who buys water by the bucket from a standpipe salesman who often pays the highest per-unit costs.

Although governments see many political hurdles in introducing water pricing policies – the principal concern being a short-term loss of votes and a secondary concern being the inflationary effect of charging for a commodity that is universally used – the benefits are increasingly being regarded as outweighing the disadvantages.

The development of a pricing policy for managing water demand does, however, require a methodology for deciding on the value of water (see above) to determine the price to be charged. Assessment of the impacts of the pricing policy before the policy is implemented is another requisite, and to do this, some sort of modelling study is required (see Chapter 6) to ensure that the impacts on all the affected stakeholders are understood.

Water as an Economic Commodity

Traditionally water has been regarded as a 'free' resource of unlimited supply with zero cost at the point of supply. Often, users have been charged for only a proportion of the costs of transfer, treatment and disposal. Opportunity costs for water are often ignored and as a consequence users have little incentive to ensure that water is used efficiently and not wasted.

The new (economic) approach to the allocation of water is to use prices and markets to ensure efficiency and that water is supplied to its most valuable uses.

In an economic sense, efficiency requires the following:

- The marginal benefit of use should be greater than the marginal cost of supply. This means that the users are able to derive greater economic benefit from the next unit of water supplied than the cost expended by the supplier in providing that extra unit of water.
- The marginal benefit per unit of resource is equal across all uses. Where the supply of water is not unlimited and the marginal units of supply have a positive cost (that is, the supplier has to expend money to develop the next unit of supply water), the value of water consumption is maximized when net marginal benefits are equal in all uses. This implies that efficiency would be increased by transferring water between users until the marginal value of the water to the users is the same across all sectors. When equality of marginal values is achieved, further redistribution of water would make no sector better off without making another sector worse off.

In theory it is possible to derive demand and supply curves which show both:

- the marginal benefit obtained from consumption and the willingness to pay; and
- the marginal cost of supply and the willingness to supply at given prices.

Where the demand and supply curves intersect defines a theoretical price at which economic efficiency and welfare is maximized. In practice, applying market principles to water management is complicated because water does not fit the economist's model of a normal commodity and of a perfect market. Often water providers occupy a monopoly situation, the logistics of transferring water between users and sectors may be difficult, and there may be values attached to water which are difficult to quantify in monetary terms; the economist's approach may need qualification in real world situations.

Valuing Water

Various methods have been developed to determine the value of water in its many uses. Those reviewed by Winpenny (1996) include:

Table 4.1 *Estimated value of water for different uses (US$ per 1000 cubic metres)*

Use	USA (Gibbons, 1986)	China (Dixon et al, 1994 Kutcher et al, 1992 Adams et al, 1994)	UK (Rees et al, 1993 Bate and Dubourg, 1994)	Zimbabwe (Winpenny, 1996)	South Africa (Hassan et al, 1995)
Industrial process	180–800	500–4000		>230	
Speciality crop	100–800		230 (fruit) 1890 (potatoes)	100–150	
Domestic	20–360			>120	
Recreational	10–400				
Navigation	generally 0 but 370 in some stretches				
Intermediate value farm crops		average: 30 at critical times: 90–100			100 (sugar)
Low value farm crops	10–60	<120	80–140 (field vegetables) 10–30 (cereals & grass)		100 (dryland crops) 0 (traditional livestock rearing)
Waste assimilation	0–20				
Industrial cooling	0–10				
Sediment prevention			0–20		
Power	0–40	20			

- willingness to pay (WTP);
- marginal cost analysis;
- 'netback';
- WTP, taking into account recycling and re-use costs;
- in-stream value for pollution assimilation;
- in-stream value for transport;
- hydroelectric generation with and without capital costs included; and
- travel cost and contingent valuation methods for amenity and recreational use.

For urban household consumers, the WTP approach has often been adapted to water pricing. This involves determining the demand curve, the relationship between the amount of water used by consumers and the charging price. This information can be obtained either by survey or from knowledge of the change in consumption following a price change. The total area under the supply/price, or demand, curve is regarded by economists as the benefit or value of the water.

For agricultural usage the value of water is often determined in terms of marginal productivity. Here the economic benefits through increased yield or quality of the crop resulting from a unit addition of water are calculated under conditions when all other farm inputs are held constant. An alternative method known as 'netback' is related to the WTP principle. By taking the gross value of the crop per hectare and subtracting all production costs, and if required, a capital recovery cost and an acceptable profit margin, the remainder can be viewed as the maximum WTP for the water.

The same methodology can be applied to industrial water valuation, but as water is usually only a small part of total production costs, it would be misleading to attribute the whole of the remainder in the value and cost calculations to water valuation. For industrial use, another method is to regard the cost of recycling water following water treatment as the upper limit on industrial WTP. The reasoning would be that if water pricing were greater than the treatment costs, industry would opt for treatment rather than buying in water.

In-stream values for water arise through its natural capacity to assimilate waste and pollutants. This value can be compared with the alternative cost of reducing the pollutants at source or the additional costs incurred in water treatment. In-stream values for water for transport can be calculated as the cost advantage of water transport over the next cheapest form of transport (Winpenny, 1996).

Values of water for amenity and tourism have been calculated using the travel cost and contingent valuation methods. The travel cost method infers the amenity value from the travel costs of visitors to the site which are then used to construct a hypothetical demand curve for the amenity or recreational value of the water body. The contingent valuation method relies on opinion surveys to reveal the value that visitors derive from the body of water.

Winpenny (1996) has reviewed the values obtained for different uses of water in different parts of the world using the methods outlined above. Although he introduces the caveat that it is important to examine the fine print associated with each valuation before considering the valuations as representative of the sector, there is a general picture that emerges: industrial uses together with speciality crops and domestic uses are always high value. Recreational uses can be high value, whilst the majority of agricultural crops, often the largest overall consumers of water, are relatively low value uses (Table 4.1).

Another approach to valuing water in terms of 'full value' and 'economic value' is provided by Peter Rogers, Professor of Environmental Engineering at Harvard University. Peter Rogers (Rogers, 1997; Rogers et al, 1998) suggests that the full value of water is made up of five components (Figure 4.1). These are:

1   **Value to users of water** This value is calculated in terms of the marginal value of product, an estimate of the per-unit output of industrial good or agricultural product for a unit of water use.

2   **Net benefits from return flows** This is the value derived from the return
flows, for example, the value derived from aquifer recharge during irrigation or downstream benefits of water diversion during hydropower
generation.

3   **Net benefits from indirect uses** This is the value of the indirect benefits
that are derived when the water diverted for one purpose is used for
another purpose. For example, wastewater from small gravity water
supply systems might also be used for irrigating domestic gardens.

4   **Adjustment for societal objectives** This is the value of water in meeting
societal objectives such as poverty alleviation, gender empowerment or
food security. In some circumstances water supplied for irrigation or
domestic use might be regarded as contributing to societal objectives.

5   **Intrinsic value** This value reflects the environmental, social, cultural and
other benefits gained from it.

Within many cultures, water has more significance than can be attributed
solely in monetary terms. In many cultures water has an aesthetic or spiritual
significance which cannot be quantified monetarily. The value we place on
'rivers running to the sea' is one example. The economic approach to the
valuation of water needs to be tempered with other appreciations of its value.
The term 'intrinsic' value of water, as defined by Peter Rogers, is one way of
ensuring that this value is taken into account in audits of water value.

If the Hippocratic Oath to the water engineer is to supply all reasonable
needs, the 'Holy Grail' to the economist is to achieve optimal economic
efficiency where marginal benefits for the resource are equalized. Within
complex real world situations, the search for optimal solutions may be fruit-
less, but a move in the right direction, towards satisfying economic efficiency
and the other objectives of IWRM, is perhaps the goal that should be striven
for, and is one that ultimately is more achievable.

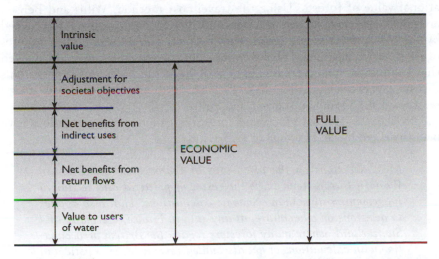

Source: Rogers (1997)

Figure 4.1 *Framework for valuing water*

The Value of Land Use

Whilst methods have been devised for valuing water in its many diverse uses, including those for water supply, irrigation of crops, hydroelectricity generation, industrial production, mining, amenity and recreational uses, and for the environment, there is also a need for methods for valuing land use. Within an IWRM context this is particularly true for land uses such as forests which, although having a high impact on water resources, may have valuable multiple uses. These may include not only primary uses for timber production and other forest products, but also secondary uses for recreation, conservation and tourism. The valuation of land uses for primary production is inherently straightforward, although tax incentives and production subsidies may significantly affect the valuation. Valuation methods for secondary uses are less straightforward and more controversial but nevertheless important; in some circumstances secondary land uses may be at least as valuable. Trade-offs need then to be considered between the value of water that may be forgone under a particular land use against the sum value of the different uses of the land.

Some of the methods that have been used for assessing the amenity and recreational value of land use are identical to those used for assessing the amenity and recreational value of water. Willis and Benson (1989) have discussed the use of travel cost and contingent valuation methods for assessing the recreational value of UK forests. They also discussed other 'market-related' methods including the hedonic price method, which links environmental assets with markets for private goods and services. The linkage of wages or house prices to environmental attributes were cited as examples that could be followed with this approach, but the practical difficulty in obtaining information on housing characteristics and sale prices of houses deterred the authors from pursuing this method for estimating the recreational value of forests. Using the travel cost method, Willis and Benson arrived at an average recreational value of £1.90 for one visit to a forest owned by the UK Forestry Commission. They estimated that the wildlife attributes of the forests contributed about 38 per cent towards this value and showed that the total annual recreational benefit from the Forestry Commission's forests lay between £14 million and £45 million per year, later to be reassessed at £53 million (Benson and Willis, 1991).

Neither this approach to valuing forest recreation nor its conclusions have been accepted by all. Hummel (1992) states:

> *Most decisions on the provisions of recreational facilities in Western Europe tend to be the result of political and technical judgements rather than economic calculations. That also applies to decisions on silviculture, at any rate in France, Germany and Switzerland, where many foresters regard the British preoccupation with calculations of net discounted revenue as simplistic and typical of a nation of shopkeepers.*

He also pointed out that the valuation of recreational facilities does not reflect 'money in the bank'; had this been the case the operational loss of the Forestry Commission would have been more than offset by the recreational income.

More recently the Forestry Commission has commissioned a study (CJC Consulting, 2003) to address, from an economics perspective, the following questions relating to forestry in England:

- What outputs are required by society from woods and forests?
- What outputs can be delivered by the private sector, and do the benefits of intervention outweigh the costs?
- What is the economic rationale that may support the use of forest policy as a means of furthering the sustainable development agenda?
- What changes are required to forestry policy or strategic delivery mechanisms?

The study concludes that 'the main case for government intervention in forestry is to deliver public good outputs in the form of urban and peri-urban amenity, recreation and biodiversity'. This focus on conservation, amenity, recreation and environment (CARE) products has become even stronger in recent years as a rationale for the existence of both the Forestry Commission and for government support to forestry in the UK, as the returns from timber continue to decline.

The question of whether forestry, on balance, is good or bad for the water environment in the UK was addressed in another study commissioned by the Forestry Commission. This report by Professor Ken Willis of Newcastle University (Willis, 2002) concludes that undertaking a reliable evaluation of the impact of forests on water for Britain as a whole is difficult, both because of a lack of relevant economic data plus the fact that the impacts of forestry on water quantity and quality are strongly influenced by site-specific factors. Ken Willis argues that there is no available comprehensive database that can readily be used to estimate the physical impact of forestry on water supply and water quality on a spatial unit basis across Britain. Furthermore, the opportunity cost of water supply and water quality improvements is also not documented on a spatial unit basis. Hence the costs and benefits of forestry on water supply and water quality cannot be mapped in any accurate, robust and reliable manner. The EXCLAIM tool that is being developed to help policymakers interpret the impacts of changing forest cover on the water regime, together with associated economic and livelihood impacts, may provide the type of framework required for undertaking the type of study identified by Ken Willis. Although primarily developed for overseas applications, the methodologies would be directly transferable to UK conditions.

Recreational and environmental benefits can accrue from other land uses in addition to forestry. Within the UK, the extension of public access to the countryside is increasingly being achieved through agreements with landowners under which government agencies purchase new rights of access to land (Crabtree, 1997). The valuation of the recreational and environmental benefits of land use is then required for specific areas to assess whether inclusion within an incentive scheme merits its costs.

Aylward et al (1998) have made an analysis of the use and non-use values of different land uses on the catchment of Lake Arenal, the source area for Costa Rica's largest hydroelectric facility and irrigation scheme. This landmark study, entitled 'Economic Incentives for Watershed Protection', takes into account both valuation, particularly non-use valuation related to watershed protection, and institutional analyses. Aware of modern research that has demonstrated that forests generally reduce water flows as compared with shorter crops (see Chapter 1), the authors state in their conclusions that:

> *by examining the issue of externalities in detail the study shows that the crucial hydrological externality (water yield) and its relative direction (positive) are contrary to that expected by previous characterizations of the problem.*

They go on to say:

> *while considerable variability can be expected in applying the valuation and institutional analyses to other sites and conditions, at a minimum this case study suggests the benefits of integrating the(se) two aspects of watershed analysis under a single framework. Additional case studies and more general theoretical work should assist in the development of a defensible consensus around rules of thumb and shortcuts in such analyses that would contribute to better policy and project formulation. Such guidance is desperately needed given the current reliance on partial analyses and outdated conventional wisdom of what constitutes watershed protection and watershed management in the humid tropics.*

For the successful integration of land and water management robust and accepted methods for valuing both water and land use will increasingly be required in the future. This is especially true where land and water are associated with environmental and recreational attributes.

Sustainability

Raising Awareness

Tragedy of the Commons

The article entitled 'The tragedy of the commons' by Hardin (1968) is now regarded as one of the seminal documents which provoked discussion and raised awareness of issues which we now conceptualize in terms of 'sustainability' or 'sustainable development'.

Referring to the tradition of a community pasture, 'the commons', Hardin gave the following example of a society that permitted freedom of action in activities that affected common property, and how it was eventually doomed to failure:

> *Picture a pasture open to all. It is to be expected that each herds-man will try to keep as many cattle as possible on the commons. Such an arrangement may work reasonably satisfactorily for centuries because tribal wars, poaching, and disease keep the numbers of both man and beast well below the carrying capacity of the land. Finally, however, comes the day of reckoning, that is, the day when the long desired goal of social stability becomes a reality. At that point the inherent logic of the commons remorselessly generates a tragedy... Ruin is the destination towards which all men rush, each pursuing his own best interest in a society that believes in the freedom of the commons.*

The publication of this article in 1968, coinciding with the first pictures of earth from space, and the new notion of 'Spaceship Earth', had a powerful resonance.

The collapse of city transport in megacities, overfishing of certain fish species and overcrowding by tourists of places of natural beauty and serenity have all been given as examples of the 'tragedy of the commons'. Land use changes resulting in adverse hydrological impacts, either in terms of quantity or quality, could equally be viewed as another example of this 'tragedy'. The salinization of much of the agricultural land of Australia and of major river systems (see Chapter 5) brought about incrementally by individual farmers' actions might be seen as a particularly pertinent example within a water resources context.

Although Hardin's article has done much to promote awareness of issues of sustainability, the general use of his narrative to predict and explain the degrading effects of increasing population pressures on natural resources has been criticized. Leach and Mearns (1996) argue that in a true commons situation, local institutions facilitate cooperation between users so that resources can be managed sustainably. The 'tragedies' only occur when the system for cooperation breaks down. There are examples in the Machakos region of Kenya (Tiffen et al, 1994) where it is claimed that increasing population densities in recent years have gone hand-in-hand with environmental recovery (see Chapter 1). Fairhead and Leach (1996) have also argued that the forest 'islands' around villages in the savannah region of Guinea are not the remnants of a previous extensive forest cover degraded by an increasing rural population, but the result of the rural population actually fostering these 'islands' in a landscape which would otherwise be less woody. The implication here is that population growth has resulted in more forest, not less (see Chapter 1).

The Limits to Growth

The book entitled *The Limits to Growth* (Meadows et al, 1972) presented a crisis scenario of the depletion of the world's resources of fossil fuels, metals, timber and fish. It is now realized that many of the assumptions on which the computer predictions were based, particularly in relation to the extent of the reserves of fossil fuels and metals, were flawed and consequently the dire forecasts that were made were mostly erroneous. Although, at that time, Meadows and colleagues successfully furthered the awareness of sustainability issues, the subsequent obvious failure of the crisis predictions has served to undermine the legitimacy of some very real concerns. The substantially revised and expanded 30-year update of the book (Meadows et al, 2005) raises again the question of the limits to growth and also presents 'overshoot' scenarios.

Brundtland and Beyond

The United Nations World Commission on Environment and Development, chaired by Norwegian Prime Minister Gro Harlem Brundtland, debated and investigated current concerns of the mid-1980s about the nature of development and the long-term consequences of certain development pathways. The report that was produced, entitled *Our Common Future*, but widely known as the Brundtland Report (UNWCED, 1987), reframed the environmental debate and laid the foundations for what was to become not only a new philosophy in our approach to development issues but also a new industry to develop the tools to implement the new philosophy.

The report provided a definition of sustainable development:

> *Humanity has the ability to make development sustainable – to ensure that it meets the needs of the present without compromising the ability of future generations to meet their own needs.*

Fresh water, together with food, energy, basic housing and health are recognized as basic human needs. Sustainability introduces notions of sound management of the world's resources that leave the resources in as good a condition for the next generation as we find them today.

The report also advanced seven strategic imperatives and seven preconditions for sustainability to be achieved. The strategic imperatives advanced were as follows:

1 Growth be revived in the developing nations, to alleviate poverty and reduce pressure on the environment.
2 Notions of equity and non-materialistic values be included in the definition of growth.
3 Essential human needs for food, housing and energy be met whilst accepting that this will necessitate changing patterns of consumption.

4   The issue of population growth should be addressed, particularly through reducing the economic pressures to have children.
5   The resource base needs to be conserved and enhanced.
6   The necessary environmental risk-management technology needs to be developed and also made available to the developing world.
7   Ecological as well as economic factors need to be taken into account in decision-making.

The preconditions for these imperatives were identified as follows:

1   Responsive political decision-making processes.
2   Economic systems which make fewer demands on resources.
3   Responsive social systems that maintain union by redistributing both the costs and benefits of development.
4   Production systems which can operate within ecological limits.
5   Technology developments that support energy- and resource-efficient solutions.
6   An international order that maintains cohesion globally.
7   Responsive, flexible, self-correcting governments.

The report suggests that the shift to sustainable development must be powered by a continuous flow of wealth from industry, but recognizes that future wealth creation will need to be much less environmentally damaging, more just and more secure.

The report has been widely applauded for taking a long-term and strategic approach, rather than piecemeal approach, to dealing with sustainability.

It has, nevertheless, been criticized for not taking proper account of the structural relationship between the economy and the environment. Clayton and Radcliffe (1996) argue that the report assumes that economic growth can co-occur with, or even enhance, certain types of natural capital, and that increased consumption in the developing world will therefore be possible without the environmental costs that have been associated with economic growth in the industrialized nations. They suggested that:

> given its relative lack of structural analysis, the Brundtland Report should not be taken as a blueprint for sustainability. It is, rather, a statement of principles.

They go on to say that:

> as a general rule, the purpose of such broad statements is to stimulate progress. It is usually desirable that such statements are eventually superseded by more detailed prescriptions for change. As part of this process of development, it sometimes becomes necessary to return to and revise some of the initial principles.

This is probably a valid assessment of the current position. The Brundtland Report has provided the stimulus for environmental organizations, industry and development agencies to rethink their strategies and to develop the detail in the processes needed to address sustainability issues. The detailed strategies, the 'blueprints' for sustainability, are now emerging, reflecting the needs of business, conservation and development interests. The emerging blueprints, the Natural Step, the Triple Bottom Line, the Sustainable Livelihoods and the Pentagon, and Integrated Economic and Environmental Satellite Accounts, are outlined below.

The Natural Step

The concepts behind the Natural Step were originated by Dr Karl-Henrik Robert, one of Sweden's leading cancer researchers and environmentalists, and are now being developed by the Natural Step Foundation. Robert was able to persuade the King, schools and industrial sponsors to back a report on Sweden's environmental problems and on the most critical avenues for action following the Natural Step approach. As a follow-up, an educational package was sent to every household in the country outlining the steps needed to make Swedish civilization environmentally sustainable for the long-term future.

The Natural Step philosophy is based on four principles or 'system conditions':

1   Substances from the Earth's crust must not be extracted at a rate faster than their slow redeposit into the Earth's crust.
2   Substances must not be produced by society faster than they can be broken down in nature or deposited into the Earth's crust.
3   The physical basis for nature's productivity and diversity must not be allowed to deteriorate.
4   There must be fair and efficient use of energy and other resources to meet human needs.

The Natural Step Foundation claims that:

> *The four system conditions provide a descriptive framework for a sustainable society. Participants on all levels – households, corporations, local authorities, nations – can systematically direct their activities to fit into this frame by requiring all secondary goals to function as natural steps in the process of achieving the four conditions of sustainability.*

The World Business Council for Sustainable Development (WBCSD) (see Appendix 1), a coalition of 125 international companies which claim a shared commitment to the environment and to the principles of economic growth and sustainable development, endorses the Natural Step approach. It is recognized that the first three principles pose major problems for industries concerned with mineral extraction and waste management. The fourth principle, they recognize, is slowly gaining acceptance in the business world whereas a decade earlier many businesses would have regarded it as outside their remit. About 50 national and international companies including IKEA and Electrolux are now training their staff in the Natural Step approach. The approach is also supported by conservation organizations (IUCN, UNEP and WWF, 1991).

The Triple Bottom Line

Whereas the Natural Step focuses on the physical aspects of sustainability, the Triple Bottom Line approach recognizes explicitly the social aspects. The ideas behind the Triple Bottom Line were developed by SustainAbility, a strategic management consultancy and think-tank concerned with foresight, agenda-setting and change management. Founded in 1987, it claims to be the longest-established international consultancy dedicated to promoting the business case for sustainable development.

The elements of the 'triple bottom line' are seen as representing society, the economy and the environment (Elkington, 1997). Society is seen as dependent on the economy – and the economy is seen as dependent on the global ecosystem, whose health represents the ultimate 'bottom line'. The 'bottom line' metaphor arose from the use of the term by business to represent the profit figure in a company's earning-per-share statement. To arrive at this figure accountants will, as part of standard accounting practice, collate, record and analyse a wide range of numerical data which relates to economic performance. This approach is seen as the model for social and environmental accounting, to allow the calculation of the social and environmental 'bottom lines'. The mechanisms for doing this are still being developed and are the subject of debate, but will need to embody the notions of 'social capital' and 'natural capital'.

Social Capital

Social capital is regarded in part as human capital, in the form of public health, skills and education, but also collectively, as society's health and wealth creation potential. Ismail Serageldin, the World Bank's vice president of environmentally sustainable development, recognizes that the fostering of human capital requires 'investments in education, health and nutrition'.

Natural Capital

Natural capital is often considered in two forms: 'critical natural capital' which is essential to the maintenance of life and ecosystem integrity, and 'renewable natural capital' which can be replaced, repaired or substituted. The methods for accounting for natural capital are slowly being developed.

The three bottom lines are not regarded as stable – but in constant flux due to social, political, economic and environmental pressures, cycles and conflicts. Elkington (1997) uses the example of plate tectonics to describe the movement of the lines:

> *Think of each bottom line as a continental plate, often moving independently from the others. As the plates move under, over or against each other, 'shear zones' emerge where the social, economic or ecological equivalents of tremors and earthquakes occur.*

SustainAbility's perceptions of the shear-zone interactions are as follows:

- **Economic/environmental** In the economic/environmental shear zone, some companies already promote eco-efficiency. But there are greater challenges ahead, for example, environmental economics and accounting, shadow pricing and ecological tax reform.
- **Social/environmental** In the social/environmental shear zone, business is working on environmental literacy and training issues, but new challenges will be sparked by, for example, environmental justice, environmental refugees and the inter-generational equity agenda.
- **Economic/social** In the economic/social shear zone, some companies are looking at the social impacts of proposed investment, but bubbling under are issues like business ethics, fair trade, human and minority rights, and stakeholder capitalism.

Sustainable Livelihoods and the Pentagon

The Department for International Development (DFID) White Paper on International Development, *Eliminating World Poverty: A Challenge for the 21st Century* (DFID, 1997) presents the concept of the stewardship of natural resources so that the needs of both present and future generations can be met. Sustainability does not rely upon a 'quick fix' solution becoming available in the future to reverse degradation. The White Paper also promotes the concept of 'sustainable livelihoods' and this, together with the management of 'the natural and physical environment' is expected to achieve the overall goal of poverty alleviation. A 'sustainable livelihood' is defined thus:

> *A livelihood comprises the capabilities, assets (including both material and social resources) and activities required for a means of living. A livelihood is sustainable when it can cope with and recover from stresses and shocks and maintain or enhance its capabilities and assets both now and in the future, while not undermining the natural resource base.*

Based on the work of the Institute of Development Studies (Scoones, 1998), five types of capital assets upon which individuals build their livelihoods are defined:

1   **Natural capital** The natural resource stocks: for example, land, water, wildlife, biodiversity and environmental resources.
2   **Social capital** The social resources (networks, membership of groups, relationships of trust, and access to wider institutions of society) upon which people draw in pursuit of livelihoods.
3   **Human capital** The skills, knowledge, ability to labour and good health important to the ability to pursue different livelihood strategies.
4   **Physical capital** The basic infrastructure (transport, shelter, water, energy and communications) and the production equipment and means which enable people to pursue their livelihoods.
5   **Financial capital** The financial resources which are available to people (whether savings, supplies of credit or regular remittance or pensions) and which provide them with different livelihood options.

The DFID approach recommends plotting assets on a five-axis graph, a pentagon. Carney (1998) concedes that the plotting of assets is necessarily subjective – the axes are not calibrated – but hopes that the analysis will provide a starting point for understanding how assets translate into livelihoods. However, the consequences for natural resource management of applying this new 'people-first', poverty-focused approach to sustainable development are not yet known. There are concerns that the poverty alleviation approaches focused at the micro-catchment scale may result in 'tragedy of the commons' type impacts at larger scales. Conversely, it could be argued that IWRM approaches, although aiming to achieve net economic benefits to basin inhabitants, may not be taking sufficient account of the poorest in society.

Equity and the Gini Coefficient

Whereas the pentagon approach of capital assets is essentially qualitative in nature, a quantitative measure for auditing equity in terms of income inequality within populations is provided by the Gini coefficient, developed by the Italian statistician Corrado Gini. The Gini coefficient is a number between 0 and 1, where 0 corresponds with perfect equality (where everyone has the same income) and 1 corresponds with perfect inequality (where one person has all the income, and everyone else has zero income).

The Gini index can be visualized through the Lorenz curve. If the income-receiving units in a population are ranked by income from the smallest to the largest and the cumulative share of income accruing to each category of the population from poorest to richest is plotted against the cumulative population share, the Lorenz curve is obtained (Figure 4.2).

If there was perfect equality (so that the first 10 per cent of the population received 10 per cent of the income and 20 per cent of the population received 20 per cent of the income, etc.) a diagonal line would be drawn across the graph. When actual income distributions are depicted on this graph, the Lorenz curve departs from the line of perfect equality. For example, the bottom 20 per cent of the population may receive only 5 per cent of the total

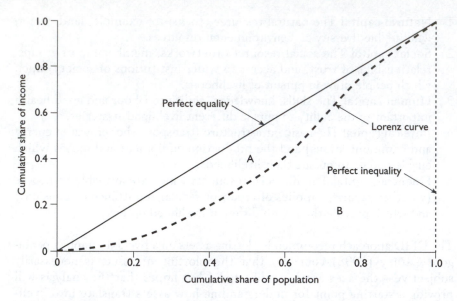

Figure 4.2 *Lorenz curve and lines of perfect equality and perfect inequality;
the Gini coefficient is given by A/(A+B) where the area between the
line of perfect equality and the Lorenz curve is A, and the area
underneath the Lorenz curve is B*

income. The Gini coefficient (G) is an expression of the ratio of the amount
of the graph located between the line of perfect inequality and the Lorenz
curve and the area of the graph below the line of equality:

$$G = A/(A+B)$$

The Gini coefficient can be calculated numerically in terms of the cumulative
population variable (X) and the cumulative income variable (Y) for a population numbering n through the formula:

$$G = \left| 1 - \sum_{k=0}^{k=n-1} (X_{k+1} - X_k)(Y_{k+1} - Y_k) \right|$$

The Gini coefficient provides a quantitative method for measuring and
monitoring the success of development efforts to achieve a more equitable
distribution of income or wealth among populations at the country, regional
or district level. At the country level, values for the Gini coefficient are given
in the United Nations *Human Development Report* (UNDP, 2004) (Table 4.2).

Although it is rarely applied as a measure of success of development at
the project level, increased use of indices like the Gini coefficient is urgently
required to evaluate the success or otherwise of development efforts aimed
at addressing poverty and improving equity. The perverse outcomes that are
believed to result from many land- and water-related policies (see Chapter 5)

Table 4.2 *Gini coefficients calculated by country*

Country	Gini coefficient
Australia	0.352
China	0.447
France	0.327
Germany	0.283
India	0.325
Japan	0.249
Mexico	0.546
UK	0.360
USA	0.408

Source: UNDP (2004)

could be more easily detected and evaluated if calculations of the Gini coefficient were performed before and after project implementation.

Human Development Index

The human development index (HDI), together with the Gini coefficient, is another quantitative measure that can be applied to evaluate the development success of a country. It measures a country's achievements in three aspects of human development: longevity, knowledge and a decent standard of living.

Longevity is measured by life expectancy at birth; knowledge is measured by a combination of the adult literacy rate and the combined gross primary, secondary and tertiary enrolment ratio; and the standard of living is measured as the gross domestic product (GDP) per capita.

The index was designed to capture the attention of policymakers, media and NGOs, and to draw their attention away from the more usual single-focus economic indicators such as GDP statistics. The aim was a greater focus on human outcomes, not economic data. The HDI was created to re-emphasize that people and their lives should be the ultimate criteria for assessing the development of a country, not economic growth or interest rates.

The United Nations Development Programme produces annual reports on human development using the HDI as one of the key indicators. The reports show both differences in HDI between countries and indicate how progress is being made (or otherwise) in meeting development objectives (UNDP, 2004).

Environmental Accounting and Integrated Economic and Environmental Satellite Accounts

Environmental movements, including the International Union for Conservation of Nature (IUCN), have long recognized that the System of National Accounts, as defined by the UN and implemented by governments worldwide, does not accurately incorporate or take account of the environment. National accounts are the economic data systems used to calculate familiar macro-economic indicators such as gross national product (GNP), GDP, savings rates and income per capita. They are built and maintained by governments, following standard accounting practices defined largely through an international process coordinated by the UN.

Environmental accounting is seen as the mechanism by which national accounting systems can be modified to account for the economic role played by the natural environment. To increase international acceptance and implementation of environmental accounting, the IUCN launched the first phase of its Green Accounting Initiative in 1996 (IUCN, 1998).

Because of its diverse membership, IUCN regards itself as well placed to contribute to the increasing acceptance of environmental accounting. Through its neutrality in the debates over approaches to environmental accounting, it is hoped that it may help the international community move towards greater agreement on methodology, which in the long run is regarded as essential for environmental accounts to achieve their full potential as a source of information for decision-making.

While much of their work is still in the developmental stages, many countries have experimented with implementing environmental accounting methods to better understand economy–environment interactions and to test environmental strategies. Norway is one of the few countries to have institutionalized environmental accounting as a routine government activity. In the 1970s, driven by concern about resource scarcity, Norway started to maintain consistent annual data on reserves and consumption of key minerals, fisheries and forests. Including these data in econometric planning models has helped policy decision-making in regard to increasing economic activity whilst complying with international conventions on air pollution reduction.

Other countries have been active in developing environmental accounting methodologies. The US Bureau of Economic Analysis (BEA) has been responsible for developing the system of national economic accounts which are used to produce the national income and product accounts, input–output accounts and balance sheets for the US economy. Responding to the need for environmental accounting (Landefeld and Carson, 1994), the BEA produced a new accounting framework that covers the interactions of the economy and the environment. This framework introduces new breakdowns that are relevant to the analysis of the interactions and extends the existing definition of capital to cover natural and environmental resources. The framework takes the form of a satellite account termed the Integrated Economic and Environmental Satellite Account (IEESA), which supplements, rather than replaces, existing accounts such as GDP.

The interactions covered are those that can be related to market activities and therefore assigned market prices. Their impacts are demonstrated through effects on indicators of production, income, consumption and wealth.

The accounts have two main structural features. Firstly, natural and environmental resources are treated like productive assets. These resources are viewed in the same way as other physical assets such as structures and equipment, and are treated as part of the nation's wealth. The flow of goods and services from them can be identified and their contribution to production measured. Secondly, the accounts provide details on all the expenditure and assets that are relevant to understanding and analysing the environment–economy interaction.

It is expected that fully implemented IEESAs would allow the identification of the economic contribution of natural and environmental resources broken down by industry, by type of income and by product.

The BEA, referring to future developments of the IEESAs, states that:

> *The plan calls for work to extend the accounts to renewable natural resource assets, such as trees on timberland, fish stocks, and water resources. Development of these estimates will be more difficult than for mineral resources because they must be based on less refined concepts and less data.*

And:

> *Building on this work, the plan calls for moving on to issues associated with a broader range of environmental assets, including the economic value of the degradation of clean air and water or the value of recreational assets such as lakes and national forests. Clearly, significant advances will be required in the underlying environmental and economic data, as well as in concepts and methods, and co-operative effort with the scientific, statistical, and economic communities will be needed to produce such estimates.* (Landefeld and Carson, 1994)

The outcome of this work has not yet been published. The IUCN has suggested that the strong business lobby in the USA, particularly pressure from the mining industry, has curtailed the progress the BEA was making on environmental accounting.

The Double Triple Win

The Double Triple Win concept recognizes that there should be a balance between the world's food production and its consumption. In the diagrammatic representation of the concept (Figure 4.3), the lower triangle refers to three components relating to sustainable production: food production must be economically viable, it must be environmentally sound and it must be organized in a manner which is socially acceptable. To be achieved, these components require good governance together with an integrated approach to land and water management. The upper triangle relates to the consumption of food. One of the components coincides with sustainable production, i.e. economic viability. In addition, the growing number of people who do not produce the food themselves must have access to food, i.e. they must earn an

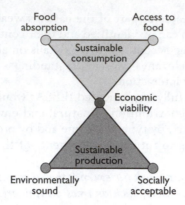

Source: SIWI-IWMI (2004)

Figure 4.3 *The Double Triple Win concept*

income to be able to purchase the food they need and want. The concept, promoted by the Stockholm International Water Institute and the International Water Management Institute (SIWI-IWMI, 2004), presumes synergies between production and consumption, between food and environment, and between consumer preferences and production potential. The challenge will be to discover synergies that combine the more productive and more socially acceptable aspects of production whilst minimizing depletion and degradation of the environment.

The Blue Revolution and Blueprints for Sustainability

These different blueprints, the Natural Step, the Triple Bottom Line, the Pentagon, and Integrated Economic and Environmental Satellite Accounts, are not mutually exclusive. Neither are they definitive. Nor are they sufficient to provide the blueprints needed by the blue revolution for addressing all land use and water resource issues or all the sustainability questions raised by the case studies discussed in this book.

Nevertheless, the existing blueprints will form the starting point for what is required. The Natural Step outlines principles for non-renewable resource exploitations and disposal of wastes and pollution into the environment but says little about social issues and how to manage trade-offs. The Triple Bottom Line brings in the social dimension but gives little guidance on how the bottom lines can be quantitatively assessed for either the social bottom line or the environmental bottom line; at present social 'accounting' is no more than social reporting. The Pentagon approach, whilst considering five forms of capital, makes no attempt to quantify them and is therefore of little value as a tool for evaluating development options. The approach used in Integrated Economic and Environmental Satellite Accounts lies closest to the requirements of the blue revolution by providing an objective, quantitative method for accounting for economic and environmental assets; but this approach takes no account of the social dimension and social assets.

Quantitative methods of asset accounting for the social, economic and environmental bottom line are needed for the blue revolution because qualitative concepts of sustainability, although an integral part of the revolution, are not in themselves sufficient. The blue revolution is not just concerned with obtaining sustainable solutions, it is concerned with obtaining solutions which satisfy all relevant stakeholders representing water resource, environmental, economic and social interests, solutions which recognize the inevitable trade-offs, in a quantifiable form, between the interests of the different stakeholders.

IMPLEMENTING THE IDEALS

Taken together, the UNCED, SAP and sustainability ideals have brought in a potent mix of new ideas for water management, the implications and ramifications of which, when applied, are only slowly being appreciated.

Perhaps most significant is the slow realization that the agricultural sector should not always be seen as the unquestioned priority user of water. Under centralized 'command' economies, concepts of food security and self-sufficiency ensured that the agricultural sector received priority treatment among water users. But agriculture is often a low value user of water and in situations of water shortage, from an economic perspective, higher value uses for supply, industry and even power generation may bring higher returns. From an economic perspective again, water diverted to the 'environment' and to sustaining wildlife and the eco-tourism industry may also be higher value uses than that of irrigation water for low-value agricultural crops. There is also recognition, in the more hydrologically enlightened countries, that forestry is a high user of water and that in water-deficient countries there needs to be serious consideration of whether, through the export of timber, they are really exporting their valuable and possibly more precious water resource. South Africa is perhaps the first country, through applying the results from its applied research programme into the water use of plantation forestry, to develop a water policy based not only on the well understood 'polluter pays' principle but extending this to the 'user pays' principle. The implications are that high water users such as foresters will be required to pay an 'interception levy' to compensate for the water that forests are removing from downstream users. The levy would be based on consideration of the extra water use from plantation forest compared with the indigenous land use. In South Africa this would normally be grassland.

Water for Agriculture or for the Environment? – Meeting the World's Food Needs

Probably one of the greatest challenges that must be faced in meeting the ILWRM ideals is in balancing water needs for food production and for nature.

Two possible interventions (see also Chapter 7) which will increase the world's food production, increased irrigation or increasing the agricultural lands on the planet by 'horizontal expansion' into the forests or rangelands, will not be welcomed by environmentalists.

But Malin Falkenmark (2003) argues from the sheer scale of the water resource assessments to meet food needs that informed trade-offs will have to be made. The problems associated with increased irrigation are well exemplified by the Aral Sea and the Yellow River. Abstraction of waters for irrigation has decreased the river inflow to the Aral Sea to 10 per cent of the natural flow, causing the lake to shrink to a small proportion of its original size with severe ecological consequences, together with the loss of a viable fishing industry. Abstractions for irrigation are also blamed for the Yellow River in China drying up for seven months in 1997.

Falkenmark argues that to find the way out of this considerable dilemma will need large-scale international attention in the next few decades and improved dialogue between water management and environmental organizations.

Finding solutions which are both practical and affordable is another key question. The EU Water Framework Directive, developed with the best of motives to help protect the environment, perhaps should have given more thought to the implementation difficulties and costs, particularly the monitoring costs. Similarly the South African National Water Act, the environmental focus of which was driven by the 'water for fish' concerns of in-stream ecologists, would entail massive monitoring costs if fully implemented. Some have argued (Quibell, 2004, personal communication) that it would cost more to implement the monitoring than it would to buy back all the existing abstraction licences, thereby removing the need to monitor but eliminating a productive and job producing sector of the economy.

Agricultural and Forestry Strategies Consistent with IWRM

To satisfy ambitions of food security and self-sufficiency, agricultural research for developing countries has traditionally focused almost exclusively on means of increasing productivity. As productivity and water use are intimately linked, agricultural and irrigation strategies, often FAO supported, generally call for greater exploitation of any remaining undeveloped water resources to be directed towards the agricultural sector, and usually towards large commercial farming operations. The requirements of other water users are not always considered in these strategies. To support the water demands of this perceived priority user of water, government water departments have placed great emphasis on expensive civil engineering activities associated with dam construction and the construction of transmission networks for irrigation schemes. The logic of this sequence of activities was rarely questioned within a command economy, and politicians could be assured of making political capital by promises of further dam construction. 'Two dams for every district' was promised by the Minister for Lands and Water Resources in Zimbabwe.

Table 4.3 *Water use by sector and contribution to GDP in Namibia*

Sector	Water used (%)	Contribution to GDP (%)
Irrigation	43.0	3
Cattle	25.3	8
Household + other	25.3	27
Mining	3.2	16
Tourism	0.4	4
Industry + commerce	2.8	42

Source: Pallett, ed (1997)

With a move from command economies to economies responding to free market forces, driven by SAP principles, the economic logic of diverting a large share of the water resources of a water-deficient country to the agricultural sector is increasingly being questioned. With increasing support for the principles enunciated by UNCED, which call for greater recognition of equity, stakeholder involvement and the environment and for treating water as an economic good, the past logic appears increasingly flawed and a new paradigm is developing. Whereas in the past it would have been heresy to doubt that agriculture should be regarded as the priority water user, these questions are now being posed in many countries. In Zimbabwe it is being asked whether agriculture should be using 80 per cent of the country's water resources when it is contributing only 16 per cent of GDP (see Chapter 6).

In proportional terms, the imbalance is even more extreme in Namibia where, although 43 per cent of the country's water is used for irrigation, it contributes only 3 per cent of GDP (Table 4.3).

These water allocation questions receive greater prominence in times of water scarcity. During the southern African droughts of 1992 and 1995 when water shortages in Zimbabwe led to closure of industries, severe rationing in cities and shortage of power (from hydroelectricity generation), the practice of using the scarce water resource for large-scale irrigation of relatively low value crops such as wheat was difficult to defend. Nor was the agricultural sector, which was receiving water at the low, heavily subsidized 'blend price' (see Chapter 6), being encouraged to use this water efficiently. Indeed the price was so low that the returns from hydroelectricity generation, if water had just been left to flow in the northern-flowing rivers into Kariba, would have been greater than the receipts from farmers for the use of this water for irrigation. Equity considerations in relation to water allocation for agricultural use are now also on the agenda. Whereas water rights were formerly associated with land tenure and were traditionally allocated on a 'first come, first served' basis, the question of need will increasingly be used as the criterion.

The UN-supported Consultative Group on International Agricultural Research (CGIAR) is now attempting to align strategies for increasing agricultural productivity within an environment of growing scarcity and competition for water through the System-Wide Initiative on Water Management (SWIM). The first paper produced under this initiative by Molden (1997) presents a conceptual framework for considering how water is used and recycled within a basin and gives a useful definition of water accounting terms. Molden also makes the important point 'that the portion of water diverted to an irrigation scheme that is not consumed, is not necessarily lost from a river basin, because much of it may be reused downstream'. An associated paper by Seckler (1996) discusses the concept of 'dry' and 'wet' water savings. Here 'wet' savings are regarded as genuinely beneficial savings to the whole system which allow other users, possibly those downstream, to make use of the savings. 'Dry' savings are those that result in no 'downstream' benefits from the savings. Any texts such as these are surely valuable if they can introduce the ideas into the agricultural community and, particularly, the agricultural irrigation community, that there are downstream users that also need water and that allowing water to flow in a river and not to use all of it for irrigated agriculture is not necessarily 'a waste', and that there may indeed be valid environmental or downstream uses for that water.

The increasing recognition of the needs of downstream users and the recognition that the environment is also a valid 'user' of water is the reason why so many countries are now developing IWRM strategies. There is a requirement now for the agricultural and forestry sectors to take full notice of these new developments which call for a more holistic appreciation of development issues; past objectives of 'increased productivity at all costs', can no longer be justified. Research priorities now need to be reassessed in the light of this new paradigm and sectoral strategies for the agricultural and forestry sectors need to be developed which align with the UNCED and SAP concepts embodied in IWRM strategies.

Priorities in Water Allocation

Historically, rules for water allocation have developed in a piecemeal fashion where the first user of the water often gains the right of usage through 'prior appropriation'. With increasing scarcity and increasing demands from the different sectors for a share of the water, this traditional 'first come, first served' principle needs to be re-examined. The question posed is how to prioritize the manifold demands for water: the demands for basic human consumption, the environment, consumption for production including agriculture, industry, power generation, household uses (other than for basic needs), and recreational and navigational uses. The question becomes even more pressing as demand outstrips supply and no new water rights can be allocated. This situation, generally known as 'closure' of the resource (when usable outflows are fully committed), has already been reached in many North African and Middle Eastern countries and in Australia (see Chapter 6), and has generated considerable political and socio-economic tensions (Chatterton and Chatterton, 1996).

Various approaches to water allocation have been advocated, but all would agree that some form of allocation is necessary when water resources come under stress. Inevitably conflicts will develop between the different sectors demanding water; without a rational water allocation policy, there can be no means of resolution.

Top-down approaches, which give priority to some users above others, is one approach; allocation through market forces and the ability to pay is another; and a third recognizes that the transfer of 'virtual' water between different sectors may be a way of making up for resource deficits.

A priority system proposed for arid southern Africa (Pallett ed, 1997), but one equally appropriate in the wetter regions of the world, places basic consumption for human survival and sanitation as the highest priority, with demands for the environment as the second. Consumption for production purposes is third, with navigational and recreational uses last. The authors argue that placing environmental needs before those of human production may appear to be idealistic, and an impractical luxury. But they argue that it is precisely in these conditions of water scarcity and increasing demand that water resources should be well cared for, so that they can sustain development both now and into the future.

Allocation through market forces, which allows sectors which are able and willing to pay a higher price for water to obtain a higher allocation, is another approach which is discussed in the next section. Politically this approach may be difficult to apply, particularly if there are powerful lobbies (often from the agricultural sector) which wish to retain the status quo, especially when the status quo has historically meant the provision of subsidized water. Another 'market force' instrument which can allow allocation transfers between users is the transferable water entitlement (TWE). This instrument allows the right to water to be bought or sold without the necessity of selling the accompanying land and is claimed to increase efficiency by aiding the transfer of water to higher value uses such as higher value crops or industrial processes (see Chapter 6).

A further approach, and one that has been claimed to have operated successfully for the last 25 years in countries in the Middle East and North Africa, involves not the direct transfer of water between sectors but the transfer of commodities whose production requires high inputs of water (Allan, 1992, 1996). This 'virtual' transfer of water means that food deficits can be made up by buying in food, particularly cereals, from more water-abundant regions and countries which have food surpluses, thereby freeing more water in water-scarce countries for higher value uses such as industry, services and domestic supply. Allan (1996) claims that it is the water demands for agriculture and plant production, even in the domestic garden, which are the uses causing economic crisis and social stress. He points out that for each person about $1000m^3$ of water is needed each year to satisfy food needs, but only $1m^3$ per year is required to drink and as little as $3.5m^3$ for domestic use. However, as much as $2000m^3$ per year is used by affluent families owning large gardens and irrigating lawns and flowerbeds in arid or semi-arid areas. By buying in food, governments can defer the painful process that would otherwise be required to manage demand and reallocate water supplies; in this way it may be possible to avoid the immediate political stress of confronting intransigent water users with the need to improve their water use efficiency. Allan points out that there are no engineering measures that could mobilize the 20–30 billion cubic metres per year of water needed to produce the grain being imported annually into the Middle East, and that current and foreseeable technologies cannot provide water at costs which can be accommodated by crop production systems.

A corollary to the argument that water-scarce countries should consider buying in 'virtual' water in the form of cereals, thereby freeing up water for higher value uses, is that water-scarce countries should consider whether it is prudent to export relatively low-value commodities which require a high water input. A case in point is the current dilemma in South Africa with regard to its commercial forestry operations. Usually forestry operations are on the hill tops and upper slopes, with fruit growing areas, industry, townships and, in some cases, game parks, downstream. The question of whether forestry should be depriving higher value uses downstream is currently an emotive issue among the different sectors (see Chapter 5).

The approaches outlined above are not necessarily mutually exclusive. Depending on the balance of priorities within a particular country or region, an element of free market forces could be invoked with a pricing policy for water, and this could be set up subject to constraints to protect aspects which are thought to require protection, for example, the poorest members of society or the aesthetic and spiritual aspects of rivers and water bodies.

In operational research terms this would mean that the model to determine the pricing policy would be set up with an objective function which might optimize basin economics subject to predefined constraints. 'Hard system' methodologies are now available to assist with this task for both water allocation (Kutcher et al, 1992; Hassan et al, 1995) and the planning of water projects using decision support systems (Jamieson, ed, 1996; Brans et al, 1986) (see Chapter 7).

THE WORLD COMMISSION ON DAMS –
RECONCILING ECONOMIC GROWTH,
SOCIAL EQUITY, CONSERVATION AND
POLITICAL PARTICIPATION

The World Commission on Dams (WCD) was born out of an IUCN and World Bank-sponsored workshop held in Gland, Switzerland, in April 1997.

Representatives of diverse interests came together to discuss the highly controversial issues associated with large dams. Although there were deep-seated differences on the development benefits of large dams, a consensus was obtained on one issue: the need for a World Commission on Dams.

The controversial issues associated with large dams are at the centre of blue revolution and ILWRM ideals: how to reconcile economic growth, social equity, environmental conservation and political participation in a changing world context.

The self-imposed task of the Commission was 'to conduct a rigorous, independent review of the development effectiveness of large dams, to assess alternatives and to propose practical guidelines for future decision-making' (WCD, 2000). The Commission was funded by a total of 53 public, private and civil society organizations, a funding model that was unique for international commissions.

The Commission completed its work with the launch of its final report in 2000 and disbanded.

The remarkable document that was produced has given us rare insights into the sectoral competition for water and the shifting power struggle between engineering, economic development, equity and conservation interests. It also highlights many of the sustainability and 'catchment closure' concerns (e.g. that rivers no longer run to the sea) that are addressed in this book. Kader Asmal in the foreword to the report states:

> *As we seek water we face an escalating crisis, even of biblical proportions. In Ecclesiastes, recall the passage:*
> > *One generation passeth away,*
> > *and another generation cometh:*
> > *but the earth abideth always...*
> > *All rivers runneth to the sea,*
> > *yet the sea is not full...*
> *The words are beautiful, haunting and, suddenly, anachronistic. For they are not true due to demands and dams during our lives. Even degraded rivers seldom totally run, but loiter in a chain of reservoirs. In some years our mightiest rivers – Africa's Nile, Asia's Yellow, America's Colorado, Australia's Murray – do not reach the sea.*

Kader Asmal also takes the optimistic view that water scarcity and competition for water can, rather than promoting conflict, be a catalyst for peace:

> *Some see in our scarcity a harbinger of troubled waters to come. They believe water scarcity inevitably locks peoples, regions and nations in a fierce, competitive struggle in which restless millions race to the bottom in fear and self-interest. And thus, they maintain, when rivers cross borders within or between nations, water scarcity leads to water stress which leads to water wars. Our Commission, and through it, this Final Report, contradicts that sentiment. We see water as an instrument, a catalyst for peace, that brings us together, neither to build dams nor tear them down but to carefully develop resources for the long term.*

The thrusts of the Report were directed in two main areas: a review of the performance of large dams and a proposed new development framework.

The review of large dams was dedicated to analysing the performance of dams based on the questions posed in an international survey: What were the projected versus actual benefits, costs and impacts of large dams? To what degree had dams delivered on developers' promises or to what degree had they fallen short? The conclusions were that large dams vary greatly in delivering predicted water and electricity services and related social benefits.

Irrigation dams have tended to fall short of physical and economic targets. Hydropower dams 'tend to perform closer to, but still below, targets for power generation, generally meet their financial targets but demonstrate variable economic performance relative to targets'. Perhaps most contentiously, the Report claims that the history of large dams reveals a 'pervasive and systematic failure' by governments and developers to assess the range of potential negative impacts and to put adequate mitigation and compensation measures in place.

The Report suggests that the positive contribution of dams to irrigation, domestic and industrial consumption, electricity generation and flood control has been 'marred in many cases by significant environmental and social impacts which when viewed from today's values, are unacceptable'.

The tone of the report is cautionary towards dams and technology. It argues not for abandoning large dam technology, nor for unrestrained reliance upon it, but for ensuring that the technology is kept under democratic control. It claims that few efforts have been made in the past to measure or monitor the benefits of dams and that dam projects have largely escaped due diligence procedures that are routinely applied to smaller development projects.

The second central and perhaps even more contentious thrust of the report is the promotion and advocacy of a new, very detailed and comprehensive development framework. (The degree of detail has been criticized in some quarters as making it impossible to take forward new dam developments) The framework comprises:

- 5 core values;
- 5 stages of decision-making before a project is approved;
- 7 strategic priorities and a planning and project cycle with criteria for assessing compliance; and
- 26 guidelines for review and approval of projects.

The five core values – equity, efficiency, participatory decision-making, sustainability and accountability – are derived directly from the UNCED ideals and the more recent United Nations Development Programme *Human Development Report* (UNDP, 2000) (see Box 4.1).

The WCD report recommends five key stages and decision points (Figure 4.4) within which decision-makers and stakeholder groups can be assured of compliance with agreed procedures and commitments. The Report claims that the benefits of this approach include lowering risks to livelihoods and cost escalation, reducing the number of disputes and encouraging local ownership.

The seven strategic priorities identified by the report are: gaining public acceptance; comprehensive options assessment; addressing existing dams; sustaining rivers and livelihoods; recognizing entitlements and sharing benefits; ensuring compliance; and sharing rivers for peace, development and security (Figure 4.5).

The Report recommends 26 guidelines for the review and approval of projects under the different strategic priorities:

Priority 1: Gaining public acceptance

1   Stakeholder analysis.
2   Negotiated decision-making processes.
3   Free, prior and informed consent.

Priority 2: Comprehensive options assessment

4   strategic impact assessment for environmental, social, health and cultural
     heritage issues.
5   project-level impact assessment for environmental, social, health and
     cultural heritage issues.
6   Multi-criteria analysis.
7   Life cycle assessment.
8   Greenhouse gas emissions.
9   Distributional analysis of projects.
10 Evaluation of social and environmental impacts.
11 Improving economic risk assessment.

Priority 3: Addressing existing dams

12 Ensuring operating rules reflect social and environmental concerns.
13 Improving reservoir operations .

Priority 4: Sustaining rivers and livelihoods

14 Baseline ecosystem surveys.
15 Environmental flow assessment.
16 Maintaining productive fisheries.

Priority 5: Recognizing entitlements and sharing benefits

17 Baseline social conditions.
18 Impoverishment risk analysis.
19 Implementation of the mitigation, resettlement and development action
     plan.
20 Project benefit-sharing mechanisms.

Priority 6: Ensuring compliance

21 Compliance plans.
22 Independent review panels for social and environmental matters.
23 Performance bonds.
24 Trust funds.
25 Integrity pacts.

Priority 7: Sharing rivers for peace, development and security

26 Procedures for shared rivers.

BOX 4.1 HUMAN RIGHTS AND HUMAN DEVELOPMENT

The UNDP *Human Development Report 2000* focuses on human rights as the basis for human development. It promotes six fundamental shifts from the thinking that dominated the 20th century:

- From state-centred approaches to pluralist, multi-actor approaches – with accountability not only for the State but also for the media, corporations, schools, families, communities and individuals.
- From national to international and global accountabilities – and from the international obligations of States to the responsibilities of global actors.
- From the focus on civil and political rights to a broader concern with all rights – giving as much attention to economic, social and cultural rights.
- From a punitive to a positive ethos in international pressure and assistance – from reliance on naming and shaming to positive support.
- From a focus on multiparty elections to the participation of all through inclusive models of democracy.
- From poverty eradication as a development goal to poverty eradication as social justice, fulfilling the rights and accountabilities of all actors.

Source: UNDP (2000); WCD (2000)

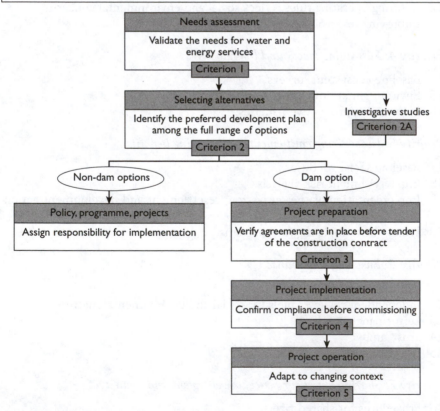

Source: WCD (2000)

Figure 4.4 *Five key decision points in planning and project development related to dams*

Source: WCD (2000)

Figure 4.5 *The WCD's Policy Framework with seven strategic priorities*

A major achievement of the WCD process was the holding together of the different stakeholders so that a partial consensus could be achieved in the views put forward in the report. However, the report has not been universally applauded or accepted. It received an enthusiastic reaction from international environmental organizations such as the IUCN and World Wide Fund for Nature, but less supportive were organizations such as the International Commission on Large Dams (ICOLD). ICOLD (2001) states that 'WCD's report is unbalanced and contains insufficient commentary on dam benefits such that anti-development groups are now calling for a moratorium on project development. This view is potentially disastrous for developing countries'. Furthermore it states that 'The procedures suggested by WCD for project evaluation are too cumbersome and serve as a huge deterrent to investment. They need to be streamlined without sacrificing intent.'

The major dam-building countries of the world were also generally critical of the report. China, with nearly half the large dams in the world, was quick to reject the WCD Final Report. The other major dam-building countries: India, Spain and Turkey were also highly critical.

Most organizations involved in the dams debate were able to agree and accept the general principles of the five core values and the seven strategic priorities. What was not generally agreed was the applicability or the practicality of the 26 guidelines.

The World Bank's Water Resources Strategy (World Bank, 2004), following the ICOLD position, is critical of three aspects:

1   Whilst accepting the rights of affected and indigenous people, the World Bank believes that adoption of the WCD principle of 'prior informed consent' amounts to a veto right that would undermine the fundamental right of the state to make decisions in the best interests of the community as a whole.
2   Whilst there is agreement on stimulating good-faith negotiations on international rivers, World Bank experience and policies are based on proactive engagement rather than disengagement from countries that are not already negotiating with their neighbours on international waters, as advocated by the WCD.
3   Whilst there is agreement on the importance of consultation and public acceptance, experience suggests that the multistage, negotiated approach to project preparation recommended by the WCD is not practical and would virtually preclude the construction of any dam.

Rather ominously the World Bank states that it will not comply with the 26 guidelines but will continue to implement its own operational policies.

The frustration felt by one of the commissioners, Thayer Scudder, at the lack of progress is expressed in his remarkable and candid book (Scudder, 2005) into the WCD process. He states:

> *It has taken me nearly 48 years to evolve this position. Readers will probably sense the anger I feel at the unacceptable and unnecessary costs that large dams have caused to tens of millions of people. Indeed, rereading sections in this monograph on the stress and trauma associated with resettlement infuriates me. I do not expect my position, or my anger, to change unless governments and project authorities begin to implement state-of-the-art guidelines.*

The issues addressed by the WCD – how to balance the needs of water for economic development whilst ensuring that equity, environmental and conservation requirements are met – are central to the blue revolution. But the Commission only addressed the more obvious concerns that are presented by large dams. Less appreciated, but arguably also very important, are the same alterations to the water environment created by smaller dams and soil water regulation structures. On the spectrum of scale ranging from a soil water conservation trench to a check dam to a village-level reservoir to a medium-size reservoir to a large dam, all these water-retention structures or soil water conservation structures have a similar function. They retain and 'regulate' flows, removing peaks and making water available for later use or as flow in the river. But all these structures come at a cost. They all increase water loss from the catchment, directly as evaporation from their open water surfaces and from the wetter surrounding riparian areas and indirectly, when water is taken from behind the retention structures for irrigation, water supply and other purposes. It is not only large dams that should be the focus of Kader Asmal's concern about stopping the rivers flowing to the sea. A sufficiently high concentration of smaller structures within a catchment, as is now happening in development projects in India and other parts of the world (see Chapter 5), will have the same effect.

UNCED TO THE MILLENNIUM DEVELOPMENT GOALS (MDGS)

The holistic management of fresh water as a finite and vulnerable resource, and the integration of sectoral water plans and programs within the framework of national economic and social policy, are of paramount importance for actions in the 1990s and beyond.

Integrated water resources management is based on the perception of water as an integral part of the ecosystem, a natural resource and a social and economic good, whose quantity and quality determine the nature of its utilization. To this end, water resources have to be protected, taking into account the functioning of aquatic ecosystems and the perenniality of the resource, in order to satisfy and reconcile needs for water in human activities.

(Agenda 21, Chapter 18, paragraphs 18.6 and 18.8, as endorsed at UNCED, Rio de Janeiro, (The Earth Summit), June 1992)

UNCED ratified the Dublin principles for the management of water. These were subscribed to by most nations and are referred to as the Dublin–Rio or UNCED principles. They have since been interpreted as follows:

- Water has multiple uses and water and land must be managed in an integrated way.
- Water should be managed at the lowest appropriate level.
- Water allocation should take account of the interests of all who are affected.
- Water should be recognized and treated as an economic good.

These principles are the cornerstones of IWRM and provide the basis for the blue revolution.

The international debate on IWRM has continued since the Earth Summit. The inter-ministerial conference on drinking water supply and environmental sanitation held in Noordwijk, The Netherlands, in 1994, reinforced the UNCED concerns. More recently, the committee on natural resources of the Economic and Social Council noted that some 80 countries, comprising 40 per cent of the world's population, are already suffering from serious water shortages and that, in many cases, the scarcity of water resources has become the limiting factor to economic and social development. It also recognized that ever-increasing water pollution had become a major problem throughout the world, including coastal zones. The UN Commission on Sustainable Development, at its second session in 1994, noted that in many countries a rapid deterioration of water quality, serious water shortages and reduced availability of fresh water were severely affecting human health, ecosystems and economic development. This Commission requested that a 'comprehensive assessment of the freshwater resources of the world' be submitted at its fifth session and to the special session of the General Assembly in 1997. This assessment was prepared by a number of UN organizations including the Department for Policy Coordination and Sustainable Development, the Department of Development Support and Management Services, FAO, UNDP, UNEP, UNESCO, UNIDO, World Bank, the WHO and the World Meteorological Organization, together with international research organizations and experts.

The report (UN Department for Policy Coordination and Sustainable Development, 1997) generally presents a rather gloomy picture of the future for the world's water resources and calls for immediate action to improve efficiency of use and to reverse degradation trends. The report notes that water use has been growing at more than twice the rate of population increase during the 20th century, and that already a number of regions are chronically water deficient:

> About one-third of the world's population lives in countries that are experiencing moderate to high water stress partly resulting from increasing demands from a growing population and human activities. By 2025, as much as two-thirds of the world population would be under stress conditions.

The British government's White Paper on International Development (DFID, 1997) again restates its commitment to the UNCED principles, but reinterprets them in relation to its new declared objective which focuses on world poverty reduction:

> We are supporting international efforts through the United Nations, other agencies and bilaterally to implement Key Principles for Sustainable Integrated Water Management as set out in Agenda 21 and reiterated at the Special Session of the UN General Assembly in June 1997.
>
> We will:
> - treat water as both a social and economic good;
> - increase our support for programmes that bring clean, safe water to poor people;
> - encourage all those who have an interest in its allocation and use, particularly women;

- *be involved in decision-making and management of water resources; and*
- *adopt a comprehensive framework that takes account of impacts of water use on all aspects of social and economic development.*

The allusion to 'a comprehensive framework that takes account of impacts of water use on all aspects of social and economic development' brings in concepts of IWRM. Some observers are critical that there is insufficient commitment to an integrated approach. Boyd (1997) of the Overseas Development Institute (ODI) states:

> *The White Paper places strong emphasis on environmental issues, and links environmental conservation with poverty reduction. However, improving rural livelihoods demands an integrated approach to natural resource and environmental management, rather than this sectoral approach which reflects conventional disciplinary specialisations.*

The Millennium Development Goals

Following on from UNCED and the other development conferences and summits held in the 1990s, a series of International Development Goals were being compiled and discussed by development organizations.

At the 55th Millennium Assembly of the United Nations, which was held at the Headquarters of the United Nations in New York in September 2000, the targets for the International Development Goals were set out and agreed unanimously by the member states, in the United Nations Millennium Declaration, 55/2 (UN, 2000). At the next (56th) meeting of the UN General Assembly, and following consultations among international agencies, including the World Bank, the IMF, the OECD and the specialized agencies of the United Nations, what had by then become known as the Millennium Development Goals (MDGs) were recognized as part of the 'Road map towards the implementation of the United Nations Millennium Declaration' (UN, 2001).

The form of the indicators that will be required to monitor the performance of the MDG targets are still under discussion. At present, 48 indicators have been proposed (see Table 4.4).

It is recognized by development organizations that the concepts underlying Integrated Water Resource Management are necessary (but clearly not sufficient) to achieving the MDGs, particularly the goals relating to extreme poverty and hunger (1), human health (4, 5 and 6) and to ensure environmental sustainability and access to water and improved sanitation (Goal 7, Target 10).

Whilst the simple linear rationale behind the MDGs, their targets and their indicators is compelling, it does gloss over the complexity of dealing

Table 4.4 *The Millennium Development Goals, Targets and Indicators*

TARGETS	INDICATORS
Goal 1 – Eradicate extreme poverty and hunger	
1 Halve, between 1990 and 2015, the proportion of people whose income is less than $1 a day	**1** Proportion of population below $1 a day 1a. Poverty headcount ratio (percentage of population below national poverty line) **2** Poverty gap ratio (incidence x depth of poverty) **3** Share of poorest quintile in national consumption
2 Halve, between 1990 and 2015, the proportion of people who suffer from hunger	**4** Prevalence of underweight in children (under 5 years of age) **5** Proportion of population below minimum level of dietary energy consumption
Goal 2 – Achieve universal primary education	
3 Ensure that, by 2015, children everywhere, boys and girls alike, will be able to complete a full course of primary schooling	**6** Net enrollment ratio in primary education **7a** Proportion of pupils starting grade 1 who reach grade 5 **7b** Primary completion rate **8** Literacy rate of those aged between 15 and 24 years
Goal 3 – Promote gender equality and empower women	
4 Eliminate gender disparity in primary and secondary education, preferably by 2005 and in all levels of education no later than 2015	**9** Ratio of girls to boys in primary, secondary, and tertiary education **10** Ratio of literate women to men aged 15 to 24 **11** Share of women in wage employment in the non-agricultural sector **12** Proportion of seats held by women in national parliament
Goal 4 – Reduce child mortality	
5 Reduce by two-thirds, between 1990 and 2015, the under-five mortality rate	**13** Under-five mortality rate **14** Infant mortality rate **15** Proportion of 1-year-old children immunized against measles
Goal 5 – Improve maternal health	
6 Reduce by three-quarters, between 1990 and 2015, the maternal mortality ratio	**16** Maternal mortality ratio **17** Proportion of births attended by skilled health personnel
Goal 6 – Combat HIV/AIDS, malaria and other diseases	
7 Have halted by 2015 and begun to reverse the spread of HIV/AIDS	**18** HIV prevalence among pregnant women aged 15 to 24 **19** Condom use rate of the contraceptive prevalence rate **19a** Condom use at last high-risk sex **19b** Percentage of 15 to 24 year olds with comprehensive, correct knowledge of HIV/AIDS **19c** Contraceptive prevalence rate **20** Ratio of school attendance of orphans to school attendance of non-orphans aged 10 to 14

TARGETS	INDICATORS
8 Have halted by 2015 and begun to reverse the incidence of malaria and other major diseases	**21** Prevalence and death rates associated with malaria **22** Proportion of population in malaria-risk areas using effective malaria prevention and treatment measures **23** Prevalence and death rates associated with tuberculosis **24** Proportion of tuberculosis cases detected and cured under directly observed treatment short course

Goal 7 – Ensure environmental sustainability

9 Integrate the principles of sustainable development into country policies and programs, and reverse the loss of environmental resources	**25** Proportion of land area covered by forest **26** Ratio of area protected to maintain biological diversity to surface area **27** Energy use (kilograms of oil equivalent) per $1 GDP **28** Carbon dioxide emissions (per capita) and consumption of ozone-depleting chlorofluorocarbons **29** Proportion of population using solid fuels
10 Halve, by 2015, the proportion of people without sustainable access to safe drinking water and basic sanitation **11** Have achieved, by 2020, a significant improvement in the lives of at least 100 million slum dwellers	**30** Proportion of population with sustainable access to an improved water source, urban and rural **31** Proportion of population with access to improved sanitation, urban and rural **32** Proportion of households with access to secure tenure

Goal 8 – Develop a global partnership for development

12 Develop further an open, rule-based, predictable, non-discriminatory trading and financial system (includes a commitment to good governance, development, and poverty reduction–both nationally and internationally) **13** Address the special needs of the least-developed countries (includes tariff and quota-free access for exports, enhanced programme of debt relief for Heavily Indebted Poor Countries (HIPC) and cancellation of official bilateral debt, and more generous overseas development aid for countries committed to poverty reduction)	Some of the indicators listed below will be monitored separately for the least-developed countries, Africa, landlocked countries and small island developing states. **Official development assistance** **33** Net Overseas Development Aid Overseas development aid total and to the least-developed countries, as a percentage of OECD (Organisation for Economic Co-operation and Development)/DAC (Development Assistance Committee) donors' gross national income **34** Proportion of bilateral, sector-allocable overseas development aid of OECD/DAC donors for basic social services (basic education, primary health care, nutrition, safe water and sanitation) **35** Proportion of bilateral official development assistance overseas development aid of OECD/DAC donors that is untied **36** Overseas development aid received in landlocked countries as proportion of their gross national incomes **37** Overseas development aid received in small island developing states as proportion of their gross national incomes **Market access** **38** Proportion of total developed country imports (by value and excluding arms) from developing countries and from least-developed countries, admitted free of duty
14 Address the special needs of landlocked countries and small island developing states (through the Program of Action for the Sustainable Development of Small Island Developing States and 22nd General Assembly provisions)	**39** Average tariffs imposed by developed countries on agricultural products and textiles and clothing from developing countries

Table 4.4 *continued*

TARGETS	INDICATORS
	40 Agricultural support estimate for OECD countries as a percentage of their GDP **41** Proportion of overseas development aid provided to help build trade capacity
	Debt sustainability
15 Deal comprehensively with the debt problems of developing countries through national and international measures in order to make debt sustainable in the long term	**42** Total number of countries that have reached their HIPC decision points and number that have reached their HIPC completion points (cumulative) **43** Debt relief committed under HIPC initiative **44** Debt service as a percentage of exports of goods and services
	Other
16 In cooperation with developing countries, develop and implement strategies for decent and productive work for youth **17** In cooperation with pharmaceutical companies, provide access to affordable, essential drugs in developing countries **18** In cooperation with the private sector, make available the benefits of new technologies, especially information and communications	**45** Unemployment rate of 15 to 24 year olds, male and female and total **46** Proportion of population with access to affordable, essential drugs on a sustainable basis **47** Telephone lines and cellular subscribers per 100 population **48a** Personal computers in use per 100 population **48b** Internet users per 100 population

Source: UNDG (2003)

with real world situations. The implication, and underlying logic, that each goal can be addressed independently, and by doing so, will allow some eventual ideal outcome is simplicity taken to an extreme. Unfortunately 'win–win' solutions are difficult to find in real life, and trade-offs involving hard decisions will be necessary to decide to what extent each of the goals should be achieved – an aspect that politicians and development practitioners are not always keen to admit. For water the trade-offs can be illustrated in terms of how water can be valued for its different uses in terms of '$ per drop', 'jobs per drop', and 'hops per drop'. Here '$ per drop' represents the demand for productive use, 'jobs per drop' represents the job opportunities that may be associated with a particular form of use and 'hops per drop' represents, as frogs could represent an indicator of ecological health, the requirement of water to meet in-stream ecological needs. Similarly for the land resource, there are conflicting demands for different productive and environmental uses together with requirements to provide jobs and liveli-hoods. Behind some of the goals we see some of the vested interests which have supported the engineer's, environmentalist's and forester's narratives which have fought to control land and water policies in the past. This is not to forget that politicians, scientists and development practitioners have their own vested interests in the development process (Chapter 5).

The challenge for the blue revolution is to find ways to achieve the objectives and desired outcomes of the MDGs, whilst recognizing that trade-offs will be necessary in finding solutions, particularly when we are dealing with real world situations where there are:

- increasingly severe and conflicting demands on the land and water resource to supply food, water and other goods and services (e.g. timber, fisheries, conservation and amenity) leading to sectoral conflicts between the water, land, power generation, irrigation and piped water, and sanitation provision sectors;
- concerns that upstream management of land and water in 'watershed development' projects generally ignores downstream impacts, particularly as it affects the lowland rural and urban poor, and transnational and coastal interests; and
- concerns that the opportunities that better resource management (ILWRM) provides in a rapidly globalizing world economy will be captured by the non-poor.

This will require increased recognition of the outcomes of different MDG policies and goals as they affect poverty and hunger, human development, economics, the environment and water resources and, in particular, that policies meeting one objective may be at the expense of meeting another:

- Improved land and water policies which do not disadvantage the poor – through confronting the complex and messy real world situation in which it is important to recognize that land and water policies and practices at international, national and local levels are generally driven, dominated and exploited by the vested interests of sectoral, powerful and wealthier groups (see Chapter 5).
- Recognition of the 'hidden food gap'. While conventional food production projections tend to focus on irrigated agriculture, assuming plausible expansion of irrigation and development of market forces, a huge 'hidden food gap' tends to characterize poor regions with large undernutrition and rapid population growth, regions which are often characterized by climatic variability in seasonal rainfall, recurrent drought years and intra-seasonal dry spells (Falkenmark, 2003).
- Ensuring that MDG-driven water and sanitation schemes do not damage the environment. There is a need to ensure that the major initiatives that are being carried out to provide piped water and sanitation schemes in developing countries are properly set within an IWRM context. Recent international concern about the 'World Water Crisis' has focused on the plight of 'the poor' (largely urban in the dominant view) and their acknowledged suffering from poor water supply, poor sanitation and hence waterborne diseases. Arguably the situation in many developing countries resembles that of early Victorian Britain in which river basin planning and management lagged provision for the urban poor by almost 150 years, by which time the largest basin management problems were those of over-abstraction and sewer discharges.

- Ensuring that 'environmental' schemes do not disadvantage poor people, damage water resources and curtail opportunities for food production. The rationale given for Indicator 25, the proportion of land area covered by forest, is that it 'provides a measure of the relative importance of a forest in a country' and, self-evidently, 'Changes in forest area reflect the demand for land for other competitive uses'. The assumption is that 'Forests provide a number of functions that are vital for humanity, including the provision of goods (timber and non-timber products) and services such as protection against flooding, habitat for biodiversity, carbon sequestration, watershed protection and soil conservation.' The claim is also made that 'the resource is not infinite and that its wise and sustainable use is needed for humanity's survival'. Whilst there is no denying the production benefits of forest together with the many conservation, amenity, recreation and spiritual benefits, it is argued (Chapter 2) that the other quoted services in relation to protection against floods, watershed protection and soil protection are mostly either highly overstated or wrong. In Chapter 5 the 'forester's narrative' which promotes such claims is discussed. No mention is made in the rationale of the water resource downsides of forestry schemes. Nor is it mentioned that competition for forest lands may be for other productive uses such as food production, which may be economically more viable for poor people together with meeting local food needs. Environmental 'wins' may be at the expense of meeting other MDGs. The notion expressed in Indicator 25 that 'while substantial areas of productive forest remain, there is now widespread recognition that the resource is not infinite and that its wise and sustainable use is needed for humanity's survival' has elements of the fervour of environmental movements of the first European colonialists who imagined that the whole Earth might be threatened by deforestation, famine, extinction and climate change (Grove, 1995; Falkenmark, 1995).

Meeting MDGs has become the aim of all international and most national development organizations. The Partnership in Statistics for Development in the 21st Century (PARIS21) organization provides data on how these goals are being met (Table 4.5). PARIS21, supported by the OECD, was launched in 1999 'to act as a catalyst for promoting a culture of evidence-based policy-making and monitoring in all countries, and especially in developing countries'.

The UN Millennium Project (UNMP, 2005) produced it own report on the MDG process 'Investing in Development'. The lead author was Professor Jeffrey Sachs, special adviser to the United Nations Secretary General and head of the Earth Institute at New York's Columbia University. The report reflects and endorses the philosophy of the MDG process that development and poverty eradication can be achieved through the simple linear process of addressing the symptoms of poverty and advocates more in the way of technocratic solutions, particularly those focused on improved infrastructure (roads, ports, energy supplies etc) and health care. Recognizing that the MDGs will not be achieved by 2015 in many countries, it calls for an immediate six times

Table 4.5 *Progress towards meeting the Millennium Development Goals*

Goal	Progress
1 Reduce the proportion of people living in extreme poverty by half between 1990 and 2015	As growth increased globally in the mid-1990s, poverty rates fell – rapidly in Asia, but little or not at all in Africa. Income inequality is a barrier to progress in Latin America
2 Enrol all children in primary school by 2015	Although enrolment rates continue to rise, they have not risen fast enough. On current trends, more than 100 million school-age children will not be in school in 2015
3 Make progress towards gender equality and empowering women by eliminating gender disparities in primary and secondary education by 2005	Getting more girls through school is essential but not enough. The gender gap may be narrowing, but girls' enrolments remain persistently behind those of boys
4 Reduce infant and child mortality rates by two-thirds between 1990 and 2015	For every country that cut infant and under-5 child mortality rates fast enough to reach the goal, 10 lagged behind – and another one moved backwards, often because of HIV/AIDS
5 Reduce maternal mortality ratios by three-quarters between 1990 and 2015	Skilled care during pregnancy and delivery can do much to avoid many of the 500,000 maternal deaths each year. But the proportion of births attended by skilled personnel rose slowly in the 1990s
6 Provide access for all who need reproductive health services by 2015	Contraceptive use is one indicator of access to reproductive health. With increasing access to reproductive health services, the rate of contraceptive use is rising in all regions
7 Implement national strategies for sustainable development by 2005 so as to reverse the loss of environmental resources by 2015	Despite their commitments at the Rio Earth Summit in 1992, fewer than half the world's countries have adopted strategies, and even fewer are implementing them

Source: Partnership in Statistics for Development in the 21st Century, PARIS21 (2004)

increase in the present UN antipoverty budget of $20 billion to $120 billion, with a further increase to $195 billion by 2015. A note of caution towards the MDG process and the Sachs approach being promoted as the only or preferred solution to meeting development goals is provided by Jens Martens (2005), Director of the European Office of the Global Policy Forum:

> *The Sachs Report largely restricts itself to the superficial allevia-tion of the symptoms of poverty. The structural causes of poverty and social injustice remain largely neglected. This weakness is a mirror image of the problem underlying the MDG strategy. The populist reduction of development to a few quantitative goals and targets and the focus on 'extreme' poverty bear within them the danger of taking political leave from more far-reaching approaches to development, particularly from concepts of environ-mentally sustainable and socially just development.*

As the dangers of promoting water-related developments without considering the more holistic impacts are now recognized – requiring an integrated approach to land and water resource management, the same more integrated approach to meeting the MDGs may also be required. It is too simplistic to assume that each can be addressed independently of the others. It will, as discussed above, be difficult to find win–win situations to meet the different goals and there will inevitably be hard decisions to be made in relation to trade-offs.

IWRM ORGANIZATIONS

The UNCED ideals and the blue revolution are leading to the formation of new international and national organizations which explicitly or implicitly accept these new directions. The international debate on IWRM has been furthered by two new non-governmental organizations (NGOs): the Global Water Partnership (GWP) and the World Water Council (WWC). Both these organizations were founded in 1996 and have similar objectives, although the GWP regards itself more as a facilitator of IWRM projects, whilst the WWC promotes itself as a 'think-tank' on IWRM issues. The English and Welsh Environment Agency, formed in 1996, is an example of a national organization which was formed with the explicit intention of taking a more integrated approach to water and environmental management and regulation.

The Global Water Partnership

The GWP, whose proclaimed ambition is to translate the Dublin–Rio principles into practice, was formally established at a founding meeting in Stockholm in August 1996. It is promoted as an international network open to all involved in water resource management, including governments of developing as well as developed countries, UN agencies, multilateral banks, professional associations, research organizations, the private sector and NGOs. The GWP intends to emphasize its comparative advantages as compared to bilateral and multilateral donors, and other agencies concerned with water and development. It claims no wish to duplicate already existing activities or compete with established donor agencies. Rather, it wishes to support those already working in the field of water and development, and thus gain from the experience and knowledge that already exists. The specific objectives of the GWP are that it will:

> support integrated water resources management programmes by collaboration, at their request, with governments and existing networks and by forging new collaborative arrangements, encourage governments, aid agencies and other stakeholders to adopt consistent, mutually complementary policies and programmes, build mechanisms for sharing information and experiences,

develop innovative and effective solutions to problems common to integrated water resources management, suggest practical policies and good practices based on those solutions, and help match needs to available resources.

The GWP is made up of four components:

1 The Consultative Group (CG).
2 The Technical Advisory Committee (TAC), consisting of professionals and scientists in disciplines related to water resource management.
3 The Steering Committee.
4 The GWP Secretariat, based in Stockholm (see Appendix 1), which provides administrative support to the CG and the TAC.

The World Water Council

The World Water Council (see Appendix 1) was formed in June 1996 with the proclaimed objectives of 'promoting awareness of global water issues and facilitating conservation, protection, development, planning and management of world water resources'.

The WWC believes there is a need for another water organization because:

Our understanding of global water policy issues suffers from the extreme fragmentation of the field into national, regional and local water authorities and a host of professional and scientific organizations established along sectoral lines. Until now there has been no overarching umbrella group able to deal with water policy issues in their entirety, identify problem areas and advocate solutions.

The WWC calls itself:

a true umbrella organization, a forum and a think-tank where all the divergent interests concerned with water issues can meet, debate, reflect and provide solutions to global water policy issues.

The Council is currently governed by a board of governors presided over by a chairman. The elected board of governors, whose members come from all geographic regions of the globe and from all sectors concerned with water management and policy issues, is chosen by a general assembly composed of all voting members. The Council is launching two long-term projects. The first is a long-term vision for water, life and the environment, a process that will lead to the systematic identification of the water-related problems facing the world in the current century and will recommend solutions. The other is a global water assessment, an effort to develop for the first time a satisfactory inventory of the world's fresh water resources.

In the first edition of *The Blue Revolution*, it was questioned 'whether IWRM, which already has to cope with many fragmented sectoral organizations involved with water management, can really afford the luxury of two international umbrella organizations to further its interests'.

Both the GWP and WWC seem to have found separate niches for their operations, the GWP focusing more on the tools required to implement IWRM at a local and catchment scale, whilst the WWC directs its efforts more to global and policy issues. Both have an important role to play in furthering IWRM and ILWRM.

The English and Welsh Environment Agency – A National Initiative

The Environment Agency was formed in April 1996 from former regulatory authorities whose remits separately included water, pollution and waste disposal. These were the National Rivers Authority (NRA), Her Majesty's Inspectorate of Pollution, and the Waste Regulation Authorities, together with smaller units from the Department of the Environment. The stated aim of the Agency is to 'protect or enhance the environment as a whole, in order to play its part in attaining the objective of sustainable development'.

The objectives of the agency set by Ministers are:

- an integrated approach to environmental protection and enhancement;
- consideration of the impact of all activities and natural resources;
- delivery of environmental goals without imposing disproportionate costs on industry or society as a whole;
- clear and effective procedures for serving its customers, including the development of single points of contact with the Agency;
- high professional standards, using the best possible information and analytical methods;
- organization of its own activities to reflect good environmental and management practice, and provision of value for money for those who pay its charges, and for taxpayers as a whole;
- provision of clear and readily available advice and information on its work; and
- development of a close and responsive relationship with the public, including local authorities, other representatives of local communities and regulated organizations.

Sherriff (1996) states:

> The creation of the Environment Agency has further strengthened the integrated approach to river basin management and has specific duties associated with sustainable development and the need to take costs and benefits into account in exercising its functions.

in other words, a clear restatement of the objectives of IWRM and the blue revolution.

One task of the Environment Agency is to consider the adequacy of water resources. It does this in a number of ways.

- It must balance the medium-term demands for, and supply of, fresh water.
- It is required to take action, as and when it considers necessary, in order to conserve, redistribute or otherwise augment water resources in England and Wales, and to secure the proper use of water resources.
- It has to manage the rate of abstraction of water in relation to the average effective rainfall.
- The Agency must also make assessments of the forecast balance between future demands and available water resources. It also prepares plans aimed at achieving a proper future balance by considering not only engineering options designed to increase supply, such as new reservoirs or transfer schemes, but also demand management options, such as leakage control and water metering.
- The Agency is also required to address the issue of the impacts of abstractions on low river flows and of the environmental consequences of these low flows. The Agency recognizes that most of the problems have been caused by 'licences of right' which were granted under the earlier Water Resources Act of 1963. These authorizations legalized existing abstractions without reference to their environmental impact.

Sherriff (1996) remarked that the recent droughts of 1995/96 resulted in a shift of emphasis from water quality to water quantity as being the top priority for water companies' future investment plans. The impacts of future climate change on water resources (Arnell, 1996) and of land use change, especially that resulting from the proposed doubling of lowland forests in the UK (see Chapter 6) are also important issues which may result in supply shortages in times of increasing future demands.

The Environment Agency (EA) operates over eight regions, which are further subdivided for administrative purposes, allowing an integrated approach to be taken at a local level. Following on from the work of the NRA, the river catchment (watershed) has been adopted as the spatial unit within which environmental decisions are made and implemented. The EA took forward the former National Rivers Authority's approach for producing Catchment Management Plans (CMPs) and built in a stronger stakeholder consultation component in the form of 'Local Environment Agency Plans'.

Local Environment Agency Plans

Local environment agency plans (LEAPs) were originally conceived as non-statutory action plans which would use the local planning process to promote inputs from stakeholders such as local authorities, industry, farming organizations, environmental groups and other agencies and individuals, including local residents. They were seen to play a central role in developing liaison between the EA and the other stakeholders, educating the public on local issues, prioritizing local environmental issues and in providing the mechanism through which they can be resolved.

The LEAP process evolved from that developed by the former National Rivers Authority for producing CMPs. It was recognized (Slater et al, 1995) that the production of many of the earlier CMPs had involved little interaction with stakeholders and that, partly as a result, the CMPs had little impact as planning tools. An exception was the Thames region of the Authority, which had developed a more systematic approach to liaison with local planning authorities and other stakeholders. It was the ethos and the procedures developed by the Thames region which largely defined the subsequent LEAPs process (Gardiner, 1992).

The production and implementation of a LEAP involves three stages:

1   Following consultation with the relevant stakeholders and analysis of the issues affecting each catchment, and an assessment of catchment uses and resources, a consultation report is produced. This then forms the basis for public consultation and discussion.
2   Following public consultation the EA then produces an action plan which details areas of work and proposed investments together with timescales, targets and estimated costs for improving environmental conditions within the catchment.
3   The implementation of the LEAP goes hand-in-hand with appraisal and monitoring, and an annual review is produced which reports on progress.

The gaps between the ideals embodied in the LEAPs and their production became apparent later. This was particularly evident with regard to the meshing of development and water resource planning. Where land use changes were occurring, being driven increasingly by conservation, amenity, recreation, environment (CARE), heritage and tourism interests, there was a clear need for the water resource benefits or disbenefits of the land use change to be taken into account in the planning equation. This had not been happening, perhaps partly because the water resource impacts resulting from land use change had not always been known or understood. But the reason may have been partly because the right questions had not been asked, perhaps because the correct institutional mechanism and institutional linkages between the development planners and water resource planners did not exist.

Evolving Environment Agency Strategies: CAMS and the 2001 Water Resources Strategy

In 2002, an internal review of the LEAPs process was completed. The Agency decided to use the LEAPs inventory of 130 previously published Local

Environment Agency Plans to continue to support local priorities but not to continue production of any further LEAP documents. Other strategies were evolving, and ultimately the work of the Environment Agency would need to mesh with the EU Water Framework Directive that was being developed.

Earlier, in 1999, the Environment Agency had also reviewed its system of issuing licences for water abstractions. A number of changes were made, the most important being the development of catchment abstraction management strategies (CAMS).

The main aims of CAMS were:

- to make information on water resources and licensing practice available to the public;
- to provide a consistent approach to local water resource management, recognizing the reasonable needs of water users and the environment; and
- to provide the opportunity for greater public involvement in managing the water resources of a catchment.

The EA launched the CAMS process in April 2001 and set out a six-year programme to develop, with consultation with local stakeholders, a CAMS for every catchment in England and Wales.

CAMS were also seen as part of the new National Water Resources Strategy that was issued in the same year (EA, 2001). This Strategy aimed to improve the environment, while allowing enough water for human uses. It was aimed to contribute to sustainable development, social progress, protection of the environment, making wise use of natural resources, and the maintenance of high and stable levels of economic growth and employment. It was designed to be flexible and phased, to thus avoid unnecessary investment while retaining the security of water supplies.

The strategy concluded that:

- in much of England and Wales, water can be a scarce resource;
- continued availability of a reliable public water supply is essential; the enhancement of supply by about 5 per cent over the next 25 years was recommended by improving existing schemes and developing new resources;
- water efficiency should be promoted actively;
- over the next 25 years, household water metering would become widespread;
- continued progress in leakage control would be necessary;
- agriculture must focus on using available water to best effect; and
- commerce and industry should pay increasing attention to water efficiency.

The Water Resource Strategy also considered the current status of water resource availability in England and Wales (Figure 4.6), together with that which might occur under different future scenarios. The future scenarios were based on the Government's Foresight framework, which looked at the

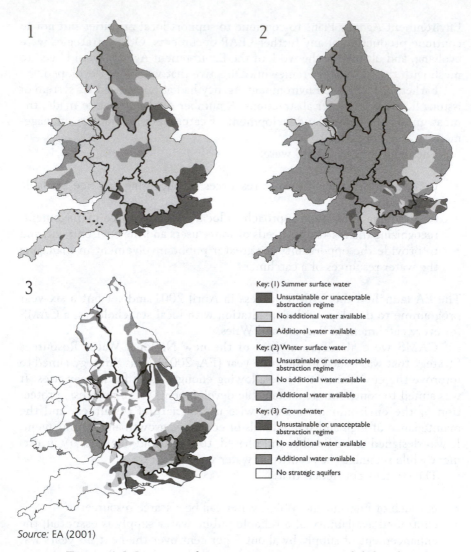

Key: (1) Summer surface water

■ Unsustainable or unacceptable abstraction regime
□ No additional water available
▨ Additional water available

Key: (2) Winter surface water

■ Unsustainable or unacceptable abstraction regime
□ No additional water available
▨ Additional water available

Key: (3) Groundwater

■ Unsustainable or unacceptable abstraction regime
□ No additional water available
▨ Additional water available
□ No strategic aquifers

Source: EA (2001)

Figure 4.6 *Current indicative water resource availability for England and Wales: 1 summer surface water; 2 winter surface water; 3 groundwater*

different ways in which our political and social values could change over time. These showed that over the following 25 years, total demand for water could fall or rise. The range of future demands is shown in Figure 4.7.

From its emergence from the previous NRA, the Agency has had to contend with continuously changing mandates which it has addressed through the proliferation of strategies and directives. These now include not only the overarching water resources strategy and CAMS but also the Restoring Sustainable Abstraction Programme, the Habitats Directive Review of Consents and the UK Biodiversity Action Plan. A major function of the EA is also in relation to 'Asset Management Planning' (AMP).

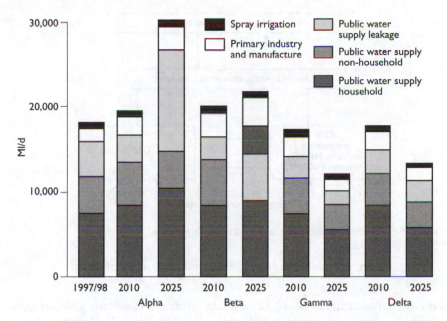

Figure 4.7 *Total water demand for England and Wales by scenario in 2010 and 2025*

Source: EA (2001)

The Office of Water Services (OFWAT) uses the AMP process to determine the programme of water infrastructure and environmental improvements that will be funded in the future and the allowable water bill price rises that the water companies can impose to raise the necessary funds. The EA is responsible for drawing up, under the National Environment Programme, the list of important nature conservation sites that are being impacted by water company activities (poor water quality or a lack of water) together with mitigation measures to ameliorate the problems.

The links between these different EA Initiatives are shown in Figure 4.8. A challenge for the future is to link with the European Environment Agency and find a way to mesh the different EA initiatives with the requirements of the European Water Framework Directive and the requirements to produce River Basin Management Plans.

The European Environment Agency

The stated aim of the European Environment Agency (EEA) is to support sustainable development and to help achieve significant and measurable improvement in Europe's environment through the provision of timely, targeted, relevant and reliable information to policymaking agents and the public.

The EEA was formally established by the European Economic Community in 1990 and became operational in 1994. It is primarily a networking organiza-

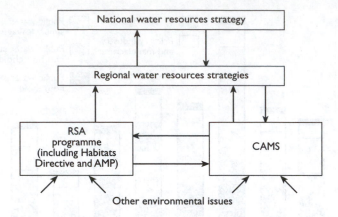

Note: RSA Refers to the Restoring Sustainable Abstraction Programme
Source: EA (2002)

Figure 4.8 *Links between CAMS and other EA initiatives*

tion based around the in-house Eionet data information system which it uses to provide advice and inputs on indicators and data flows. It plans to extend this to a shared European integrated spatial information system in line with the Inspire (infrastructure for spatial information in Europe) and global monitoring for environment and security (GMES) initiatives.

The Agency works across four major thematic areas: tackling climate change, tackling biodiversity loss/understanding spatial change, protecting human health and quality of life, and the use and management of natural resources and waste.

The Agency has adopted a 'policy cycle' approach to improving European policy in these four key areas (Figure 4.9). Information about the state of action of policy implementation within Europe is collated by a new network of European environmental protection agencies and it is planned that this process will be strengthened through an active stakeholder process in support of scenario development, policy evaluation and data quality assurance.

THE EU WATER FRAMEWORK DIRECTIVE

The driving force behind the EU Water Framework Directive (WFD) was the concern from environmentalists about the quality of Europe's lakes and rivers. The Directive (EUROPA, 2000) came into force on 22 December 2000 and replaces earlier, piecemeal EU water legislation. It expands the scope of water protection to all waters and sets out clear objectives that must be achieved by specified dates. It is the most substantial piece of EU water legislation to date, requiring all inland and coastal waters to reach 'good status' by 2015. It will do this by establishing a river basin district structure within which demanding environmental objectives will be set, including ecological targets for surface waters. The Directive sets out a timetable for the initial transposi-

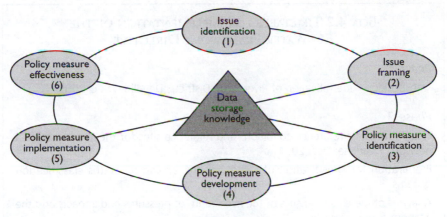

Source: EEA

Figure 4.9 *The European Environment Agency's proposed policy cycle, supported by data, information and knowledge*

tion into laws of Member States, and thereafter for the implementation of requirements.

The Directive requires Member States to establish river basin districts and for each of these a river basin management plan. The Directive envisages a cyclical process where river basin management plans are prepared, implemented and reviewed every six years. There are four distinct elements to the river basin planning cycle: characterization and assessment of impacts on river basin districts, environmental monitoring, the setting of environmental objectives, and the design and implementation of the programme of measures needed to achieve them.

Although the Directive sets regulatory standards which must be met by partner countries, it is not evident that much account has been taken of the costs or the economic viability of meeting these standards. Implementation of the directive is now posing a number of problems for member states, both technical and financial.

The Water Framework Directive raises technical questions in relation to the definition of the status of water bodies. The Directive demands that by 2015 all water bodies must have at least a good ecological status or potential. To define this status requires the identification of a number of reference sites so that these can be used as yardsticks for the conditions in the other water bodies. The WFD has given normative (i.e. baseline) descriptions for the biological/chemical/physical definition of a reference site, where 'reference sites are areas without any influence from human activity'. But areas without human influence do not exist in Europe today and this poses the question of how to define this ideal. It has been suggested that the problems of finding or defining reference sites may to some extent be overcome by finding the least-impacted areas and then making paleo-botanical investigations in the sediments to determine the past situation. The first projects to determine the reference situation in wetlands have already been launched in Spain.

BOX 4.2 TIMETABLE FOR IMPLEMENTATION OF THE EU WATER FRAMEWORK DIRECTIVE

Phase 1

Transposition – Identification of River Basin Districts, Deadline: Dec. 2003

Phase 2

Establishment of reference conditions and reference sites for the inter-calibration network, Deadline: Dec. 2004

Preparation for specification of values for the ecological status classification systems

Analyses of the characteristics of the river basin, of pressures and impacts and the economics of water use

Phase 2a

Establishment of community criteria for assessing groundwater (Commission proposals), Deadline: Dec. 2002

Individual Member State action in the absence of adoption criteria, Deadline: Dec. 2005

Phase 3

Operational monitoring programmes, Deadline: Dec. 2006

Phase 4

Publication of River Basin Management Plans, Deadline: Dec. 2009

Source: EEA

Whether the EU Framework Directive's targets are achievable by partner countries by the specified dates or will later be seen as 'aspirational', only time will tell. Conservationist and environmentalist NGOs are already critical of the progress and the quality of the efforts of member states in meeting the targets. The European Environmental Bureau and the World Wildlife Fund carried out a survey in 2004 among NGOs to determine the progress and compliance of the Member States. As their missions are primarily environmental and not so much concerned with the costs of implementation, their reports (EEB, 2004; EEB and WWF, 2004) are, understandably, very critical of progress and of missed opportunities.

Overall, the reports summarizing the views of 22 NGOs paint a rather dark picture as to the quality of WFD transposition and implementation. They claim low levels of NGO participation in the transposition and implementation process, lack of transparency in issues such as river basin characterization and inter-calibration, and failure to make clear the WFD's overall objective 'to achieve good status by 2015' within transposition legislation. They also point out the massive delays in implementing the directive.

Balancing the requirements of water for the environment with the financial costs in relation to economic and social development is a major challenge for the blue revolution. Clearly, meeting the environmental objectives of the Water Directive targets will not come without costs, including capital costs for building and replacing waste water treatment plants, costs for assessment and long-term monitoring, and costs for training the necessary staff required to fully implement the directive. For the established EU countries this may not be too large an extra burden compared with dealing with the previous piecemeal water legislation. For the EU Accession countries this may be too large a step for the existing human and financial resources to accommodate.

Chapter 5

Policies, Power and Perversity

Professor Tony Allan (Allan, 2003) of the School of Oriental and African Studies (SOAS) London Water Research Group, King's College, London, states that:

> *The history of water management over the past two centuries has been shown to have been subject to a sequence of sanctioned discourses. A discourse is sanctioned or not by the extent to which the policy is the result of what social theorists call a 'hegemonic convergence'. When coalitions come together they are partial in their selection of assumptions and information to feed into the policymaking discourse. Self-serving assumptions and information gets on to agendas, gets discussed and influences policy outcomes. Unwelcome information is relegated to appendices or ignored.*

In this chapter an attempt is made to understand how some present land and water policies, and some climate change policies, have developed, evolved and continue to be implemented, despite overwhelming evidence to show that in many cases the policies themselves are based on a flawed understanding of the physical interactions (the myths, see Chapter 2) and/or that the policies are having perverse outcomes, i.e. the opposite to those that were intended. The terminology of the 'sanctioned discourse', as coined by Tony Allan, is used together with the term 'narrative', which in this context refers to the story that particular groups develop, embellish and publicize to promote their particular cause.

By the nature of things, the blue revolution may be accused of creating its own sanctioned discourses by singling out policies for scrutiny and neglecting others. But here five are investigated, those which are believed to underlie:

1 **Watershed development** The promotion of watershed development for livelihood and poverty reduction benefits.
2 **Flood control policies** The long-standing and continuing struggle between engineering and forestry/environmental interests for domination of resources to 'control the flood'.

3 **The world's biggest experiment?** The Natural Forest Protection Programme and the Sloping Lands Conversion Programme.
4 **The world's greatest environmental challenge?** Climate Change and the Clean Development Mechanism.
5 **Markets for watershed services** 'Silver bullet' or 'fools gold'?

In the last section of the chapter the case is made for better evaluation of these policies in relation to outcomes and consideration of these policies in relation to others which are based less on the sanctioned discourses and narratives of engineers, foresters and environmentalists.

WATERSHED DEVELOPMENT PROGRAMMES – BENEFITING THE POOR?

In recent years, watershed development programmes promoting soil water conservation measures, forestry and groundwater-based irrigation have been extremely successful in many semi-arid areas of India and China as well as elsewhere in the world. Agricultural production has increased and the livelihoods of large numbers of people have been enhanced. However, this success has not always come without a cost.

Within watershed development programmes the implementation of soil water conservation structures, forestry and groundwater-based irrigation schemes have generally all been promoted to local communities and NGOs as 'good things'. The sanctioned discourse among watershed development programme managers and NGOs is that as all these interventions are 'good things', more must be better. This translates into programmes where the success of a programme is measured by the number of soil water conservation structures constructed, the area of forest planted and the area of groundwater-based irrigation schemes developed.

Many groups benefit. A thriving industry has developed in many parts of India to construct soil water conservation structures with benefits both to the building companies and to the programme implementers, through bribes and 'kick backs'. To a similar, although possibly lesser, extent the same applies to forestry and irrigation interventions. With such vested interests at stake it is perhaps unsurprising that the sanctioned discourse is reinforced by those involved and benefiting from these programmes. The parties involved in the programmes neither wish to take notice of nor publicize any possible downsides that might be associated with these programmes.

Causes of Catchment Closure

Although it should be stressed that in the right circumstance the above interventions can indeed be hugely beneficial and be in the wider public interest, problems can arise when these 'good things', all high water using land uses, are implemented in excess or in combination such that the total evaporative loss from a catchment becomes close to the amount of input rainfall and the catchment approaches the 'closed' or no-runoff condition.

Soil Water Conservation – As a High Water User

Charles Batchelor and colleagues (Batchelor et al, 2001, 2003) were perhaps the first to recognize and show that soil water conservation measures such as check dams, contour bunding and contour trenching, are not, as popularly imagined, always benign technologies. Although these structural interventions may well have the intended benefits of reducing the movement of sediments, increasing the recharge of water into the soil and 'smoothing out' peak flows, these benefits should be seen in relation to the 'costs'. The costs arise because the water surface behind the structure and the wet 'riparian' zone around the structure will almost certainly be evaporating at a higher rate than that from the land use prior to the installation of the structure. When such measures are used sparingly within a catchment there will be very little change to the overall water balance. But when used in excess (Figure 5.1) there can be a very significant effect, leading to reduced catchment flows and catchment closure.

When catchments are already approaching or have reached closure, as is the situation in many catchments in southern India, the promotion of further soil water conservation measures as a solution can only be regarded as 'soil water conservation madness'. In these circumstances there can be no overall benefit. The catchment closure problem will be made worse and the 'owner-ship' of water will effectively move 'uphill' as new structures appear in the landscape.

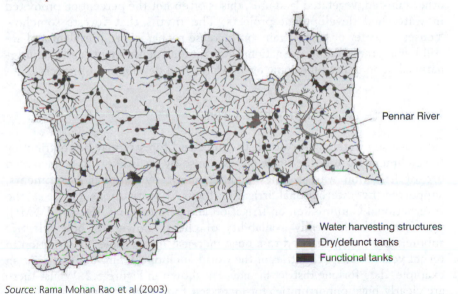

Source: Rama Mohan Rao et al (2003)

Figure 5.1 *High density of soil water conservation structures located in one of the catchments of the Andra Pradesh Rural Livelihoods Project*

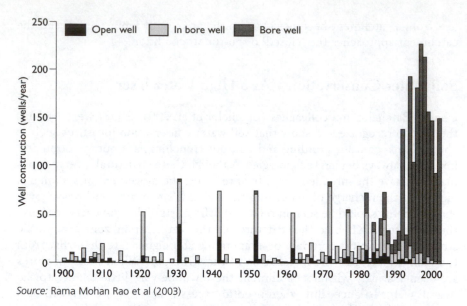

Source: Rama Mohan Rao et al (2003)

Figure 5.2 *The number of wells of different types constructed during the 20th Century in Kalyandurg District, Andra Pradesh, India, showing the large increase in borehole construction in the last decade of the century*

Forestry – As a High Water User

Although the scientific evidence (Chapter 2) shows that forests, and particularly plantation forests, generally evaporate considerably more water than other rain-fed, vegetated land uses, this is often not the perception promoted in watershed development projects. The myths that forests somehow 'conserve' water or 'attract rain' or 'increase recharge' are prevalent and are still being promoted by the national government departments and the international donors that fund some of the watershed development projects.

Irrigation – As a High Water User

Although soil water conservation structures and forestry may be contributing to catchment closure, the single biggest cause by far is likely to be increased use of irrigation waters. The encouragement by national governments, supported by international irrigation-focused institutions (such as the International Commission on Irrigation and Drainage (ICID) and IWMI), together with the ready availability of cheap 'down the hole' electric submersible pumps has led to a huge increase in borehole construction in recent years in many countries of the world, including China and India. As an example, data for one district in India are shown in Figure 5.2. Whilst there are clearly huge opportunities for increased food production from irrigated agriculture, its continued promotion by international institutions and national governments, without recognition or acceptance of the water resource

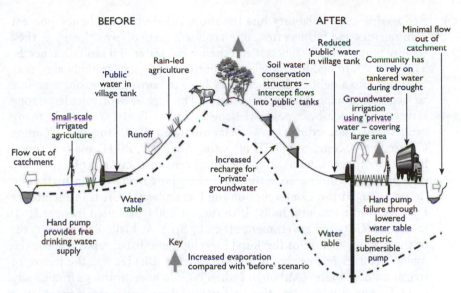

BEFORE

AFTER

'Public' water in village tank

Rain-led agriculture

Small-scale irrigated agriculture

Runoff

Flow out of catchment

Hand pump provides free drinking water supply

Water table

Soil water conservation structures – intercept flows into 'public' tanks

Increased recharge for 'private' groundwater

Reduced 'public' water in village tank

Minimal flow out of catchment

Community has to rely on tankered water during drought

Groundwater irrigation using 'private' water – covering large area

Hand pump failure through lowered water table

Water table

Electric submersible pump

Key

Increased evaporation compared with 'before' scenario

Source: Calder et al (2004)

Figure 5.3 *Impact of catchment interventions on water flows and availability of 'private' and 'public' water*

constraints, is both dangerous and irresponsible. As demonstrated below, the consequences can be severe.

Perverse Outcomes Resulting from Catchment Closure

As catchments approach closure a number of downsides, or perverse outcomes, become apparent. Charles Batchelor and his colleagues were instrumental in highlighting some of these problems through a series of well produced and well argued reports on the Karnataka and Andra Pradesh Rural Livelihood Projects (Batchelor et al, 2001, 2003). Similar concerns have also been expressed by Marcus Moench and colleagues from consideration of catchments in both India and Nepal. The course of events can be identified as follows:

1   Together with very little river flow out of the catchment there is a long-term trend towards the lowering of groundwater tables resulting in dry wells, boreholes and seasonal water shortages (Figure 5.3).
2   Where water tables are too deep to be accessed by handpumps, water tankers are now seen supplying and charging poor people for water that until recently they would have obtained for free (apart from maintenance costs) from their own boreholes.
3   The gap between the rich and poor widens. As the demand for water rises, shallow wells are rapidly being replaced by deep boreholes that require machinery and funds to drill. In many cases less vulnerable people have the resources to continue exploiting the diminishing water supplies, further contributing to inequitable distribution and use of resources.

4   Reduced water availability hits the most vulnerable and hence poorest communities and farmers first, often robbing them of even the water they require to maintain livelihoods and their basic water and sanitation needs. The poorer farmers, if they wish to continue accessing groundwater, may be thrust into a debt cycle where they have to borrow increasing amounts to extract reducing quantities of water. The high rate of suicides among farmers has become a political issue in India. There are clearly many causes but, according to C. Hanumantha Rao, former Planning Commission Member, (*Times of India*, August 1, 2004) many farmers have committed suicide after spending tens of thousand of rupees on digging wells, finding no water, and then borrowing to dig further in desperation. At the Conference on the Groundwater Crisis in Anantapur District, Andra Pradesh, India, 19th August 2004, attended by over 1500 farmers, NGOs and government officials, Sri Y. V. Malla Reddy, Director of the Ecology Centre of the Rural Development Trust, reported that the major factor in 75 per cent of the 400 farmer suicides was the failure of irrigation borewells. (Although Indian NGOs have in the past cynically used farmer suicide statistics to further their particular causes, it is believed that there is a genuine basis for the Anatapur claims.)

5   The promotion of irrigation that involves mining groundwater resources and substantial lowering of water tables is unsustainable in the long term and leads to 'boom' and 'bust' cycles in agricultural production.

The excessive promotion of forestry, irrigation and soil water conservation measures within watershed projects may result in other perverse and inequitable outcomes which disadvantage the poor and benefit the rich. In some situations the ownership of water may be effectively transferred from communal to private owners. Forestry, soil water conservation measures, check dams and other physical structures all tend to reduce surface flows of water which might otherwise have flowed into village reservoirs (tanks) for communal use. On the other hand, private landowners generally benefit from the structures and interventions on their land which increase recharge and the availability of the 'private' groundwater they can access. They also benefit from the increased growth rates of forests which have greater access to soil water.

Inter-sectoral Conflicts – Power and Climate Change

Watershed projects promoting groundwater-fed irrigation may also be contributing to inter-sectoral, water and energy resource conflicts: in some southern Indian States as much as one-half of all the electricity generated is being used for pumping groundwater for irrigation purposes – from ever greater depths as groundwater tables recede. The unsustainable nature of the problem is well recognized even though the solutions may not be so well recognized. Tushaar Shah, Principal Scientist at the Institute for Water Management Institute (IWMI) has stated (Shah, 2005) that in India, groundwater irrigation is central to the livelihoods of farmers and to reverse trends would require cutting the present rate of groundwater use by 70 per cent or more in many regions, 'even if possible, doing this would throw out of gear millions of rural livelihoods and cause massive social unrest'.

But is this not a somewhat short-sighted and dangerous attitude? If the problem is not tackled now the consequences will surely be worse in the future. Whilst it continues, we are also seeing in countries which have major problems with depleting groundwater tables (India and China in particular) massive wastage of electrical power as water tables are 'chased down'.

New methodologies involving 'allocation equity' and 'green water' policy instruments, discussed in Chapter 7, may be of value in addressing the demand management issues that clearly need to be tackled now, before situations worsen. Controlling this massive waste of electric power could also be seen as a major achievement in terms of reducing greenhouse gas emissions from the increased numbers of power stations required to pump groundwater (power stations which have often been provided under donor aid – another example of perversity). With estimates of around 200km^3 of water being pumped each year for groundwater-based irrigation in India, and presumably similar, if not greater, quantities being pumped in China (derived from FAO Aquastat, 2004), there is clearly scope for benefits to many sectors if means can be found to implement a management system which allows sustainable use and prevents excessive lowering of water tables.

A Donor–Government-Sanctioned Discourse?

Even though some of the problems associated with watershed development projects have been recognized, many donor- and government-funded programmes and government policies appear to be exacerbating the situation:

- The widespread promotion of forestry programmes by donor organizations and forestry interests as a means to increase groundwater recharge is, in the vast majority of circumstances, not only deeply flawed in that forestry is more likely to reduce recharge rather than increase it, but it is also dangerous in that it obfuscates the real and pressing issue of regulating and controlling the exploitation of depleting groundwater aquifers for irrigation waters.
- Watershed development projects in India and elsewhere have often focused on (expensive) supply side measures directed at increasing storage, infiltration and recharge whilst doing little to manage demand.
- International irrigation institutions and national government policies have actively encouraged the creation of boreholes for groundwater irrigation.

Could donors and government departments be involved in their own sanctioned discourse with regard to watershed development projects? Watershed activities such as forestry and soil water conservation structures are generally promoted as benign technologies that are at the very least

Box 5.1 Water-related myths

Water harvesting is a totally benign technology

Although water harvesting technologies can produce huge benefits, intensive drainage line treatment, in particular, can significantly reduce water resource availability to 'downstream' communities. In some cases, this negative trade-off does not matter; in others, severe hardship can result.

Planting trees increases local rainfall and runoff

The reality is that forests exert a small, almost insignificant influence on local rainfall and, notwithstanding a small number of exceptions, catchment experiments generally indicate reduced runoff from forested areas compared to those under shorter vegetation.

Runoff in semi-arid areas is 30–40% of annual rainfall

Although localized runoff and runoff from individual storms can be high, annual runoff at the micro-watershed scale (or greater) in semi-arid areas tends to be much lower than 30–40%.

Rainfall has decreased in recent years.

With few exceptions, studies of long-term rainfall records that have used data from a single set of rain gauges have not shown a significant decrease (or increase) in mean annual rainfall.

Aquifers are underground lakes

The reality is that check dams and other water-harvesting structures usually have only localized impacts on groundwater levels and aquifers rarely behave like underground lakes. Or put another way, localized recharge in one place rarely leads to an immediate rise in groundwater levels many kilometres away.

Water use of crops depends mainly on crop type

A common misconception is that the daily water use of agricultural* crops is directly related to the crop type and that evaporation rates are many times higher from some crops than others. The reality is that, assuming that a crop is well supplied with water and has a full canopy (the crop completely shades the ground), the daily rate of evaporation is driven primarily by the meteorological conditions (e.g. radiation, wind speed and dryness of the air).

Aquifers, once depleted, stay depleted

A pessimistic view of aquifer depletion is that this is an irreversible process. The reality is that in most cases aquifers can be re-established or replenished as long as the balance between recharge and extraction is swung towards recharge. This can occur as a result of increased recharge, decreased extraction or both.

Note: * The qualifier 'agricultural' has been added here by the author as there can be large differences in water use between short crops which are usually agricultural and tall crops such as forests – see Chapter 2.
Source: Rama Mohan Rao et al (2003)

'poverty neutral'. If a discourse develops, often based on water-related myths (see Box 5.1; Batchelor et al, 2001, 2003; Calder, 1999, 2000; Calder and Gosain, 2003; Saberwal, 1997), it may lead to a self-reinforcing tendency between government and donor agencies to disregard information and arguments that contradict the received wisdom as to the best solutions to water-related problems for the poor. There is evidence to indicate that a 'sanctioned discourse' is pursued even when circumstances radically change, as happens when a region moves from water surplus into water deficit. In water deficit conditions there is overwhelming evidence to show that many present donor and government water-related policies and practices are doing little to benefit the poor.

The Way Forward

While confusion reigns about the real benefits of watershed development interventions, and there are suspicions that many vested interests would like to preserve present watershed development policies, some very real questions are posed concerning how outcomes can be improved. Clearly there are both technical and governance aspects that need to be addressed.

In relation to the technical issues it is clear that many watershed development programmes have reaped benefits through the promotion of soil water conservation measures, forestry and groundwater-based irrigation. The question is: under what circumstances might these interventions result in beneficial or untoward outcomes?

It is suggested that to resolve this question consideration should be given to two issues:

1   The sustainability of land uses within the watershed with respect to evaporative use. It is important to determine if the long-term precipitation (P) still exceeds the total long-term evaporation (E) from the present land uses, comprising for example dryland agriculture, rangelands, forestry and irrigated areas (i.e. to determine if $P > E$).

2   Whether surface flows (Q_s) exceed an agreed minimum flow (Q_m). Minimum flow criteria could be defined variously. Conventionally, criteria would be defined in terms of an agreed seasonal or annual minimum volume flow. Alternatively, for reservoired catchments, criteria could be defined in terms of return periods of surface flow exiting the catchment; a return period of one year, for example, or a more severe criterion of, say, five years. The Q_s/Q_m criteria could then be regarded as positive if the return period for flows was less than one year or five years. This definition would then approximate conditions of whether the final reservoir (or 'tank' using Indian terminology) of the catchment has spilt within the last year or within the last five years.

The four combinations resulting from this analysis indicate preferred options for the management of evaporation from land uses and for the management of surface flows. Using the Falkenmark green and blue water terminology (see chapter 7) these could be referred to as the green water and blue water management options:

1 **P > E, Qs > 0**
   Green Water Management: Opportunities for enlarged areas of land uses with increased evaporation, for example irrigated areas and forestry.
   Blue Water Management: Benefits may be gained from further SWC measures and water retention structures. Increase density of structures, rehabilitate structures.
2 **P < E, Qs > 0**
   Green Water Management: Reduce areas of land uses with increased evaporation, for example reduce irrigation and forestry. Increase areas of 'water providing' land uses such as dryland agriculture.
   Blue Water Management: Only local benefits (at the expense of downstream users) will be gained from further soil and water conservation (SWC) measures and water retention structures. Consider increasing efficiency of existing structures through measures such as deepening (to reduce evaporative losses through reducing the surface to volume ratio).
3 **P < E, Qs = 0**
   Green Water Management: Reduce areas of land uses with increased evaporation , for example reduce irrigation and forestry. Increase areas of 'water providing' land uses such as dryland agriculture.
   Blue Water Management: No overall benefits from further SWC measures and water retention structures. Consider reducing density of structures and/or increasing efficiency of existing structures through measures such as deepening.
4 **P > E, Qs = 0**
   Green Water Management: Opportunities for enlarged areas of land uses with increased evaporation, for example irrigated areas and forestry.
   Blue Water Management: No overall benefits from further SWC measures and water retention structures. Consider reducing density of structures and/or increasing efficiency of existing structures through measures such as deepening.

Quadrant 1 exhibits benefits from further soil water conservation (SWC) measures; quadrants 3 and 4 exhibit no benefits; quadrant 2 shows local benefits but at the expense of downstream users.

This approach, shown in the 'quadrant' diagram, Figure 5.4, may help to direct development funds to those situations where further structural measures are likely to have an overall benefit (quadrant 1) and to scale back investments in catchments which are approaching conditions of catchment closure (quadrants 3 and 4). The approach also makes clear the interconnecting management options regarding green and blue water mangement and shows that in quadrants 2 and 3 development efforts would be much better directed at green water management, by reducing catchment evaporation losses, than by managing blue water through further water retention

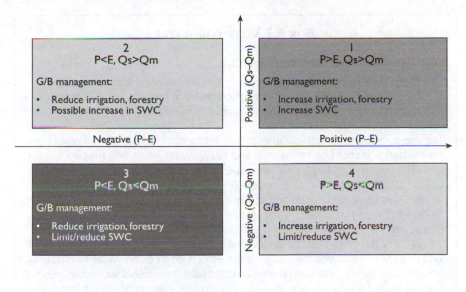

Note: E and P represent average annual evaporation and precipitation respectively. Qs and Qm represent actual and agreed minimum flows respectively. Minimum flow criteria could be defined variously – for example, a proportion of the volume flow in a median rainfall year; reservoir spill return periods of, say, one or five years.

Quadrant 1 exhibits benefits from further soil water conservation (SWC) measures; quadrants 3 and 4 exhibit no benefits; quadrant 2 shows local benefits but at the expense of downstream users.

Figure 5.4 *Catchment conditions that can be used to identify green and blue water management options and whether benefits would be derived from further soil water conservation measures and water retention structures*

measures. There are many examples in India where water tables have been lowered to 1000 ft, where no water has spilled from the village tank in the last five years, yet investments in further soil water conservation measures are still taking place.

The 'quadrant' approach may help to identify the technical issues which relate to watershed investments but the question of governance in land and water management remains. Professor Ashvin Gosain, of the Indian Institute of Technology in Delhi, one of the leaders in developing hydrological models linked to GIS technologies and the programme leader entrusted with analysing the impact of climate change on India's water resources (Gosain and Tripathi, 2003; Gosain and Rao, 2004; Gosain et al, 2003) has indicated that what is required, perhaps even more than improved technical knowledge, is good governance (Box 5.2, see also Chapter 7). Gosain argues that 'good governance, together with better communications between scientists and policymakers, should help to keep the water barons at bay and help the poor to access water at affordable prices'. Marcus Moench and colleagues (Moench et al, 2003) have also highlighted the importance of good governance in meeting South East Asia's water problem (Chapter 7).

BOX 5.2 VOTE FOR WATER

Low base-flows and livelihoods in India

> *Every state has its own water laws, but what we need is coherence, so that we can make a real difference on a much larger scale.* (Professor Ashvin Gosain, Indian Institute of Technology, Delhi)

The old people in Jhaniari village in India's Himachal Pradesh still remember the time when you could go to the well and draw water when you needed it – for free. The young ones today only know the water tanker that comes once a week to sell water for more than a rupee per 20-litre bucket! In the state of Tamil Nadu, to raise this issue to the attention of officials at the highest levels, farmers even fielded a 'Water Candidate' in the recent election campaign. The wells are dry, and so are the hill slopes. Better go and plant trees?

No, say the researchers from Newcastle University and the Indian Institute of Technology in Delhi who are studying the effects of trees on water in Himachal Pradesh and Madhya Pradesh. The researchers have found that too many trees on the hill slopes – and elsewhere in the catchment – actually reduce the water output of the wells. And too many deep wells have been drilled already. What is needed more than anything else is good governance of the area, keeping the water barons at bay and allowing the poor access to water at affordable prices.

This project is contributing to the national debate on trees and water. It is supplying geo-referenced information and a simple modelling tool that show how water tables have changed over past years in relation to deforestation and afforestation measures, groundwater mining for dry-season irrigation and other watershed interventions.

A recent workshop, organized by the project team in collaboration with the Overseas Development Institute's RAPID (Research and Policy Development) project, demonstrated the need for better communication between policymakers and researchers. The workshop was seen as the start of a powerful relationship that can change policy and make things happen, based on solid research evidence.

Source: DFID (2004)

CONTROLLING THE FLOOD – FORESTERS, ENVIRONMENTALISTS AND ENGINEERS

In many countries of the world there is a growing disparity between the public perception and the scientific evidence relating to the causes of floods, their impacts and the benefits of mitigation measures.

It is suggested that this disparity has arisen through the extensive promotion of certain land uses and engineering interventions by vested interest groups. What we see is a conflict between different narratives and 'sanctioned discourses', supported by environmentalists, foresters and engineers. In the absence of any effective dissemination of the scientific evidence that would allow a contrary view to be taken, these discourses have gained considerable momentum in many countries.

This disparity may have resulted not only in the wastage of development funds (possibly to the extent of tens of billions of dollars per year) on unachievable targets, but also in unwarranted blame being placed on upland communities whose practices have generally had only marginal impacts on downstream flooding.

It is recognized that the interaction of floods and society is a highly complex subject: floods may have both natural and anthropogenic causes; floods have beneficial as well as detrimental effects; the effects of land use change and engineering interventions may be site specific to the extent that not only the magnitude but also the direction of the effect may vary between sites and vary also with the size of the flood. However, what is recognized with some certainty is that simplistic and populist land management solutions, such as oft-advocated solutions involving commercial afforestation programmes, cannot ever represent a general solution and will, in most situations, have at best marginal benefit and at worst negative impacts (see Chapter 2). Similarly, structural engineering interventions, although in the short term providing protection to flood-affected communities in one area, may have the effect of transferring the problem downstream and may also introduce other unforeseen adverse environmental and economic impacts (see, for example, Kissimmee structural interventions, Chapter 6).

An attempt has been made to summarize the factual basis for understanding forest and flood interactions in Chapter 2. Clearly there exists a gulf between this knowledge and the public perception. On the one hand we have science, which admits complexity, incomplete knowledge and uncertainty qualified by caveats and which sadly makes a very unexciting story – a story that the media and popular press are unlikely to consider even on the slowest of news days – and on the other hand we have simplistic, yet highly dramatic, public perception.

Why have we arrived at this disparity of perceptions? It would be facile to blame the situation on the media, who often reflect public perception, rather than drive it. How has this public perception developed? What do we need to do to reconcile the two differing views on this issue given that popular wisdom appears to be largely inconsistent with scientific knowledge? Drawing heavily from and building on the approach of Calder and Aylward (2005), an attempt is made below to trace the social factors and the different narratives and discourses which characterize the public perception of the causes and impacts of floods. The research into the power struggles between the different vested interest groups in America benefited very greatly from the insights provided by Jim Smyle of the World Bank and Russ La Fayette of the US Department of Agriculture (USDA) Forest Service.

Floods and People

Floods may be caused by natural events, by human activities, or combinations of both. Regardless of their cause, floods have a profound effect on people and the economy. Year by year floods leave over 3 million people homeless

and affect the personal and economic fortunes of another 60 million people
(WCD, 2000). A single flood in a small, centrally-located province in
Vietnam, Thua Thien Hue, in 1999 led to the deaths of 400 people and
damage to property worth $120 million, or one-half of the annual provincial
GDP. Floods pose a particular threat in Asia, where flood-related economic
losses exceeded those in North America and Europe between 1987 and 1996
(Berz, 2000).

How different actors respond to floods – be they individuals or organizations – is determined by perceptions of the impacts of floods, whether direct
or indirect, for good or bad. These perceptions may be influenced by many
factors, including first-hand experiences, received and conventional wisdom,
scientific observations, the 'sanctioned discourse', and the expected gains and
losses from staking out a position or taking a particular course of action.

To understand the history of responses to floods it is important to understand that there are many players and much at stake. Within a catchment, the
lowland farmers and fishermen, as, for example, in Bangladesh, will often
welcome the annual flood to bring down sediments rich in nutrients, and
water of sufficient volume, to support their livelihoods. Too much may cause
them problems, but too little will be a disaster. Elsewhere, where communities have encroached onto the floodplain and are not reliant on floodplain
waters for their livelihoods, they will view the flood with distrust and as a
danger, often as a plague to be blamed on any plausible external cause. Upland
communities, who are generally affected less (for good or bad) by floods, are
usually the least vociferous players in the game.

But these are not the only players or the most powerful. Many of the
technical specialties have tended to see solutions in terms of their own
focused discipline. Many foresters were early and effective players and have
long promoted forests as being a key remedy for floods. By so doing they have
ensured political support and funding for afforestation and reforestation
programmes. Similarly, engineers traditionally have seen floods as an opportunity to put in place expensive structures to either store and detain floods
(dams) or 'carry the water away' (channels). (More recently, under pressure
from environmentalists as well as a growing realization of the negative impacts
of structural measures, engineers have secured more work by re-engineering
or dismembering these structures in order to restore rivers, wetlands or other
waterways to their 'natural' state).

Scientists are not disinterested players either. Hydrologists, agronomists,
soil scientists, economists and social scientists all have an interest in securing
funding related to floods and have a vested interest in providing knowledge.
When floods make a front page story, inevitably a disaster story, the media
appear repeating the popular wisdom regarding cause and effect. These
arguments, even if outdated and mistaken, are uncritically repeated by those
NGOs and government departments who benefit from the message, under-
scoring the failure of scientists to convey their findings in a coherent and
understandable fashion to the general public.

Meanwhile, politicians will interpret the (mixed) signals as best they can
with an ear to where the votes and expenditures lie. Development organiza-

tions may try to take account of these disparate views but will generally opt for the solution that is most easily defended and causes the least disruption in budgetary allocations. Without greater efforts by scientists to explain their position, this is likely to remain the one supported by conventional (received) wisdom.

Forests and Floods – Contrasting Perceptions, Knowledge and Practice

The following is an excerpt from a letter to the *Oregonian* newspaper regarding Hurricane Mitch in 1998:

> *Contrary to the television images, the devastation wrought by [Hurricane] Mitch was no mere act of God but a far more human tragedy. Misguided government policies and poor farming practices – the two are interrelated – had already pushed the region to the brink of ecological collapse. The torrential rains only gave it a final push ...*

The public perception, promoted by the popular press, the writings of some environmentalists and conservation agencies, projects an unwavering, 'stirring' and 'evangelical' view of the relationship between forests, deforestation and floods.

The Environmentalist's Narrative

Lester R. Brown of the highly influential Worldwatch Institute, writing about the 1998 floods in China states:

> *Over the last few weeks, the world has been following the floods in China's Yangtze basin, the worst in 44 years. ...*
>
> *The Chinese government is treating this disaster as an act of nature, and indeed it is. Floods during the monsoon season from June through September in southern China are a regular occurrence. But there is also a human hand in this year's floods in the form of deforestation and intensive land development. The Yangtze basin is home to 400 million people, making it one of the most densely populated river basins on earth....*
>
> *With such a density of population, the human pressure on the land is everywhere. To begin with, the Yangtze river basin, which originates on the Tibetan Plateau, has lost 85 percent of its original forest cover. The forests that once absorbed and held huge quantities of monsoon rainfall, which could then percolate slowly into the ground, are now largely gone* (Brown, 1998).

A very similar message is contained in the writings of the well-known environmentalist Norman Myers about the consequences of deforestation in the Himalayas:

> *The Himalayan forests normally exert a sponge effect, soaking up abundant rainfall and storing it before releasing it in regular amounts over an extended period. When the forest is cleared, rivers turn muddy and swollen during the wet season, before shrinking during drier periods... Flood disasters are becoming more frequent and more severe* (Myers 1986).

These views and narratives seem so plausible, perhaps because we have heard them so many times, that we might think that they are incontrovertible truths. But, when we consider the scientific evidence (Chapter 2), we might arrive at a different conclusion.

The Hydrologist's Response

Thomas Hofer of the University of Berne's Geography Institute, referring to the 'environmentalist's concern' states:

> *The hypothesis regarding the impact of human activities in the Himalayas on the ecological processes in the lowlands can be explained by the following, superficially convincing sequence; population growth in the mountains, increasing demand for fuelwood, fodder and timber, uncontrolled forest removal in more and more marginal areas, intensified erosion and higher peak flows in the rivers, severe flooding and siltation on the densely populated and cultivated plains of the Ganga and Brahamaputra. The apparently convincing conclusions have been subscribed to carelessly by some scientists and adopted by many politicians and journalists in order to identify the so-called culprits* (Hofer, 1998a).

Hofer goes on to give examples of the 'stirring statements' laden with 'sensation and conflict potential' which are the usual lifeblood of many environmental journalists and many conservation organizations:

> *It is clear that this certainty of cause and effect is not reflected in the hydrologist's response nor are statements such as 'Flood disasters are becoming more frequent and more severe in the Himalayas' in harmony with the scientific analysis of the hydrological record carried out by the Berne Institute. In the light of the scientific studies such as Hofer's where he states that in the Ganga-Brahmaputra-Megha lowlands neither the frequency nor the magnitude of flooding has increased over the last few decades, or those of Marston and colleagues who claimed that 'results demon-*

strate that... variation in bank-full discharge [ie flood flows] can
be explained as a function of drainage area alone; forest cover did
not add explanatory power should we still accept these popular
perceptions uncritically? (Hofer, 1998a; Marston et al, 1996)

Together with the environmentalist's narrative we can see other narratives
operating which have influenced policies on how we deal with floods.

The Forester's Narrative

A particularly illuminating study and interpretation of the narrative relating
to linkages between deforestation and intensified flooding is provided by
Vasant K. Saberwal (Saberwal, 1997) of the Institute for Social and Economic
Change, Bangalore, India. Saberwal proposes a number of theses. He argues
that the institutional context in which the discourse has taken place, has, in a
sense, shaped or directed the discourse. Over time, he claims, 'one observes a
two-way process, whereby bureaucracies may use science to inform a particular rhetoric; at the same time, bureaucratic rhetoric comes to influence the
scientific discourse itself and, thereby, the very nature of science.'

Saberwal shows that the narrative influenced Indian foresters as early as
the 19th century and argues that the discourse (narrative) of today has
emerged from a diversified set of views held by European, American and
Indian foresters and environmentalists in the 1920s, evolving into the
'uniform and alarmist rhetoric that characterizes forester and environmental
positions today'. Saberwal claims that since the 1930s the ideas within Indian
and American forestry have diverged, being more quantitative in the former
and more qualitative and rhetorical in the latter, due, he believes, to differences in the nature of opposition to forester viewpoints. A synopsis of the
understanding of floods by foresters in the early 20th century comes from
Gifford Pinchot, a leading conservationist of the time and the force behind
the creation of the US Forest Service (USFS). From the observation that
infiltration rates vary from bare ground to forest, inference is made to the
(non-quantitative) conclusion that forests protect against floods. How much
protection forests offer is not made explicit, nor does Pinchot take important
downstream variables such as hydraulic attenuation into account.

Rain which falls over a bare slope acts differently. It is not
caught by the crowns nor held by the floor, nor is its flow into the
streams hindered by the timber and the fallen waste from the
trees. It does not sink into the ground more than half as readily
as in the forest, as experiments have shown. The result is that a
great deal of water reaches the streams in a short time, which is
the reason why floods occur. It is therefore true that forests tend
to prevent floods. But this good influence is important only when
the forest covers a large part of the drainage basin of the stream.
Even then the forest may not prevent floods altogether. The forest
floor, which has more to do with the fallen rain water than any

other part of the forest, can affect its flow only so long as it has not taken up all the water it can hold. That which falls after the forest floor is saturated runs into the streams almost as fast as it would over bare ground.

... in mountain countries, where floods are most common and do most harm, the forests on the higher slopes are closely connected with the prosperity of the people in the valleys below.

...Water in motion was nature's most powerful tool in shaping the present surface of the earth. In places where the slopes are steep, the structure of the ground loose, and the rainfall abundant, water may work very rapidly in cutting away the heights and filling the valleys. The destruction of the forest in such a region exposes the surface to the direct action of falling rain and is certain to be followed by the formation of torrents. (Pinchot, 1905).

It is important to note that the discussion of the effect of forest cover removal and the resultant increase in flood damage resulted from decades of poor land stewardship in the USA, from its early settlement period until the late 1800s. Uncontrolled logging, wildfires, grazing and farming denuded millions of acres, with resulting increases in soil loss, sedimentation and flooding. The science of watershed management was in its infancy and there were many opinions concerning both the cause and solution to flooding and related impacts. It seemed obvious to many that the loss of forest cover and increased flood damage were closely linked and the return of forest cover was important to the amelioration of flooding.

In the USA the vigorous debate over the environmental consequences of deforestation was related to inter-agency competition over appropriate methods of flood control. Engineers involved in flood control programmes criticized the non-quantitative basis of claims by the USFS regarding the importance of forests as a tool in flood control and developed their own 'sanctioned discourse'. Efforts by the USFS to counter these charges through empirical research led to the Wagon Wheel Gap experimental catchment research programme that began in 1910 and ran through until the late 1920s. The work at Wagon Wheel Gap did not provide all the answers to the forests/flood question but opened the door to additional studies in forests around the nation. This led to the establishment of numerous long-term forest watershed research facilities, including the Coweeta Hydrologic Laboratory (North Carolina), Hubbard Brook (New Hampshire), Parsons (West Virginia), H. J. Andrews (Oregon), Beaver Creek (Arizona) and others. These experimental studies, as opposed to observational studies, in the most part used rigorous experimental design with the inclusion of both control catchments and those subject to treatment (for example, felling or planting) and provided the basis for a quantitative understanding of the impacts of forests on the water regime.

Unfortunately the quantitative results of the Wagon Wheel Gap programme did not fully support the sanctioned discourse being developed by the USFS, that forests acted as a sponge, and thus would not assist USFS in its on-going budgetary battles with the Army Corps. Undeterred, the USFS published the experiment results with a front- and back-end that supported forests role as a 'sponge' that reduced flood flows (Bates and Henry 1928). While this is just one such case, it provides an example of how a perception can be traced back to a substantive source. The difficulty is that the source may not warrant the confidence with which it is entrusted and, in any event, should yield to the results of further studies. As detailed in the next section, the Army Corps, as well as the Department of Interior's Bureau of Reclamation, went on to become the dominant federal agencies in flood control efforts, particularly related to channels and reservoir systems. The Forest Service grew over time to include over 191 million acres of National Forests and Grasslands in 45 states and territories, with a mission of proper land management of uplands as well as related streams, lakes and wetlands. The lingering legacy, however, is that the public, and even many foresters, still subscribe to the simplistic intuitive notion of the forest as sponge and flood protector.

In contrast, in India the opposition to the forester's view came from non-technical officials of the revenue department. Saberwal indicates that the narrative developed as 'Indian foresters were drawing on the writings of US foresters, and a wider international scientific context, doing so in a highly selective fashion to bolster their case for the introduction of more stringent conservation measures'. The same lingering legacy remains in India as in the USA, a legacy which has underpinned the promotion of forestry as an effective means of reducing flood risk (and as a means of improving water resources) in a multitude of watershed development programmes, funded by both national and international agencies, throughout India.

Forsyth (1998, 2002) argues very cogently that resolution of the narratives and the 'so-called problems, such as Himalayan environmental degradation' will require the integration of social and natural science. He argues that we will need to find ways to allow critical debate about biophysical processes at the same time as acknowledging social constructions of the environment if we are to avoid the uncritical acceptance and propagation of the environmental 'myths'.

The Engineering Flood Control Narrative

In the early to mid-1900s engineers in America prevailed in the power struggle over what were the best mechanisms to control floodwaters. With flood control as their explicit objective, engineers around the world have spent over 50 years creating structural approaches such as dams and dikes (levees) to prevent floodwaters inundating the flood plain together with, in many situations, the straightening and deepening of the natural channel. In the USA alone the federal government spent $38 billion on flood control between 1960 and 1985, largely through its Army Corps of Engineers.

According to the International Commission on Large Dams, some 13 per cent of large dams, or over 3000 worldwide, have a flood control function. As

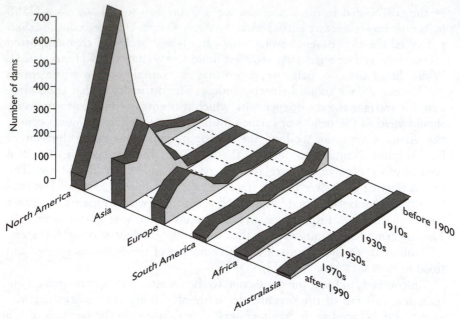

Source: International Commission on Large Dams, WCD (2000)

Figure 5.5 *Number of flood control dams built in each decade and by each region, 1900 to 2000*

can be seen from Figure 5.5, North America and Asia have been the biggest proponents of large dams for flood control. According to the World Commission on Dams, China has more large dams with a flood control function than any other country and Japan is number three on the list.

These accomplishments both spring from a powerful engineering 'narrative', together with its own sanctioned discourse, and feed into its continuing development. The engineering culture of the western world, developed and moulded by the industrial revolution, was one of pioneering advance, of conquering previously insurmountable barriers to progress, of ever-greater feats of engineering scale and excellence. Career development for engineers has traditionally been seen through association with large engineering projects – the larger the better.

That society has been transformed, and generally for the better, by engineering efforts, is undeniable. No more so than from the efforts of our water engineers who, in Victorian times, laid the basis for the improved health of nations through recognition of the need for, and through making available, adequate and wholesome supplies of water to meet the needs of households as well as many businesses. Concerns arise when the engineering narrative and the engineer's sanctioned discourse allows for no other options. Japan is perhaps an extreme example of what can happen with the proliferation of public works spending, at huge costs to the economy but with little obvious social or environmental benefit, when the engineer's sanctioned discourse becomes engrained in the political system.

In the 1900s in the USA, the water engineer turned his attention to 'taming the river' in order to reduce the damage to societies who had chosen to live and work in flood plain areas. As discussed above, it is here that the different narratives and sanctioned discourses intersect. For foresters and environmentalists the outcome was less than ideal. For engineers the outcome was the unleashing of the full power of man's ability to modify his environment to suit his own ends. However, the narrative is still being written, and even for engineers there is a downside.

The culmination of this engineering tradition with respect to flood control is perhaps best exemplified by the efforts of the US Army Corps of Engineers who, in 1954, started the engineering works which changed the natural 166-km winding path of the Kissimmee River, in Florida, into a 90km long, 9m deep, 100m wide canal. But this amazing feat of engineering, completed in 1960, illustrates many of the difficulties often associated with engineering solutions to flood control. The project also illustrates the turning point in the American perception of the benefits of engineering interventions.

The project hugely altered the hydrology and ecology of the river basin and it was widely seen as an environmental disaster (with efforts to restore the river being contemplated) even before the project finished. The engineering works caused between 12,000 and 14,000ha of wetlands to drain and dry up, with the consequent loss of the wetland flora and fauna. The changes in the flow regime also created conditions suitable for invasive plant and animal species, many of which were regarded as pests.

Traditionally, flood defences were provided as individual local schemes with little consideration as to their cumulative impact across the wider river catchment, their impact on the aquatic and coastal environment or, indeed, their economic impact. These engineering interventions have now been recognized as having other negative impacts, unforeseen at the time of construction, which are not necessarily those applying solely to the environment. There is a danger that engineering structures designed to transport the water quickly away from one flood area will, through removing the natural storage function of the floodplain, exacerbate flooding downstream. In developing regions, account has now been made of the reliance of flood plain dweller livelihoods on flood recession agriculture and in-stream fisheries. Flood defence works have often effectively ended natural floods and flood cycles, putting these communities at risk.

It now seems self-evident that individual flood alleviation schemes cannot be considered in isolation and that what happens in one part of the catchment will have effects on other areas some distance away. Returning to the Kissimmee example, environmental concerns were raised at the time of authorization, but governmental water resource management processes were, at that time, relatively single-minded. The aim was simple: flood damage reduction in the most cost-efficient fashion. With increasing environmental awareness, and as the negative environmental impact of the project became increasingly apparent, the state and federal government introduced in 1976 initiatives and research programmes aimed at gaining the knowledge required to restore the integrity of the river and retrieve some of the lost environmental benefits. In 1992 Congress approved the Corps of Engineers recommendation to undertake a river restoration programme, which was aimed, essentially, at getting the Corps to fill in the canal they had originally dug and this, perhaps the world's first major watershed restoration project designed to reverse the impacts of earlier engineering works, is now underway.

Reconciling the Narratives and Power Struggles – Integrated Flood Management and Watershed Management

We are left then with two broad narratives. On the one hand, we have the engineering flood control narrative and sanctioned discourse, which is still evolving and making progress; in some advanced industrial democracies such as Japan, not only is the movement towards engineering solutions still very strong but the provision of aid funds to other countries, often channelled through the Asian Development Bank, is promoting engineering interventions throughout the whole South East Asian region. On the other hand, we have the forest and floods narrative where, in many countries and in many institutions, the public perception and environmental concerns remain unchanged and apparently out of touch with the last 50 years' worth of scientific research. How these narratives currently intersect and how this intersection may provide for future progress on all fronts can best be seen by examining the two practical and policy manifestations of these narratives: integrated flood management and watershed management.

Towards Integrated Flood Management

Within river systems, flooding is the natural way for the system to discharge the water arising from the occasional large rainfall event. There is no problem at all until people decide to use some of the natural flood plain for their own use, and choose to protect against inundation. We then face the dilemma of protecting against a natural hazard for the benefit of mankind that has chosen to live and work in flood plain areas. (Institute of Civil Engineers, 2001)

Increasingly, attitudes to managing flood risk are moving away from structural, engineering solutions to those which are consistent with working with natural processes and promoting biodiversity and sustainable rural development. According to the WCD (2000) the impetus for this shift arises from a number of major destructive flood events in the last few decades, which subsequently led to significant changes in flood policy around the world including:

- the coastal flooding of 1953 that led to the Delta works in the Netherlands;
- the 1988–1989 floods in Bangladesh that led to the Flood Action Plan and the National Water Management Plan; and

- the Upper Mississippi floods of 1993, the Rhone floods in 1993, the 1997 floods in the Rhine and the 1998 flood in China that drew attention to the role of non-structural catchment measures.

The switch from flood control to integrated flood management recognizes the fallibility of engineers and engineering at the same time that it recognizes the difficulty of controlling human behaviour. In an ideal world, engineers would either build 100 per cent effective flood control structures or no person or economic activity would be allowed to locate in a flood hazard zone. The reality, of course, is that neither is possible. Promotion of the notion that floods can be, or are being, controlled has been a cause of strife for people and businesses which have consequently moved into these 'protected' areas. The costs of flood control rise rapidly if structural responses are to adequately cope with low annual probability, 50–1 or 100–1 chance floods (i.e. those with 50 and 100 year return periods) or even more remote events, so that the flood control that is provided often fails to provide protection against the 'big one'. The results, of course, are major natural disasters, costing business, taxpayers and insurers massive amounts of money – which over time is leading to a rethink with regard to flood control being a realistic objective.

The new approach recognizes intervention strategies in flood management and has led to a gradual shift from a focus on structural responses to flood control to introducing or expanding the role of non-structural responses as part of integrated strategies for floodplain management. The WCD provided a straightforward summary of the components of an integrated approach to flood management (see Table 5.1), which grouped responses as acting to reduce the scale of floods, isolate the threat of floods or increase people's capacity to cope with floods.

This type of approach is also evident in the Mekong River Commission's (MRC) promotion of 'Integrated Floodplain Management', which illustrates the 'new engineering approach' to flood management. The MRC views Integrated Floodplain Management as an integrated and coordinated mix of four types of management measures that reflect the flooding, flood risk and flood hazard characteristics of the particular floodplain; the specific social and economic needs of the flood-prone communities; and environmental and

Table 5.1 *An integrated approach to flood management*

Reducing the scale of floods	Isolating the threat of floods	Increasing people's capacity to cope
Better catchment management	Flood embankments	Emergency planning
Controlling runoff	Flood proofing	Forecasting
Detention basins	Limiting floodplain development	Warnings
Dams		Evacuation
Protecting wetlands		Compensation Insurance

Source: Calder and Aylward (2005)

resource management policies for the floodplain. The four management measures are as follows:

1 **Land-use Planning Measures** These are aimed at 'keeping people away from the floodwaters'. Land-use measures on the floodplain aim to ensure that the vulnerability of a particular land-use activity is consistent with the flood hazard on that area of land, i.e. the objective is to keep people and vulnerable activities out of the most hazardous areas of the floodplain.
2 **Structural Measures** These are aimed at 'keeping floodwaters away from the people'. Typical structural measures include flood mitigation dams, embankments and flood detention basins. Development and Building Controls can be seen as a particular kind of structural measure for urban and settlement areas, aimed at reducing flood damage to buildings. Typical building controls include minimum floor levels to eliminate nuisance flooding, and the use of building materials and building designs that enable rapid and effective cleanup after a flood.
3 **Flood Preparedness Measures** These recognize that – no matter how effective the above types of management measures are – an overwhelming flood will always occur. They aim at 'getting people ready for floods before they come'. In a number of cases, Flood Preparedness and Emergency Measures may be the only type of management that is feasible or economically justified. Flood preparedness measures embody flood forecasting, flood warning and raising the general flood awareness of the potentially affected population groups. The MRC Flood Forecasting System is now underway and three- to five-day flood forecasts are published daily on the internet (www.mrcmekong.org).
4 **Flood Emergency Measures** These deal with the aftermath of such an event by 'helping affected people to cope with floods'. Flood Emergency Management, like Floodplain Management, is a process that typically encompasses preparation, response and recovery. In addition to flood preparedness, the flood emergency management process embodies evacuation planning and training, emergency accommodation planning and flood cleanup planning, with the restitution of essential services and social and financial recovery measures.

Floods and New Policy Developments

The science of the causes of floods admits uncertainty and imprecision in the prediction of land use impacts on the flood regime. The interaction between forests and soils and how they co-evolved over different time periods ranging from years to thousands of years and how soil properties will ultimately change with changes of vegetation cover remains a particularly 'grey' area in our knowledge. In these circumstances, and taking account of the precautionary principle, we should be wary of advocating new courses of action which alter the present situation when we are not sure of the precise outcome. For example, we should be wary of allowing deforestation to occur on steep slopes or on soils that are recognized as being easily erodible.

On the other hand, it could be argued that we should be equally wary of investing significant proportions of very limited development funds in 'remedial' programmes (often afforestation programmes) when the scientific perception is that at best they will have marginal hydrological benefits, and at worst negative hydrological impacts. The 'best' situation we might expect, from studies in America's Pacific Northwest, is an approximately 10 per cent diminution in floods at the small scale (100km^2); at larger scales we seem to have little evidence for any beneficial effect. Of particular concern would be reforestation programmes, which involve extensive road construction, or other management activities involving extensive cultivation or drainage activities that might lead to increased flooding.

The recognition in the US Pacific Northwest that the engineering management activities associated with forestry, particularly those involving road construction, can significantly increase flood peaks and modify runoff timing has resulted in a situation not entirely dissimilar to the Kissimmee example, in that engineering works are now being reversed. Many National Forests are carefully analysing their transportation needs, then decommissioning and recontouring unneeded portions of the road network to halt continued environmental damage while restoring hydrologic function and ecological resilience.

In the UK the Forestry Commission, whose ethos and working practices would traditionally have been expected to be associated with the 'forester and environmental positions', has recently radically changed its position in relation to forest and flood issues to that of fully supporting the science perception. This is evidenced in recent publications (Forestry Commission, 2002) where not only is it admitted that '...the scope for forests to reduce the severity of major floods that are derived from an extended period of very heavy rainfall is rather limited' but also that forestry management practices such as those involving deep ploughing and drainage practices can actually enhance flood risk. This recognition of the hydrological impacts has resulted in a move away from these forms of land preparation activities in the UK in recent years. Many forestry operations in the USA are employing less intensive site preparation and management practices, both to limit environmental impacts as well as to reduce costs for practices which have little practical benefit.

The UK Forestry Commission's report, *Climate Change: Impacts on UK Forests*, does however suggest another important role for forests in relation to floods. In Chapter 5 of this report, Tom Nisbet (2002) states that 'One location where forestry could make a net positive contribution to flood control is in the actual floodplain itself. The removal of river embankments in less sensitive locations would allow floodwaters to spread out and thus help to reduce downstream flood peaks at high risk sites.' He also cautions that floodplain forest expansion is not totally without risk – 'consideration needs to be given to sites that could be threatened by the backing-up of floodwaters, problems of restricted access to rivers and the impact of higher water use on water supplies during periods of summer drought'. The recognition by the UK's Environment Agency of the higher water use of forests and their probable impacts in terms of reducing summer water flows is probably the reason why there has been little take up of this suggestion so far in the UK. Floodplain areas also tend to be areas with high values for agricultural crop production.

The plethora of misinformation, misperceptions and myths surrounding the relationships between forests, trees and land-use activities on one hand and catastrophic floods on the other, is just as prevalent in Asia as it has been in the USA and the UK. Partly through the lack of a clear science message in relation to forest and water interactions, many interest groups have selectively reproduced and propagated conventional wisdoms and developed sanctioned discourses which best suit their purposes. Foresters have long been suspected of propagating many of the forest and water myths in 'defence of their trees' and their agency agendas. More recently, environmentalists have picked up on the 'forests protect against floods' message as a means of promoting forest preservation.

Foresters, of course, not only wish to plant trees; they also want to log them. A particular situation in which the forester's sanctioned discourse, or what from the forester's perspective has been called 'the useful myth' (Kaimowitz, 2000), seems to have backfired, is in relation to the oversold benefits of forests in relation to flood mitigation and erosion control. China and other South East Asian countries have invoked policies including logging bans which have severely impacted on forestry interests and on millions of people whose livelihoods are dependent on the forestry and logging industries.

So when the 'useful myths' are oversold and are detrimental to forestry interests, it is time to address them. David Kaimowitz, Director General of the Centre for International Forestry Research (CIFOR), a research organization supported by the Consultative Group on International Agricultural Research (CGIAR), was successful in inserting an article in *New Scientist* (Kaimowitz, 2004) in an attempt to tone down the forest and flood narrative (Figure 5.6):

> There is not a shred of scientific evidence to suggest that logging or deforestation play significant roles in massive floods. And the myth is doing great damage to farmers who need forests to survive.

Many governments have used the myth about deforestation causing major flooding to force poor farmers off their lands and away from forests. Yet most of those farmers have no other way of making a living. After the Yangtze River floods of 1998, for example, the Chinese government imposed a logging ban that put over one million people out of work. And several South East Asian governments have used floods as an excuse to prohibit the traditional farming practices of ethnic minorities.

Source: *New Scientist* (2004) Illustrator: Andrzej Krauze

Figure 5.6 *Cartoon in 'The great flood myth' article*

The article by David Kaimowitz, whilst addressing the forest and floods myth, also alludes to some of the other policies which have been developed around it. Some of these are discussed below.

CHINA: THE WORLD'S BIGGEST EXPERIMENT? – THE NATURAL FOREST PROTECTION PROGRAMME AND THE SLOPING LANDS CONVERSION PROGRAMME

The major floods in China in 1998 precipitated the early announcement of the Natural Forest Protection Programme (NFPP), which stipulated the protection of natural forests throughout the country and imposed a complete ban on logging in the upper reaches of the Yellow and Yangtze Rivers. The erosion-prevention programme named the Sloping Land Conversion Programme (SLCP) was announced at the same time.

The stated purpose of the SLCP, as announced by Prime Minister Zhu Rongji, was to reduce environmental degradation. The SLCP called for the re-vegetation of 31 million hectares of land on steep slopes (greater than 25°). The state promised to subsidize 2.55 tons of grain and about US$36 per year to farmers for every hectare of such cropland converted to forestry around the upper reaches of the Yangtze. (The subsidies vary somewhat between provinces; in the north-west provinces the subsidy now amounts to 1.5 tons of grain and about US$36 per hectare for 2 years for conversion to grass and for 5–8 years for conversion to trees and shrubs).

Whilst China's system of government has undergone very rapid transformation over recent years to a form of capitalist Marxism, from a control economy to one which is now more open and decentralized, the pace of the transformation may have left some environmental policies with a 'ragged edge'. China, the world's fastest growing large economy, is struggling to find policies which promote modernization and development whilst minimizing environmental damage. The 'ragged edge' NFPP and SLCP policies appear to presume many of the forester's and environmentalist's narratives (see also the THED narrative, Chapter 1). Irrespective of whether these policies and programmes will achieve their intended beneficial environmental, flood protection and water resource (both quantity and quality) outcomes, there are concerns that there will be other negative aspects associated with these programmes both within China and in neighbouring countries:

- Increased logging in neighbouring countries. There are concerns that the increased demand for imported timber, created by logging bans in China and other South East Asian countries, has increased logging, both legal and illegal, in surrounding countries. The *Polex* newsletter (2004), under the title 'China imports the world's forests', states 'The great sucking sound continues…. Ten years ago, China was the seventh largest importer of forest products. Today it is the second. That has provided new opportunities for many exporters, but it has also fuelled illegal logging and forest destruction'.
- Turning present biodiversity hot spots into biodiversity cold spots. With the rapid implementation of the SLCP, there is a substantial threat of turning areas which might currently be regarded as biodiversity hot spots into biodiversity cold spots. A panel of scientists from the Chinese Academy of Sciences (Ministry of Water Resources, China, 2003) states that in too many areas only one kind of tree was planted under the programme and that natural (leave alone) rehabilitation would have been more effective than planting a monoculture.
- High compensation, but in too short a time? The compensation rate amounts to as much as US$417/ha in the SLCP as against US$116/ha in the comparable US land retirement Conservation Reserve Program. The programme puts farmers at risk of having to find their own markets for new tree products and assumes that there will be a future market for

these products at a date in the future when compensation has ceased (in 5–8 years).

The China Council for International Cooperation on Environment and Development (CCICED), a task force co-chaired by Professor Shen Guofeng of the Chinese Academy of Engineering (CAE) and Dr Uma Lele of the World Bank, sponsored a group of international and national experts to look at the 'giant experiment' of the NFPP and SLCP. The report (World Bank, 2002) entitled *Implementing the Natural Forest Protection Program and the Sloping Land Conversion Program: Lessons and Policy Recommendations* found that the blanket application of the current logging ban is not the best way to achieve conservation with development.

The report, perhaps not unexpectedly following more the 'forester's narrative' rather than addressing the highly political and contentious issues raised by the THED, nevertheless, found that in the case of the NFPP the impacts on local livelihoods were extensive and, in many cases, severe 'even the state-owned forestry enterprises and their staff, which have received the bulk of the compensation provided by the Government, are experiencing crisis-level impacts in many areas'. The report found that the SLCP, which requires conversion of sloping agriculture land back to forest and grasslands through provision of free grain to farmers involved in the scheme, is leading to a distortion of local markets and puts downward pressure on prices, therefore decreasing incomes for farmers who are not involved in the SLCP and who still rely on crop production. Given these lessons, the report recommended the following actions:

For the NFPP:

- Remove the ban on logging from collectively owned forests where appropriate, ensuring clarity and predictability in tenure security.
- Develop an exit strategy to move from the logging ban on state-owned forests to sustainable management of the forests.
- Develop a detailed forest–land use plan which ensures protection of old growth natural forests.
- In the interim, compensate collective forest holders for losses caused by the ban and increase the level of compensation to those impacted by the logging ban on state-owned forests.

For the SLCP:

- Develop a strategy to engage other sector agencies in reducing sedimentation from engineering works.
- With the active participation of local officials and representatives of stakeholders, improve the targeting and implementation of the programme by adopting specific environmental targeting criteria and more market-based mechanisms such as bidding.
- Develop a 'sustainability' strategy to continue the positive benefits of the programme following the end of the subsidies. This 'sustainability' strat-

egy would include an aggressive piloting and advancement of alternative
funding sources for these payments for ecosystem services, including a
redesigned Ecosystem Compensation Fund and promotion of new
markets and payment schemes for carbon sequestration.
• Build capacity at all levels for more decentralized flexible, multi-sectoral
approaches to policy, planning, implementation, monitoring and evaluation in the affected provinces.

The NFPP and SLCP were policies driven by the State Forestry
Administration (SFA). The central precepts, that forestry is necessarily always
good for preventing erosion and the best way to reduce floods, have not gone
unquestioned by other Ministries. A panel of academics from the Chinese
Academy of Sciences have voiced their concerns about the policies, recognizing also the water resource downside of forestry in reducing water flows and
aquifer recharge. These appeared in the form of suggestions on the official
website of the Ministry of Water Resources (Ministry of Water Resources,
China, 2003).

The problems associated with the NFPP and SLCP are becoming an 'open
secret' in official circles in China and are being discussed (perhaps rather
guardedly) in the press. The *China Daily* of 14 October 2004 (*China Daily*,
2004) reports Li Zibin, vice-minister of the National Development and
Reform Commission, saying 'It is unjustified to claim the five-year reforesting
efforts were to blame for the country's declining grain harvest'. Li stated that
China had reconverted 7.86 million hectares of farmland to woods and had
planted trees on 11.33 million hectares of bare hills and land between 1999
and the end of 2004. Although a National Bureau of Statistics' survey
indicated that the conversion of cultivated land into woodland has incurred
an annual grain loss of 6.5 million tons, Li claimed that 'thanks to efforts
protecting and improving production capacity of the remaining farmland, a
per-unit yield rise has enabled the affected areas to increase grain output by 5
million tons a year, meaning that the annual reduction is actually 1.5 million
tons'. Li explained that the reason for China's grain production dropping from
512.3 million tons in 1998 to 430.7 million tons in 2003 was the loss of arable
land by urbanization and industrial expansion and by the trend to convert
land to cash crops. But whatever other factors are at work, the removal of
7.86 million hectares of farmland is clearly a very significant land use change
for any country. Xu Jintao, a researcher with the Agricultural Policy Institute
of the Chinese Academy of Sciences, is quoted in the *China Daily* as saying
'the country should slow down its pace of converting more cultivated land
into forest in the west'.

The indications are that shortages of both grain and money are already
leading to reduced subsidies, and it is suspected that even these may not last
until the end of the two/five/eight years of payments promised earlier for
conversion from arable to grass/shrub/tree cover.

The official monitoring programmes of the NFPP and SLCP are viewed
as 'too academic' and are very expensive to operate except at very low
sampling frequencies. Almost all the field data are on inputs and on the

numbers of trees planted and their early survival. There is very little information to allow the Government to judge the real success or otherwise of these programmes or to determine who are the winners and losers. It is suggested (Chapter 7) that research aimed at determining these real impacts would not only be of value to the government in China in developing future land use policies but would, through linkage with the 'World's Biggest Experiment, present one of the best opportunities for really progressing our scientific understanding of the biophysical and socio-economic impacts associated with such changes in land use.

It may be that under the leadership of the new Chinese Prime Minister, Wen Jiabao, there will be opportunities for more open discussion of government policies which might allow the development of less polarized and more evidence-based land and water policies in the future.

THE WORLD'S GREATEST ENVIRONMENTAL CHALLENGE? – CLIMATE CHANGE AND THE CLEAN DEVELOPMENT MECHANISM

The British Prime Minister, Tony Blair, called climate change the world's greatest environmental challenge in a speech made in September 2004. Calling for more action to combat climate change he claimed that 'our effect on the environment, and in particular on climate change, is large and growing' and that 'our efforts to stabilize the climate will need, over time, to become far more ambitious than the Kyoto Protocol'.

But, in developing policies to address unwelcome impacts of climate change, we need to be sure that the policies created by the Kyoto Protocol, and under any later global agreements, do not themselves create unwelcome outcomes, particularly unwelcome local outcomes that might outweigh the global benefits.

'Win–win' solutions are hard to find but one that could perhaps be described as a 'triple-win' has already been identified in Chapter 4. If means and policies (see Chapter 7) could be found to manage the demand for groundwater for irrigation in countries such as India and China, not only would this represent a huge win in terms of reduced power consumption and reduced associated greenhouse gas (GHG) emissions, but it would also benefit water resources and the livelihoods of the poor.

The present Kyoto Protocol also includes three market-based instruments known as the Kyoto Mechanisms that allow countries to earn or buy carbon emission credits outside their borders:

- The Clean Development Mechanism (CDM) is a way to earn credits by investing in emission-reduction projects in developing countries.
- Joint Implementation is a way to earn credits by investing in emission-reduction projects in developed countries that have taken on a Kyoto target.

- International emissions trading (IET) will permit developed countries that have taken on a Kyoto target to buy and sell credits among themselves.

There is a concern that trading might constitute a 'let out' for some developed countries, allowing them to avoid domestic actions to reduce emissions. This has fuelled a debate over whether there should be a 'cap' on the amount countries are allowed to trade. But at present the CDM represents one relatively cheap and easy way in which industrialized countries might meet the GHG emission reduction targets by, for example, investing in a 'sink' project, such as an afforestation programme, in a developing country if it can be shown that it sequesters GHGs. The CDM is also mandated to 'assist developing countries in achieving sustainable development'. What constitutes sustainable development is decided by the host party.

The CDM is unique among the Kyoto Protocol mitigation actions because of its joint objectives of contributing to climate change reduction and to sustainable development. The aim is to assist developing countries to meet their emissions commitments without disadvantaging the livelihoods or sustainable development in the host country. But it is clear that for this to be achieved and for perverse outcomes to be avoided, particularly in relation to CDM-based forestry schemes, it will be necessary for the host country to understand clearly the biophysical and socio-economic impacts of the forestry intervention.

In some respects the issues are similar to those discussed above for the NFPP and SLCP: will the proclaimed benefits of the policies be achieved effectively and if so, at what economic cost and at what cost in relation to other possible negative outcomes? With regard to CDM forestry these can be summarized as follows:

- Concerns relating to the 'permanence' issue. Will CDM forestry interventions sequester carbon in the long term – what is the risk of failure? On the 'free' market, sink-based carbon trades for as little as $1 per ton compared with approximately $10 per ton for industrial carbon emission avoidance. The difference is based on the perception that sink carbon is more 'risky'. It is stored in 'pools' which are inherently more unstable than fossil fuel reserves left in the ground, and which are subject to sudden and unintended loss due to fires, weather events or pest outbreaks – all of which become more unpredictable in a situation of climate change. Furthermore, it is hard to guarantee the integrity of the social arrangements necessary to protect sink carbon over the long term: political disturbance, the demands of development and the uncertainties of the international legal framework could all conspire to reverse the sink processes.
- Concerns that the technical and economic costs of repeatedly verifying the carbon stored, whilst maintaining the integrity of the project over relatively long periods of time, may exceed the value of the benefit and that the CDM actions taken may simply displace activities promoting

climate change to other locations, resulting in no net benefit (the 'leakage' issue).
- Negative environmental impacts including reduction in water yield.
- Negative impacts on biodiversity.
- Negative social impacts and impacts on livelihoods.

The effectiveness of CDM programmes needs to be assessed in relation to the overriding objective of the UN Framework Convention on Climate Change (UNFCCC, 2004) to 'prevent dangerous anthropogenic interference with the climate system' (the Kyoto Protocol with its CDM clause is an instrument of the UNFCCC). CDM programmes involving sinks are generally heavily focused on carbon dioxide, the main, but not the only, greenhouse gas. There is a danger that some sink activities that store carbon might also increase the emission of other gases, methane (CH_4) or nitric oxide (N_2O), which could promote the formation of tropospheric ozone or radiation-absorbing aerosols. Such sink programmes run the risk of having a highly reduced, or even negative net radiant forcing benefit (Sampson and Scholes, 2000), that is, they might have perverse outcomes in relation to climate change mitigation. Other perverse outcomes have also been documented in which the carbon uptake resulting from increased forest growth has been more than offset by the reduction in surface albedo (reduced reflectance of incoming solar radiation) brought about by the dark forest cover (Hansen et al, 1998).

Together with possible climate mitigation benefits, other sustainability issues need to be considered (Huq, 2002; Jin and Liu, 2000). Lands that can be converted to forests typically provide a range of ecosystem services to local people, the nation and the globe. The principal concern is that raising the prominence of one of these services – climate change mitigation, a benefit experienced at the global scale – may impact negatively and significantly on the provision of other services. In particular we need to consider whether the promotion of forestry as a land use in rural watersheds through the mechanism of carbon sequestration credits will reduce downstream water resources, be detrimental to rural livelihoods of neighbouring communities and aggravate downstream water resource conflicts. One of the difficulties in reconciling forest policy in relation to both water and climate change is that there are not only different government ministries dealing with the issues but also separate research communities addressing them (climate, development, forestry and water).

In monetary terms the benefits accruing to carbon and water may be quite similar (Calder, 2000). Taking estimates of 250mm and 400mm per year as the average loss of water under deciduous hardwood and pines/eucalypts respectively (Bosch and Hewlett, 1982) and average values for water for agricultural or industrial water use as US$100 per 1000m³, the loss in value of water under hardwood forestation would be US$ 250/ha and under pines/eucalypts US$ 400. Bruce Aylward (Aylward, 1998; Aylward et al, 1998) suggests, from studies in Latin America using a carbon price of US$20/ton, that carbon sequestration credits arising from forestation would amount to around US$200–500/ha.

Steve Bass and colleagues from the International Institute for Environment and Development (IIED) (Bass et al, 2000) have considered some of the socio-economic impacts of the CDM in relation to: what is the added value of land-based carbon offsets? What might their impacts be on rural livelihoods? Are rural people and their farming and forestry systems well-suited to the provision of carbon offsets? How can rural people benefit? They conclude that if the CDM is to meet sustainability objectives, then 'International carbon offset policy, standards, and accounting and certification protocols must be built upon sustainable forestry, land use and livelihood criteria'. National institutions need to be strengthened to act as brokers between a global carbon offset marketplace and potential local suppliers with their own particular needs and interests. Local carbon offset organizational and project management capabilities need to be efficient, equitable and competitive. This could be done by building on mechanisms that already work well in relation to sustainable land use and multiple rural stakeholders, for example, rural development banks, NGOs and extension systems.

MARKETS FOR WATERSHED SERVICES – REWARDING THE POOR?

Policies involving the use of markets for environmental services (MES) or payments for environmental services (PES) are being explored in many countries of the world. In simple terms 'environmental services' can be regarded as the flow of valuable services that natural systems provide to society. In some situations environmental services can provide similar services to those that can be achieved by man-made physical interventions involving check dams or water treatment works, for example, erosion control and water quality (and can then be substitutable). There are good examples where such schemes, particularly with regard to water quality and water treatment, have been very economically successful. To avoid costly fines for not meeting federal government regulatory water quality requirements, New York City officials negotiated payments to upstream landowners for better watershed management at a cost of $1.5 billion, which was far less than the cost of a proposed filtration plant, estimated to cost $6–8 billion (Forest Trends, 2003; City of New York, 2004). Equally successful have been the payment schemes put in place by Perrier Vittel S. A., the world's largest bottler of natural mineral water, to ensure the quality of their water sources. Realizing that protection of water sources is more cost-effective than building filtration plants, Perrier Vittel used the PES mechanism to reduce nitrates and pesticides through encouraging farmers to improve animal waste management and to reduce the use of agrochemicals and through promoting afforestation schemes to landowners (Perrot-Maître and Davis, 2001).

The success of such schemes has led to many organizations, including development organizations, promoting them as 'win–win' mechanisms where not only can environmental services be maintained at less cost than man-made structural interventions, but equity and poverty-alleviation benefits could be achieved through 'rewarding the upland poor for environmental services'.

Whilst the concept is very appealing, closer scrutiny of the following aspects indicates caution:

- the underlying motives behind some of the schemes;
- the biophysical understanding upon which they are based;
- whether there are any 'buyers'; and
- who is actually benefiting from existing schemes.

The International Fund for Agricultural Development (IFAD) supports a programme for developing mechanisms in Asia for rewarding the upland poor for the environmental services (RUPES) they provide. It has the stated goal: To enhance the livelihoods and reduce poverty of the upland poor while supporting environmental conservation on biodiversity protection, watershed management, carbon sequestration and landscape beauty at local and global levels.

The programme is coordinated by the World Agroforestry Centre (ICRAF), which also coordinates the 'Alternatives to Slash-and-Burn Programme' (ICRAF, 2004), a programme which has been criticized for supporting many of the narratives underlying the THED sanctioned discourse, i.e. that it is a programme claiming that the consequences of slash and burn are devastating in terms of climate change, soil erosion, watershed degradation and loss of biodiversity and implicitly that something needs to be done about the (ignorant) upland tribes perpetrating this damage. Forsyth (2002) has shown how this narrative can so easily be exploited by vested interest groups such as the Royal Forestry Department in Thailand to impose tree planting programmes on agricultural land against the will of local farmers.

Accepting that the motives behind RUPES are as proclaimed, and that the conceptual basis for RUPES has recently been redefined (van Noordwijk et al, 2005), the programme, which has been running for some years, has yet to demonstrate much in the way of new take-up of market mechanisms or indeed that there are any 'buyers' willing to pay hard cash for such services. As scepticism about the THED sanctioned discourse grows and the real role of forests in relation to the water environment becomes better understood, it may be unsurprising that buyers of environmental services are less willing to part with their money unless they can be offered something real and tangible in exchange.

An alternative approach, exchanging services for services, may be more successful. RUPES is now investigating agreements for maintaining environmental services in exchange for confirmation of resource access rights, such as land tenure, or the provision of infrastructure such as rural roads, schools and clinics or the confirmation of favourable marketing arrangements for upland products.

Manrique Rojas and Bruce Aylward (Rojas and Aylward, 2003) offer some very interesting insights into the underlying motives behind markets for environmental services schemes in Costa Rica, motives which presumably may also apply to forest-related market schemes in other parts of the world. They pointed out the cynical nature of forestry interests in Costa Rica at the time when a structural adjustment programme was being negotiated with the World Bank. The terms of the agreement required the elimination of subsidies to the productive sectors, including the forestry sector. The forestry interests saw market mechanisms, MES or PES schemes, as the ideal way of 'repackaging' the outlawed subsidies in a way that would be acceptable to the World Bank. Rojas and Aylward state:

> However, 17 years of subsidies to the forestry sector had allowed room for the creation of an influential institutional framework to support and lobby in favour of the forestry sector's interests. These groups exerted pressure and opposed the complete elimination of forestry subsidies.
>   These proximate variables, including:
> * the development of forestry incentives in Costa Rica;
> * the transition to give subsidies to forest conservation in addition to reforestation;
> * the pressure from international financial institutions to eliminate subsidies; and
> * the internal pressure to keep the forestry subsidies,
> when combined with the broader expectations for market opportunities associated with climate change, ecotourism and certification all served as a basis for the legal definition of Payments for Environmental Services (PES) that emerged in the Forestry Law of 1996.

In relation to the biophysical understanding upon which many market-based systems are founded, the statement by the Vice President, Environmentally and Socially Sustainable Development Section of the World Bank (http://www.biodiv.org/doc/reports/fin-wbank-en.pdf), conveys well the 'public' perception by stating:

> The hydrological services provided by forests, such as clean and regulated water flow, and reduced sedimentation, for example, are typically only noted when natural disasters, flooding, siltation of reservoirs and scarcity of water occur as a result of the removal of forest cover.

But this message makes no mention of the reduction in total water flows that will almost certainly occur from forested lands compared with those under shorter vegetation types (Chapter 2). The supposed 'regulatory' benefits of forests on water flows are seen to be largely illusory on inspection of the available hydrological evidence. Whilst at the small catchment scale and for medium-sized flood events (in hydrologists jargon, the mean annual flood) there is evidence that forests can reduce floods typically by the order of 20 per cent (Hewlett and Bosch, 1984), there is no evidence that either at the large catchment scale or for the largest (and most damaging) flood events that forests provide any significant flood mitigation benefit (Chapter 2). In terms of augmenting dry season flows, all the available hydrological evidence indicates that forests reduce both annual flows and dry season flows compared with other vegetation types (Chapter 2). It is necessary also to be wary of universal claims of clean water and reduced sedimentation. Whilst natural forests generally display very low rates of soil erosion, this does not necessarily apply to plantation forests, which are subject to logging and road making (major causes of sedimentation). In highly polluted environments common in much of the developed and, increasingly, the developing world, forested catchments often have poorer water quality as a result of increased deposition of atmospheric pollutants compared with catchments under shorter vegetation types.

The excellent and detailed study carried out by Natasha Landell-Mills and Ina Porras of the IIED (Landell-Mills and Porras 2001) is also very revealing with regard to the underlying basis, the implementation and the outcomes of payments for environmental services mechanisms. They particularly question what market creation means for poor people:

> *The critical question is whether markets for forest environmental services can contribute to poverty reduction, while at the same time achieving efficient environmental protection. In short, do markets for forest environmental services offer a 'silver bullet' for tackling economic, social and environmental problems in the forestry sector, or are they simply 'fools' gold'?*

Drawing on a total of 287 case studies over a range of developed and developing countries in the Americas, the Caribbean, Europe, Africa, Asia and the Pacific, the implications for poor people of various types of market mechanisms were investigated. In relation to markets for watershed services they arrived at the following cautionary conclusions:

> *Amidst the flurry of activity to promote payments for watershed protection, little attention has been given to impacts. Questions need to be asked as to whether markets provide a preferable mechanism for delivering watershed services to tried and tested regulatory systems. The literature provides little insight on this issue. For the most part, studies offer superficial reviews of economic, social and environmental benefits with virtually no assessment of costs. Moreover, the literature fails to convince us that markets offer the optimal way of achieving improved watersheds. The lack of attention to equity impacts of emerging payment schemes raises a number of concerns.*

Concerns over equity impacts are reinforced by the analysis of constraints to market development. Even where the gains from trade are significant, the significant transaction costs involved introduce serious barriers to entry for anyone lacking financial resources, managerial and coordination skills, technical knowledge and political connections. Moreover, the following factors will increase the costs of participating in emerging markets: the greater the number of individuals living in a watershed, the weaker the government's regulatory capacity, the less reliable the hydrological data, and the less secure the property rights. While developing countries face severe hurdles in establishing markets for watershed protection, it is the poorest groups in these countries that risk marginalization. Governments have a critical role to play in ensuring markets work for the benefit of all sections of society, not just the most powerful.

A more recent study, carried out by the Centre for Land Use and Water Resources Research (CLUWRR) and IIED (Hope et al, 2005), under the cluster of forest- and water-related projects funded under DFID's Forestry Research Programme, investigates these issues in more detail. The study again is set in Costa Rica. It considered the following questions:

- Who are the rural poor, and will MES schemes release their primary development constraints?
- What have been the drivers of land-use change in tropical forested areas and will MES schemes reduce forest land use conversions which disadvantage the poor?
- Should government and donors allocate funds to MES schemes with the aim of rural poverty reduction?

The findings of this study are also far from sanguine about the benefits of payment mechanisms in relation to the rural poor. It is claimed that the Costa Rican PES programmes create a market distortion that promotes land speculation in upper watershed areas, particularly in strategic areas such as above hydropower reservoirs where buyers for market services may exist. Furthermore, it is believed that the logic of the presently constructed PES programme is not so much directed towards providing 'incentives' to improve land management practices but more towards 'compensation' for benefits deferred. In agreement with the earlier (Landell-Mills and Porras, 2001) study it is recognized that there are justifiable concerns that PES policies might lead to land evictions of the poor as wealthier elites are provided with incentives to gain control of land resources. Sven Wunder, a forest economist at CIFOR, has argued (Wunder, 2001) that promoting policies that generate increased competition for land in tropical forests is unlikely to improve the livelihoods or welfare of the rural poor. Where small farmers in Costa Rica, as in much of the rest of Latin America, hold land only through squatters' rights, the lack of legal documents of tenure not only makes it difficult for them to enter into PES agreements but it also increases their vulnerability to land forfeiture. The CLUWRR report also suggests that in Costa Rica the poor are more often located in the lower rather than upper parts of the catchment and concludes that:

It appears both inequitable and dubious that the downstream poor will be willing, or able, to pay for environmental services from upper watershed land owners (rich or poor) that are currently shrouded in beliefs rather than science (Calder, 2004), and where the establishment of functioning watershed markets is found in a handful of micro-watershed cases globally (Landell-Mills and Porras, 2001), whose institutional structures are more common to industrial, developed countries rather than dispersed, unorganized and weak rural multitudes common to the great watersheds and floodplains of Sub-Saharan Africa and South Asia, where the majority of the world's poor live.

Government and donors might well ponder such uncertainties and potentially perverse outcomes of promoting MES for 'pro-poor' development.

PREVENTING PERVERSITY – THE NEED TO EVALUATE POLICY OUTCOMES

As discussed above, forest, land and water policies are often claimed to be maximizing pro-poor and environmental benefits. Even if these claims are taken at face value closer scrutiny generally shows that little attention has been paid to the impacts that changing land use may have on water availability within a catchment. The result is that changes in land use, which may be promoted as part of watershed development programmes or for carbon credits, may reduce the availability of water for downstream users. In arid areas, where water is already scarce, this can have profound impacts on more vulnerable groups. Moreover, these land-use changes, particularly those

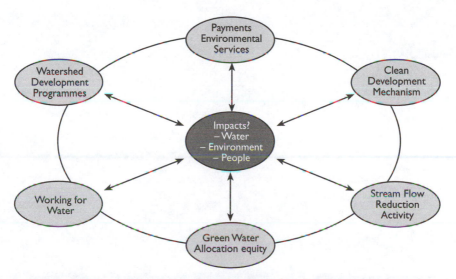

Figure 5.7 *How different land- and water-related policy instruments may impact on water, the environment and people*

involving combinations of afforestation, irrigation and soil water conservation programmes, may lead to rivers drying out completely and catchment closure.

Policies leading to large-scale afforestation are being promoted in China under the NFPP and SLCP and in India within Watershed Development Projects. Forestry is also being promoted under the CDM and PES schemes. In contrast, in South Africa the Working for Water Programme, together with stream flow reduction activity, 'allocation equity' and 'green water' instruments (see Chapter 7), aims to mitigate adverse environmental and water resource impacts of land-use change (often in connection with fast-growing trees).

It is believed that many of these policy instruments (Figure 5.7) may not be delivering the intended benefits either to the environment and water resources or to the livelihoods of vulnerable groups. The promotion of watershed development projects which encourage further groundwater-based irrigation may also be making a significant contribution to increased greenhouse gas emissions through the extra power required to pump from depleting groundwater tables. To progress the blue revolution and to achieve better outcomes from these instruments will require the political will to allow critical evaluation of these instruments, and the political will to share knowledge and to learn from recent policy developments (Chapter 7).

Chapter 6

Water Resource Conflicts

There are many causes of land-use and water resource conflicts. They arise because of land-use demands ranging from the most fundamental – for land to provide both basic food supplies and water of sufficient quantity and quality to satisfy basic human needs for drinking and sanitation – to the more aesthetic, for example, the desire to have attractive land uses such as forests and water bodies as visual enhancements to the landscape. Tensions between the many different users –agriculture, forestry, industries, power and mines; urban and rural consumers; amenity, ecology and environmental users – exist in many parts of the world. Rights of access to water and equity considerations are highly emotive political considerations, as is the question, in some countries, of how water can be shared across international river basins. Consideration of the sustainability of the land and water resource for both present and future generations, always of paramount concern in some cultures, is now more appreciated by the western world. Although the land use and water resource issues and concerns are often as diverse as the different countries' cultural, economic and technical development, there is, nevertheless, a certain common approach as to how governments treat the issues. This commonality has manifested itself as a steadfast reluctance to deal with the issues, particularly those that are not attractive from the point of view of gaining short-term political capital: to defer and fudge the issues as long as possible, has been the norm. Lack of awareness and lack of research may sometimes have been mitigating factors, but even where land use and water resource issues have been well researched and understood, the vision and enthusiasm for facing and taking up the issues is often lacking. Increasing pressures on governments, both external and from within, are now becoming such that procrastination is no longer an option. In some more enlightened countries, the revolutionary tide has turned.

Some of the major resource conflicts in the Nile basin, Zimbabwe, Malawi, India, Australia, USA, UK, New Zealand, the Philippines, Panama and South Africa, and how these relate to the blue revolution, are outlined below.

Plate 6.1 *The Nile Basin*

THE NILE – A TRADITION OF POLITICAL CONFLICTS

The modern history of the exploitation of the Nile waters demonstrates the past ascendancy of the traditional, single-minded, engineering approach to river and water resource management. It also demonstrates how this approach has led to significant economic benefits for the riparian countries of the Nile, particularly Egypt. History also shows a tradition of political conflict between many of the states exacerbated, if not caused, by these engineering developments. More recently the environmental and socio-economic impacts of these developments have been questioned and it is these concerns which are likely to moderate, if not halt, future large-scale developments.

Nine African states share the Nile catchment, which covers one-tenth of Africa and provides water to the world's longest river. Together with the political boundaries, the catchment has within it well-defined climatic, social and religious divides stretching from the desert in the north, with an Islamic tradition, to the well-watered mountains of Ethiopia in the south, the home of a mostly Christian population.

An authoritative history of the early engineering developments on the Nile and the involvement of British engineers and hydrologists who brought them about has been given by Collins (1990). Newson (1992a, 1997) supplements this history with insights into the mechanisms and reasons behind the various basin development schemes.

Engineering Developments and Water Sharing

The first phase of engineering developments in modern history began with the construction of the dam at Aswan in 1902. Claims on Nile water by Egypt had been established through long historic use. But, in the early part of the 20th century, increasing use of the upstream waters of the Nile by Sudan for irrigation necessitated some form of agreement over the sharing of the waters between the two states, and this led to the Nile Waters Agreement of 1929. The agreement served only to partition flows between the two states; ideas for the development of the basin as a whole and for increasing its storage came later. Engineers saw the Sudd – the wetland region in southern Sudan which detains and evaporates about half the Nile flows – as a major obstacle to developing the water resources of the basin. In 1925, the Egyptian government approved a scheme to 'canalize' the Nile through the Sudd to reduce evaporation losses, but the Sudan government was not adequately consulted or involved in the decision-making process and the proposals came to nothing. By 1938 a number of ways of channelling the Sudd had been evaluated and the Jonglei Canal Diversion Scheme became the scheme preferred by Egypt. Again through lack of consultation with the British in Sudan, the scheme did not progress (Collins, 1990).

The second phase of major engineering – involving the construction of the Aswan High Dam a little upstream, and within the reservoir of the original dam built in 1902 – became a source of major international conflict. Refusal by the USA in 1956 to fund the construction of the dam led President Nasser to nationalize the Suez Canal as a means of generating internal funds. Later the former Soviet Union funded the construction of this, the world's largest dam with 180 water gates and 12 power-generating units supplying 2.1 million kilowatts of electric power.

Conflict and Conflict Management

The competition over access to the Nile's waters by the riparian states continues. Upper riparian countries are starting to develop their water resources to meet growing population needs. Since Egypt would be particularly affected by additional water withdrawals in the upper basin, growing tensions exist between Egypt and these upstream states. Ethiopia's plan to divert the Blue Nile's water for irrigation projects causes particular concern to Egypt as this tributary supplies 80 per cent of the Nile water entering Egypt.

Treaties, basin organizations, commissions and 'initiatives' are all now playing a part in conflict management. In 1959 Egypt and Sudan established a treaty on water allocation whereby Sudan receives 18.5 and Egypt $55 km^3 yr^{-1}$. Riparian countries of the Kagera, an important tributary of the Nile, created a basin organization in 1977, and Tanzania, Rwanda, Burundi and Uganda are now part of it. Egypt has also unsuccessfully attempted to create a basin-wide organization, the failure of which was seen as being in part due to civil wars in Ethiopia, Sudan, Rwanda and Burundi, and also to political tensions between Egypt and Sudan. In 1992 the 'Nile Basin Initiative' was launched by the Council of Ministers of Water Affairs of the Nile Basin States (COM) to promote cooperation and development in the basin. Six of the riparian countries – the Democratic Republic of Congo, Egypt, Rwanda, Sudan, Tanzania and Uganda – formed the Technical Cooperation Committee for the Promotion of the Development and Environmental Protection of the Nile Basin (TECCONILE). One of the first activities of TECCONILE was the preparation of an action plan, and after two workshops, one in Entebbe, Uganda, in June 1994 and the second in Cairo, Egypt, in November 1994, the 'Nile River Basin Action Plan' (NRBAP) was developed. The NRBAP defined 22 development projects covering integrated water resource planning and management, capacity building, training, regional cooperation, and environmental protection and enhancement. The organization holds the promise of not only resolving water conflicts on the Nile, but also achieving true integrated water resource management for the basin. However, the report of the sixth meeting of the COM held in Arusha, Tanzania, in March 1998 shows that although there have been many achievements, there is still a long way to go before that goal can be reached. The report makes the following observations:

• The Nile River constitutes a key natural resource in our respective countries whose potential largely remains underdeveloped in most of the countries. There are emerging conflicts over access and use of the resource among the countries.

- Five out of the ten poorest or least-developed countries in the world are found in the Nile Basin.
- Strengthened cooperation and collaboration is needed to remove the current impediments, including inequity in the access and use of the resource, and set a framework and mechanism to promote equitable allocation and use of Nile waters for socio-economic development of the riparian countries.

The report also recognizes that 'as time passes by we must find a solution to managing and sharing the resources of our precious basin' and 'a shared vision can only be legitimized by action on the ground, action that benefits the peoples and particularly the poor and the disadvantaged in the Nile Basin.'

Trade-offs: Economics, the Environment, Society and Sustainability

The water resource developments on the Nile illustrate the complexity of the issues and the temporal and spatial trade-offs that need to be considered within IWRM.

On the one hand, engineering developments provide irrigation water, hydroelectricity, regulated flows and the avoidance of damaging and life-threatening floods, improved navigation for river transport and, perhaps most importantly, the potential through irrigation for feeding growing populations who can benefit from the developments. The Aswan High Dam development also provided the electric power for supplying the chemical fertilizer and steel plants which allowed industrialization in Egypt and Sudan.

On the other hand, engineering developments may be introducing a number of unforeseen problems with different spatial and temporal dimensions. Increased irrigation from the Nile waters following the construction of the dams is resulting in rising groundwater levels, increased salinity and water-logging which, although providing economic benefits for the present generation, may be leaving possibly insurmountable environmental rehabilitation problems for the next. The reduction of the natural deposition of silt on the downstream floodplains now has to be compensated for by the addition of some 13,000 tonnes of lime-nitrate fertilizer (Loucks and Gladwell, 1999). The reduction in the sediment load carried by the Nile is resulting in coastal erosion, as had been predicted. Fish catches have been reduced to about half those before the Aswan High Dam was built (ibid). Although major international efforts resulted in the translocation of some historic monuments, others were lost under the reservoir. The loss of land under the reservoir also forced the translocation of some 100,000 Egyptian and Sudanese Nubians.

It is now realized that the engineering developments planned for the Sudd would not have been without environmental and social costs. The present economy of the area is dependent on the natural environment and the grazing

provided by the river through the annual cycle of river flow and the flooding
of the floodplains (Sutcliffe, 1974). Any changes in the relation of the river to
the bank and floodplain would be expected to have an exaggerated effect on
the vegetation. The water evaporated in the Sudd cannot be regarded as a total
loss (Howell et al, 1988) as it is an essential component of the local grazing
and fishing economy of the Jonglei area. Benefits to downstream users would
have been at the expense of the communities living in the Sudd who have
made use of the water from time immemorial and which is theirs by right.

ZIMBABWE AND ITS WATER RESOURCE MANAGEMENT STRATEGY

The government that came to power in Zimbabwe at independence in 1980
invested heavily in health and education and, through parastatal organizations,
fostered rural development and the productive sectors in an attempt to
reduce socio-economic disparities. This led to an increase in public expenditure, which for most of the 1980s amounted to 45 per cent of the GDP.
Although social indicators improved, particularly in health and education, per
capita income stagnated. Large government spending reduced incentives for
private investment and fuelled inflation, while shortages of imported goods
constrained investment and growth. The population grew faster than job
creation, widening the disparities in income levels. In 1991, the government
proposed a policy agenda that formed the basis for the Structural Adjustment
Programme (SAP). The World Bank supported this with a US$125 million
structural adjustment loan (SAL) and a US$50 million structural adjustment
credit (SAC), both approved in 1992 and finalized in 1993.

The beginning of the adjustment programme coincided with the severe
southern African drought of 1992 and left Zimbabwe in its worst recession
since independence. The drought badly affected the implementation of the
SAP but it also brought to the attention of all Zimbabweans, in the most
dramatic fashion, not only the crucial importance of water in a country which
is subject to frequent droughts, but also the desperate need to have a better
way of managing the country's water resource.

Traditionally, water resource developments in Zimbabwe had been geared
towards providing water to the commercial agricultural sector through the
construction of impoundment reservoirs and irrigation canals. Currently,
annual surface water usage averages $4.7 \times 10^9 m^3$ of an estimated potential of
$8.5 \times 10^9 m^3$. Agriculture accounts for approximately 80 per cent of this usage
and it is generally the large commercial agricultural sector that has been most
vocal in calling for the remaining $3.8 \times 10^9 m^3$ to be brought into production,
even though it generally recognizes that the easiest and least costly sites have
already been used. The focus on the agricultural sector was in response to the
desire, both before and after independence, for the country to be self-suffi-
cient in food production.

During the droughts, agriculture was not the only sector to be affected.
Mining and manufacturing industries suffered restrictions and sometimes

Water Resource Conflicts **181**

closures. Supplies to the major cities and urban areas were restricted and hydroelectric generation was also reduced. There was also a greater recognition that although the agricultural sector was important to the economy, contributing 16 per cent of GDP, this was at the expense of it being the major water consumer. Questions about the balance of priorities were raised by some city dwellers in Harare, suffering water restrictions, who, during the drought of 1995, saw large commercial farmers irrigating wheat (a low value crop) on the outskirts of Harare. In contrast, in Mutare, one of the provincial centres, the commercial farmers complained that their livelihoods were put at risk when, during the same drought, as an emergency measure and after due process, abstraction licences were revoked without compensation and water which would otherwise have been used for irrigating crops was used to supply the city.

Other questions raised were whether the agricultural sector, if providing only 16 per cent of the GNP, should be the most privileged user of water and whether the price it was paying for the water was too low. Bearing in mind that in the early 1990s the agricultural sector was paying for water at the 'blend price' of 35 Zimbabwe dollars per 1000m^3 – a value less than the value of the power generated if it had just been left to flow in the northern-flowing rivers into Kariba – this could be considered a fair question!

The competing demands from the different sectors for Zimbabwe's water, highlighted so dramatically during the droughts, led to other water-related conflict. Increasingly, questions of equity, the right for all people to have equal access to Zimbabwe's waters irrespective of whether they had land tenure, became an issue. It was also appreciated that the environment was a valid user of water and that other downstream users and nations also had rights to the water.

The single-minded drive by the agricultural sector to develop the remaining unexploited resource for agricultural production, as called for in Zimbabwe's FAO-supported irrigation strategy, could be seen against the downside of increased environmental damage as evidenced by more 'dry' rivers, such as the Save, and less water for the downstream nations of Mozambique and South Africa.

These were some of the tensions which led to general recognition throughout virtually all sectors and at all levels in society in Zimbabwe that something had to be done quickly to redress the balance, to properly take into account the equity, environmental, economic and transnational issues.

Zimbabwe has now adopted a programme for the development of a National Water Resources Management Strategy (den Tuinder et al, 1995; Calder, 1997), supported by four national donor organizations, GTZ, DGIS, NORAD and DFID. The programme has a wide remit to develop a new Water Act and the structure for the proposed new Zimbabwe National Water Authority (ZINWA) and to develop a strategy consistent with UNCED and SAP principles.

Malawi: Land Use Change and Lake Levels

Malawi, a country with a fifth of its area occupied by Lake Malawi, the fifth-largest lake in Africa and one of the deepest, usually regards and presents itself as a country well endowed with water resources. If it were true, it would be fortunate, as the economy of the country is heavily reliant on its water resources and the lake. Virtually all the country's electricity is generated from hydroelectric schemes on the Shire River, which drains the lake. The fishing industry on the lake provides most of the country's protein food supply. The tourism industry is centred on the lakeside hotels. The ecology of the lake is unique, containing many hundreds of species of cichlid fish and ranks high in the UNESCO classification of World Heritage sites. The lake also provides an important national and international network for water-borne transport. But sadly the sanguine view presented of a country with secure and abundant water resources is a chimera.

Although the functioning of the lake is so critical to the viability of Malawi, until recently little was known about the reasons for the large changes in lake level that have occurred over the last 100 years for which records exist. For example, during the early 20th century there was no outflow from the lake and it became an inland drainage system. Various explanations have been put forward to account for these changes including tectonic movement, blockage of the lake outlet and linkages with sunspot cycles.

To address this issue, a team of researchers from the UK and hydrologists from the Water Department of the Ministry of Works in Lilongwe carried out a water-balance modelling study of the lake using the historic rainfall and lake-level data. The study was carried out to determine the cause of these changes and to determine to what extent these changes in level might have been the result of land-use changes, the most significant of which has been the clearance of the dry deciduous miombo woodland for rain-fed agriculture.

The evaporation model which was developed (Calder et al, 1995) considered the catchment to be composed of one of three surface types – forest, agricultural land or water. Values for the parameters for the model were derived from previous land-use evaporation studies carried out in India.

Using the recorded rainfall data for the previous 100 years, and by applying the present relationship between lake level and the outflow from the lake (stage/discharge relationship) for the whole period, the model was set up to generate predicted lake levels. With a value of 64 per cent for the forest coverage of the catchment, this model was able to describe well most of the major fluctuations in level during the period from 1896 to 1967, both seasonally and annually (Figure 6.1). (An exception was a period in the 1930s when the stage/discharge relationship for the lake may have been affected following a prolonged period of no outflow in the early part of the century.)

The overall agreement between prediction and observation indicated that variations in rainfall alone, without invoking any other changes in either evaporative demand or the hydraulic regime of the lake or other esoteric explanations such as sunspot cycles, was sufficient to explain lake level changes during this period.

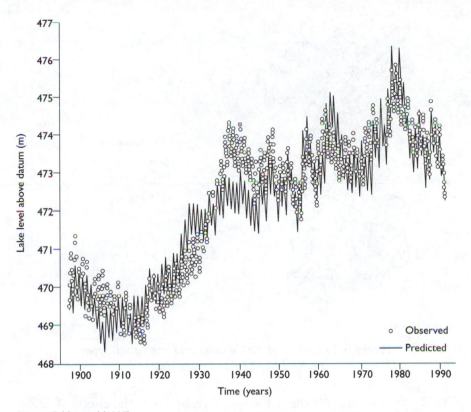

Source: Calder et al (1995)

Figure 6.1 *Lake Malawi levels: observed and predicted*

For the more recent period, model predictions which take into account a decrease in forest cover of 13 per cent over the period 1967–1990 (consistent with measurements of the decrease in forest cover for this period) agree well with observations both annually and seasonally. Without this decrease in forest cover, it is predicted that the lake level would have been almost 1m lower than that actually observed before the onset of the southern African drought of 1992. As the country is reliant on the lake for hydroelectricity generation, fisheries, tourism and transport, any further lowering of the lake level would have caused much more serious disruption, implying a significant benefit to water resources of the removal of the miombo woodland.

The model has also been used, in association with the development of a Water Resources Management Strategy for Malawi, to investigate how proposed irrigation developments would affect the water balance of the lake and lake levels (Calder and Bastable, 1995).

The modelling methodology used for Malawi has been extended through the use of geographic information system (GIS) methods to allow the convolution of rainfall and climate patterns with patterns of land use in Sri Lanka, the lowlands of the UK (Calder et al, 1997b) and in the Lake Malawi and Zambezi Basins (Figures 6.2 and 6.3).

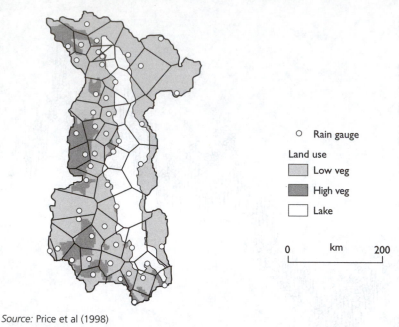

Source: Price et al (1998)

Figure 6.2 *Location of rain gauges and vegetation types on the Lake Malawi catchment*

The Zambezi Basin study shows the spatial variability in the effects of deforestation on runoff (Table 6.1). The change in mean annual runoff expected as a result of a 1 per cent reduction in the natural forest cover of the major sub-catchments of the Zambezi ranges from zero for the Rioc (where mean annual runoff is zero) to 3.33mm for Malawi.

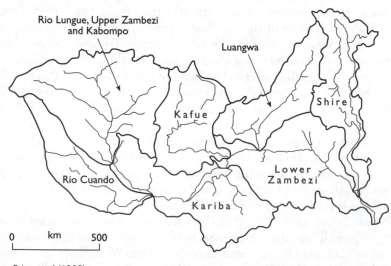

Source: Price et al (1998)

Figure 6.3 *Zambezi catchment and major sub-catchments*

Table 6.1 *Average change in mean annual runoff expected as a result of clearance of the natural forest for rainfed agriculture on the major subcatchments of the Zambezi*

Subcatchments of the Zambezi	Catchment Area (km²)	Increase in Mean Annual Runoff for a 1% reduction in natural forest cover (mm)
Lungwé Bungo, Kabompo and tributaries		2.87
Chobe	133,593	0.00
Kariba (tributaries between Victoria Falls and Kariba Dam)	223,364	0.74
Kafue	157,638	2.66
Luangwa	149,438	2.86
Shire	157,231	3.33
Lower Zambezi	237,393	2.05

Source: Price et al (1998)

These GIS developments should provide not only more accurate predictions of the hydrological impacts of land-use change, but also a more general modelling approach for investigating forest/land-use impact problems worldwide.

A general feature of these studies is that the conversion of indigenous forest to rain-fed agriculture, whether in the wet or dry climatic regions of the world, is likely to result in an increase in annual runoff. Recognition of the impacts of land-use change is therefore important in both assessing and managing fresh water resources, whether at the local or regional scale.

India: Eucalyptus, Irrigation, Power and Water Resources

The complexity and interrelations of water resources, and social, economic and political dimensions related to land use, reach extreme proportions in India. The tensions and passions generated by the issues are manifest at all scales. Without the strong framework of India's federal government, the conflicts between the states of Karnataka and Tamil Nadu over the sharing of the waters of the Cauvery River may well have escalated. Groundwater tables are dropping in most Indian states, mostly as result of increased groundwater abstractions. The largest volume of the abstraction is directed to the agricultural sector for irrigation. To provide the power for pumping the water from the ground to the surface, up to two-thirds of all the electric power generated in some southern Indian states is used for this purpose alone. These rates of abstraction are clearly unsustainable and may be causing damage to some aquifers where, through compaction, their physical properties are being permanently altered. Yet at present there are neither legal nor economic controls nor the political will to address the situation. There are neither licensing arrangements for borehole drilling nor requirements for obtaining a water right for abstracting groundwater. Economic controls are minimal as the farmers receive the electric power at heavily subsidized rates and there are also many cases of illegal connections and farmers receiving power without any payment. The political will to address the situation is largely absent as politicians rely on the farmers' vote for their support. The situation is in desperate need of the blue revolution, an integrated approach to resource management, but the two triggers for the revolution, an official recognition of the problem and the will to tackle it, are not in place.

The Eucalyptus Concern

Other land-use and water resource issues have been well recognized in India, one of the 'hottest', not only in India but worldwide, being related to the hydrological impacts of *Eucalyptus* species. Approximately half of all plantation forestry in the tropics and sub-tropics is composed of *Eucalyptus* species. Their high growth rates and their ability to grow within a wide range of site conditions make them attractive species for both commercial and social forestry applications.

The large-scale planting of such exotic species has aroused deep-seated anxieties in India and in many other tropical countries. Eucalyptus plantations were thought to cause serious socio-economic problems at the village level and adverse environmental impacts, particularly in relation to high water use, erosion and nutrient depletion. They were often presented as the principal culprit for the lowering of groundwater tables. The uncertainty and the worries that existed are illustrated in 'The Tree that Caused a Riot' (*New Scientist*, 18 February 1988).

In the absence of hard evidence to the contrary, speculation by the press and by some local environmental groups raised the controversy to such a pitch that in parts of Karnataka State in southern India, farmers ripped out eucalyptus seedlings from government nurseries and plantations. Yet other farmers in Karnataka saw eucalyptus as a valuable source of income and were keen to plant it in their fields (Plate 6.2). And eucalyptus trees can have other benefits. As providers of a fast-growing source of timber, firewood and pulp, they can help to reduce the pressure on the few remaining indigenous forests as wood sources and thus aid conservation efforts. Through saving foreign exchange on the importation of pulp they have obvious economic benefits.

Clearly, information was required on the potential hydrological impacts so that decisions could be made in the context of IWRM. As a result of a comprehensive research programme and detailed studies in India, South Africa, South America and Australia, hard evidence now exists on the hydrological impacts of these plantations. The results do not show *Eucalyptus* species to be quite as villainous as they have often been portrayed, but neither do they show them to be without hydrological disbenefits. What they do show is a complex pattern of interactions, some of which may be seen as beneficial and others as

Plate 6.2 *Bark stripping after felling eucalyptus plantations*

adverse. Although the research providers have done their work and major advances in knowledge have been achieved, the use of this knowledge for land management purposes has been less spectacular. This is perhaps unsurprising as the issues are complex and the tools for holistic resource management (see Chapter 7) have only recently been developed.

Eucalyptus species are beneficial in having high plot water use efficiencies. They probably produce more biomass per unit of water evaporated on a plot basis than any other tree species. Their high growth rates make them very attractive plantation species and in some countries, such as Australia, their ability to reduce and hold down water tables is a very great advantage in salinity control. Offsetting these advantages is the high water consumption, which needs to be considered together with other socio-economic and environmental factors. The challenge for future forest managers and hydrologists is to design sustainable forestry systems for *Eucalyptus* species which minimize some of the adverse hydrological impacts that have been identified, whilst being compatible with the social and economic needs of the local people. All this needs to be set within the context of integrated water resource management.

An outline of the research findings from one study directed at resolving the eucalyptus concern is given below.

Land Use and Water Resource Field Study in Karnataka

To answer the questions raised about the environmental impacts of fast-growing tree plantations, and to devise ways in which some of the adverse effects could be minimized, studies of the hydrology of eucalyptus plantations, indigenous forest and an annual agricultural crop were initiated at four main sites in Karnataka.

Three of these sites were in the low-rainfall zone (800mm per annum) at the Devabal and Puradal experimental plantations near Shimoga and the Hosakote experimental plantations near Bangalore. The soils were of different depths, approximately 3m at Devabal and Puradal and greater than 8m at the Hosakote site. The fourth site was at Behalli in the high rainfall zone (2000mm per annum) on deep soils (greater than 8m) (Figure 6.4).

The research was carried out jointly by Indian and British organizations, the Karnataka Forest Department, Mysore Paper Mills and the University of Agricultural Science, Bangalore, in India, and the Institute of Hydrology and the Oxford Forestry Institute in the UK.

Measurements were made of the meteorology, the plant physiology, soil water status, rainfall interception and the direct water uptake of individual trees using tracing measurements. Measurements were also made of the growth rates of the trees.

Water Use Results

Although the different experimental methods for determining water use operated over different time and space scales, the water use measurements obtained from the physiological, soil moisture, interception and tracing studies were generally much the same at all the sites. The deuterium tracing method, developed during the Karnataka project, proved to be a very effective and powerful method for determining transpiration rates of whole trees. This new

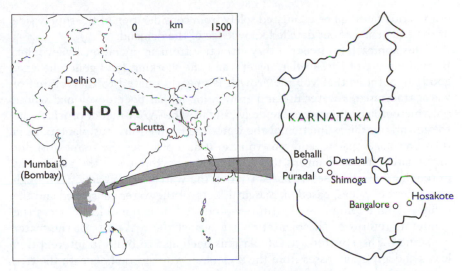

Figure 6.4 *Location of the eucalyptus environmental impacts study sites in Karnataka, southern India*

method revealed a surprisingly 'tight' and simple relationship between the individual tree transpiration rate for young eucalyptus trees and the cross-sectional areas of their trunks (see Chapter 3, Figure 3.5). The relationship implies that, irrespective of the size of tree, sap velocities are the same. As water in the soil becomes scarce and water stress develops, the same linear relationship between transpiration rate and basal cross-sectional area appears to hold, even though the sap velocity decreases. This finding, together with the empirical relationship that in water-limited conditions volume growth is related to the volume of water transpired, provided the basis for a simple water use and growth (WAG) model (Calder, 1992b) that is applicable in India and other water-limited parts of the semi-arid tropics. Conventional methods for estimating the water use of vegetation are based on the assumption that evaporation is primarily determined by meteorological 'demand', a function of solar radiation and atmospheric temperature, humidity and turbulence. Conventionally the 'supply' side of the equation, where regulation is imposed through stomatal controls exerted by the plants, is considered to be of secondary importance. In temperate conditions where generally neither atmospheric demand is very great nor soil water severely limiting, these methods are very appropriate and successful. In the dry zones of India, on the other hand, it appears that the roles are reversed: water supply rather than meteorological demand primarily determines evaporation. The restrictions imposed by soil water availability, and for the young eucalyptus plantations, tree size, are so profound that, on a day-to-day basis, they limit the amount of evaporation that can take place. During the Indian dry season the meteorological demand imposed by the hot dry climate is far in excess of the water supply. Although the meteorological demand provides the energy and driving force for evaporation, it does not, when viewed over time scales of a few days, control the evaporation rate. This implies that for these supply controlled conditions, evaporation rates can be estimated solely from consideration of the supply side of the equation without detailed knowledge of the demand.

This approach is of course very attractive from an operational viewpoint. By making use of these relationships and the working (and generally very good) hypothesis that volume growth is linearly related to the volume of water transpired, a water use and growth model has been developed whose only meteorological input is the daily rainfall. The WAG model provides the framework for the estimation of the water use from eucalyptus plantations in relation to age, spacing and growth rate. It also provides the framework for investigating the mechanisms that control the growth rates of the plantations in relation to water use – what is termed the water use efficiency. Through assignment of values, based on marginal costs, of the water consumed and the value per unit volume of the timber produced, it is possible to assess the economic returns of the plantation set against the real costs of the water consumed. These water-use calculations need also to build in interception losses and any other losses from the understorey or bare soil beneath the tree canopy. One feature of eucalyptus plantations is that although water consumption is high, transpirational water use efficiency is also high, so that for a given amount of water transpired the volume of timber produced is probably as high as that from any tree species. Bearing in mind that interception losses and understorey losses are essentially a 'fixed overhead' loss per year of water not usefully employed, the high growth rates of *Eucalyptus* species means that these overheads are a small proportion of the total water consumed. On a plot basis the water use efficiency is probably as high if not higher than that of any known tree species.

The main water use findings were as follows:

• In the dry zone, the water use of a young eucalyptus plantation on medium-depth soil (3m) was no greater than that of the indigenous dry deciduous forest.
• At these sites, the annual water use of eucalyptus and indigenous forest was equal to the annual rainfall (within the experimental measurement uncertainty of about 10 per cent).
• At all sites, the annual water use of forest was higher than that of annual agricultural crops (about twice that of finger millet).
• At the dry zone, deep soil (greater than 8m) site, the water use over the three (dry) years of measurement was greater than the rainfall. Model estimates of evaporation were 3400mm as compared with 2100mm rainfall for the 3-year period. These results were later confirmed by an experiment carried out on an adjacent 'farmer's field', where measured soil moisture depletion patterns under eucalyptus from the date of planting were shown to be much greater than those under other tree species (Figure 6.5). They indicated that roots were penetrating the soil at a rate exceeding 2.5m per year and were able to extract and evaporate an extra 400–450mm of water in addition to the annual input of rainfall.
• At none of the sites was there any evidence of root abstraction from the water table. Where this has happened in Australia at a site where the

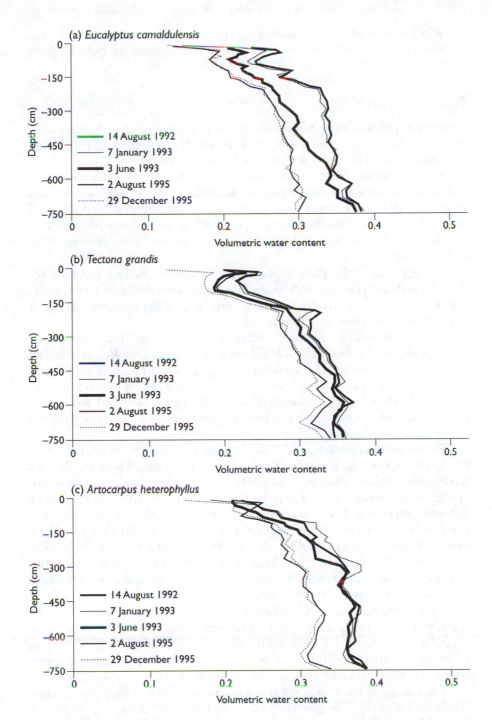

Figure 6.5 *Volumetric water content profiles recorded beneath the*
Eucalyptus camaldulensis, Tectona grandis *and* Artocarpus heterophyllus
plots, Hosakote, India

water table is relatively shallow, there are reports of annual eucalyptus water use of 3600mm in areas where the rainfall is only 800mm (Greenwood et al, 1985).

Erosion Results

Contrary to previous expectations and earlier published results, the Karnataka study established that some tree species are much worse than others in their potential for inducing raindrop splash-induced soil erosion.

Measurements of the modification of raindrop size by different tree canopies were obtained using a purpose-built, opto-electronic device known as an optical disdrometer. Its use in India immediately provided new and hitherto unforeseen results on drop-size modification and erosion potential that have great relevance to the choice of tree species for erosion-sensitive environments.

Experiments at the Puradal and Hosakote sites show that not only are there large differences in the drop-size spectra beneath different tree species, but that each species, irrespective of the drop size of the incident rain, has a characteristic spectrum (see Figure 1.5).

For the three different trees studied, Caribbean pine (*Pinus caribaea*), eucalyptus (*Eucalyptus camaldulensis*) and teak (*Tectona grandis*), the median volume drop diameters of the through-fall ranged from 2.3mm to 4.2mm. The corresponding drop kinetic energies beneath the different trees, assuming that the drops reach terminal velocity, differ by a factor of about nine between Caribbean pine with the lowest kinetic energies and teak with the highest kinetic energies.

The erosivity of natural rainfall is related to its intensity. As rainfall intensity increases, the size of raindrops generally increases also. There is a defined relationship between drop size and rainfall intensity from which the erosivity of the characteristic spectra may be related to the erosivity of rainfall of different intensities. The characteristic spectra for Caribbean pine, eucalyptus and teak correspond to the spectra of natural rainfall that would be expected with intensities of 48mmh^{-1}, 200mmh^{-1} and an essentially infinite rainfall intensity, respectively. These intensities can be interpreted as the 'break even' intensities at which the erosive power of rainfall of higher intensity would be moderated by the canopy.

Clearly, the canopies of Caribbean pine and eucalyptus, species exotic to India, will have a moderating effect for high-intensity storms. But there is no naturally occurring rainfall intensity for which the indigenous teak can exert a moderating effect; it will always produce a modified spectrum for drops falling at terminal velocity that is more erosive than the natural rainfall.

The canopy of the tree is not the only canopy affecting drop-size modification and erosion. The presence of an understorey canopy, close to the ground where drops cannot reach terminal velocities, is very effective in ameliorating splash-induced erosion. Where the understorey has been removed through fire or biological competition, the potential for erosion is very much increased (see Plate 1.1).

Water Use Efficiency

The recognition that water is a valuable resource in its own right and that forests generally evaporate more water than other crops, provides a powerful incentive for trying to improve the water use efficiency of plantation forests.

Both growth rates and water use efficiency of the eucalyptus plantations in the dry zone in India are low by world standards. To some extent climatic factors, which are not amenable to manipulation, are responsible for the low water use efficiencies. (High vapour pressure deficits as a result of increasing atmospheric demand are known to decrease water use efficiency, while high temperatures, leading to high rates of maintenance respiration, also have a depressing effect on water use efficiency.) Nevertheless, it is believed that there is still great potential for improvements through, for example, species selection, removing nutrient and water stress, and improved silvicultural practices such as optimal spacing and weeding.

These aspects were studied in a controlled environment facility at the Hosakote site where three tree species – *Eucalyptus camaldulensis*, *Tectona grandis* and an indigenous species *Dalbergia sissoo* – were grown on 10x10-m plots under different conditions of water and nutrient stress. The different stresses were imposed by water treatments of 0, 2.5, 5.0 and 7.5mm applied each day, irrespective of rainfall, through a drip irrigation system and nutrient treatments of zero, one and four times a standard application rate, applied in the dry form on all plots twice a year.

Results from the first two years of the experiment showed up to five-fold increases in growth rates on plots which received both water and fertilizer treatments compared with the control plots (Figure 6.6). Although water applications alone lead to large increases in growth rate, there was no evidence to show that purely transpirational water use efficiency was improved.

Water Resource Implications

The hydrological studies carried out in southern India on plantations of exotic tree species, indigenous forest and an agricultural crop show a varied and complex pattern of hydrological impacts. In summary, the water resource implications of afforestation with exotic species are as follows:

- **Erosion** The net rainfall size spectra associated with such exotic species as *Pinus caribaea* or *Eucalyptus camaldulensis* make their plantation preferable, from a soil conservation perspective, to T. grandis, which has a characteristic net rainfall spectrum of potentially much greater erosivity. The common occurrence of fires beneath teak plantations, which destroys the protective understorey, is another reason for not planting teak on sites sensitive to erosion.
- **Water use** At the Devabal and Puradal sites where the water use of eucalyptus plantations has been compared with that of indigenous forest, there is no evidence that Eucalyptus species use more water than the indigenous dry deciduous forest. They do, nevertheless, use more water than a typical annual crop – about twice as much as ragi, a finger millet.

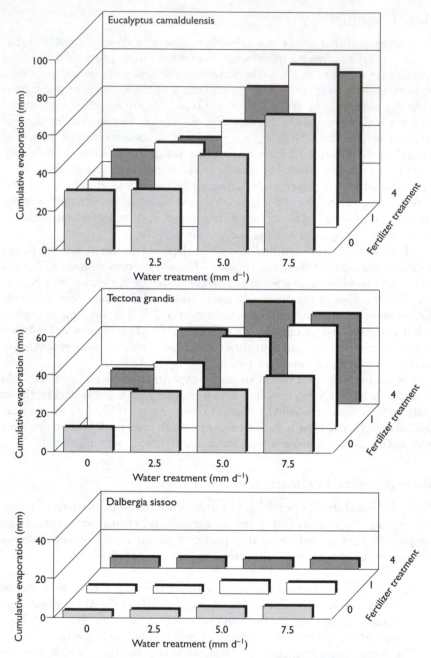

Figure 6.6 *Stand volumes recorded in September 1993 for*
Eucalyptus camaldulensis, Tectona grandis *and* Dalbergia sissoo
(top to bottom) for a range of water and fertilizer treatments

- **Water use** The Hosakote findings, which show much higher water use from young eucalyptus plantations than from young plantations of other tree species, and water use greater than the rainfall input, have important and serious water resource implications.
- **Water use efficiency** Although the water use of eucalyptus plantations is much higher than that of other tree species, the water use efficiency, expressed on a plot basis, is also much greater for the eucalyptus plantations. For the same amount of water consumed, on a plot basis, a higher return in terms of useful biomass will be achieved from the eucalyptus plantations.

Sustainable Management Systems

From the research experience outlined earlier, it is suggested that the potentially adverse aspects of plantation forest practices can be curtailed through the adoption of the following:

- **Rotation** Where soil water 'mining' occurs, then one strategy which may prove advantageous, particularly on deep soils, would be to rotate eucalyptus with agricultural crops. A five-year period under an agricultural crop should allow the soil water reserves, depleted by say ten years of forestry, to be replenished. From studies in other arid zones of the world, there is evidence that deep-rooted trees bring up nutrients from deep soil layers to the surface. If this is true of *Eucalyptus* species in India, then there would be dual benefits from rotation; the trees would replace nutrients the agricultural crops remove whilst the agricultural crops would replace water that the trees have removed.
- **Patchwork Forestry** The forest water use results indicate that recharge to the groundwater under large areas of either plantation or indigenous forest in the dry zone in India is likely to be small and will not, on average, be more than 10 per cent of the rainfall. However, if plantation forests were grown as a 'patchwork', interspersed with annual agricultural crops, much of the adverse effects on the water table would be alleviated as up to half the annual rainfall should be available for recharge under the agricultural crops.
- **Irrigation** In theory it would be possible to optimize a 'patchwork' design with irrigated areas of forestry. Using irrigation, it should be possible to grow the same volume of timber on one-fifth to one-tenth of the usual land area, leaving the rest for rain-fed agriculture. There may also be economic advantages of this type of scheme. If the plantations were located close to the pulp mills, transport costs would be minimized, which could halve total production costs.

AUSTRALIA AND SALINIZATION

Background

Salinity and its avoidance or management has been an enigma in Australia. On one hand there has been a wide understanding of the inherently salty nature of the environment and the inevitability of salinity. On the other, there has been a high propensity to ignore the problem and believe that for some reason salinity will not develop in any specific area.

This quotation (Robertson, 1996) is a vivid illustration of the frequently occurring situation worldwide where, when land use and water resources decisions need to be taken promptly, and although there is no lack of research or knowledge, the issues are fudged and deferred. No rational reasons are given, although self-interest and short-termism may be suspected.

Robertson makes the case that the early explorers in Western Australia regularly encountered and reported saline land and water: 'with exception of rivers flowing out from the Darling Ranges, WA rivers are beds of salt, pools of brine and brackish water'. The relationship between land clearing and salinity was widely recognized by the turn of the century – where natural forests on catchments had been ringbarked, increased salinity had been recorded in streams and reservoirs. In an early publication, Wood (1924) clearly demonstrated that there was both salt stored within the landscape and in groundwaters and that when native vegetation was cleared, this resulted in increased salts in the upper soil horizons and surface water.

Robertson concluded 'Unfortunately, despite this and a more of knowledge, research and experience, the "not here" syndrome has prevailed and we are still seeing salinity expand'. Some authorities ominously believe that if steps are not taken quickly, as much as 48 per cent of Australia's agricultural land will go out of production, irreversibly, within the next few decades.

The Salinization Process

It is now generally believed that salinization of the landscape has occurred over geological timescales. Windblown salts from the ocean and salt in rainfall have led, in the generally low-rainfall and high-evaporation climate of much of Australia, to a gradual build up of salt in the soil profile. Hingston and Gailitis (1976) showed that accretion of salt from oceanic aerosols was between 100–200kg ha^{-1} yr^{-1} in high-rainfall coastal areas, falling to 10–20kg ha^{-1} yr^{-1} at a distance of 300km from the coast. At these rates of accretion 10,000 years would have been sufficient to account for the measured salt concentrations in the coastal zone, but continuous accretion from the late Pleistocene would have been necessary to account for the measured concentrations in the more arid interior. The indigenous *Eucalyptus*-dominant vegetation, widespread over much of Australia, has established an evaporative regime that is in almost exact balance with the rainfall input. The balance is such that salts within the root zone are flushed through to the saline water table below, but the evaporation rate from the natural forest is sufficient to prevent the water tables rising, either into the root zone and killing the vegetation, or rising to the surface and seeping into watercourses. In this precariously balanced ecosystem, human intervention has had serious consequences. Clearance of the indigenous forest has realized the danger of raised water tables leading to incidents of saline seeps developing in low-lying areas where the water tables reach the surface. The huge civil engineering exercises of the 1950s and 1960s, sometimes, as in the Snowy Mountains Project, involving the reversal of flow direction of the rivers, have resulted in mixed blessings. Although in the short term, agricultural productivity has been increased, this has been at the expense of longer-term environmental and ecological damage. Excess irrigation waters from these schemes are a major contributing factor to higher water tables, increased leaching of salts into the watercourses and the possible irreversible damage that is being done to the ecology and environmental health of the major river systems such as the Murray-Darling.

Management Options

A range of options has been recognized as beneficial in controlling and, hopefully, reducing dry-land and river salinity. These options can loosely be grouped under three headings: land management, engineering solutions and economic tools.

Land Management

Replanting trees and shrubs in the recharge areas of a catchment will increase the evaporation, through increased interception and probably also increased transpiration, and reduce recharge and groundwater levels. This will alleviate salinity problems in seepage areas by both lowering water tables and lowering the level at which seepage takes place, hence reducing the land area affected, and also by reducing the volume of seepage waters. The Western Australian Department of Agriculture (1988) recognizes that while it may not be economic to carry out large-scale planting, it recommends planting on identified specific recharge areas within a catchment, especially if these areas are small and do not produce economic crops. In and around the highly saline seepage areas, replanting with salt-tolerant shrubs such as saltbush (*Atriplex*) for forage production has been advocated (Malcolm, 1990) and is being incorporated into whole farming systems.

In areas where dry-land salinity problems are less extreme, changes in cropping pattern have been advocated. The replacement of shallow-rooted grasses with deep-rooted alfalfa was found to be very effective for salinity control in the Northern Great Plains of the USA (Halvorson and Reule, 1980). In Australia the growing of deep-rooted lupins in the rotation of grain crops has been advocated rather than short-rooted clover, for the same reasons. Perennial pasture has also been shown to be effective in reducing recharge. A rotationally grazed stand of lucerne used 433mm of water annually compared with 231mm for an adjacent wheat crop (Western Australia Department of Agriculture, 1988).

Engineering Solutions

The state and federal governments of Australia have traditionally favoured engineering solutions to control salinity problems. Various engineering schemes have been tried or proposed. These include the interception of saline groundwaters and the diversion of the excess water (returns) from irrigation schemes to evaporation pans or directly to the major rivers, such as the Murray River. Direct pumping of groundwater to lower water tables has also been tried with some success in some agricultural areas, but a major problem with this type of solution is the disposal of the saline effluents. Disposal to rivers is the common option, but often serves only to salinize the vital water supply for the less fortunate users who happen to be located downstream. If downstream users also drain their fields or pump groundwater in a similar fashion, rivers will undergo progressive salinization until their ecology is destroyed and lower reaches become unfit for human use or irrigation. Piping the effluents for discharge into the sea has been considered, but is generally thought not to be cost effective. The combination of engineering solutions with land use management has been claimed to be most effective. Some success in salinity control in the wheat belt of Australia has been obtained through the combined use of land drains for groundwater interception together with eucalyptus plantations in recharge areas.

Economic Tools

In most countries irrigation water has an artificially low price (see Chapter 4) and is heavily subsidized by governments. Australia is no exception. In the early 1990s subsidization was of the order of A\$300 million a year (Simmons et al, 1991). Increasingly it is recognized that subsidized and low prices for water lead to inefficiencies in use that contribute to waterlogging and salinization problems. Increasing the price for irrigation water is one method that can be adopted for encouraging efficient water use. In Victoria, gravity surface water supplies were being charged at A\$12.0 per 1000m^3 in the early 1990s, but the policy is now to increase charges at 2 per cent above inflation until the full supply cost of A\$22.5 (at 1989 values) is reached (Evans and Nolan, 1989).

Another method, which has been used in the USA and also in some states of Australia, is the transferable water entitlement (TWE) or transferable water right. This is a mechanism by which a market for water can be achieved by allowing entitlements to be bought and sold without the necessity of buying and selling the accompanying land. The use of the mechanism is expected to increase efficiencies in a number of ways, including the transfer of water to higher-value uses and higher-valued crops. It is also expected to lead to the increased adoption of water-saving irrigation technologies, because the saved water can then be sold. Decreased use of irrigation of unsuitable land and where economic returns are low, perhaps because of existing water-logged or salinized conditions, might also be anticipated.

Another economic tool involves salinity credits. The theory is that the Murray-Darling Basin States can earn salinity credits by carrying out land management and engineering schemes that reduce salinity in the Murray-Darling River. They can then construct drainage and aquifer pumping schemes which increase salinity in the river network, provided that the salinity increase does not exceed their credit. The flaw in this approach, as pointed out by Macumber (1990), is that the amount of salt that needs to be disposed of from the aquifers is far in excess of any possible credits that could be achieved.

Research and Integrated Management

Australia has committed much in the way of research funds to investigate and address the issue of salinization. The equity, economic, ecological and sustainability issues related to salinization are all researched and fairly well understood. However, although the technology and awareness are in place, the salinization problem has not even been contained let alone resolved.

Why this should be the case in one of the most environmentally and ecologically aware countries in the world is not immediately obvious, and does not augur well for the blue revolution. Where does the problem lie? Could it be that the direct incentives for the different stakeholders are not in place? Perhaps the farmer, attending a meeting on integrated catchment management and hearing about the benefits of land management as a means of salinization control, may ask himself on the way home 'what is in it for me?'. Why should he forgo production on his most productive land by planting trees when the benefits may well accrue not to him, but the landowners downslope? Or perhaps the farmer thinks that delaying another year will not make much difference and he can get another year's grain crop. Perhaps the politicians feel that there are no votes in pressing through measures which will cost their electorate hard cash in the short term – even though the long-term benefits are patently obvious to all.

This is perhaps the greatest challenge of the blue revolution: to develop methods to recognize and capture the human dimension and the aspirations and motivations of the different stakeholders. From an appreciation of the different viewpoints it may be possible to put in place management philosophies which can provide recognizable incentives to all parties. The Comprehensive Assessment of the Freshwater Resources of the World, produced for the Commission for Sustainable Development (UNDPCSD, 1997), hails the Murray-Darling Basin Commission as a successful example of the integrated water management approach:

The Murray-Darling Basin covers one-seventh of Australia, and accounts for half the country's gross agricultural production. As demands for water increased, reservoirs were constructed to increase the available supply to individual states. In recent years, use approached the sustainable yield of the basin as a whole, and pressure mounted for sharing the resource between jurisdictions. In 1985, a Basin Commission was formed and in 1989, agreement was reached on sharing. The next issue requiring resolution was soil salinity that had the potential to expand to 95 per cent of the total irrigated area within 50 years. The three upstream states were the primary beneficiaries of water diversion, while the damage caused by salinity was most severe in the downstream state. An agreement was reached on joint funding of remedial measures and collaboration was initiated, driven primarily from the community level. Action has been under way for four years, and the spirit of collaboration continues as a demonstration of integrated water management success.

This view is heartening and it is certainly to be hoped that the Commission is successful in its task. Unless this can be achieved and the issues are really handled and resolved in an integrated way, the ominous conclusions of Robertson, foretelling of an environmental disaster of enormous proportions, will almost certainly happen. There is clearly little time to waste if an irreversible disaster is to be prevented. Already some experts are proclaiming that the Murray-Darling basin is irretrievably lost as a fresh water system and that it should now be regarded as a saline conduit to remove irrigation drainage waters and saline seeps to the ocean.

USA: PIONEERING APPROACHES AND PRACTICE

The zeal of the pioneer is evident in North America's history of river and water resource management. The influence and dynamism of the engineering community in 'taming the river' and 'draining the swamp' was such that there are now more than 50,000 major engineering structures – dams of over 25 feet in height – within the USA and many of the major river systems have reaches which have been 'straightened' or canalized. The dams served the USA well in terms of flood control, water supply and hydroelectric generation. But by the late 1960s and early 1970s a new, more questioning, attitude towards the benefits of further engineering developments was beginning to influence decision-making. This coincided with the beginnings of the environmental movement, activism by conservationists and landowners, and a growing awareness of resource scarcity. The better appreciation of the environmental and social costs associated with many engineering developments has profoundly changed America's approach to these developments. Indeed, not only is it now more difficult to obtain the necessary agreements to allow new engineering developments, but in some cases river rehabilitation programmes have been initiated which are actively reversing the alterations that had been made to river and water resource systems, to pursue a more 'natural' environmental regime. Arguably, the USA, which was once at the vanguard of the engineering approach to water resource development, is now at the vanguard of the movement towards a more natural and more environmentally sustainable and socially acceptable water resource regime. The power of this new movement is evident through the new approaches demonstrated in the sustainable management of aquifer systems such as the Ogallala, the very strong environmental focus now displayed in the management of the Great Lakes, and the social and environmental orientation of both the Heritage Rivers Initiative and the Kissimmee River restoration programme, which are described below.

The American Heritage Rivers Initiative

In the State of the Union Address of 4 February 1997, President Clinton pledged:

> *Tonight, I announce that this year I will designate ten American Heritage Rivers, to help communities alongside them revitalize their waterfronts and clean up pollution.*

Following up on this pledge, President Clinton signed an executive order establishing the American Heritage Rivers Initiative (see Appendix 1, p315), a new programme to help communities restore and revitalize waters and waterfronts. The initiative has three objectives: natural resource and environmental protection, economic revitalization, and historic and cultural preservation. It encourages communities to come together around their rivers and develop strategies to preserve them. It was expected that Americans would look toward rivers as sources for improving community life and that the American Heritage Rivers Initiative would 'integrate the economic, environmental and historic preservation programs and services of federal agencies to benefit communities engaged in efforts to protect their rivers'.

The new approach was further illustrated in a later speech made in North Carolina (President Clinton, 30 July 1997), to designate 14 American Heritage Rivers:

> *Who are we, such brief visitors on this Earth, to spoil the rivers and other treasures that were here so long before we arrived? We must work together, as this community has done for generations, to preserve all these sacred gifts for all time.*

The American Heritage Rivers programme is structured to support 'outstanding community-based efforts designed to ensure the vitality of the river in community life for future generations'. It was set up as a locally driven programme on the assumption that the stakeholders, the local communities, 'know best what they need'.

Once a heritage river is designated, a full-time contact, called a 'River Navigator', coordinates efforts to match community needs with available resources from the existing programmes.

Kissimmee River Restoration

Before engineering works for flood control, the Kissimmee River meandered from its origin in Lake Kissimmee to the northern shore of Lake Okeechobee. The extensive 18,000-ha floodplains of this Florida river provided a wide range of wetland habitats with over 35 species of fish, 16 species of wading birds, 16 species of waterfowl, river otters, and many species of invertebrates, amphibians and reptiles.

The flood control project was conceived and designed between 1954 and 1960, a time which predated much of the environmental law that came about in the USA in the late 1960s and early 1970s: the Clean Water Act of 1972, the National Environmental Policy Act of 1969, and the Endangered Species Act of 1973.

At the time of authorization, and when construction began in 1961, environmental concerns were expressed, but governmental water resource management processes were, at that time, relatively single minded. The aim was simple: flood damage reduction in the most cost-efficient fashion.

That was what was done. As part of the Central and Southern Florida Flood Control Project, the US Army Corps of Engineers carried out the engineering works which improved the navigation and flood control by transforming the natural 166-km winding path of the Kissimmee River into a 90km long, 9m deep, 100m wide canal, known today as the C-38 canal.

The project hugely altered the hydrology and ecology of the river basin. It was widely seen as an environmental disaster and efforts to restore the river were being contemplated even before the project finished. The engineering works caused between 12,000 and 14,000ha of wetlands to drain and dry up, with the consequent loss of the wetland flora and fauna. The changes in the flow regime also created conditions suitable for invasive plant and animal species (many of which were regarded as pests). Disturbance has often been attributed as a causal factor in invasion either through natural disturbance or through human alteration to the natural system (Ewel 1986).

The Act of 1976 initiated a series of state and federal initiatives and research programmes aimed at gaining the knowledge required to restore the integrity of the river in order to retrieve some of the lost environmental benefits. After 15 years of research and planning, the state of Florida finally adopted, in 1990, the South Florida Water Management District's restoration plan and sought authorization and joint funding for the plan from the federal government.

With enactment of the 1992 Water Resources Development Act, Congress approved the Corps of Engineers' recommendation to undertake a river restoration programme, which was aimed, essentially, at getting the Corps to fill in the canal they had originally dug.

Source: Kissimmee River Restoration Project

Plate 6.3 *Kissimmee River, Florida, USA*

This, perhaps the world's first major watershed restoration project designed to reverse the impacts of earlier engineering works, is now underway. By March 2001, the first phase of the Kissimmee River Restoration Project had been completed. About 7.5 miles of the canal had been filled and new river flow-ways recreated to restore the 'braided river' floodplain marshes of the Kissimmee.

With regard to the Kissimmee River Restoration, M. K. Loftin, the Assistant Director of the Water Resources Division and Project Manager for the Kissimmee River Restoration, South Florida Water Management District, stated at the Kissimmee River Restoration Symposium, held in Orlando in October 1988, that 'environmental problems are emotional; environmental issues, political; and environmental solutions, technical' (EPA, 1992). More projects like the Kissimmee Restoration may be required to achieve the desired balance of economic, environmental and social objectives in IWRM.

LAND USE, PRODUCTION, THE ENVIRONMENT AND AMENITY IN THE UNITED KINGDOM

Although the earliest studies of water and land-use issues can perhaps be ascribed to Switzerland and France in the 19th century, followed in the early 20th century by Hubbard Brook in the USA, the UK began to make a significant contribution by the 1950s. The catchment studies in East Africa (Pereira et al, 1962) funded by the British ODA (in the early 1950s), the catchment and process studies initiated by Frank Law in the Yorkshire Pennines, and the later inception of catchment and process studies at Plynlimon and Thetford, were all seminal in the development of land-use/hydrological studies in the UK. The theoretical framework for measuring and estimating evaporation provided by Howard Penman and John Monteith, both Fellows of the Royal Society, established British science in this area, a contribution arguably unequalled anywhere else in the world. British scientists have also made major contributions to research into land use hydrology elsewhere in the world. The UK has also been a world leader in the development of methodologies for IWRM and was perhaps the first country to fund the development of modelling methodologies which link the water resource, economic and ecological aspects of land management (see Chapter 7).

Yet although the funding of research may be a requirement for proper water resource and land use management, is it sufficient? If the Rural White Paper on England (HMSO, 1995) is to be used as a criterion, the answer must be 'no'. Although this well-meaning White Paper captures the public desire for the amenity aspects of rural land use, there is a singular unawareness of the interlinking water resource issues. Is this the fault of the scientists for not disseminating their results or the policymakers for not taking the trouble to make themselves aware of them? Have the scientific results been poorly and ambiguously presented? Has there been a lack of involvement of stakeholders in defining and carrying out the research? Has the populist scientific press been slow to take up the issues? The answer is probably 'yes' to all these questions. Although all the ingredients have been present, the proper mix and end-product have not been obtained. The poor linkage between land-use research in the uplands and its application in land-use management is decried by Newson (1997) in his seminal book on land and water issues: *Land, Water and Development*. He states that:

> *three years after the acceptance of a paper on the hydrological impacts of afforestation in the UK by the hydrological community, the Secretary of State for the Environment in the UK Government made the following statement in Parliament: "As regards afforestation, its percentage and its effects on catchment areas...I am advised there is a lack of clear scientific evidence."* (*Hansard*, 21 March 1980)

Newson has attempted to 'put the knowledge base of hydrology in a policy context' through later publications (Newson, 1990, 1991, 1992b) and these have resulted in a slow, but measurable, policy readjustment to the original research. This book continues that theme in the hope that the UK, together with countries such as South Africa, can take benefit from the results of its own land-use research.

An outline of some of the contributions to land-use hydrological research, tracing the conflicts that have arisen in the uplands and lowlands of the UK and the development of modelling methodologies to assess the impacts of the land-use changes, are given below. The development of modelling methodologies for addressing forest-impact issues is given at some length as these methods have subsequently been found to have wide application and have formed the basis for land-use impact modelling in other temperate and tropical regions of the world.

Impacts of Water Resource Developments on the Environment

In recent years some of the most controversial water-related conflicts in the UK have arisen not so much from the effects of environmental and land-use changes on water resources, but from the effects of water resource developments on the environment and ecology.

Of particular concern have been the groundwater and river abstractions by water companies (see Chapter 4) which have led to low summer flows in rivers and, in some circumstances, dried-up river beds on what were normally perennial rivers. Increasingly, the water resource planner must really take into account and balance the needs of the environment with the economics of water resource developments and water demands (Smith, 1997). But this balance may not be easy to achieve. Foster and Grey (1997) state that sustainable groundwater management requires maximizing the use of aquifer storage to reduce water supply costs while limiting environmental impacts, and maximizing groundwater protection to reduce water supply treatments while not unduly restricting land-use activities. They argue that achieving this balance is difficult because groundwater systems are complex and sometimes slow to react to change.

Environmental bodies have been active in developing initiatives and programmes which are aimed at reducing the environmental impact of these actions. English Nature's wildlife and fresh water initiative details a plan of action for conserving Sites of Special Scientific Interest (SSSI), whilst the Ministry of Agriculture, Fisheries and Food has a water level management plan programme in force which is specifically directed at protecting wetland SSSIs. The Royal Society for the Protection of Birds (RSPB) has published a report entitled *Practical Implications of Introducing Tradable Permits for Water Abstractions*, which claims that the present method of regulating abstractions, using abstraction licensing, does little to discourage the wasteful use of water. Tradable permits for water abstractions would operate in a similar way to the transferable water entitlements or transferable water rights that are used in the USA and some states of Australia (see above), and would be expected to increase the efficiency and allocation of water use by farmers, some of whom presently have too much water and others not enough for their requirements. The RSPB believes that tradable permits would reduce the pressures on the environment and help maintain water levels at key wetland sites. Studies have been made to examine the practical extent to which water rights can be traded within the existing regulatory system, which have led to proposals being made to deregulate existing legislation to allow trading to proceed (Streeter, 1997).

Increasing pressure from the public and environmental bodies will ensure that land and water resource planners will have to take full account of nature conservation and the environment in all future planning decisions. The environment secretary has recently accepted recommendations from the Joint Nature Conservation Committee for the addition of 33 plant and animal species to the list of those receiving protection under the Wildlife and Countryside Act. This now includes water voles, whose range and numbers have declined rapidly because of the introduction of American mink. Developments which disturb the riverbank homes of water voles will now be illegal. But achieving the balance between water resource developments and the impacts of these developments on basin economics, ecology and the environment is clearly no easy task and tools are being developed (see Chapter 7) which can assist land-use and water resource planners in this task.

Upland Afforestation Conflicts

Since the mid-1950s, when Frank Law (Law, 1956), engineer to the Fylde Water Board, published the results of his studies from Stocks Reservoir in the Lancashire Pennines, a controversy has continued over the effects of upland afforestation on evaporation and the water resources of the UK. Originally, the concern centred on the effects of spruce afforestation of upland moorland water catchments that were being used for supply purposes; then, by the late 1970s, the deleterious effects of afforestation on hydroelectric power generation were recognized. By the late 1980s the hydrological effects of extensive larch plantations became an important issue: food surpluses being generated within the European Community had resulted in reduced subsidies to farmers and had consequently increased the probability of marginal agricultural lands (not always in the uplands) being afforested.

By the late 1970s, studies carried out by the Institute of Hydrology and other organizations had validated Law's conclusion of enhanced evaporation rates from upland forests. Nevertheless, doubts were expressed that because most of the experimental studies had been carried out in the relatively warm climates of Wales and England, primarily on grass and forest vegetation, the results could not necessarily be applied in Scotland. In Scotland the climate is cooler and snow can form a significant component of the annual precipitation, and heather rather than grass moorland predominates. Further studies, involving both process and catchment experiments were executed to quantify these effects through process studies at a number of upland sites and catchment experiments located at Balquhidder in central Scotland (Calder, 1990). Although quantity concerns were originally predominant, questions of water quality later came to the fore. In the high-pollution climate of the UK, the process responsible for the high evaporative losses from forests – enhanced aerodynamic transport arising because of the high aerodynamic roughness of forest canopies – is also responsible for the much higher rates of gaseous and particulate pollutant deposition to forests. These high deposition rates meant that forested catchments in the UK, and the streams emanating from them, were generally more acid, than those from upland grassland catchments.

Upland Land Use Research at Plynlimon

An example of the use of process studies in conjunction with catchment experiments to examine the effect on water use of land-use changes associated with forestry is provided by the studies carried out by the Institute of Hydrology at Plynlimon, Central Wales. The catchments are located at the source of the Rivers Wye and Severn in steep upland topography (Plate 6.4).

The annual precipitation is of the order of 2400mm (Table 6.2) and is distributed fairly evenly throughout the year. Most of the precipitation occurs as rain; the snow contribution is very variable, but averages 5 per cent per year. The rain is mostly of low intensity, generated from frontal systems enhanced by the orographic effect of the hills. Streamflow is perennial, although storm runoff forms a major proportion of the flow. The soils are predominantly peaty, overlying mudstone and shale drifts on the slopes. Peat of up to 3m in depth occurs on the hilltops and in the valley bottoms where it overlies glacially deposited boulder clay. The Wye catchment is under grass cover; 70 per cent of the Severn catchment is under coniferous forests, mostly Norway and Sitka spruce, with 30 per cent under moorland grass.

Plate 6.4 *The forested Severn catchment at Plynlimon, Central Wales*

Measurements at Plynlimon

At Plynlimon the processes controlling transpiration have been measured using a number of techniques. These include the use of a 'natural' lysimeter (see Plate 3.1), together with neutron probe and tensiometric measurements of soil moisture (Calder, 1990), plant physiological measurements of stomatal conductance and leaf water potential, and 'tree cutting' measurements of water uptake from excised trees (Roberts, 1978).

A number of techniques were also used to measure the evaporation arising from the proportion of the rainfall that is intercepted by the vegetation and re-evaporated before it reaches the ground, i.e. the interception. These techniques included conventional through-fall troughs and stem-flow gauges,

Table 6.2 *Measurements from the Plynlimon forest lysimeter, February 1974 to October 1976*

Period	Precipitation (mm)	Interception (mm)	Transpiration (mm)
6 Feb–31 Dec 1974	2328	685	289
1 Jan–31 Dec 1975	2013	529	335
1 Jan–1 Oct 1976	1103	366	277
Total	5444	1580	901

Note: The precipitation was recorded at the nearby Tanllwyth gauge within the Severn catchment.
Source: Calder et al (1982).

plastic-sheet net rainfall gauges (Calder and Rosier, 1976) and gamma transmission measurements (Calder, 1990).

Plynlimon Process Study Results

These process studies conclusively demonstrated that at Plynlimon the reduced runoff per unit area from the forested catchment is principally the result of the increased interception losses from the forest. The higher interception losses are generated because of the increased turbulence and lower aerodynamic resistance to the transport of water vapour and heat between the forest surface and the atmosphere. This leads to higher evaporation rates from the forest in wet conditions compared with grassland. The enhanced evaporation rates occur both during rainfall and immediately afterwards from the wetted vegetation surface; about half the interception loss occurs during rainfall.

The transpiration from the forest is typically about 10 per cent less than that from grassland as a result of physiological controls imposed by the forest (lower stomatal conductance). Because of the high and seasonally even rainfall climate at Plynlimon, periods with soil moisture deficits sufficient to limit transpiration are not common.

Upland Research and Land-use Evaporation Models

The two results – that interception losses from tall vegetation are likely to be greater than those from short vegetation and that, when soil moisture is non-limiting, forest transpiration is likely to be similar to but less than that from grass – have general significance. They can, with few qualifications, explain the results from the majority of the world's 'forest/grass' catchment experiments (see Hewlett and Hibbert, 1967). A third generalization, applicable in more arid regions where large soil moisture deficits occur, is that the greater rooting depth and the resultant greater soil water availability to forests compared with grass and agricultural crops, leads to higher transpiration rates from forests. So, during drought periods, evaporation losses from forests may also be higher than those from grasslands, but for different reasons.

The qualifications to these generalizations mainly concern the observations from four south-east Australian catchments (Langford, 1976) which, after forest fires, showed a decrease in runoff in subsequent years of 24 per cent compared with runoff from a catchment that escaped the fire. This apparently anomalous result, one of the few examples of forest removal decreasing runoff, was explained by Greenwood (1992) in terms of the unique forest structure. He pointed out that the forest, which was composed predominantly of exceptionally tall (98m) Eucalyptus regnans (some of the world's tallest trees), had a minimal canopy which reduced both interception and transpiration losses. Following the fire, the germination of seeds and the subsequent regrowth rapidly led to the leaf area per unit ground area exceeding that of the former forest canopy.

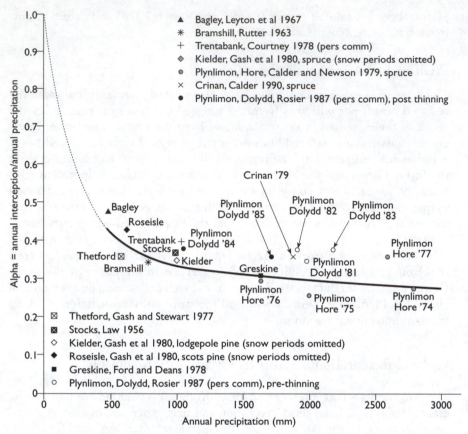

Figure 6.7 *Observations of the annual fractional interception loss from forests in the UK*

To make use of the upland land-use research findings for water resource management the development of evaporation models was required. The development of these models, which now have a much wider application outside the UK uplands, is described below.

The 1979 Forest Impact Model

Based on the upland research findings, a semi-empirical model was developed by Calder and Newson (1979) for estimating the annual and seasonal differences in runoff from afforested, upland catchments in the UK, which were previously under grass cover. These catchments receive rainfall throughout the year and periods with large soil moisture deficits are uncommon. This original forest-impacts model was parsimonious in both data requirements and in the number of model parameters, and was designed to be of practical value as an operational tool for water resource assessment. This ethos has been preserved in later developments of the model which now have a wider range of applications. The original (1979) model requires information on annual or daily rainfall, annual or daily Penman (E_T) estimates of evaporation, and the proportion of the catchment with complete canopy coverage.

For the calculation of annual evaporation, the assumptions inherent in the method are as follows:

- Evaporation losses from grassland are equal to the annual Penman potential transpiration estimate for grass, E_{Ta}.
- Transpiration losses from forest are equal to the annual E_{Ta} value multiplied by the fraction of the year that the canopy is dry.
- The annual interception loss from forest, with complete canopy coverage, is a simple function of the annual rainfall, P_a (Figure 6.7).
- Soil moisture deficits are insufficient to limit transpiration from grass or trees in this (wet) area of the UK.

This leads to the equation for the calculation of annual evaporation:

$$E_a = E_{Ta} + f(P_a\alpha - w_a E_{Ta})$$

where:
α = the interception fraction (35–40 per cent for regions of the UK where annual rainfall exceeds 1000mm),
w_a = the fraction of the year when the canopy is wet ($\sim 0.000122P_a$),
f = the fraction of the catchment area under forest cover.

Use of aerial photographs for upland UK forests has shown that, typically, for areas marked on maps as extensive forests, the f value is about 0.66; the remaining area comprises roads, gaps between forest blocks, riverbanks, clearings and immature plantations with unclosed canopies.

The Calder-Newson model indicates that in the wet upland regions of the UK, annual evaporation rates from forested catchments (with 75 per cent of their area afforested, equivalent to 50 per cent canopy coverage) may exceed those from grassland by 100 per cent and runoff will be reduced, typically by about 15–20 per cent.

This simple model has been used to investigate the effects on water supplies of afforesting the catchments of the major UK reservoirs. It was also used, in the early 1980s, to provide information for the Centre for Agricultural Strategy's investigations into the feasibility of proposals to increase greatly the proportion of upland forestry in Britain. It has been used subsequently in many studies into the effects of afforestation on water resources in the UK.

Annual Model: Forest/Heather/Grass

Research on the evaporative characteristics of heather (*Calluna vulgaris*) in the UK uplands has established that transpiration losses are lower, but interception losses greater, than those for grassland. These observations (Table 6.3) suggest that the annual interception losses from heather can be estimated from an equation of the form:

$$E_a = \beta E_{Ta}(1 - w_a) + \alpha P_a$$

where $\beta = 0.5$ and $\alpha = 0.2$.

This equation indicates that evaporation from grassland and heather moorland will be similar when both are growing in regions that experience an annual rainfall of about 1250mm. In regions with annual rainfall greater than this, the higher interception losses from heather will outweigh the reduced transpiration from the heather and the total annual evaporation from heather will be greater than that from grass; the converse is true for annual rainfall less than 1250mm.

Table 6.3 *Interception and transpiration observations for forest, heather and grass summarized in terms of the average interception ratio α, the daily interception model parameters, γ, δ, and the ratio of actual to Penman E_T evaporation, β*

Site	Period	Interception Parameters			Transpiration fraction (β)
		α	γ (mm)	δ (mm^{-1})	
Forest					
All sites interception: (Plynlimon, Dolydd, Crinan and Aviemore)		0.35	6.9	0.099	
Plynlimon Forest Lysimeter	1974–1976	0.3	6.1	0.099	0.9
Dolydd	1981–1983	0.39	7.6	0.099	–
Crinan	1978–1980	0.36	6.6	0.099	–
Aviemore	1982–1984*	0.45	7.1	0.099	–
Heather					
Model estimate derived using automatic weather station data and measured interception parameters	1981	–	2.65	0.36	
Crinan, neutron probe	1981–1983	–	–	—	0.58–0.67
Law's heather lysimeters	1964–1968	0.16	–	–	0.25–0.5
Sneaton Moor lysimeter	1980	0.19	–	–	0.25–0.5
Grass					
Wye catchment, Plynlimon (indicates annual evaporation consistent with Penman E_T)					1.0

Note: *Not including snow periods.
Source: Calder (1990)

Daily Model: Forest/Heather/Grass

To investigate the seasonal variation of the effects of a land-use change among forest, heather and grassland, the same approach was adopted with the incorporation of an interception model which operated on a daily timestep.

The model incorporated the two-parameter exponential relationship:

$$I = \gamma(1 - \exp(-\delta P))$$

where I is the daily interception loss (mm) and P is the daily precipitation (mm). With parameter values $\gamma = 6.91$ and $\delta = 0.099$, the model was found to fit well with coniferous forest interception losses recorded at a number of upland sites in the UK.

Seasonal evaporative losses were obtained by summing the daily evaporation estimates, E_d, as given by:

$$E_d = \beta E_T(1 - w) + \gamma(1 - \exp(-\delta P))$$

Here the transpiration is estimated as the product of β, termed the transpiration fraction, a climatologically derived daily Penman E_T estimate, and a term $(1-w)$ which represents the fraction of the day that the canopy is dry and is able to transpire (where w is the fraction of the day the canopy is wet = $0.045P$ for $P<22$mm; $w = 1$ for $P=22$mm). This equation has been validated by comparison with soil moisture and interception measurements at different sites in the uplands of the UK. Estimates of the parameters α, β, γ and δ for the different vegetation types and the sources from which they were derived are shown in Table 6.3.

Although the interception component of the model is based more on empiricism than theoretical reasoning, the parameters can be attributed some physical meaning. The γ parameter can be considered to represent the mean daily interception loss which would be obtained with an infinitely high value for the daily precipitation, essentially the maximum interception loss per day. The δ parameter governs the rate at which interception loss increases with increasing precipitation (whilst not allowing interception to exceed the precipitation). Consideration of more detailed experimental and physically based modelling studies of the interception process (Calder, 1996b; Calder et al, 1996), which led to the development of the two-layer stochastic interception model, allows further insights. This model, which takes into account the dependence of the rate of wetting of vegetation on drop size, indicates that the γ term will primarily be influenced by local climate and the aerodynamic and wetting properties of the canopy. The δ term will be controlled mainly by the wetting properties of the canopy. It is expected that from the knowledge gained from the further development and calibration of the more physically based interception models, it will eventually be possible to better identify the model parameters for use in operational evaporation models. These may take the form of the two-parameter exponential model or a 'collapsed' or simplified version of this model.

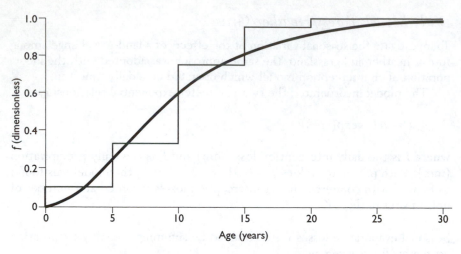

Figure 6.8 *'Effective' forest cover against age function*

The seasonal model, as for the annual model, is appropriate for conditions similar to those of the UK uplands where soil moisture stress is an infrequent occurrence. The model, as described, is strictly applicable only to mature stands of vegetation. For catchments with a high proportion of immature forest, it was suggested that, as a working hypothesis, the fractional canopy coverage parameter (f) could be related to age on the basis of an S-shaped function originally postulated by Binns (in Calder, 1990, p122). Suggested values for f for upland UK forests were $f = 0.1$ for trees aged 0–5 years, 0.33 (6–10 years.), 0.75 (11–15 years), 0.95 (16–20years) and 1.0 for trees older than 20 years (Figure 6.8).

The HYLUC Model

From these studies, evolved the HYdrological Land Use Change model (HYLUC), which now exists in a spatially distributed form that allows the convolution of rainfall and climate patterns with patterns of land use through linkage to a GIS. The HYLUC model also incorporates additional components which take into account the effects of limiting soil water availability on transpiration (not usually required in the wet uplands of the UK). It also includes an improved and more general method for estimating the w term, a growth function that allows the treatment of immature forests and an option to allow seasonal variability in the interception parameters.

Limiting Soil Water Availability The methodology for determining the effects on transpiration of soil moisture limitations follows the modelling approach used to describe the soil moisture regime under grassland sites (Calder et al, 1983) which used a moderating function (m) which limits as soil moisture is depleted, according to the relationship:

$m = 1$ (for $\delta s < {}^{s_m}2$)
$m = 2$ $(1 - {}^{\delta s}s_m2)$ (for $\delta s = {}^{s_m}2$)

where δs is the soil moisture deficit and the parameter s_m is the maximum available water and represents the asymptotic value towards which the soil moisture deficit approaches. (It may also be regarded as approximately the total water available in the profile to the crop between the 'field capacity' and 'wilting point' values.)

Wet Day Fraction (w) The fraction of the day for which vegetation canopies remain wet during and following rainfall was estimated simply from the ratio of the daily interception loss and the maximum daily interception loss, for the particular vegetation type, using the relationship:

$$w = \gamma(1?\exp(-\delta P))/\gamma$$
$$= 1-\exp(-\delta P)$$

Growth Function

To take into account the hydrological response of the forest in the HYLUC model in the early, immature phase of the forest cycle, a one-parameter function incorporating exponential terms has been used to describe the Binns sigmoidal function (Figure 6.8). The 'effective' fractional canopy coverage from fully forested plots is described by:

$$f = 1-\exp(-g_f a + 1-\exp(-g_f a))$$

where:
f is the 'effective' fractional canopy coverage,
g_f is a 'growth factor', taken as 0.00047 (d^{-1}),
and a is the age of the forest (d).

Following the reasoning used in the original derivation of the model, the 'effective' fractional canopy coverage over the whole catchment can then be calculated as:

$$f = f_a(1-\exp(-g_f a + 1-\exp(-g_f a)))u_j$$

where:
f is the 'effective' fractional canopy coverage of the catchment,
f_a is the fraction of the catchment area forested (fraction designated on a map as forest),
$(1-u_j)$ is the fraction of the forested area occupied by road and river channel borders and gaps in the forest, taken as one-sixth. (This compares with the value of one-third which was used in the earlier model when immature forest within the overall forested area was also included).

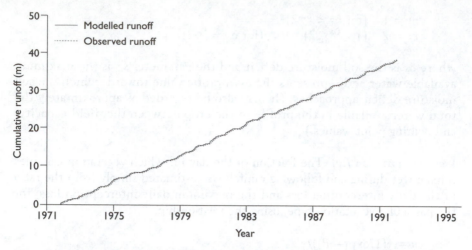

Figure 6.9 *Cumulative runoff observed and predicted with the GIS version of the HYLUC97 model for the forested Severn catchment at Plynlimon*

Seasonal Variability The 1997 version of the model (HYLUC97) also incorporated an option to allow seasonal variability in the interception parameters, which is particularly relevant to the treatment of deciduous forests.

Upland Forest Impact Predictions

Application of the GIS-linked versions of the models shows that they are able to describe changes in flow resulting from afforestation practices in both the Plynlimon experimental catchments (Figure 6.9) and for river catchments in Scotland (Figure 6.10).

The HYLUC97 model has also been applied to lowland forests in the UK, upland forests in New Zealand and variants of the model have been applied in Malawi and the Zambezi basin as described elsewhere in this chapter.

Trees and Drought: Lowland Conflicts

Quantity versus Quality

Among the recommendations of the UK Government's 1995 White Paper on Rural England (DOE, 1995) was a proposal to double the area of forests within England by the year 2045. The combination of this proposal together with government recognition of the real possibility of climate change resulting in hotter, drier summers and wetter winters, has raised questions (House of Commons, Environment Committee, 1996; DOE, 1997) concerning the possible impacts on UK water resources and the water environment of the combined effects of climate change and such a large change in land use.

Interactions between water quality and quantity were also recognized as an issue. Woodlands were thought to protect water supplies from nitrate

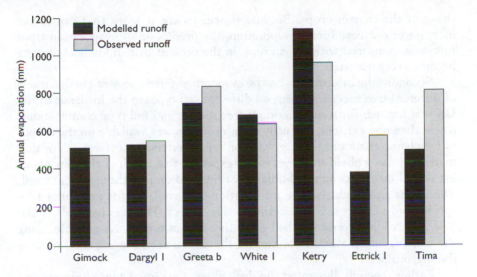

Figure 6.10 *Annual evaporation, modelled and observed, from seven upland forested catchments in the UK*

pollution associated with agriculture and the Forestry Commission argued that this expected benefit needed to be balanced against any reduction in water yield. Nitrate concentrations within UK groundwaters have been steadily rising over the past 20 years due to leaching losses from intensive agriculture. This trend was expected to continue for at least the next 10–15 years. Many sources, particularly those within the Triassic sandstone aquifer in the UK Midlands, were close to, or exceeded, the mandatory 50mg/litre standard for potable water. On the basis of the expected protection afforded by forests in relation to nitrate pollution, boreholes had been sunk within existing forest on the sandstone aquifer to tap the low-nitrate water (nitrate concentrations less than 10mg/litre) for blending purposes. The Forestry Commission's argument was that if it could be shown that significant recharge of low-nitrate water was occurring beneath the forest, the development of such sources could avoid the need for expensive nitrate removal treatment.

Clearly, to be able to follow the philosophy of ILWRM it is important to be able to assess the water quantity impacts of lowland afforestation both now and in the future, when climate change may have occurred, and to set these within the context of other water quality, environmental, economic and socio-economic impacts. Unfortunately, it was difficult to make an accurate prediction of the water quantity impacts of UK lowland afforestation, even under the present climate, for two reasons.

The first reason is that in the lowlands of the UK, both the effects of higher interception losses from forests and greater transpiration during dry periods are important, but neither predominates. Furthermore, in periods of no rainfall, but periods when soils are sufficiently wet to offer no restriction to the availability of soil water to either short crops or forests, it is usually found that forest transpiration rates are actually around 10 per cent less than those of the shorter crops. Because processes are at work that can either increase or decrease forest evaporation, the prediction of evaporation from forest, as compared with short crops, in the present British lowland climate becomes very uncertain.

Secondly, the information on the evaporative differences of combinations of different tree species growing on different soil types in the lowlands of the UK was limited. For some important tree species and soil type combinations, it was then non-existent. Virtually no information was available on the evaporative characteristics of trees growing on soils overlying sandstone, or for that matter on 'brownfield sites', yet it was expected that much of the new planting would take place in the Midlands of England on just these types of soil. There was also doubt, where information was available for particular tree species and soil types, as to whether it was correct. This was particularly the case for broadleaf forest on chalk soils; thus, it was not always possible, using the existing information, to be sure of the direction of the impact, let alone the magnitude.

Earlier research illustrated the difficulties. One important study, carried out at Thetford Forest in the east of England in the early 1980s (Cooper, 1980), showed that recharge under the pine forest was reduced by as much as 50 per cent compared with grassland. Here the trees were able to tap water from the underlying chalk, whereas the grass, because of shorter rooting, had limited access to water stored in the overlying sandy soil. A second study (Harding et al, 1992), at Black Wood in southern England as referred to in Chapter 3, concluded that beech afforestation of grassland overlying the chalk would increase recharge by 18 per cent. A third study (Hall et al, 1996b), commissioned by the Department of Trade and Industry (DTI) to investigate the water use of fast-growing coppice poplar and willow plantations growing on clay soils in southern England, indicated evaporative differences similar in magnitude to the Thetford results.

Recognizing these difficulties and the importance of resolving the question of the water resource impacts of the proposed large increase in forest cover in the UK, the then Department of the Environment, Transport and the Regions (DETR) commissioned a scoping study to investigate the possible range of water resource impacts associated with woodland on chalk and sandstone. This study involved running the HYLUC97, GIS-based evaporation model with trial model parameters derived from earlier work (Calder et al, 1997b, 1999) at the Black Wood chalk site and Greenwood Community Forest site (sandstone) in the Midlands of the UK.

The Black Wood Anomaly

Published results on the water use of forest in lowland England indicated a range of impacts, with the Black Wood results alone indicating increases in runoff or recharge as a result of afforestation. Although the measurements of soil moisture depletion recorded in the chalk soils beneath the beech forest at the Black Wood site in southern England are accepted as being reliable (see Chapter 3 and Figure 6.11), it has been questioned (Calder et al, 1997b)

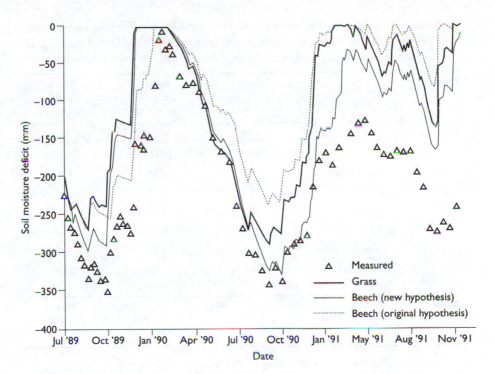

Figure 6.11 *Model predictions of soil moisture deficits due to evaporation at the Black Wood site for beech (original and new hypotheses) and grass, together with the observed soil moisture deficits under beech*

whether these measurements necessarily support the hypothesis that beech forest water use is less than that for grassland. This is an important question because the interpretation given by Harding et al (1992) has left the UK water industry with the sanguine view that broadleaf afforestation of grassland areas will be of positive benefit to water resources, a view that is, to say the least, unusual in the world context.

The earlier conclusions drawn concerning the evaporative losses from forest at the Black Wood site were partly based on assumptions of very significant drainage (~150mm) taking place from the soil/chalk profile during soil moisture deficit conditions; such assumptions were required for consistency with transpiration calculated using measured stomatal conductance. To investigate whether alternative interpretations were possible for the Black Wood results, a 'limits'-type model (a version of HYLUC97) was used to explore different hypotheses. The hypotheses investigated were the original assumption made about the drainage function for the chalk and a new function implying much reduced drainage (~25mm) (Calder et al, 1997b). The version of HYLUC97 used was standard except for the use of an exponential 'step length' function (Calder et al, 1983), to represent freely available water and to model soil moisture deficits in relation to soil moisture availability, to be consistent with the approach used by Harding et al (1992).

Table 6.4 *Evaporation model parameters representing different vegetation covers on different soils where step length relates to available soil water, β is the transpiration fraction and γ and δ are interception parameters*

Chalk		Grass	Beech (original hypothesis)	Beech (new hypothesis)
	Source	Calder et al (1983)	Harding et al (1992)	Calder et al (1997b)
	Step Length	160	1000	1000
	β	1	0.75	0.9
	γ	0	2.23	4.46
	δ	–	0.21	0.099
	Winter γ	0	1.84	3.68
	Winter δ	–	0.108	0.099

Sand		Grass	Pine	Broadleaf (new hypothesis)	Mixed forest
	Source	Calder et al (1983)	Cooper & Kinniburgh (1993)	Cooper & Kinniburgh (1993)	
	Step Length	53	83	83	83
	β	1	0.9	0.9	0.9
	γ	0	4.6	4.46	4.6
	δ	–	0.099	0.099	0.099
	Winter γ	0	4.6	3.68	3.68
	Winter δ	–	0.099	0.099	0.099

Clay loam		Grass	Pine	Broadleaf (new hypothesis)	Mixed forest
	Source	Calder et al (1983)	Cooper & Kinniburgh (1993)	Cooper & Kinniburgh (1993)	
	Step Length	75	200	200	200
	β	1	0.9	0.9	0.9
	γ	0	4.6	4.46	4.6
	δ	–	0.099	0.099	0.099
	Winter γ	0	4.6	3.68	3.68
	Winter δ	–	0.099	0.099	0.099

Source: Calder et al (1997b)

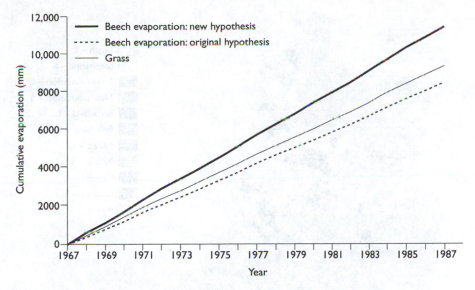

Figure 6.12 *Predicted cumulative evaporation for different land uses at the Black Wood chalk site (1967–1987)*

The HYLUC97 model predictions of soil moisture deficits due to evaporation alone (without incorporating a drainage function), obtained with model parameters relating to the original hypothesis and the new hypothesis, are shown in Figure 6.11. For comparison the measured soil moisture deficits are also shown in the figure. The model parameters relating to the original hypothesis (Harding et al, 1992) and the new hypothesis, which were obtained partly from 'default' values (Calder, 1990) and partly by adjusting the interception model parameters to give a better fit to the observed soil moisture deficits, are given in Table 6.4.

Model predictions of the cumulative evaporation from grass and beech forest, assuming both hypotheses, are shown in Figure 6.12. The new hypothesis would indicate that, as a long-term average, the annual evaporation from broadleaf forest (beech) is 105mm higher than that from grassland. The average recharge (assuming no runoff from the chalk site) would be reduced by 38 per cent as a result of broadleaf afforestation of grassland. This predicted reduction of recharge of 38 per cent should be seen in contrast to the increase in recharge of 15 per cent predicted by the earlier Black Wood study.

Forest Impacts in the Midlands

Following the original study of Harding et al (1992), the models developed at the Black Wood chalk site were extended to estimate the impacts of afforestation on sites overlying the Nottingham Triassic sandstone, one of the most important aquifers in the UK (Cooper and Kinniburgh, 1993). As Cooper and Kinniburgh used the same model parameters as Harding to describe the

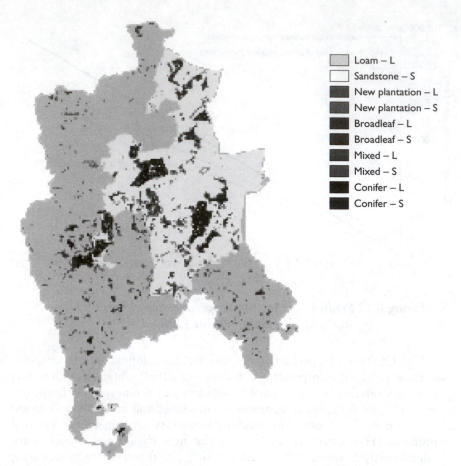

Loam – L
Sandstone – S
New plantation – L
New plantation – S
Broadleaf – L
Broadleaf – S
Mixed – L
Mixed – S
Conifer – L
Conifer – S

Figure 6.13 *GIS display of forest cover in the Greenwood Community Forest*

evaporative response of broadleaf forest at the Nottingham sites, it is not surprising that they drew similar conclusions: that broadleaf afforestation of grassland on the Nottingham Triassic sandstone would also increase recharge.

Nevertheless, if the reservations concerning the use of these parameters to describe the evaporative response of forest on chalk are well founded, the same reservations must apply to the conclusions drawn of reduced evaporation from broadleaf forest, as compared with grass, on sandstone. To investigate the range of possible impacts resulting from broadleaf afforestation on sandstone sites, a similar modelling study to that outlined above for Black Wood was carried out. This study used essentially the same new hypothesis model parameters derived for broadleaf forest, but adjusted to take into account the different soil water availability expected on sand and clay-loam soils in the Midlands. The chosen study area was the Greenwood Community Forest in Nottinghamshire. Nottinghamshire County Council supplied land-use information relating to forest cover and the distribution of agriculture and grassland, together with information relating to the geology and soil type as GIS files (Figure 6.13).

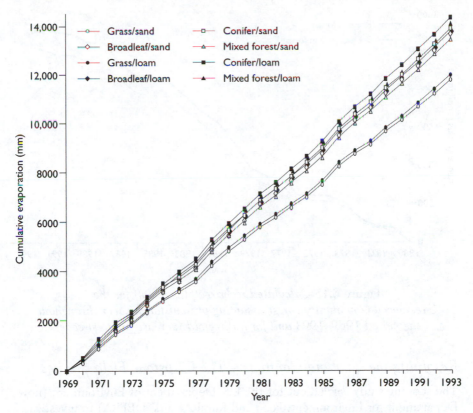

Figure 6.14 *Predicted cumulative evaporation for different land uses at the Greenwood Community Forest (1969–1993)*

Application of HYLUC97 then allowed the calculation of the range of impacts associated with the two scenarios (Calder et al, 1997b). The model predictions of seasonal evaporation, assuming essentially the same 'new hypothesis' model parameters relating to the chalk site but with different parameter values relating to soil water availability (Table 6.4), are shown in Figure 6.14.

The new hypothesis assumption would indicate that as a long-term average, the annual evaporation from broadleaf forest on sand soils is 93mm higher than that from grassland and that the average recharge plus runoff would be reduced by 51 per cent as a result of broadleaf afforestation of grassland. For broadleaf afforestation on clay-loam soils, the predicted reduction in recharge plus runoff would be 62 per cent.

The calculated cumulative recharge plus runoff from the Greenwood Community Forest assuming the present forest cover is shown in Figure 6.15. Also shown is the calculated cumulative recharge plus runoff for a threefold increase in forestry, where it is assumed that the increase occurs in proportion to the present distribution of forestry on the different soil types. Over the 24-year period from 1969 to 1993, the calculated average reduction in recharge plus runoff from the Forest as a result of an increase in forest cover from the existing 9 per cent to 27 per cent is 14mm (11 per cent reduction).

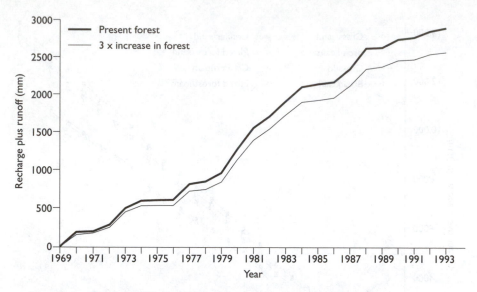

Figure 6.15 *Calculated recharge plus runoff for the Greenwood Community Forest assuming present forest cover throughout the period 1969–1993 and for a threefold increase in forest cover*

Resolving the Lowland Conflicts – The Clipstone Field Studies

The scoping study carried out for the UK Department of Environment (now Department for Environment, Food and Rural Affairs, DEFRA) to investigate the range of possible water resource impacts resulting from increased afforestation of lowland England indicated hugely different projections depending on whether model assumptions were based on the 'Black Wood anomaly' or on the results of other lowland forest studies.

The Black Wood study had indicated that broadleaf afforestation of grassland overlying chalk or sandstone bedrock would have beneficial impacts on water resources by increasing recharge by 17 per cent and 25 per cent, respectively, under beech and ash on chalk soils compared with that under grassland.

Alternatively, if the results from other lowland studies are believed to apply at Black Wood (on the chalk soil), the predictions of reduced recharge would be very detrimental to water resources. Of primary concern, if this alternative scenario was correct, were the local implications of increased forestry in areas where water resources were already being utilized to the limit or where low flows in rivers were causing environmental concerns.

The Black Wood results were clearly of great significance to forestry interests and fitted well with the forester's narrative that forests are necessarily always good for the water environment, that they 'conserve water' and always provide water of high quality.

But the questions raised with the House of Commons Select Committee for the Environment had introduced some scepticism of some elements of the forester's narrative. The very significant loss of water yield from forested catchments in the uplands of the UK was well recognized by all parties. As

Plate 6.5 *Neutron probe access tube installation (to 9m) for soil moisture measurements at the oak site at Clipstone, part of the New Sherwood Forest*

Plate 6.6 *Neutron probe access tube installation (to 9m) for soil moisture measurements at the heath site at Clipstone, part of the New Sherwood Forest*

Plate 6.7 *Neutron probe access tube installation (to 9m) for soil moisture measurements at the grass site at Clipstone, part of the New Sherwood Forest*

Plate 6.8 *Neutron probe access tube installation (to 9m) for soil moisture measurements at the pine site at Clipstone, part of the New Sherwood Forest*

the majority of the proposed new planting in England was planned for the Midlands, it was crucial to determine what the real impacts would be.

To resolve these questions a stakeholder group was formed comprising forest, water and land interests: a research team from the University of Newcastle upon Tyne (CLUWRR), Loughborough University and the UK Forestry Commission; the funding body (then the Department of the Environment, more recently the Department of the Environment, Transport and the Regions, and now DEFRA); the EA; the local County Council and water company; and an agricultural extension agency.

The Clipstone Field Studies – Water Quantity   Under the direction of the stakeholder group, field studies were initiated in February 1998 at Clipstone Forest, part of the new Sherwood Forest in the Midlands of the UK, to test and refine the scoping study results. The water use of four different vegetation types comprising oak, heath, grass and pine was investigated principally through the use of neutron probe (Figure 6.16) and capacitance probe measurements of changes in soil water content. The Forestry Commission also funded additional studies on the water quality implications of one of the vegetation types – Corsican pine woodland. The observation period was from February 1998 to April 2002.

These records were complemented by local and near-local measurements of rainfall and other meteorological variables that allowed the calculation of potential evaporation. Regional estimates of potential evaporation were also obtained from the Meteorological Office.

The soil moisture profiles, obtained by the neutron probe at approximately two-week intervals under the different sites between 1998 and 2000, are shown in Figure 6.16. The most obvious difference between sites is the uniformly and consistently drier soil conditions beneath the pine, especially at depth. This is in sharp contrast to the situation beneath the shorter vegetation types.

The soil moisture deficits recorded for the top 2m of soil for grass, heath, oak and two pine sites at Clipstone are shown in Figure 6.17, together with the HYLUC97 model predictions of soil moisture deficit using model parameters (Table 6.5) which were optimized for each site (Calder, 2003; Calder et al, 2003a). Table 6.6 shows the recharge calculated for the measurement period for the different vegetation types. (It should be noted that in this application of HYLUC97, both the interception parameter (γ) and the transpiration-related parameter (β) were optimized for both winter and summer periods.)

The long-term cumulative recharge plus runoff values for a sand soil for grass, oak and pine vegetation cover were obtained by running the HYLUC97 model with the locally calibrated HYLUC97 parameter values (Table 6.6) and a long-term (~30 year) climate record (Figure 6.18).

These results indicate that the initial predictions of the percentage reductions in recharge from forest compared with grassland, obtained in the scoping study, were broadly correct. The latest predictions (Calder, 2003; Calder et

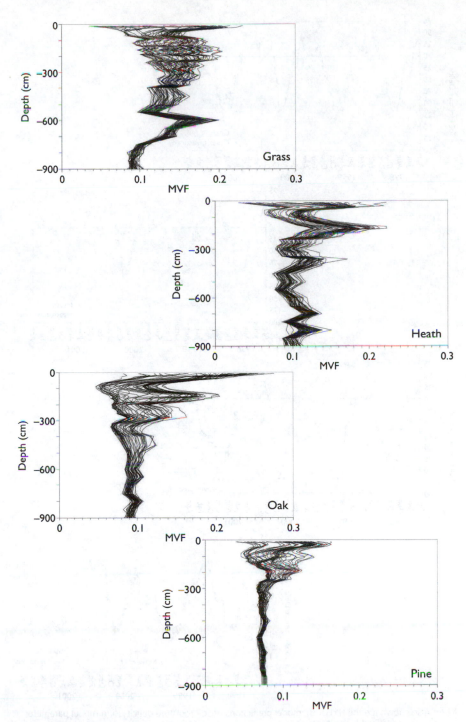

Note: MVF refers to moisture volume fraction
Source: Calder et al (2003a)

Figure 6.16 *Range of volumetric water content recorded under each site at Clipstone, 1998–2000*

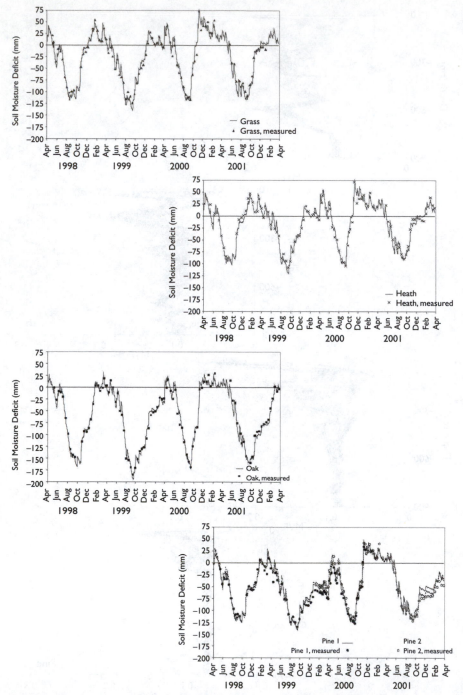

Note: Also shown are the HYLUC97 model predictions of soil moisture deficit using model parameters which were optimized for each site
Source: Calder et al (2003a)

Figure 6.17 *Soil moisture deficits recorded for the top 2m of soil for grass, heath, oak and two pine sites at Clipstone*

Table 6.5 *HYLUC97 optimized parameter values calibrated for the Clipstone sites using the mean of all soil moisture neutron probe access tube measurements of soil moisture deficit together with the root mean square (RMS) prediction error (indicating goodness of fit)*

HYLUC97 parameters for a sand soil	Grass	Heath	Oak	Pine 1	Pine 2
Available water (mm)	179	157	288	173	162
	(179 + 21)	(171 + 10)	(264 + 21)	(169 + 9)	(172 + 17)
β	0.88	0.82	0.99	0.76	0.84
	(0.93 + .03)	(0.81 + .02)	(1.00 + .05)	(0.85+ .06)	(0.81 + .05)
Winter β	0.98	0.78	0.82	0.89	0.95
	(0.99 + .02)	(0.78 + .02)	(0.82 + .03)	(0.84 + .04)	(0.90 + .07)
γ (mm)	-	2.3	3.0	3.5	4.2
		(2.3 + .3)	(3.6 + .5)	(3.5 + .7)	(4.2 + .5)
Winter γ (mm)	-	1.4	0.7	4.1	2.9
		(1.46 + .1)	(0.8 + 1)	(3.9 + .5)	(3.0 + .6)
Drainage half-life (days)	12	14	4	15	13
	(10 + 1)	(13 + 1)	(4 + 1)	(12 + 2)	(10 + 1)
RMS error (mm)	10.8	8.8	8.2	8.6	7.9
	(12 + 1)	(11.8 + 0.2)	(12 + 1)	(12 + 2)	(11 + 2)

Notes: In parentheses are shown the HYLUC97 optimized parameter values and standard errors calibrated using the individual neutron probe access tube measurements of soil moisture deficit together with the site average RMS error. The transition days between winter and summer and between summer and winter are set as 17 June and 7 November. The interception δ parameter has been set equal to 1/γ
Source: Calder et al (2003a)

al, 2003a) indicate that long-term recharge rates beneath oak will be reduced by one-half (48 per cent) and by three-quarters (75 per cent) under pine compared with grassland (Figure 6.18). It should be noted that for a year of average annual rainfall, no recharge will occur beneath the pine forest. It is only for years of significantly higher than average rainfall and storm events, such as the very wet autumn of 2001, that significant recharge will take place beneath pine forest.

The Clipstone Field Studies – Water Quality Before the field studies began at Clipstone, there was an expectation that, even if the water resources beneath the predominantly Corsican pine forest at Clipstone were reduced in quantity, the quality of recharge water would be good. This appeared to be confirmed by the quality tests on water being abstracted by Severn Trent plc from boreholes located within Clipstone Forest. However, once the study had commenced, the soil water quality monitoring that was being carried out by the Forestry Commission researchers using collector trays to intercept saturated flow percolating through the upper 30–60cm of soil appeared to indicate otherwise. Indeed, some of the poorest quality water in terms of nitrate concentrations had been obtained from the soil profile under pine. These were above World Health Organization recommended limits (Table 6.7).

To help understand the processes which influenced these results, a drilling programme was carried out in the spring of 2001 to obtain water quality

Table 6.6 *HYLUC97-derived values for the field capacity at each site together with the four-year value of recharge plus runoff predicted using the mean of all tubes at a site*

HYLUC97-derived values	Grass	Heath	Oak	Pine 1	Pine 2
field capacity (mm)	312	279	317	248	239
	(317 + 23)	(282 + 7)	(321 + 12)	(242+ 8)	(238 + 10)
Predicted recharge	804	755	542	192	251
plus runoff,	(766 + 51)	(719 + 16)	(510 + 21)	(236 + 58)	(269 + 22)
Mar 1998 –					
Mar 2002 (mm)					

Notes: In parentheses are shown the HYLUC97-derived values and standard errors for the field capacity at each site together with the four-year value of recharge plus runoff predicted using the individual neutron probe access tube measurements of soil moisture deficit. The significance of the use of the individual neutron probe access tube measurements is that they provide an estimate of the uncertainty (standard error) of the recharge estimate.
Source: Calder et al (2003a)

samples beneath the root zone. The samples taken during the drilling programme, which extended to >30m, showed that the high nitrate (and chloride) concentrations measured in the soil extend beneath the root zone to a depth of about 4m.

In high pollution (industrial) climates the deposition of most atmospheric pollutants, in both the gaseous and particulate forms, is likely to be higher for forests because of the reduced aerodynamic resistance of forest canopies compared with that of shorter crops. The high deposition load together with high evaporation from the pine forest is sufficient to explain the high concentrations of nitrate (and chloride) observed beneath the pine forest at Clipstone.

The analysis of the chloride concentration profiles by Dr Tom Nisbet and other Forestry Commission researchers not only provided a cross-check on the nitrate results in terms of reflecting similar spatial and depth distributions but also provided a valuable cross-check on the estimates of recharge which were obtained through measurement and modelling studies of soil water content (discussed above). The chloride balance estimates of recharge given in the final report to UK DEFRA (Calder et al, 2003b) indicated a long-term annual recharge rate of some 25–30mm for the pine. Interestingly the Forestry Commission researchers' results for recharge under pine were even less than those from the other studies. But within experimental uncertainty, the chloride-derived results are consistent with the values of 34 ± 8mm for the original pine and 38 ± 3mm for new pine predicted by the HYLUC97 modelling studies (Figure 6.18).

Taking a value of 0.07 for the volumetric water content of the sandstone at depth beneath the pine (Figure 6.16) and a value of 35mm per year as the long-term recharge rate would indicate that a 'piston flow' pulse of water would be moving at ~0.5m per year. So it may be another 20–40 years before the nitrate pulse reaches the water table (depending on the location of the water table as influenced by abstractions by Severn Trent plc and future precipitation rates).

Table 6.7 *Mean (and standard deviation) of the chemical composition of soil water draining through the upper 30–60cm of soil under grass, oak and two pine sites (original pine and clear-felled pine) showing very high nitrate concentrations under pine*

Site	Total volume (mm)	pH	Conductivity (µS)	Colour (hazen value)	$N(NO_3)$ (mg l^{-1})	$N(NH_4)$ (mg l^{-1})	$P(PO_4)$ (mg l^{-1})
Grass							
mean	223.8	6.7	192.2	270.2	4.1	0.46	1.6
SD		0.53	77.6	82.4	2.7	1.7	0.53
Oak							
mean	445.3	4.0	142.6	389.0	0.54	0.44	0.08
SD		0.40	49.3	196.7	0.68	0.90	0.09
Original pine							
mean	88.9	3.8	271.1	187.5	10.1	3.4	0.17
SD		0.24	72.1	81.3	3.2	4.2	0.16
Clear-felled pine							
mean	112.2	4.0	149.6	147.5	4.7	0.27	0.03
SD		0.25	39.8	100.4	1.8	0.91	0.05

	Total volume (mm)	K (mg l^{-1})	$S(SO_4)$ (mg l^{-1})	Cl (mg l^{-1})	Na (mg l^{-1})	Ca (mg l^{-1})	Mg (mg l^{-1})
Grass							
mean	223.8	7.3	4.4	18.0	5.2	27.0	2.3
SD		5.1	2.5	18.2	2.2	9.9	1.2
Oak							
mean	445.3	4.2	6.7	10.7	4.6	2.8	1.6
SD		2.0	1.8	4.3	1.1	1.4	0.59
Original pine							
mean	88.9	7.7	11.8	19.8	6.8	8.4	2.9
SD		0.16	3.3	2.8	5.5	1.7	2.8	0.60
Clear-felled							
mean	112.2	3.1	7.7	5.5	3.4	4.4	1.6
SD		0.81	4.6	2.9	1.5	2.1	0.62

Source: Calder et al (2003b)

The implication for the lowland water resources of England and Wales is that afforestation of arable or grassland with pine will not bring about the expected benefit in terms of lower nitrate concentrations. More importantly, nitrate levels in groundwater under existing pine forest could be expected to rise in the future, adding to the existing nitrate problem affecting waters draining agricultural areas.

In contrast, woodland planting with broadleaves such as oak might be expected to improve water quality by reducing both nitrate and phosphate

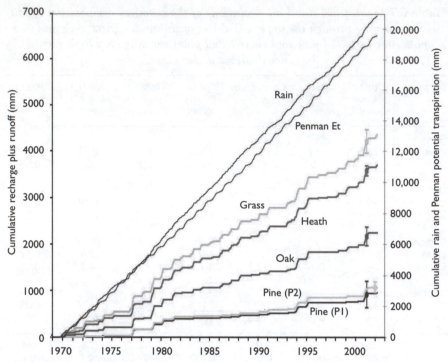

Notes: P1= original pine site, P2 = new pine site; Penman potential transpiration (right hand scale)
Source: Calder et al (2003a)

Figure 6.18 *Cumulative recharge plus runoff predicted for a sand soil for grass, oak and pine vegetation covers using the locally calibrated HYLUC97 parameter values together with cumulative values of measured rainfall and Penman potential transpiration*

levels to low values – although similar borehole investigations to those carried out under the pine at Clipstone are required to fully confirm these expectations (sanguine expectations of the water quality benefits of pine were later proven to be unfounded!).

What was not explained by the Clipstone study (it was not part of the study aims) was how the groundwater flow net beneath Clipstone Forest, which largely consists of pine, is able to supply relatively good quality water to the Severn Trent plc boreholes, even though the current study indicates low recharge rates of poor quality water beneath pine. The regime implies sources of recharge beyond the forest on agricultural land. However, these are areas from which high concentrations of nitrate are known to have leached (hence the past designation of this area as a nitrate vulnerable zone). If abstraction rates are reliant on 'mining' old, high-quality water from the aquifer beneath the forest, and not on using water that is currently being recharged, the current situation is clearly not sustainable in the long term and water quality and yield will ultimately fall.

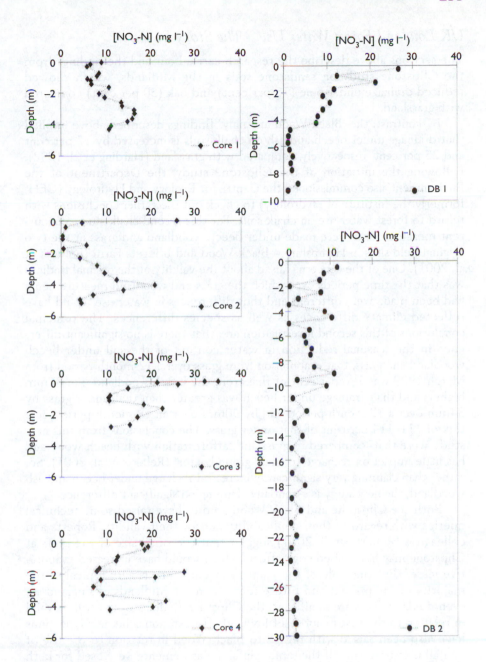

Notes: New pine site
Source: Calder et al (2003)

Figure 6.19 *NO_3-N concentrations in pore water extracted from each of the six boreholes drilled to different depths beneath Corsican pine at Clipstone – illustrating the very high concentrations in the top ~10m*

UK Lowland Forest Water Use – The Story So Far

The sections above describe the research carried out and the findings from the Clipstone study on sandstone soils in the Midlands, which showed reduced drainage under pine (75 per cent) and oak (50 per cent) compared with grassland.

By contrast, the 'Black Wood anomaly' findings described above implied that drainage under beech and ash on chalk soils is increased by 17 per cent and 25 per cent, respectively, compared with grassland (Harding et al, 1992). Following the initiation of the Clipstone study, the Department of the Environment also commissioned the Centre for Ecology and Hydrology (CEH, formerly the Institute of Hydrology) to check out the earlier conclusions with regard to forest water use on chalk soils. For this second chalk study, concurrent measurements were made under beech woodland and grass at the two original field sites in Hampshire – Black Wood and Bridgets Farm (Roberts et al, 2001). One of the concerns raised about the validity of the original findings was that the time periods over which the grass and woodland measurements had been made were different and thus differences in water use would have reflected climate differences as well as species differences. The principal conclusions of this second investigation are: that there is no significant difference in the seasonal reduction in water content of the soil under beech woodland and grass; that evaporation from grass over a 12-month period from March 1999 was 106 per cent of that from the beech woodland, i.e. 36mm higher; and that drainage under beech was greater than that under grass by 34mm over a 12 month period and by 90mm over an 18 month period, ie a flux of 111–114 per cent of that under grass. The conclusions from this new study were that 'compared to grassland, afforestation with beech woodland has little impact on recharge to chalk groundwater' (Roberts et al, 2001). So, rather than claiming very significantly increased recharge under beech and ash woodland, the new study is essentially claiming no significant difference.

Both the Clipstone and Black Wood studies have raised some technical queries with regard to their applicability and/or their validity. Roberts and colleagues (Roberts et al, 2001) suggest that the small size of the plots at Clipstone may have raised edge effects which would have increased evaporative losses. But the scale of the planting at Clipstone is very typical of the majority of the present and future forestry in the Midlands of England so, even if edge effects are significant, the Clipstone findings would still be valid in relation to the vast majority of lowland afforestation schemes. Questions have also been raised with regard to Black Wood in relation to the use of rainfall measurements. If the same rainfall measurements were used for both the grassland and forest sites, rather than using rainfall measurements from canopy gauges above the forest (which are prone to underestimate rainfall), the water balance calculations would have indicated increased evaporation from the forest at Black Wood.

But, given that there are still some remaining technical queries, the studies have shown a much improved picture of the likely impacts of lowland afforestation and, very importantly, the probable variation in impacts due to soil type. The Clipstone studies show long-term recharge reduced by 75 per cent under pine and 50 per cent under oak compared with grassland growing on the sandy soils in the Midlands of England – the region originally planned for a large increase in forest cover. The most recent Black Wood study now suggests little difference in water use between forest and grassland on chalk soils. The crucial soil type dependency of these results is probably due to the unique physical nature of chalk, which can retain large volumes of water between 'field capacity' and 'wilting point'. Earlier modelling studies (Calder et al, 1983) have shown that the available water accessible to grass rooting into chalk soils in southern England is unlimited in most years such that grass transpiration would be taking place at near to potential rates (compared with sandy soils where soil water stress would significantly limit transpiration from grass). The probably higher rates of transpiration from grass in these circumstances would tend to balance the higher interception losses expected from trees.

The studies have also shown that the traditional forester's narrative of forests always providing good quality water does not always reflect the facts. The nitrate concentration in the soil water beneath the pine stands at Clipstone exceeds the World Health Organization's limits for drinking water. This raises serious concerns for the future as nitrate levels in groundwater under existing pine forest would be expected to rise, adding to the existing nitrate problem affecting waters draining from agricultural areas.

Whilst broadleaves such as oak might be expected to provide good quality water, low in nitrates and phosphates, the same might also be expected of heathland, which would have the added benefit of not reducing water yield (50 per cent for the site at Clipstone).

NEW ZEALAND: WATER ISSUES AND LAND USE

The Perception of Water Issues

On any worldwide comparison, New Zealand must rate high as a country with abundant water resources. Twelve metres or more of water fall each year on parts of the Southern Alps in the South Island. And with only 3.4 million people occupying a land area of 270,000km^2, the population pressure is low. Taken together with a low-pollution climate and generally high-quality waters, it would be easy to assume that water resource issues were not a major concern in New Zealand and that water resource conflicts would be minimal.

Yet this sanguine view is not wholly true. Although abundant, New Zealand's water resources are not well distributed. Average annual rainfall at Milford Sound on the west coast of the South Island is 6240mm, but a little more than 100km eastwards, at Alexandra in central Otago, the rainfall is only 340mm. The eastern areas of both islands have dry summers and experience soil moisture deficits sufficient to limit horticultural development. Hydroelectric power stations supply a major part of New Zealand's power requirements, but in the South Island much of the rainfall on catchments falls in summer, whereas electricity demand peaks in winter. In these high-flow

Table 6.8 *Estimated economic value of New Zealand's water resources*

Activity	Value (NZ$ million)
Water supply (agriculture, industry, domestic)	450
Waste disposal	450
Fresh water fisheries	100
Recreation and amenity values	500
Hydroelectric power generation and thermal plant cooling	800
Gravel resource replenishment	40
Total	2340

Source: Mosely (1988)

rivers, floods are a common hazard and high flows are commensurate with high rates of sediment transport. Water quality has been affected in some catchments by effluents from urban areas and facilities such as dairy and wood processing plants, by runoff enriched by fertilizer and animal wastes from agricultural areas, and by sediment introduced by accelerated erosion (Waugh, 1992). Water-based recreations such as boating and fishing are popular pastimes in New Zealand and the amenity aspects of high-quality waters are appreciated. As in so many countries, irrigation, which uses $1.1 km^3 yr^{-1}$, is the largest consumptive user of water, but is not the highest value use (Table 6.8).

Waugh (1992) predicted increasing conflict between water conservation interests and farmers needing irrigation water to support pastoral agriculture, cropping and horticulture in New Zealand.

From a world perspective, these hydrological concerns might seem neither unusual for a developed country nor particularly severe. For cultural and traditional reasons this is not how the issues are perceived in New Zealand, particularly in relation to waste disposal. Whereas the European settlers, following the tradition of European settlers elsewhere, showed no particular appreciation for the environment and were happy to throw their waste and effluent into watercourses, this is not a practice that the Maori inhabitants would condone or accept. The 'new' concept of sustainability is not new to the Maori, who regard water as the essential ingredient of life – a priceless treasure left by ancestors for the life-sustaining use of their descendants (Taylor and Patrick, 1987).

In the early 1950s concerns about the impacts of land-use change and upland land use on water yield and other aspects of hydrology led to New Zealand embarking on a major programme of land-use change catchment studies to quantify the impacts. In many ways the issues and the impacts are not too dissimilar to those in the UK and similar methods have been used to research the impacts. The modelling methodologies used to describe and predict the impacts of land-use change on water yield are outlined below.

Land-use Change and Impacts

Major changes in New Zealand's land cover followed the Polynesian settlements about 1000 years ago. Prior to the first settlement, forest is thought to have covered 75 per cent of the 26.5 million hectares of land. By the time the Europeans arrived only about 11.3 million hectares of forest remained and by 1950 the area of native forest had been reduced to about 5.7 million hectares, much of it on poorer, mountainous land. About the same area of land remains under native tussock grass (Fahey and Rowe, 1992). Planting of exotic forests over large areas began in the 1920s and by 1990, 1.3 million hectares had been established. About 9 million hectares are under improved pasture. The country's economic growth was dependent on these land-use changes, but it was soon recognized that these alterations of land use were having important impacts on the hydrology, particularly in relation to the quantity of water, floods and erosion.

The land-use impacts section of the Forest Research Institute (now Landcare Research New Zealand Ltd) operates three paired-catchment experiments in the South Island. These are at Maimai, to investigate the impacts of harvesting native beech forest; at Big Bush to determine the impacts of establishing *Pinus radiata* plantations; and at Glendhu, to determine the impacts of converting native tussock grassland to pine. To illustrate how land-use change methodologies have a general application in helping with the resolution of water resource conflicts, the use and application of the HYLUC97 model, largely developed and calibrated for use in UK conditions, to New Zealand conditions, is described below.

The Glendhu Study

Proposals to convert large areas of tussock grassland in the upland of east Otago to pine plantation have raised concerns about the impacts on both water quantity and quality. In 1979 the former New Zealand Forest Service established a paired-catchment study in the Glendhu forest in the upper Waipori catchment, where water quantity impacts were a major concern to hydroelectric generating plants located downstream. The aims were to investigate the streamflow behaviour and water balance of lightly-grazed tussock grassland and to assess the impact of afforestation on annual water yields, storm peak flows, water chemistry and sediment yield. Only the impacts on water yield are described here.

The Glendhu paired-catchment experiment was instrumented in 1979 with rain gauges and flow-measuring weirs and data collection began on 10 October 1979 (Fahey and Watson, 1991; Fahey and Jackson, 1997). The two catchments, GH1 and GH2, were originally both under native tussock grassland (dominated by the species *Chionochloa rigida*). In 1982, after a three-year calibration period, 67 per cent of GH2 was planted with *Pinus radiata*. Catchment GH1 was retained under the original vegetation as the control catchment.

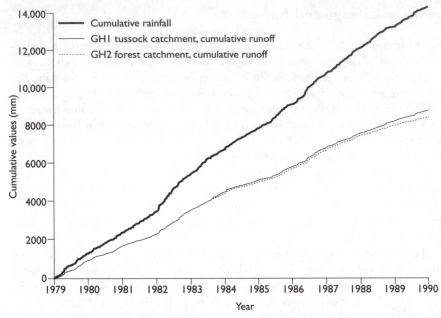

Figure 6.20 *Cumulative rainfall and runoff recorded from the Glendhu catchments*

Changes to the Flow Regime The cumulative rainfall and flow record from the catchments is shown in Figure 6.20.

The very close agreement between the runoffs measured from the two catchments during the calibration period implies a very high degree of integrity and internal consistency of the data from these catchment studies. From 1987 onwards it can be seen that the cumulative flow recorded from GH2, the forested catchment, is less than that from the control, GH1, and that the divergence becomes increasingly pronounced as time progresses. The difference in slope for the more recent period, 1991–1994, indicates a reduction in runoff of 27 per cent for the forested catchment compared with the control.

Application of the HYLUC97 Model to Glendhu Application of the HYLUC97 model to the Glendhu tussock grass catchment showed that good agreement between predicted and observed runoff could be achieved with parameter values only slightly modified from those measured for heather moorland containing *Calluna vulgaris* (Calder, 1990) in the uplands of the UK (Table 6.9).

A 10 per cent reduction in the γ parameter, which determines the maximum daily interception loss, from 2.65 to 2.4, allows good agreement both seasonally and in the long-term totals of flow (Figure 6.21).

By incorporating the HYLUC97 standard upland forest growth function (see above) and the same parameter value derived for spruce plantations in the UK, the HYLUC97 model was also able to describe the change in the flow regime that was measured at Glendhu as the forest grew (Figure 6.21).

Table 6.9 *Evaporation model (HYLUC97) parameters representing tussock and pine vegetation on soils with high water availability*

HYLUC97 parameter Source	Heather Calder, 1990 (measured)	Tussock grass Calder, 1990 (based on heather parameters)	Pine Calder, 1990 (identical to conifer parameters)
s_m	200	200	380
β	0.5	0.5	0.9
γ	2.65	2.4	6.91
δ	0.36	0.36	0.099
Winter γ	2.4	2.4	6.91
Winter δ	0.36	0.36	0.099

Note: Where s_m relates to maximum available soil water, β is the transpiration fraction and γ and δ are interception parameters.

The modelling study confirms the significance of forest impacts on water yield and provides a modelling framework for estimating the impacts of afforestation in other upland areas of New Zealand.

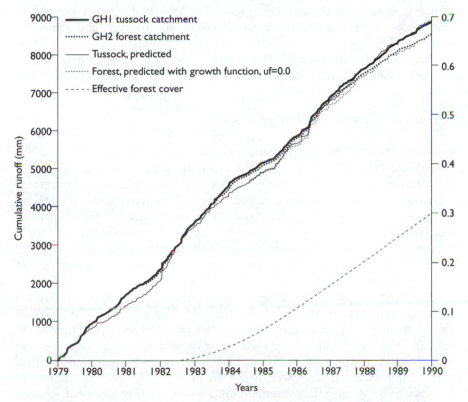

Figure 6.21 *Cumulative runoff measured and predicted for tussock catchment GH1, together with cumulative runoff measured and predicted for forest catchment GH2, using the forest cover/age function*

THE PHILIPPINES: BIG CITIES, SMALL CATCHMENTS

The rapid industrialization and urbanization of the major population centres in the Philippines, together with logging, agricultural and irrigation developments in the headwater catchments, have induced environmental and water resource concerns which, in terms of both range and severity, exemplify many of the problems that face large cities in the developing world. Whilst increasing populations and expanding industries demand more water, the ability to meet demands is being reduced by siltation, nutrient, herbicide and pesticide pollution of surface waters, together with pollution and often saline intrusions within the groundwater aquifers.

The Philippines is a country made up of more than 7000 islands, and many of its provincial centres, including Metro Manila, are coastal. The economic boom of the early 1990s has resulted in rapid development which has often been to the disadvantage of the environment, so that air quality, water quality and quantity, degradation of the land and marine ecology are all issues of great national concern. But pressures for further development are leading to increased urbanization, which is now moving from the coastal plains into the headwater catchments. Regulations on development are in the hands of many government departments (Tolentino, 1996) which have not always been successful in demonstrating an integrated approach to land and water resource planning.

The problems affecting the Philippines' second city, Cebu, are illustrative of these issues and a novel grass-roots approach to IWRM is described below.

Cebu – A City with Water Stress

Concerns about Cebu's water supplies were first voiced in the mid-1970s. The Water Resources Centre of the University of San Carlos in Cebu City detected an increasing intrusion of sea water into Cebu's aquifer system which was attributed to overextraction. By 1997 the water demand in Metro Cebu was estimated at 240,000m^3 per day of which only 115,000m^3 per day was being supplied by the government-owned and controlled water supply corporation. The deficit was being met by uncontrolled extractions from private wells, whilst industrial needs were being met by a combination of water purification and desalination.

The land use on the three headwater catchments which supply surface water to Cebu was another cause for concern. The original forest cover on these catchments had been cleared for timber products and agricultural activities and this had seriously degraded water quality. Efforts to improve land management on the catchments had been hindered by questions of land ownership between land owners, tenant farmers and occupiers. Questions of jurisdiction between local government units and national government agencies had also compounded the problem.

An Asian Institute of Management report (Tañada, 1997) claimed:

The initial response to the water crisis by the local government units was slow and tentative in some cases. Towns and cities in Metro Cebu had few specific programs in informing the local residents about the water situation. Frequently, local officials, including mayors, councillors, development council members, as well as local line agency personnel, had little or no knowledge about water resources problems, let alone strategies for solving them. They did not have access to relevant information and frequently made decisions based mostly on political and/or economic considerations without regard for their long-term consequences. Their decisions were also not based on a holistic approach.

The forestry lobby advocated reafforestation with fast-growing tree species as the panacea, in the fond belief that this will automatically cure all water quality and quantity problems. Tañada (ibid) says, with perhaps some understatement:

the challenge of finding a common point for cooperation or compromise between the various groups is not an easy task. The absence of an integrated management of resources and comprehensive land use policy for the watersheds has left the area open to unregulated and inappropriate land use.

Cebu Uniting for Sustainable Water – A Citizens' Initiative for IWRM

The perceived failure of governmental planning has resulted in a pressure group, Cebu Uniting for Sustainable Water (CUSW) being set up to address these land and water resource issues (Tañada, ibid). Formed out of a coalition of several organizations in Metro Cebu, CUSW regards itself as a citizens' initiative. Since its formation in 1995 it has been working towards developing a land-use plan for the watersheds. It realizes that the real test of its success will be whether the plan is eventually adopted by the leaders of Metro Cebu.

At its general assembly in April 1997, CUSW had 77 institutional and 66 individual members covering many sectors. With such a range of public and private, social- and business-oriented interests represented (Table 6.10), CUSW encountered dissenting opinions, not only outside but also within the group.

CUSW claims not to take a hard line against development nor does it claim to be an environmental group. It claims to be seeking schemes which allow development, but which are compatible with maintaining the watershed so that the supply and quality of the water are enhanced. CUSW recognizes that the interests of the people who live in the area and survive from the land have to be considered – displacement is not feasible, socially or economically. The

Table 6.10 *Sectors represented by 'Cebu Uniting for Sustainable Water'*

Sectors represented by CUSW

Farmers	Fisherfolk	Business	Professionals
Youth	Academia	Religious	Political leaders
Local government	Landowners	Hill-land residents	
NGOs	Line agencies	Women	Health
Urban poor	Cooperatives	Civic	Labour
Interested individuals			

Source: Nacario-Castro (1997)

eleven objectives that CUSW hope to see incorporated in the Cebu Watershed Management and Development Plan (Nacario-Castro, 1997) are as follows:

1   Integration of watershed communities.
2   Respect for prior right over alienable and disposable lands.
3   Protection and promotion of biodiversity.
4   Adherence to a watershed resource management plan.
5   Use of biodegradable and non-toxic substances.
6   Installation of control systems for noise reduction and against potable water contamination and atmospheric pollution.
7   Respect for the dynamism of local culture.
8   Promotion of human security agenda.
9   Incorporation of a method for measuring social impact.
10   Non-discrimination of local residents.
11   Extended accountability of project developers.

Cebu – Further IWRM Initiatives

Under the sponsorship of the British Council, a Watershed Protection and Management Seminar was held in Cebu in November 1997. The seminar was attended by all sectors concerned with the management of land and water resources in the Philippines and the output of the seminar was a statement subscribed to by the organizations represented. This statement, which is consistent with the stated objectives of the CUSW Watershed Management and Development Plan, is a framework to improve watershed management.

The required components of this framework are:

• a National Watershed Management body with operating units at the watershed level;
• an Integrated Watershed Management plan including land use;
• survey, studies, data-based planning, consultation and participation on the part of stakeholders;
• data and decision support system;
• development of management programmes;
• programme evaluation and assessment;

Plate 6.9 *The Bridge of the Americas crossing the Panama Canal*

- monitoring and promulgation;
- resources: financial and technical; and
- commitment, vision, and understanding of strategy process.

Implementation programmes are:

- legislation of ordinances for watershed management including land tenure and water rights;
- education, training and workshops for stakeholders;
- establishment of a national authority;
- body for enforcement, implementation, monitoring and facilitation;
- establishment of a decision support system;
- creation of a water information system;
- pollution control;
- appropriate technology; and
- water pricing policy, costing, valuation of resources and fines.

Activities and delivery mechanisms consist of:

- pilot programme on small basin;
- fund sourcing;
- coordination among groups;
- legislation and policy;
- community participation;
- capacity building and technical support;
- provision of livelihood opportunities;

- education (proactive), dissemination – all stakeholders;
- networking – all stakeholders;
- coordinating body;
- review existing process;
- development of an implementation plan.

CENTRAL AMERICA – AFFORESTATION AND THE PANAMA CANAL

The Panama Canal

The continued functioning of the Panama Canal is a central concern of the Government of Panama. The ownership of the Panama Canal was transferred from the Government of the USA to the Government of Panama at the beginning of the new millennium. During the period leading up to the change of ownership, major changes were also taking place in relation to the institutional understanding of land-use and water resource issues. This is now leading to a reconsideration of government policies with respect to the management of the canal watershed.

With United States Agency for International Development (USAID) support, a Regional Plan (Intercarib/Nathan Associates, 1996a,b) had been produced earlier which advocated a massive reforestation (104,000ha) of the lands in the Panama Canal watershed that were under agricultural use, primarily for livestock production. The report was based on the assumption (perceived wisdom) that the reforestation programme would have a positive impact on water quality, quantity and erosion, and would lead to an increase in annual and dry season flows. The proposals in the report were enshrined in a Panamanian Law, Law 21, in 1997. The Government of Panama later requested the World Bank to support them in designing a project that would assist them in carrying out their responsibilities in the watershed under Law 21.

As part of the preparatory phase of the project design, the World Bank's Senior Natural Resource Specialist, Jim Smyle, commissioned various consultancies and scoping studies to investigate the current land use in the catchment together with the hydrological and economic impacts of the proposed change in land use. The Centre for Land Use and Water Resources Research at Newcastle University carried out the scoping study into the hydrological impacts of the proposed land-use change (Calder et al, 2001).

Impacts of Forest on Annual Flows

The study of the impacts of forest cover on annual flows involved the application of the HYLUC97 spatially distributed evaporation model using local information on land cover and land use (Figure 6.22), and previously published 'default' forest and non-forest parameter values (Calder,1999).

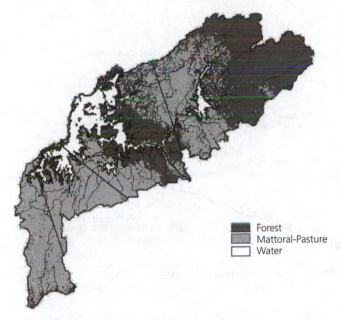

Forest
Mattoral-Pasture
Water

Source: Calder et al (2001)

Figure 6.22 *Existing land cover/land use in the Panama Canal watershed*

The model was shown to be able to describe the recorded flow regime for three of the major sub-catchments of the Panama Canal Watershed and for three of the experimental catchments operated by the Smithsonian Tropical Research Institute, within an error (~10 per cent) which was essentially commensurate with the experimental error of the observations. The results in terms of cumulative flow for two of the catchments, the partially forested Trinidad and the fully forested Chagres, are shown in Figures 6.23 and 6.24.

The predicted reduction in runoff on conversion of full pasture to full forest plantation (calculated as cumulative runoff under plantation cover less cumulative runoff under pasture, as a percentage of runoff under pasture) ranged from 18 per cent for the Chagres catchment (3420mm annual rainfall) to 29 per cent for the drier Trinidad catchment (2222mm annual rainfall).

Analysis of Forest Impacts on Dry Season Flows

An analysis of the impacts of forest cover on dry season flows, referred to here as low flows, was carried out on the historical daily flow record supplied by the Panama Canal Authority. The aim was to investigate whether there was any statistically significant change in the low flow response that could be associated with known vegetation (deforestation) changes in the Panama Canal watershed. The analysis was carried out with respect to three of the major sub-watersheds: Chagres, Trinidad and Cirí Grande.

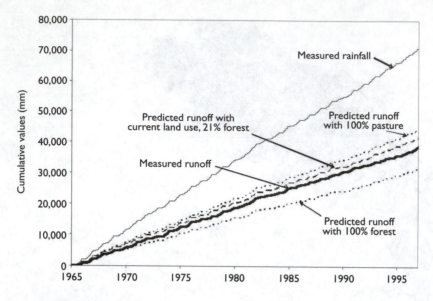

Source: Calder et al (2001)

Figure 6.23 *Comparison of actual streamflow with HYLUC97 model predictions in a deforested catchment (21% forest cover), Rio Trinidad, Panama*

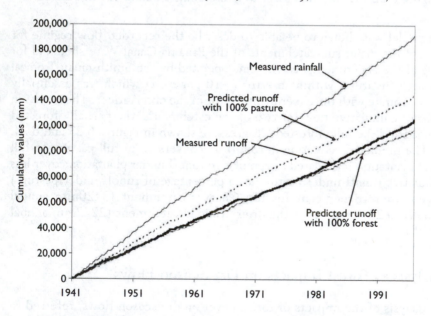

Note: missing runoff measurement in middle of record (1970) evidenced by no increases in the cumulative values
Source: Calder et al (2001)

Figure 6.24 *Comparison of actual streamflow with HYLUC97 model predictions in a forested Catchment (99% forest cover), Rio Chagres, Panama*

The Chagres sub-watershed has seen little to no land-use change during the analysis period, remaining largely under primary forest cover. It is not clear precisely when deforestation took place in the Trinidad and Cirí Grande sub-watersheds. A study of the Panama Canal watershed carried out by Intercarib S.A. and Nathan Associates (Intercarib S.A. and Nathan Associates 1996a,b) suggests that Trinidad and Cirí Grande were largely deforested during the 1952–1976 period, however, remote-sensing data compiled by the later Panama Canal Watershed Monitoring Project (PMCC, 1999) contradicts this view. While coverage is limited, the Panama Canal Watershed Monitoring Project data suggests that large-scale deforestation in these two watersheds occurred in the late 1970s and 1980s.

For each of the sub-catchments, where records were complete, Chagres (1933–1996), Cirí Grande (1947–59, 1981–96) and Trinidad (1947–1996), the following analyses were undertaken:.

- cumulative annual minimum 7- and 30-day runoff volume against time (Figure 6.25);
- flow duration curves for periods which appear to have different gradients (Figure 6.26 and Table 6.11); and
- decade means (where possible) and standard errors of annual minimum 7-day discharges against time (Figure 6.27).

The gradients of the plots of cumulative annual minimum runoff volume against time for all three catchments are fairly uniform (Figure 6.25). They do indicate breakpoints at 1970/71 on the Chagres (decrease) and Trinidad (increase), as well as slight decreases in the Trinidad and Cirí Grande gradients after 1980.

The flow duration curves for the periods divided by these breakpoints are shown in Figure 6.26. These curves describe the historical probability of exceeding a given discharge level. The value of the discharge which is exceeded 95 per cent of the time (Q95) is commonly used as an index of low flows and was used in this study. These values are shown in Table 6.11. The table indicates a modest increase in low flows in the case of Trinidad and Cirí

Table 6.11 *Q95 values estimated for Rios Chagres, Cirí Grande and Trinidad catchments, Panama*

Catchment	Years	Q95 (m³/s)
Rio Chagres	1933–50	7.7
	1951–69	8
	1971–96	7
Rio Cirí Grande	1947–59	0.9
	1981–96	1.1
Río Trinidad	1947–69	0.7
	1970–80	0.8
	1981–96	1.1

Source: Calder et al (2001)

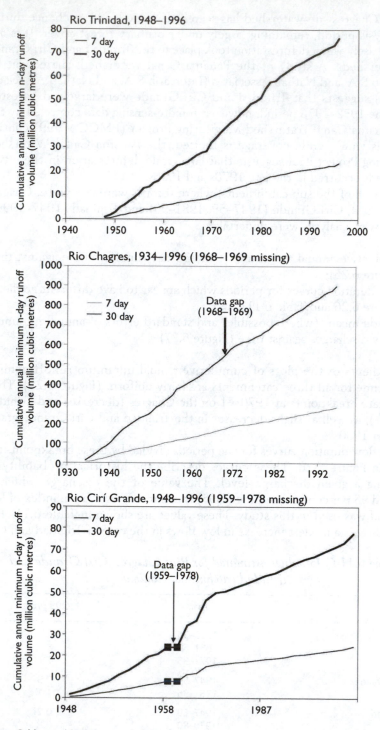

Source: Calder et al (2001)

Figure 6.25 *Cumulative annual minimum 7- and 30-day runoff volume against time for Trinidad, Chagres and Cirí Grande catchments, Panama*

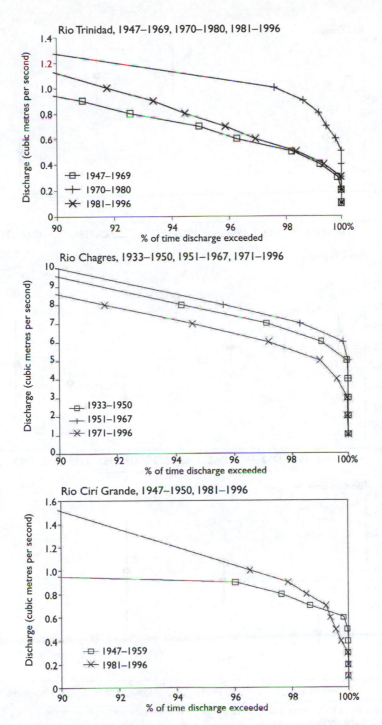

Note: for Cirí Grande a 2-year period of data of questionable quality immediately after missing data (1979–1980) was excluded from the analysis

Source: Calder et al (2001)

Figure 6.26 *Flow duration curves for selected periods for Trinidad, Chagres and Cirí Grande catchments, Panama*

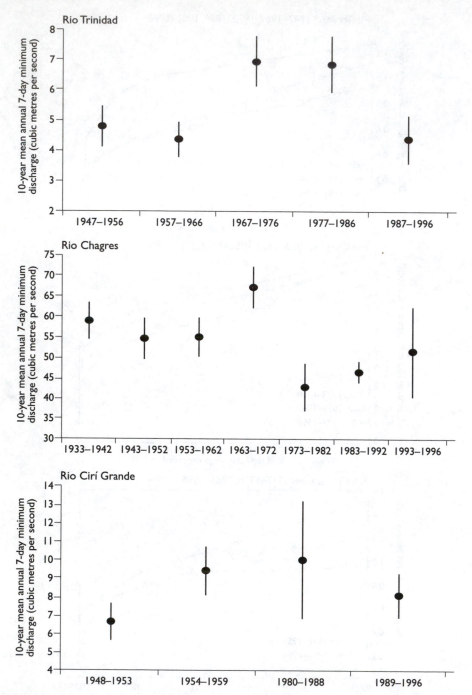

Note: the analysis for Chagres and Trinidad are for 10-year periods; for Cirí Grande the analysis is for 6-, 8- and 9-year periods
Source: Calder et al (2001)

Figure 6.27 *Period means and standard errors (vertical bars) of annual 7-day minimum discharges for Trinidad, Chagres and Cirí Grande catchments, Panama*

Grande from 1980 onwards, but a decrease in low flows in the case of Chagres.

As the final step in the analysis, the means and standard errors for the 7-day minimum low flows were calculated (Figure 6.27). The results of these analyses indicate considerable variation in the low flow response with time for the catchments that did not experience any land-use change and those that did. On the catchments that did experience deforestation, there is no evidence for a monotonically increasing or decreasing trend which could be taken to be associated with what was believed to be a monotonically decreasing forest cover with time. The conclusion drawn was that the analysis provides no evidence for a significant linkage, either positive or negative, between the changes in land use that have occurred on the catchments and the low flow response.

It should be pointed out that the analysis was carried out without access to stage discharge calibrations in low flow conditions. It is recognized that only small offset errors in the stage/discharge relationship can lead to significant discharge errors in low flow conditions. If access to the calibration data were made available, this might allow periods of high uncertainty to be excluded and provide a better basis for the analysis of the historical record.

Although it was not within the scope of the original study, another approach to detecting a low flow response to land-use change can be provided through modelling. Later versions of HYLUC (HYLUC03) now incorporate a soil and groundwater storage and flow routing component for understanding and predicting the impacts of land use not only on annual flows but also on low flows. Use of this type of model also provides insights and helps to clarify the key processes within a catchment which might determine the low flow response under different conditions of vegetation type and geology. This type of model would show, for example, that if the capacity of groundwater stores (supplying low flows) within a catchment were of moderate depth (such that they were always full at the end of the wet season irrespective of whether the vegetation above had high or low evaporative properties), the drainage from these stores, providing much of the dry season flow, would be the same. On the other hand, if the groundwater store had a larger capacity such that it was not always filled when under a high evaporative vegetation type, then we would expect a much reduced dry season flow. Thus, although we would always expect the higher evaporation from forests compared with short crops to result in reduced annual flows, the effect on low flows might be significantly modified by the geology over the range between a zero signal and one that is the same degree as the reduction in annual flow. In the same way these models are also able to explore the range of infiltration properties that would be required under different vegetation types to significantly influence dry season flows.

It is possible that the interplay of these different environmental factors on the Panama Canal watershed is such that although annual flows are reduced under forest, there is no marked effect on low flows, or at least to the extent of one that can be detected within the 'noise' arising from year-to-year climate variation and measurement error. This hypothesis could now be tested through the application of HYLUC03-type models.

Conclusions

The study, rather than supporting the conventional wisdom that afforestation would increase flows to the canal reservoirs which would enhance the capacity of the canal, indicates that annual flows would be reduced and, if there is no significant enhancement of low flows resulting from afforestation, the capacity of the canal will be reduced by around 10 per cent. Aylward (2002), reviewing the hydrological and socio-economic issues relating to the Law 21 proposals for the Panama Canal, concludes that 'Further analysis of the low flow issue is therefore essential'.

In addition, the scoping study suggested that expected benefits of an afforestation programme in terms of erosion control are also unlikely to be achieved. To date, virtually all of the commercial planting within the watershed is with teak and herbicides are usually applied to reduce competition from understorey weeds. With regard to the discussion above relating to scientific and public perceptions, the scientific perception would indicate that this is a situation which may lead to not only very much increased rates of soil erosion compared with the current pasture system, but also a possible decrease in water quality.

The utility of the research in helping to identify development options was recognized at the World Bank Watershed Management Workshop held in Washington in February 2005 (Box 6.1), and the Panama Canal Authority is now recommending this approach for other sectoral programmes within the watershed. The Panama Canal Authority is now planning alternative developments for securing more flow to the canal. These include a massive enlargement of the area of the catchment through further dams and tunnels to divert the water into the original catchment. This has been opposed by various environmental groups because of the loss of indigenous forest and the displacement of indigenous peoples that would result. There appears, not unsurprisingly, to be little interest from international donors in funding these proposals. The strategic interest of the USA in the functioning of the canal also seems to be on the wane. The USA sees global warming, in some respects, as being beneficial to its interests. One aspect of this is the expectation that the North West passage, the sea route from the Pacific to the Atlantic via the north of the American continent, will, through melting of the pack ice, be open to commercial shipping in the next few years. If and when this happens, the strategic value of the canal to the USA will diminish considerably. Shipping would no longer be restricted in size by the locks of the Panama Canal. The North West passage would represent a considerably cheaper and possibly politically more secure option than sending ships through the southern route, the Panama Canal.

> ## Box 6.1 Conclusions and impacts of the Panama Canal Watershed (PCW) research programme as presented at the World Bank Watershed Management Workshop, Washington, February 2005
>
> Analysis of development options for the PCW.
> Under the full reconversion scenario of Law 21:
>
> - Water shortages under the full reconversion scenario suggest a **loss of $700 million** to the Panamanian economy from downstream effects of changes in water quantity.
> - From the perspective of the global shipping industry, the **extra cost** to the global economy of shipping via alternative routes could be **as high as $4 billion**.
>
> Implementation of the full reforestation programme of lands currently under pasture: minimum cost of **$250 million**. Benefits are insufficient to outweigh the investment cost and potential loss of Canal function due to change in the hydrological regime. *This option yields negative economic returns*.
>
> Implementation of *'moderate' alternatives* (shift to sustainable agriculture, improved ranching or silvopastoral uses, agroforestry, and reforestation in critical areas): Cost: **$40 to $60 million**. Analysis shows positive *economic returns*.
>
> *Conclusion:*
>
> **A less extreme implementation of Law 21 may achieve both environmental and economic improvements in the management of the PCW.**
>
> 1. Intersectoral rural development and WSM programme developed and subsequently approved by 'Interinstitutional Commission for Watershed Management (CICH). Programme has 8-year time horizon and focuses on 'moderate' alternative.
> 2. CICH passes resolution requesting Ministry of Finance to require public- and donor- financed programmes in PCW be compatible with approved programme.
> 3. Panama Canal Authority requests other sectors (represented in CICH) to follow same approach in order to define their sectoral programmes/approaches to WSM in the Panama Canal Watershed.
>
> *Source:* Presented by J Smyle

Japan: Crumbling Foundations, Public Works and Green Dams

The Context – Public Works at Any Cost

There is a huge and growing concern in Japan that the Ministry of Land, Infrastructure and Transport is pushing through large public works projects even though often there is no obvious benefit to society, and in many cases obvious dis-benefits to the environment (Seaman, 2004; Kerr, 2001). Japan spends 6 per cent of its GDP on public works, whilst other advanced industrial democracies (AIDs) spend between 2 and 4 per cent. Public works spending is twice as high as spending on social security, whereas in other AIDs it is about half. Neither the presently ruling Liberal Democratic Party, nor the Democratic Party of Japan when it was in power in the 1990s, appears to have the power to control this powerful Ministry. Since the end of World War II, the Ministry has taken effective control of how it uses the public works budgets and only offers 'explanations' to the governing party and the tax payers on project spends. It appears unresponsive to public concerns and this apparent lack of Government control has raised questions within Japan as to whether the country can still truly be regarded as operating under a democracy.

The opposition party, the Democratic Party of Japan (DJP), (http://www.dpj.or.jp/english/policy/19hc-elec.html) have proposed ways to break the vested interests structure surrounding public works:

> It is essential to change the way Japan provides social infrastructure. At present, the most basic elements of sound financial management, such as cost-benefit analysis, consideration of value-for-money or mechanisms to balance priorities between various budgets, simply do not exist. High cost structures, vested interests and widespread collusion have been protected, but waste is rampant, and the country has built up a mountain of debt. All of this has occurred in the name of economic stimulus. The DPJ will drastically reform public works spending, making efficiency the priority in providing social infrastructure. The money saved will be used to cover deficiencies in employment policy, strengthen social security, and tackle national debt.

The DPJ also claim that:

> Because of collusion between politicians, officials and construction companies, Japan's public works are high cost and many are of dubious value. While ensuring that the country provides the necessary social infrastructure, the DPJ will reduce public works spending by 30 per cent over 5 years, by eradicating collusion, forcing down costs, cutting waste and adopting PFI (the Private Finance Initiative) as a model for government-private sector partnership.

As part of the DPJ's policy to reduce spending on public works they recommend the move from concrete dams to 'green dams':

> The DPJ's policy to preserve water will depend not on concrete dams, but on measures to conserve forests and natural environments, as 'green dams'. Measures, such as direct payments to promote forestry, will create jobs in the countryside.

In relation to forest and water policy the DPJ again promote the 'green dam' concept:

> *The basis for laws on forestry policy will be the 'green dam' concept, so as to preserve and develop water resources, land and wildlife.*

The Engineering versus Environmental/Forestry Conflict

The current engineering versus environmental/forestry conflict in Japan has a remarkable resonance with the conflicts between engineers and foresters in America in the 1920s, who were both claiming to have the solution to flood control. Yet in Japan there is an extra dimension: the polarization between engineering and forestry vested interests is reflected in the ministries. The Ministry of Land, Infrastructure and Transport promotes public works and engineering interventions, whilst the Japanese Forestry Agency promotes 'Green Dams' as the solution to flood control. Professor Kuraji Koichiro of the University Forest in Aichi, part of the University of Tokyo, has pointed out (Kuraji, 2005) the fallacy of relying on forests (Green Dams) as the principal solution to flood control. The Japan Water Agency and the River Bureau of the Ministry of Land, Infrastructure and Transport have also identified the ineffectiveness of forests in ameliorating major floods. These organizations have argued that forest soil, which has the capacity to absorb a proportion of small storm rainfall and ameliorate small floods, will be fully saturated and have no ameliorating effect for the largest storms. This would almost certainly be the case for storm events with 100-year return periods, the event magnitude which is used as the design rainfall for the flood control plans of Japan's rivers. The discussions in Chapter 5 would indicate that there is no single 'silver bullet' solution to flood control. Forestry, although able to mitigate smaller floods, will have little or no effect on the largest and most damaging floods (see Chapter 2, Figure 2.6).

Promoting an Integrated Approach to Flood Management

The discussions in Chapter 5 indicate that reliance on either concrete dams or 'green dams' for flood control is misplaced. Green dams are certainly ineffective in controlling large flood events. Concrete dams may also fail in certain circumstances. An integrated approach to floodplain management recognizes these deficiencies. In summary, the integrated approach recommended in Chapter 5 advocates four measures:

1   **Land-use Planning Measures** aimed at 'keeping people away from the floodwaters'. The objective is to keep people and vulnerable activities out of the most hazardous areas of the floodplain.

2   **Structural Measures** aimed at 'keeping floodwaters away from the people'. Typical structural measures include flood mitigation dams, embankments and flood detention basins. Typical building controls include minimum floor levels to eliminate nuisance flooding, and the use of building materials and building designs that enable rapid and effective cleanup after a flood.

3   **Flood Preparedness Measures** recognize that, no matter how effective the above types of management measures are believed to be, an overwhelming flood will always occur. They aim at 'getting people ready for floods before they come'.

4   **Flood Emergency Measures** deal with the aftermath of such an event by 'helping affected people to cope with floods'. The flood emergency management process embodies evacuation planning and training, emergency accommodation planning, flood cleanup planning with the restitution of essential services and social and financial recovery measures.

SOUTH AFRICA: FORESTS AND WATER

The Revolution – Civil Rights and Water Policy

> *The dictionary describes water as colourless, tasteless and odourless – its most important property being its ability to dissolve other substances. We in South Africa do not see water that way. For us water is a basic human right, water is the origin of all things – the giver of life.* (South African White Paper on Water Policy)

For a country which has so courageously faced and resolved inequities in its attitudes toward, and its political treatment of, different racial groups, it would perhaps not be surprising if South Africa were prepared to exhibit the same virtues in dealing with its land-use and water resource issues. It might be expected that under such circumstances South Africa's *White Paper on Water Policy* would display new approaches to dealing with the issues. In the event the White Paper demonstrates such remarkable vision and awareness of the issues that it must be regarded as the model for other countries to follow and must place South Africa at the very forefront of the blue revolution.

Both Africa's spiritual and secular appreciation of water is well captured in the poems taken from the White Paper:

> *From water is born all peoples of the earth. There is water within us, let there be water with us. Water never rests. When flowing above, it causes rain and dew. When flowing below it forms streams and rivers. If a way is made for it, it flows along that path. And we want to make that path. We want the water of this country to flow out into a network – reaching every individual – saying: here is this water, for you. Take it; cherish it as affirming*

your human dignity; nourish your humanity. With water we will wash away the past, we will from now on ever be bounded by the blessing of water.' (Mazisi Kunene)

Water has many forms and many voices. Unhonoured, keeping its seasons and rages, its rhythms and trickles, water is there in the nursery bedroom; water is there in the apricot tree shading the backyard, water is in the smell of grapes on an autumn plate, water is there in the small white intimacy of washing underwear. Water – gathered and stored since the beginning of time in layers of granite and rock, in the embrace of dams, the ribbons of rivers – will one day, unheralded, modestly, easily, simply flow out to every South African who turns a tap. That is my dream.' (Antjie Krog)

South Africa has the political will to address water, land-use and forestry issues and a governmental structure which is almost uniquely suited for the purpose: both the water and forestry sectors are within the same ministry, the Department of Water Affairs and Forestry (DWAF). To achieve the goal of 'Equity, efficiency and sustainability in the supply and use of water in South Africa', Professor Kader Asmal, Minister of DWAF, has initiated the National Water Conservation Campaign and conservation projects which include the Working for Water Programme (DWAF, 1996) (see below).

South Africa has also carried through a programme of adaptive forest hydrology research that has made use of knowledge gained in other parts of the world and supplemented this with research on forest–water interactions in South African conditions. This carefully executed research, carried out in close collaboration with stakeholders with forestry interests and downstream user and environmental interests, has resulted in findings which are not only widely disseminated but are also accepted by these different groups.

This has led South Africa not only to endorse the conventional 'polluter pays' principle, which requires the polluter of the environment to either pay for its remedial treatment or to pay society in recompense for the loss of environmental quality, but to originate a new principle, the 'user pays' principle. This requires land uses that consume large amounts of water, such as forestry, to pay what is now commonly becoming known as an 'interception levy'. South Africa is unusual in having the awareness and confidence to address the issues and the confidence in its research to advance this new approach.

Water and Land-use Issues

Water has always been a major concern in South Africa. The average annual rainfall amounts to 440mm, of which less than 10 per cent reaches the rivers. In the 1920s, farmers' associations and other organizations petitioned the government to investigate why many of South Africa's rivers were drying up.

At the time there was a drive to encourage tree planting. The forester's myth of the hydrological benefits of forests was under suspicion. There were concerns that extensive plantations of exotic pine, eucalypts and wattle were reducing water supplies, exhausting the soil and promoting erosion. The issue of forestry and water supplies was discussed at the Fourth Empire Forestry Conference hosted by South Africa in 1935, and as a result a research station was established at Jonkershoek in the south-western Cape with the task: 'to determine how normal afforestation, as carried out in State plantations, would affect climate, water conservation and erosion'. Dr C L Wicht, founder of the station, devised an experimental design of catchment research which was based on the paired-catchment principle as used at Emmental in Switzerland and Wagon Wheel Gap in Colorado, USA. But Dr Wicht was quick to realize that no two catchments of the eight identified for research at Jonkershoek were even remotely comparable. He devised a novel approach:

> *Each stream is to be studied independently and compared with itself before and after treatment. In each case all factors which might influence streamflow will be observed and correlated. It is hoped that such analysis will disclose general trends common to all catchments. On the basis of these trends it may be possible to generalize as to the effects of afforestation on streamflow in the winter rainfall region.* (Wicht, 1939)

It was this attention to detail that ensured that the potential of the catchment study approach was maximized so that any identified changes in the flow regime could be correctly attributed to either the change in land use or to other climatic or environmental variables. This 'belt and braces' approach entailed extra costs in the operation of both the calibration period and the paired-catchment comparison period, and delays in obtaining the final result (because of the extra time required for the calibration). With hindsight, this was clearly justified by the achievement of unambiguous and indisputable results: results which, because they are so clear-cut and unmistakable, have been accepted by both the scientific and policymaker communities. Since 1972, the Forest Act has required timber growers to apply for permits to establish commercial plantations on new land or sections of land which have not been planted for five years, and applications may be rejected on the grounds of high water use. Robust empirical models now exist (Scott and Smith, 1997) for calculating the reduction in total and low flows to assist with this task. This acceptance of the findings of the carefully conducted research in South Africa has led to them being used as the basis of water and land management policy. In other countries discussion and debate is still clouded by the 'forester's myth' and by short-term and sometimes poorly conducted research which has given ambiguous results. This research has also led to the question 'should South Africa, a water-scarce country, be exporting its water in the form of forests?'

Upland Water and Land-use Conflicts

Mountains are the dominant influence on South Africa's surface water resources. Only 20 per cent of the country receives more than 800mm of rain and most of this is in mountainous areas. For such a water-deficient country, the provision of water from the uplands, maximal in quantity and quality, is of vital concern.

The forests require at least 800mm of rain to grow at economic rates, so these same mountain catchments come under pressure both for afforestation and for water gathering. Commercial forests consist almost entirely of exotic species and form a large and important industry with plantations occupying almost 1.2 million hectares (Bands et al, 1987). Nowhere are the conflicts between forestry and water interests more extreme than in South Africa.

The predominant indigenous vegetation cover in the mountains is not forest. Under the influence of periodic bushfires, grassland and unique fynbos communities have evolved as the natural vegetation cover, with patches of indigenous forest being confined to small areas on cool and protected sites. Together with demands for water and economic-driven demands for timber, there are now ecological demands for the fynbos to be conserved.

Upland Land Use, Ecology and Hydrology Interrelationships

Understanding of the interrelationships between land use, hydrology and ecology is essential for the sustainable and multi-use management of South Africa's mountainous areas. The hydrological research programme centred at Jonkershoek, which by the 1960s had become even more focused on ecological concerns, is providing that understanding. The catchment studies provide unequivocal evidence for the reductions in streamflow that will occur as a result of afforestation with commercial species (Table 6.12).

The studies also destroy the forester's myth that forests 'attract rain'.

> *Forests are associated with high rainfall, cool slopes or moist areas. There is some evidence that, on a continental scale, forests may form part of a hydrological feedback loop with evaporation contributing to further rainfall. On the Southern African subcontinent, the moisture content of air masses is dominated by marine sources, and afforestation will have negligible influence on rainfall and macroclimates. The distribution of forests is a consequence of climate and soil conditions – not the reverse.* (Bands et al, 1987)

The studies also confirmed that periodic fire and its management were essential not only for the maintenance of the natural vegetation, but also for the maintenance of the soil mantle, the unique fauna and water yield. To maintain the ecology of the fynbos, fire is needed at intervals of between 10 and 30 years to germinate seedlings. Fire intervals shorter than about 6 to 10 years

Table 6.12 *Impact of afforestation on streamflow determined by catchment studies in South Africa*

Experimental catchment	Natural vegetation	Rainfall (mm)	Natural runoff (mm)	Afforestation	Streamflow reductions (mm)
Bosboukloof Jonkershoek	Fynbos	1300	600	*Pinus radiata* (57%) (1940)	330 at 23 years
Biesievlei Jonkershoek	Fynbos	1430	660	*P. radiata* (98%) (1948)	400 at 15 years
Tierkloof Jonkershoek	Fynbos	1800	1000	*P. radiata* (36%) (1956)	500 at 16 years
Lambrechtbos Jonkershoek	Fynbos	1500	530	*P. radiata* (84%) (1961)	170 (mean 8 to 16 years)
Catchment 2 Cathedral Peak	Grassland	1400	750	*Pinus patula* (75%) (1951)	375 at 17 years 440 at 22 years
Catchment A Mokobulaan	Grassland	1150	250	*E. grandis* (100%) (1969)	403 at 5 years
Catchment B Mokobulaan	Grassland	1040	220	*P. patula* (100%) (1969)	100 at 5 years (tentative result)
Catchment C Mokobulaan	Grassland	1200	180	Control	–
Catchment D Westfalia	Indigenous forest	1700	720	*E. grandis*	200 at 3 years

Source: Bands et al (1987)

eliminate many plant species, whilst protection from fire for more than 30 years results in senescence. Burning of the fynbos also increases water yield; the burning of 23-year-old fynbos resulted in streamflow increases of 200mm in the first year after burning (Bands et al, 1987). Burning of grassland has a negligible effect on water yield because of the winter dormancy of grass and its rapid regrowth to full canopy in the spring.

A major threat to the fynbos ecology and to the water yield from these upland areas is from the invasion of alien shrubs and trees. Two of the most dangerous species are the Australian shrub, silky hakea (*Hakea sericea*), and the Mediterranean cluster pine (*Pinus pinaster*). A major programme of IWRM directed at eliminating or controlling these invaders, to conserve water yields and the ecology of these areas whilst providing economic returns and employment opportunities, is now underway.

Invasive Trees

Probably nowhere else in the world is the tight link between land use and water resources better appreciated than in South Africa. Not only have research programmes been geared to determining the impacts of plantation forestry, for forest and land management purposes, but research is now being directed at the impacts and management of invasive species, some of which have 'escaped' from the commercial forests. These invaders have much the same impacts as forest plantations in reducing streamflow, but in the unmanaged state they also have other deleterious hydrological effects. The increased amount of plant material, the above-ground biomass, in invaded fynbos areas is three to ten times higher (Versfeld and van Wilgen, 1986) leading to increased fuel loads in the event of a fire. When fire occurs, the intensity is much greater and may well be sufficient to sterilize the soil, killing the seeds of indigenous plants. High-intensity fires will also lead to water repellency in soils which have been associated with high rates of surface runoff and soil erosion in storms following fires (Scott, 1993; Le Maitre et al, 1996). The hydrological consequences are higher floods and increased siltation of watercourses and reservoirs.

It has been standard forestry practice in South Africa to avoid planting trees in the riparian zones of afforested catchments, to reduce the risk of soil erosion close to the stream channel and to avoid any increase in water use by riparian vegetation. Invaders are no respecters of forestry practice and often spread rapidly into these riparian areas (Dye and Poulter, 1995). It has been demonstrated that removal of infestations of self-established riparian trees can have huge effects on streamflow. Dye and Poulter (ibid) have shown that removal of a strip of self-sown *Pinus patula* and *Acacia mearnsii* along a 500m riparian zone at Kalmoesfontein increased streamflow by 120 per cent. Even more dramatic are reports of a stream in Mpumalanga (DWAF, 1996) which, before the clearing of a 500m strip of riparian *Eucalyptus grandis*, disappeared within 50m of entering the stand. About three weeks after clearing the eucalypts the stream was visible for 200m in the stand, and after one month it was running through the stand. It was postulated that it had taken about a month for the stream and rainfall to recharge the water table, restoring a perennial stream from a dry streambed.

The hydrological dangers from invading trees are not just local in their impact. It has been calculated (Le Maitre et al, 1996) that unless curtailed, invaders will eventually reduce the water supply to Cape Town by 30 per cent. It has also been shown that the cost of water from the best dam option is several times more expensive than the cost of water yielded through clearing the invading aliens (DWAF, 1996).

Working for Water

> *Through the clearing of invasive alien plants, the Working for Water Programme is helping us to secure vital water supplies. It typifies the aspirations of the Reconstruction and Development Programme. Already it has brought hope and dignity to thousands of South Africans by creating jobs and business opportunities, and by empowering local communities to care for water and their natural environment.* (President Nelson Mandela)

Table 6.13 *Water resource, ecological and social benefits following the clearing of invasive plants*

No clearing	20-year clearing programme
Water	
Total infestation of catchments in 40–50 years	Far greater long-term water security
Loss of ~3000 million m³ of water per year	Optimal flow in rivers in dry seasons
Cost to replace lost water ~R12000 million	Cost to clear invader plants ~R900 million
Very high price of water and seasonal shortages	More affordable and assured supply of water
Massive soil erosion and siltation of dams	Greatly reduced soil erosion and dam siltation
Greater scouring of rivers and increased flooding	Reduced scouring of rivers and flooding
Ecological	
Extinction of over 1000 plant and animal species	No extinction of plants and animal species
Some rivers, estuaries, wetlands and aquifers will dry up	Enhanced ecological functioning of water systems
Massive impacts of fires on life and property	Greater stability and diversity in ecological systems
Social	
Greater levels of unemployment	4000 direct jobs for 20 years
Increases in crime and non-payment of services	Empowerment, community-building, human dignity
Lost opportunity for social development	Benefits for health, welfare, social stability
Migration of rural communities to urban areas	Migration of urban communities to rural areas
Loss of productive agricultural land	Possible increase in productive agricultural land
Loss of use of wild flowers, thatching grass, herbs	Very profitable harvesting of 'wild' resources

Source: Working for Water Programme

South Africa's Working for Water Programme is directed at controlling invasive alien species of shrubs and trees for ecological and water conservation purposes, but it is recognized that its greatest challenge is to optimize the opportunities for reconstruction and social development. The well-executed adaptive ecological and hydrological research has provided the base which has given politicians the confidence to initiate such an expensive and innovative IWRM programme, sure in the knowledge that the benefits are going to outweigh the costs. The options of clearing or not clearing the invaders are clearly spelled out in the programme's publicity material, an extract of which is given in Table 6.13.

In the opinion of the Department of Water Affairs and Forestry:

by cutting down invading alien plants (such as wattles and pines), we significantly enhance the availability of water. Invasive alien plants grow and spread. If we fail to eradicate them, they will strangle our water supplies. In essence, either we pay now, or we pay more later.

The South African National Water Act

The South African National Water Act (NWA) of 1998 is arguably the leading example of water legislation based on IWRM principles. With the election of the post-apartheid government in 1994 the opportunity existed for not just incremental adjustments to existing policies but also a complete rewriting of policies that would meet the new political imperatives and integrated resource considerations. Furthermore, the emergence of a new water resources paradigm (Gleick, 2000) based on IWRM had matured with the acceptance of the Dublin–Rio principles in 1992 and South Africa was uniquely placed to take advantage of this. The drivers behind the creation of the National Water Act can thus be considered to be both political and hydrological.

Political drivers:

- To move away from the colonial rules and regulations of well-watered European countries, which considered the interests of a dominant group with privileged access to land and water.
- To move towards laws that focus on the dry and variable climate in South Africa, and promote use which is optimal for the achievement of equitable and sustainable economic and social development.
- To legitimize water use only if it is beneficial to the public interest.
- To meet the basic human need for water and to maintain ecological sustainability of river systems.

Hydrological drivers:

- All water in each phase of the water cycle needs to be treated as part of the common resource and will be subject to a water charge. This has given rise to the inclusion of Stream Flow Reduction Activities (SFRAs) as legitimate water users in the NWA.
- A vast pool of experimental evidence that forests of exotic tree species reduce streamflow resulted in forestry being listed as the first SFRA. Forestry is therefore subject to a water use charge.
- Scarcity and sensitivity of South Africa's water resources. South Africa is an arid country with only 1200 m3 of fresh water available for each person per year. More than 50 per cent of all the available fresh water resources is already used, compared to 5 per cent and 10 per cent of neighbouring arid countries (Namibia and Botswana).

Innovative Land and Water Policy from South Africa – The SFRA

In South Africa, forestry has historically been recognized as an important water user and concerns for the protection of water resources have led to the control of commercial afforestation and forestry practices since 1972, when a system known as the Afforestation Permit System (APS) was implemented. The APS has since been superseded by the implementation of the new National Water Act (NWA) (Act no. 36 of 1998). According to the NWA, forestry is now known as a 'stream flow reduction activity' (SFRA) and as such must be licensed as one of 11 categories of water use. A stream flow reduction activity is defined as '… any activity (including the cultivation of any particular crop or other vegetation) … [that] … is likely to reduce the availability of water in a watercourse to the Reserve, to meet international obligations, or to other water users significantly' (NWA Section 36(2)).

In Chapter 4 of the NWA the general principles for regulating water use (as part of the National Government's responsibility to manage the scarce water resources) are set out. 'Water-use' is defined in section 21 of this chapter of the act, and includes, among others 'engaging in a stream flow reduction activity'. Only forestry is presently a registered SFRA (DWAF, 2003). Another section (section 36) of the Act sets out the guidelines for determining whether a land-based activity (in addition to forestry) should be declared an SFRA and hence added to the list of water users. Once a land-based activity is declared as a water user, the activity is then subject to water use entitlement, similar to all the other water users. Licences are granted by the provincial Licence Assessment Advisory Committees after consideration of the estimated overall water use per quaternary catchment provided by the provincial departments of DWAF. Water use licences are granted or declined based on consideration of all water use needs in the catchment and whether the proposed use is deemed 'beneficial'. The panels have adopted the responsibility for ensuring good forestry practice in terms of both society and the environment.

Equity and fairness underlie the development of the SFRA concept with the intention of introducing the concept to all users of water in whatever form it is used. Thus, whether water is made use of from a catchment in liquid form, water which in the Falkenmark (1995) terminology is defined as 'blue' water and is water which can be abstracted from streamflow or groundwater, or whether it is made use of in vapour form through evaporation, termed 'green' water, the same regulations would, in principle, apply.

In some regards, the control of commercial afforestation by the erstwhile 'Permit System' and the subsequent declaration of forestry as a SFRA, could be considered a water resource management tool which considers the linkages between terrestrial vapour flows in the form of green water (arising in the most part through transpiration from vegetation which enables vegetative growth, agricultural crop production and biomass production in trees) and blue water (streamflow). However, the somewhat misleading focus on blue water in the declaration of SFRAs does little to promote this concept.

Furthermore, it could be argued that the issue of 'beneficial use' is considered largely in social and environmental terms and receives inadequate economic consideration.

Difficulties with the implementation of the SFRA policy range from administrative to political to hydrological, but are not regarded as insurmountable and much progress has been made in implementing the policy. Since declaration of an SFRA implies a certain amount of control by Government over land-based activities, and potentially also has financial implications for land owners, implementation of the policy has understandably met with resistance from affected landowners. The large-scale production of sugar cane within South Africa has alerted Government to this land use being identified as a potential SFRA, and growers are now contesting the proposed declaration on the basis of how the SFRA is defined within the Act. Their main argument is that 'significance' of streamflow reduction has to be proved for each particular area before a land-based SFRA activity can be declared. They maintain that the variation in climatic, soil, water demand and economic and social conditions makes this nearly impossible. The Government has offered its own interpretation of the Act, along with simplified criteria to be used to declare and regulate SFRAs. A consultative process and negotiation is presently underway.

Affected land owners have also questioned the terminology used in the Act. In the drafting of the South African NWA, early discussions regarding SFRAs proposed an associated levy known as a 'resource conservation charge'. This has now been implemented as a 'water resource management charge', currently calculated on a per hectare basis for SFRAs. Some role-players in the forest industry have called this a 'rain tax'. However, this is disingenuous – rather, it is suggested, and using 'green water' terminology, it would be more appropriate to regard this levy as a charge for an ecosystem service. The service would be the production of the biomass in a forest stand and the levy would be based on the estimate of the changes in green water flows caused by the transformation from a natural, or baseline, land use to a commercial land use involving afforestation.

Implementation of a policy of water use regulation relating to land-based activities is admittedly cumbersome, expensive and creates an administrative burden. Being classified as a 'water use' in terms of the Act will require first of all registration as a user, it may further require licensing, determining the water use, and also payment of a water resource management charge. Considering the shift from large to small growers in forestry and sugar cane, the task of registering and keeping track of these activities could be considerable. However, these difficulties should be weighed against the need for fairness and equity in a country where water is recognized as having high value in all its uses whether for supply, crop production or ecology. Institutional arrangements to deal with the administrative issues are now far advanced.

The hydrological difficulties pertaining to implementation of the SFRA policy lie firstly in the measurement of water use of a land-based activity. The term SFRA and the way it is defined in the Act unfortunately complicate measurement of evaporation (green water). The term 'stream flow reduction activity' and the way it is defined in the NWA implies that evaporation from a land-based activity should be expressed and measured in terms of its effect on streamflow (hydrograph) only. Besides making it very difficult to assess water use in this way, it partly defeats the objective of accounting for green water in order to identify its use in each phase of the hydrological cycle (Ashton et al, 2002). (It is recognized that a revision of the definition and terminology used in the Act may be required.)

A second problem with determining water use of a land-based activity is to define the baseline vegetation to which the water use of an activity should be compared. It was proposed by Government, and generally accepted, that the natural vegetation types that would potentially have grown in a particular area should be used as the baseline. The implication was that measurement of water use of a crop (land-based activity) would now require also the determination of the water use of a potential natural vegetation type. Detailed vegetation maps are now available in South Africa and numerous projects are under way to determine water use of the different vegetation types. This leads to the issue of accuracy to which water use of land-based activities can be estimated. Scientists are now challenged with developing methodologies to calculate the water use of crops, as compared with natural vegetation, under a very wide range of conditions in both space and time. The production of acceptable methodologies which preserve an acceptable degree of accuracy will require innovative approaches to modelling complex situations, and a process of negotiation and agreement between a wide range of users.

Recent Developments in Linking 'Statutory' and Markets Approaches

The Working for Water (WfW) programme of the South African DWAF can be considered, alongside the SFRA, as another innovative 'statutory' policy instrument related to land and water management. Although closely focused on the potential blue water benefits associated with removing invasive alien plants (IAPs), particularly forestry species from infested catchments, the WfW programme is not bound by the same limits applying to the SFRA legislation and terminology and thus has the flexibility to more fully explore new options for the management of both land and water resources. In this regard, consideration has been given to market-type approaches for rewarding or compensating land owners who clear IAPs from riparian zones with water use licences for commercial forests elsewhere in the catchment (Jewitt et al, 2000) and more recently the possibility of granting a water use licence to a mining concern in return for the clearing and maintenance of stretches of river infested by IAPs (Marais, personal communication). Other opportunities for water-related market mechanisms in South Africa have been reviewed by King and colleagues (King et al, 2003).

Chapter 7

Integrated Land and Water Resource Management

CONCEPTS AND PRINCIPLES

The crucial need to integrate the land component in integrated water resource management, fundamental to the blue revolution, is becoming increasingly recognized. The term integrated land and water resource management (ILWRM) is now accepted terminology for the philosophy or process underlying the integrated management of land and water resources.

Land and water management occurs at different levels within society ranging from that exercised by donors and governments to that exercised by individuals. The blue revolution must recognize the different mechanisms and different governance systems that exist in society for managing land and water, and ensure that wherever possible these can access the best available science-based evidence and can operate in an open and transparent manner without recourse to the 'sanctioned discourse'.

Unlike earlier quests for the development of a tightly defined 'water resources master plan' there is increasing recognition that ILWRM is more likely to be achieved if it is structured as an incremental, evolving iterative process. Earlier attempts at finding optimal solutions (in the linear programming sense) to the conflicting demands on the land and water resource have been largely abandoned in favour of 'satisficing' or workable solutions involving incremental change without requiring unnecessarily abrupt and disruptive changes. ILWRM must accommodate means of obtaining progressive commitments from stakeholders to new developments and initiatives. This new paradigm that is developing is the essence of the blue revolution. Technological, or 'hard', methodologies and solutions cannot ever, on their own, be sufficient. They need to be blended and tempered with 'soft' methods that can deal with the human dimension. The 'hard' tools, for example, computer-based geographic information system-linked (GIS-linked) hydrological models, need to be constructed so that they can incorporate socio-economic models which can then be used to evaluate and compare different development options.

ILWRM involves the coordinated planning and management of land, water and other environmental resources for their equitable, efficient and sustainable use. ILWRM programmes need to be developed alongside, and not in isolation from, economic structural adjustment and other sectoral programmes. For ILWRM strategies to be implemented, fragmentation of institutional responsibilities must be reduced.

ILWRM objectives encompass the UNCED principles:

- Water has multiple uses and water and land must be managed in an integrated way.
- Water should be managed at the lowest appropriate level.
- Water allocation should take account of the interests of all who are affected.
- Water should be recognized and treated as an economic good.

ILWRM strategies seek to ensure:

- a long-term viable economic future for basin dependants (both national and trans-national);
- equitable access to water resources for basin dependants;
- the application of principles of demand management and appropriate pricing policies to encourage efficient usage of water between the agricultural, industrial and urban supply sectors;
- in the short term, the prevention of further environmental degradation and, in the longer term, the restoration of degraded resources; and
- the safeguarding of local cultural heritage and the local ecology as they relate to water management and the maintenance and encouragement of the potential for water-related tourism together with linkages between tourism and conservation.

ILWRM strategies should recognize that:

- solutions must focus on underlying causes not merely their symptoms;
- issues must be approached in an integrated way; and
- in general, development of sound resource management and collective responsibility for resources will take place at the sub-regional or village level.

ILWRM implementation programmes should:

- comprise an overall strategy that clearly defines the management objectives, a range of delivery mechanisms that enable these objectives to be achieved, and a monitoring schedule that evaluates programme performance;
- recognize that the development of water resource management strategies may require research to assess the resource base and, through the use of models and the development of decision support systems, to determine

the linkages between water resource development and the impacts on the environment, socio-economics, equity and ecology; and

- ensure that mechanisms and policies are established that enable long-term support to programmes of environmental recovery.

The blue revolution is dependent on these tools and these 'integrating' methodologies and they are being rapidly constructed. They are being recast in both the hard mould, which captures all our recent advances in information technology and the physical and environmental sciences, and in the soft mould, which contains our new appreciation of the complexity and importance of the human players in unstructured real world systems, systems where tensions and conflicts abound and where the linkages between different interest groups are ill defined. They are being developed so that society's appreciation of land use and water resources in relation to conservation, amenity, recreation and environment (CARE) issues can be quantified. Most importantly, these tools are being designed and constructed to work and mesh together. The success of this design will be of crucial importance to the success and rapid advance of the blue revolution.

LAND AND WATER GOVERNANCE

Although Water Governance and holistic and integrated approaches to water resources management feature strongly in the international water agenda, in many countries water governance is in a state of confusion. The specific water governance issues vary. In some countries there is a total lack of water institutions, and others display fragmented institutional structures (sector-by-sector approach) and overlapping and/or conflicting decision-making structures. In many places conflicting upstream and downstream interests regarding riparian rights and access to water resources are pressing issues that need immediate attention; in many other cases there are strong tendencies to divert public resources for personal gain, or unpredictability in the use of laws and regulations and licensing practices, which impede markets and voluntary action and encourage corruption and other forms of rent-seeking behaviour. (UN World Development Report, 2003)

Solution of many of the problems and perverse outcomes in relation to land and water policies and watershed development projects (as identified in Chapter 5) rests primarily in the realm of governance.

The *United Nations World Development Report* (UNESCO, 2003) defines governance as the exercise of economic, political and administrative authority to manage a country's affairs at all levels. It comprises the mechanisms, processes and institutions through which citizens and groups articulate their interests, exercise their legal rights, meet their obligations and mediate their differences.

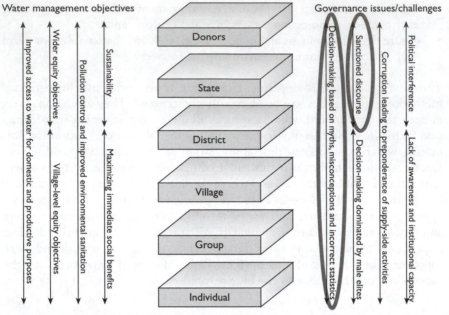

Water management objectives

Governance issues/challenges

Note: Shown circled are the major challenges related to 'myth busting' and eliminating the 'sanctioned discourse'
Source: Batchelor (2005)

Figure 7.1 *Water management objectives and governance challenges at different levels in society*

In a land and water context, governance is considered as the range of political, social, economic and administrative systems that are in place to develop and manage land and water resources, and the delivery of water services at different levels of society. Thus, governance relates to the way decisions are made rather than the decisions themselves. In many developing and developed countries the core challenge in ILWRM is that of land and water governance, particularly in relation to the deeper political and societal foundations on which day-to-day decisions and courses of action rest. Recognition of the land and water objectives at different levels in society and the governance challenges they face at the different levels (Figure 7.1), may assist the task of identifying the correct 'entry points' on which to initiate actions (Batchelor, 2005).

Recognition that the administrative boundaries of governance systems do not match spatially and identically with the physical boundaries of land and water systems (Figure 7.2) is another issue that must be taken into account within ILWRM.

It is also recognized that difficult ILWRM decisions will have to be made if both poverty reduction and environmental sustainability are to be addressed effectively. In some countries the issues are seen as a conflict between 'water for fish' and 'water for people'. Although some 'win–win' solutions may exist, it is likely that meeting the joint objectives of long-term environmental sustainability and poverty reduction will almost inevitably involve negative trade-offs (Batchelor, 2005).

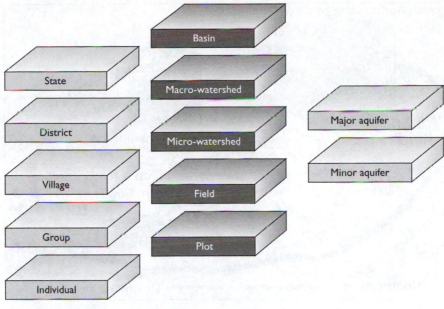

Source: Batchelor (2005)

Figure 7.2 *Governance systems need to recognize the disjuncts that exist between hydrological and administrative boundaries*

Marcus Moench and colleagues (Moench et al, 2003) have argued, from consideration of case studies of river basins in India and Nepal, that the challenge for water management in South Asia is neither primarily about the ability of governments, non-governmental organizations (NGOs) or communities to choose between one or other set of technically viable solutions to water problems, nor is it really about integration or planning mechanisms for resolving multiple demands on and disputes over a limited water resource base. They argue that the core 'water' challenge is one of governance, particularly the deeper 'constitutional' foundations on which day-to-day decisions and courses of action rest.

They state:

> *Since both natural and social conditions are changing and are subject to substantial uncertainty, we cannot make linear plans that will solve water problems for our lifetimes or for future decades. Instead, we need the capacity (information, fora and processes for decision-making, legal and regulatory mechanisms, executive capabilities, and governance with embedded dispute resolution mechanisms) to enable society to respond to constraints that could be local or regional, short or long term, political, economic or technical. This is the real challenge.*

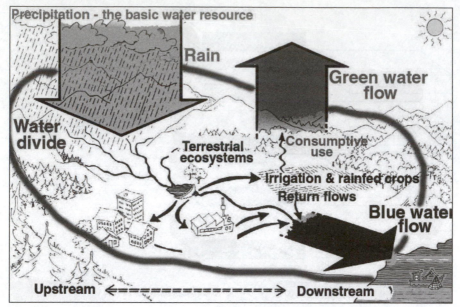

Source: Falkenmark (2003)

Figure 7.3 *Falkenmark's green and blue water terminology, which has been very effective in conveying to non-hydrologists the importance of evaporation (green water) and the management potential for managing green water as part of the hydrological cycle*

ILWRM Methodologies

Green and Blue Water Terminology

Professor Malin Falkenmark, senior scientist at the Stockholm International Water Institute, introduced the green and blue water terminology (Falkenmark, 1995) as a means of conveying to non-hydrologists the importance of evaporation (green water), and the potential for managing evaporation, as part of the hydrological cycle (Figure 7.3). This terminology has had widespread take up. More 'colours' have been introduced by other groups to subdivide the type of water but it is not clear whether this has actually increased or confused understanding and detracted from the simplicity of the original concept. The concept has been used very effectively by Malin Falkenmark to revisit and raise awareness of the question of how the world is eventually going to meet its food needs. The concept has also been used in relation to South Africa's land and water policies, which were originally geared to managing (blue water) flows in rivers but which can now increasingly be seen to be considering, and attempting to manage, the green water component also.

Green and Blue Water Approaches for Evaluating the Water Requirements for the World's Food Needs

In Chapter 2 it was mentioned that some of the early global sustainability concerns, such as those of Meadows and colleagues in their book, *The Limits to Growth* (Meadows et al, 1972), were later discredited when some of the crisis scenarios that were laid out did not in fact happen. But if we look more closely at how, until now, some of these crises have been avoided, it suggests that these may not have been solved but have just been deferred to the (perhaps not too distant) future.

Gordon Conway, President of the Rockefeller Foundation, (Conway, 1999) and Conway and Toenniessen (1999, 2003) have argued that the green revolution, one of the great technological success stories of the second half of the 20th century, through the introduction of scientifically bred, higher-yielding varieties of rice, wheat and maize, allowed overall food production in the developing countries to keep pace with population growth, with both more than doubling. They state that the benefits of the green revolution reached many of the world's poorest people:

> *Forty years ago there were a billion people in developing countries who did not get enough to eat, equivalent to 50 per cent of the population of these countries. If this proportion had remained unchanged, the hungry would now number over two billion – more than double the current estimate of around 800 million, or around 20 per cent of the present population of the developing world. Since the 1970s, world food prices have declined in real terms by over 70 per cent. Those who benefit most are the poor, who spend the highest proportion of their family income on food.*

But they also argue that the gains in food production provided by the green revolution technologies have reached their capacity, yet the world's population continues to rise. They call for increased efforts in plant biotechnology research to increase food production.

They are critical of current market-based models of food production which attempt to mimic the workings of a world market in which demand for food is met by supply. Although these models suggest that the world population growth rate will be matched by a similar growth in food production and that world food prices will continue to decline, it is clear that most developing countries will not be able to afford the cost of buying food in international markets to meet local demands. In the model produced by the International Food Policy Research Institute (IFPRI), the total shortfall in food production per year in developing countries in 2020 will be some 190 million tons and the model predicts this can be met by imports from the developed countries. But Conway argues that the flaw in this logic is that the poor will be simply priced out of the market. The market-based projection models will not take account of the needs of the poor because their needs are 'hidden'.

Table 7.1 *The hidden and total food needs by the year 2020, assuming a cereal need equivalent to 3000 calories per person per day*

	Hidden food gap	Imports	Total food gap (the need minus production and imports)
East Asia	—	55.8	55.8
South Asia	160.0	22.7	182.7
West Asia/ North Africa		68.5	68.5
Sub-Saharan Africa	187.5	26.1	213.6
Latin America/Caribbean	11.6	15.0	26.6
Total developing countries	359.1	188.1	547.2

Note: Figures are millions of tons
Source: Conway (1999)

Conway has taken a different approach to forecasting food requirements based on the minimum energy need requirement for a person to remain healthy. Taking a value of 3000 cereal calories per day to cover food, livestock feed, seed, storage losses and waste during processing, Conway calculates the total food gap, in terms of cereals, of 214 million tons for Sub-Saharan Africa and 183 million tons for South Asia in the year 2020. If all this food were to be supplied by the developed countries, it would require nearly 550 million tons, some three times that (190 million tons) predicted by the market model (Table 7.1).

Malin Falkenmark (2003) recognized the significance of the 'hidden food gap' and asked what will be the water resource implication and water needs of another big increase in food production to meet the world's growing food requirements. Based on crop water requirements to produce different foods, the composition of different diets, and the food needs for a nutritionally acceptable diet, a per-capita water requirement of 1300m^3 yr^{-1} in consumptive water use (i.e. green water use where water is lost to the system through evaporation) has been suggested (Falkenmark and Rockstrom, 2004). (It should be noted that this figure is irrespective of whether the roots get the water directly from rainfall or from applied irrigation water. It should also be noted that this figure is about 70 times that of a suggested figure of 50 litre day^{-1}, which represents estimates of household level water requirements for drinking and sanitation, Gleick (1996)).

By taking account of the extra 1300m^3 required each year for each extra person on the planet and the extra water requirement to raise the nutritional level of all the undernourished individuals in the world of today, Falkenmark and Rockstrom (2004) arrived at the following global amounts of additional green water:

by 2025: + 3800km^3 yr^{-1}

by 2050: + 5600km^3 yr^{-1}

Falkenmark highlighted the magnitude of the quantities involved by indicating that the next generation will require an additional amount of green water that is equivalent to ALL blue water use by humanity today. By the second generation another 60 per cent will be needed.

At the regional scale the predictions between the present time and 2025 were:

Sub-Saharan Africa   3.1 times the present $(460–1450 km^3 yr^{-1})$
Asia (except Russia)   2.2 times the present $(2830–6210 km^3 yr^{-1})$

Falkenmark suggested three possible sources for this extra water:

1   Irrigation, i.e. redirecting even more water from rivers (blue water) to meet green water requirements.
2   Increased 'crop-per-drop' efficiency, i.e. losses in current agricultural water use (irrigated as well as rain fed) could be put to productive use.
3   Horizontal expansion by which green water now used for plant production by natural ecosystems (forests, grasslands) would be used for production of crops instead.

Falkenmark and Rockstrom (2004) analysed the potential contribution by 2050 of meeting needs from these different sources:

Irrigation: maximum $800 km^3 yr^{-1}$
Crop-per-drop improvements   maximum $1500 km^3 yr^{-1}$
Horizontal expansion   minimum $3300 km^3 yr^{-1}$

Clearly diverting further blue water for irrigation will not be welcomed by environmentalists who feel the need to conserve most of the remaining streamflow for the benefit of aquatic ecosystems (Chapter 2, Chapter 5, IUCN 2000). Furthermore, even if this option were environmentally acceptable, it would only provide one-seventh of the extra green water requirement.

More effective might be crop-per-drop improvements, particularly if these can be applied to dry land agriculture.

But ultimately, the implication of the analyses by Malin Falkenmark and Johan Rockstrom are that, assuming current world population projections are correct (and unless a presently unknown way of producing food can be found), there will be a need to enlarge the present agricultural lands on the planet. This can only be achieved by expansion into the current rangelands or forests of the world. Both of these options are likely to be as unpopular to environmentalists as transferring more river water for irrigation.

Where rangelands are suitable for dry land agriculture, the conversion could lead to huge improvements in the ratio of the amount of food produced per unit of green water evaporated. Water requirements for meat production have been estimated to be $\sim 5 m^3 1000 kcal^{-1}$ based on grain-fed meat-producing cattle (Pimentel and Houser, 1997; Gleick, 2000). This is ten times the water requirement for the same value of vegetarian food: Rockstrom (2003) has suggested 0.53m^3 1000kcal^{-1} as an average value for cereal and vegetable crops. Rockstrom also points out that much of the world's meat production is from grass-fed cattle and has estimated ratios of as much as 10–30m^3 1000kcal^{-1} under these conditions – implying a 20–60 times higher water requirement than for vegetarian foods. But if this conversion were to occur it would require not only the loss of rangeland, which like forests may have high environmental values, but a change of food habits to more vegetarian food.

These are some of the hard decisions that will need to be made if the world's population is to be fed. Meeting the Millennium Development Goals (Chapter 2) will require more than progress on each of the food, water and environmental fronts. It will require some hard trade-offs and the recognition that win–win solutions are not always possible in achieving food production and environmental goals.

Green Water Policy Instruments

For decades South Africa has been at the forefront of both research into the hydrological impacts of land-use change and the development of innovative land and water management policies.

South Africa was among the first countries to recognize the need to reserve water for the environment. The environmental lobby, driven by in-stream ecologists, was very effective at promoting its cause and the concept of the 'ecological reserve' was incorporated into the National Water Act (Chapter 6). The focus of many of South Africa's land and water policies has been towards maintaining and allocating the water in streams and rivers, the blue water component of the hydrological cycle. Certain land uses which are recognized as having high evaporative characteristics, which can reduce streamflow (only commercial forestry at present), are being defined as 'Stream Flow Reduction Activities' (SFRAs). The aim is to charge owners of SFRA land uses for the water they consume.

The 'statutory' or regulatory approach to managing land and water that South Africa has adopted with the SFRA can be contrasted with the 'market' approach discussed in Chapter 5. Both have similar aims and objectives even though they arose as the result of very different 'drivers'. Both are experiencing difficulties in implementation.

A question that arose during the course of the Catchment Management and Poverty (CAMP) project (CAMP, 2004) was whether, from consideration of the policy processes leading to the development of the SFRA and the market approach, lessons could be learned that would assist with the development of improved but similarly intentioned land and water policy instruments in South Africa and other countries. The aim was an approach which is 'transparent', defensible, robust to implement and has low transaction costs whilst still meeting environmental, economic efficiency and poverty alleviation benefits. It was suggested that through development and extension of the SFRA principles and casting this as a 'green water policy' instrument, possibly with a 'compensation' or 'incentive' component, some of the above aims might be better achieved. What was proposed was to build on some of the best aspects of the statutory and market approaches whilst trying to minimize the implementation difficulties.

Casting SFRA-type legislation with the focus on how vegetation affects the primary process of evaporation from a catchment (green water) rather than the secondary consequences on streamflow (blue water) would be expected to have the following benefits:

- It would assist with both the writing of legislation and the implementation of policies by simplifying the legal definition of terms. This would be achieved by focusing on the more readily calculable and defensible methodology for estimating evaporative differences from different vegetation types (a methodology which is well advanced and generally accepted in countries such as South Africa) rather than the much more complex and less generally accepted methodologies required for predicting the secondary impacts of different vegetation types and land uses on streamflow.

- It would highlight the importance of evaporative loss as determined by land use within a catchment (water that is effectively 'lost' to the catchment and can never reappear in the stream) and help distinguish this water loss function from the streamflow regulation function of land use. Although from theoretical considerations different types of land use (through, for example, differences in soil properties) might be expected to have different effects on seasonal streamflow, in practice the magnitude of these effects is usually insufficient to allow easy quantification, or even detection, without the use of very detailed measurement and analytical techniques. Whether or not it can be proved that the streamflow regulation function is significant and beneficial for a particular land use it is argued that this function should not be confused with the evaporative 'water loss' function. The regulatory function is replaceable or substitutable by other interventions such as the construction of reservoirs or check dams, but no intervention can replace the water which has been evaporated and lost from the catchment.

- It would help to identify the value of a land use and whether, in the context of the South African NWA, the land use is a beneficial user of water in the public interest (where the declared aim of the act is to 'promote the sustainable, beneficial use of water in the public interest'). This could be achieved through not only assessing the social, ecological and economic benefits of the land use on a land area basis but also by assessing these benefits on the basis of green water use (Hassan et al, 2002). The green water focus enables the establishment of new green water indexes of beneficial use:
  - social: jobs per drop;
  - ecological: an indicator is required for overall ecological value expressed per unit of green water – hops per drop has been suggested as reflecting frogs as an indicator of ecological health!); and
  - economic: dollars per drop.

- It would more easily allow the development of compensation mechanisms which might enable the transfer of payments from 'excess water users', for example, forests, to 'water provider' land uses, for example, annual cropping, particularly annual cropping with a weed-free dry season.

If this option were incorporated into the green water policy instrument then some of the poverty alleviation and equity aspects, aimed for in the 'market' approach, might be more easily realized. The same questions relating to transaction costs and whether small farmers without legal land tenure could benefit from such schemes, identified for market-based instruments, would still need to be addressed. If the transaction cost in setting up compensation payment schemes dealing with large numbers of farmers, some without land tenure, is regarded as prohibitive, an alternative may be to channel compensation funds to communities for communal benefit rather than directly to individual farmers. A model for a communal benefit programme might be for improved land management programmes of the type that are being piloted in South Africa by CSIR if it can be ensured that these programmes still deliver 'water provider' benefits.

South Africa is not the only country devoting attention to the management of green water. In China the Hai Basin Integrated Water and Environment Project, funded by the Global Environment Facility, is introducing innovative green water management methodologies through the allocation of units of evaporation to each administrative county within the basin. It is recognized that the portion of irrigation water consumed through evaporation (green water), locally termed the net extraction, is the amount of water lost to downstream users and the environment. It is expected that managing water resources in terms of evaporation (net extraction) will encourage farmers to maximize the benefits from each allocated evaporation unit. This could be achieved through reducing the evaporation and transpiration which does not contribute to productive plant growth by, for example, reducing waterlogged areas, by irrigating when evaporation is lowest (at night instead of during the day), by using moisture-retaining mulches, and by replacing open irrigation canals and ditches by pipes. Irrigation scheduling and deficit irrigation are other methods that can be employed to significantly increase yield per unit of evaporation.

The crucial water resource driver for this project is the massive overexploitation of water resources within the basin, leading to both groundwater overdrafting (excessive depletion of groundwater levels) and much-reduced flows to the ecologically sensitive Bohai Sea. In this basin, where Beijing is located, groundwater is being pumped (mostly for irrigation) at a rate of 26 billion cubic metres a year, a rate which is estimated (World Bank, 2005) to exceed the recharge by as much as one-third.

The innovative Hai Basin project, task managed for the World Bank by Doug Olson and Liping Jiang, will estimate evaporative water use over the whole basin using remote sensing techniques with sufficient resolution to identify and monitor water use at the farm plot scale, and will then use this information to calculate and allocate evaporation units for each county in the

Table 7.2 *Objectives, drivers, perceptions of land and water interactions, and actual and anticipated implementation problems associated with different land and water policy instruments*

Land and water policy instrument	Declared objectives	Drivers	Perceptions of land and water interactions	Implementation problems (actual and anticipated)
SFRA-charge imposed on excess water use from registered StreamFlow Reduction Activities – forestry and others (potentially) sugar cane, bamboo, jatropha). Markets for Watershed Services – Payments made by downstream beneficiaries of 'watershed services' to upstream land owners and land managers. Evaporative Loss, Land Water Use Charge – green water policy instrument (building on SFRA) but with a compensation mechanism for 'water providing' land uses.	To meet equity, ecological and economic efficiency objectives of the National Water Act (NWA). To meet economic, social (poverty alleviation), environment objectives.	Public and institutional (farmers, ecologists, downstream communities) concerns about the reduction in streamflow caused by commercial forestry. Forestry interests who see market mechanisms as a way of: 1 promoting and financing 'forest protection' and 'sustainable forest management'; 2 circumventing prohibitions on subsidies to 'productive sectors'.	Based on decades of detailed scientific research from catchment experiments and process studies in RSA and awareness of similar studies elsewhere in the world (Bosch and Hewlett, 1982). Traditional public and foresters' beliefs that forests are necessarily good for all aspects of the water environment.	Commercial interests (forestry and sugar cane) question terms, definition and methodologies for estimating land use impacts on streamflow. 1 General absence of groups willing to pay for services. 2 Mechanisms may not be sustainable in the long term unless real benefits (based on science understanding of land and water interactions) can be demonstrated. 3 Little evidence that the poor can benefit – richer farmers and landowners with land title appear to benefit most from existing schemes.
Evaporative Loss, Land Water Use Charge – green water policy instrument (building on SFRA) but with a compensation mechanism through use of the compensation mechanism for 'water providing' land uses.	To meet equity, ecological and economic efficiency objectives together with possibly poverty alleviation through use of the compensation mechanism.	To merge the best components of the SFRA and markets approach to achieve the declared objectives whilst minimizing implementation difficulties.	As for the SFRA above.	1 Implementation problems may be reduced through simpler definition of terminologies and simpler methodologies for estimating evaporation from different land uses (rather than impacts on streamflow). 2 If transaction costs in dealing with large numbers of farmers, some without land tenure is high, an alternative may be to channel compensation fund to communities for improved land management programmes.

basin. The aim is to work with farmers to reduce evaporation to sustainable allocation levels whilst maintaining, if not raising, farm incomes. To assist this task evaporative water use calculations will be correlated with data on crop production and farmer incomes to show the range of yields and incomes per unit of evaporative water use (using essentially similar dollar-per-drop indices that have been derived in South Africa). Recognizing that the productivity of irrigation water is the result of a host of factors, including plant breeding, soil fertility, fertilization, tillage, weed control, soil moisture management, drainage, soil salinity, irrigation scheduling and cropping pattern changes, the project will also work with farmers to improve irrigation and cultivation practices.

The attributes and relative benefits of the different policy instruments are summarized in Table 7.2. More generally, the development of green water policy instruments would also have the potential benefit of focusing attention directly on the issue of what should or should not be considered high water consuming land uses. In some countries the traditional mythology that forests are necessarily always good for the water environment, and that forests are 'providers' of water, still persists..

Malin Falkenmark has used the blue and green water terminology very effectively to highlight the value and importance of the evaporative (green water) component of the hydrological cycle in relation to the crucial question of meeting the world's food needs. The terminology may have similar value in highlighting the opportunities for managing green water in a catchment management context. In particular, when catchments are at or approaching closure, it provides the more positive management option of promoting a move from other land uses to dry land agriculture, than the more negative approach of revoking abstraction licences or curtailing commercial forestry. Falkenmark (2003) has suggested that in a regional context sub-Saharan Africa has considerable opportunity for the 'horizontal expansion' of agriculture into forested or rangeland regions. Green water policy instruments may be one way of promoting this expansion of dry land agriculture.

Allocation Equity

South Africa's apartheid history has left a legacy of inequity, not least in terms of water allocation, which is now being addressed under the Water Allocation Reform Programme (Box 7.1). Whereas the past emphasis had been on 'getting more water', then 'using water more efficiently' (Dent, 2000), the present dominant focus of attention is 'allocating water equitably'. It is increasingly recognized (Turton, 1999) that to achieve peaceful, holistic and equitable progress in southern Africa there is a need to broaden participation and also democratize the process of water allocation. The need is seen as important and urgent in a region beset with conflict and inequalities.

One example of these inequalities can be seen in the Steelpoort Catchment of the Oliphants river system. Here there is the dramatic visual contrast of former homeland areas, where many households have no water in

BOX 7.1 WATER ALLOCATION REFORM – EXTRACTS FROM THE SPEECH BY MS BUYELWA SONJICA, MINISTER OF WATER AFFAIRS AND FORESTRY, 12 APRIL 2005

Today we are declaring WAR; WAR on wasteful use, WAR on inequity in water use and WAR on poverty.

The WAR I am talking about is Water Allocation Reform. Over the past ten years, my department focused on the delivery of basic water supply and sanitation. This was important in restoring the dignity of the lives of our people. In the second decade, having ensured access to clean water for more than 10 million people, the agenda is shifting towards ensuring fairness in access to water for productive purposes and fairness in sharing the benefits from that use.

The National Water Act, through which we will address this matter, is a remarkable piece of legislation – one of the finest pieces of water legislation in the world. It is, to my mind, particularly fine not only because it comprehensively addresses the balance of protection and use, but also because it specifically addresses the issue of redressing the inequities of the past. It is built on the three principles of sustainability, efficiency and equity – three principles that we need to address in water allocation. Three principles that, as custodian of the nation's water resources, I must ensure are adhered to.

Achieving the principle of equity is a particular challenge. As I have mentioned, access to natural resources, including water, is still a predominantly white (and male) privilege. This needs to change. We need to ensure that water can be made available to black entrepreneurs, to women, to the disabled. We need to ensure that water is available to a wide range of users, from small scale farmers and SMMEs to the biggest and most wealthy industrial and agricultural users. We need to make water available in a way that will sustain and grow the first economy while allowing the second economy users to develop into the first economy. And all this we must do in a water scarce country where our water resources are already fully allocated in many catchments and where environmental needs have often been neglected. This is no small challenge.

The 'Water Allocation Reform Framework' addresses this by suggesting methods that could be used to:

- take proactive steps to meet the water needs of historically disadvantaged individuals, women and the poor;
- ensure participation by these groups;
- establish partnerships to build capacity to use water productively because it is not enough to give access to water and expect poor people to prosper if they do not have the land, the start up capital or the skills to grow products or to access markets.; and, through all this,
- to promote the sustainable, efficient and beneficial use of water in the public interest.

In South Africa and internationally, water resources management has often been seen as a highly technical process. Through our approach, however, we want to demonstrate that people sit at the centre of water allocation. The water allocation reform process is fundamentally a socio-political process. However, in order for it to be effective; it must be based on sound and appropriate technical, economic and environmental approaches.

> Just as there are growing demands on our water resources, there are equally loud demands to address the inequities in access to and use of our water resources. To balance these demands, it may be necessary to reallocate water between users, where some water may be taken from existing users to give to those who have none. This is a complex process, and will require extensive consultation with stakeholders in that particular catchment if it is to achieve the goal of equity *and* sustainable and efficient use in the public interest. We will not serve the public interest if water is wasted or used unproductively – there will be less food produced and less jobs created.
>
> *Source:* Speech by Ms. Duyelva Sonjica, 12 April 2005

their homes or easy access to water, a drab and dry land, yet, over the hill, a green landscape exists, bristling with shiny new rotating arm irrigation systems which are squirting jets of water into the air. South Africa has arguably led the way in world terms in developing, in the National Water Act, innovative water policy where the focus is on equity, efficiency and sustainability. But the development of new policies is not sufficient to address past injustice; the Act has to be implemented. One of the more critical and contentious aspects of this implementation will be the reallocation of water, using compulsory licensing (compulsory licensing allows for the reallocation of water by requiring all existing and potential new water users in a catchment, which includes commercial forestry, to reapply for a licence to use water).

Some would argue that this reallocation has to be done quickly or patience will run out and, in a situation similar to Zimbabwe where inequitable land ownership between white and black farmers became a crisis issue, inequitable sharing of water might become the major divisive issue in South Africa. Others argue that existing users of water are making productive use of the resource, are contributing to employment and growth and, importantly, have the capacity for responsible use of water. It is therefore clear that the way in which water is reallocated between users is an extremely sensitive but important issue, which can have severe economic, social, political and environmental consequences if mishandled (DWAF, 2005).

Whilst Falkenmark and Rockstrom (2004) have highlighted the importance of finding a balance between water sharing for food and the environment, in some parts of the world there is the even more pressing issue of finding ways to share water equitably among people. New approaches and innovative thinking may provide solutions not only for South Africa but also for the rest of the world. These approaches need to be practical and affordable, and to focus on and address key concerns and not waste time and resources on minor concerns. As Gavin Quibell, a South African expert on allocation issues, described the situation 'if it isn't broke, don't fix it' (2004, personal communication).

Allocation Equity is a mechanism that is currently being developed by DWAF for the equitable allocation of catchment runoff among all users, including the poorest, whilst ensuring that the water use remains in the broader 'public interest' and that changes in allocation are negotiated in a

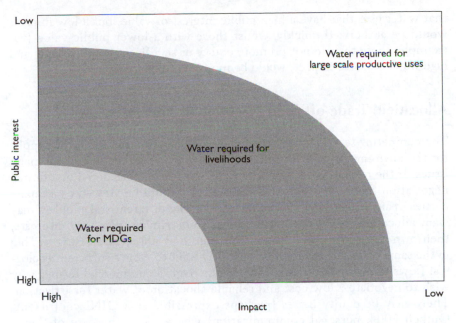

Source: DWAF (2005)

Figure 7.4 *The approach proposed by DWAF for addressing licensing issues taking account of both the public interest and water resource impact*

sensitive and transparent manner between users. The Department of Water Affairs and Forestry (2005) recognizes that the 'public interest' includes not only a move towards greater equity in water use but also the sustainable and efficient use of water, the protection of aquatic ecosystems and the maintenance of the existing water-based economy together with maintaining investor confidence in the country. Sustainable development 'should reflect a balance between social justice, economic efficiency and ecological integrity'.

Inherently this approach recognizes that achieving more-equitable allocation and use of water promotes social stability and is therefore, in itself, in the public interest. Over and above this, the process aims to promote shifts in water use towards more beneficial water uses that realize improved net social benefit: greater economic returns and employment opportunities, non-market benefits and intangibles. In this way the approach aims to maximize the beneficial use of water without impacting negatively on the most vulnerable groups.

This approach explicitly takes account of both the public interest and the impact of water and land uses as part of the water use authorizing process. At one extreme, the water required to realize the MDGs (low impacts on water availability but high on the public good) will get a priority allocation that will not require a licence. At the other extreme, water required for larger-scale commercial uses (high impacts on water availability) would require careful consideration and authorization depending on their expected impacts and public benefits. This balance between impact and public benefit, which is reflected in the authorization process, is shown in Figure 7.4. It is expected that water uses that have a high public interest or value, but a low impact, would be authorized quickly, whilst those with a lower public value (for example, those that do not promote equity or significant employment) and high water resource impact, would be more carefully considered.

Allocation, Trade-offs and Negotiation Theory

The competing sectoral demands for water allocation for food, for supply, for the environment and for industry involve many stakeholders and many issues. If the resolution of these demands were to be considered in a formal negotiation theory context, the negotiations would be viewed as a 'many parties, many issues' conflict (Raiffa, 1982). The different stakeholders may want allocations to meet certain criteria to maximize their own interests, their own 'payoff function'. Payoff functions may not always be expressible in the same units. An environmentalist may want to ensure sufficient ecological flows to maintain salmonid fish in the river; a commercial farmer may wish to negotiate a low cost and reliable allocation of water for irrigation. There may be equity issues (perhaps expressible as a GINI coefficient, Quibell 2004, personal communication) where, as in the case of South Africa, 'black emerging enterprises' will be given preference in relation to water allocations. A community may wish to maximize livelihood benefit, perhaps expressed in terms of job creation. A catchment manager may wish to avoid a catchment reaching closure or not meeting minimum ecological flow requirements through curtailing non-productive uses which are not in the public interest such as alien invasive trees. There are also likely to be volumetric demands for industrial, household and possibly downstream transnational users.

Clearly, finding an allocation 'solution' will involve trade-offs. Because the different players will have objectives which are in different units (ecology, equity, money, job creation), it is not possible to express the problem as the minimization or maximization of an objective function unless each objective is converted to the same units (a common currency), which may or may not be feasible or desirable.

The different trade-off options might be quite complicated. A commercial farmer might prefer to receive a lower allocation of water if he knew that he would receive the allocation for a guaranteed or longer time in the future, knowing that by accepting this agreement he would be able to reliably plan an investment in irrigation equipment. Agreements to remove alien invader trees might be rewarded by water rights or agreements to move requests for water allocation to a higher public interest category.

In South Africa there is a debate as to whether the cessation of what is regarded as an 'illegal activity' (it is illegal to allow alien invasive trees to remain on your land) should be rewarded with water rights. However, this difficulty might be circumvented by viewing the exercise as in the public interest and thereby giving greater preference, through a quicker response to a request for a water allocation, to a landowner willing to expend efforts in the public interest.

The application of green water policy instruments opens up a whole new range of policy options. Farmers might be willing to consider dry land farming, if offered an incentive or payment, thus increasing the area of a land use which effectively releases more water into the system than that from an indigenous baseline vegetation. Tradable water rights might be another option, but there are concerns that powerful elites might be in a position to buy out the other players.

One approach to addressing these issues, favoured in the 'traditional' approach to watershed management based on the principle of the social planner where a central authority 'takes care' of the needs and interests of the various groups and sectors in the basin, is through multi-criteria analysis. But this approach has not always been found to be very effective in a land and water resource management context. The values assigned to the weightings that need to be given to the different objectives to reduce them to a common currency totally influence the outcome. Without agreement between all the stakeholders the 'arbitrariness' of an external agency deciding the weightings reduces the acceptability of this approach.

Another approach to finding allocation solutions and to supporting negotiations between stakeholders is through negotiation theory. Within the context of ILWRM there may be a number of advantages obtained through the use of negotiation theory and bargaining models. The decentralization of land and water management and the focus on stakeholder involvement create new problems for government departments which have previously had experience of only centralized, top-down management methods. The formation, in many countries, of catchment management authorities or river basin authorities entrusted not only with ultimate responsibility for management (and being the final arbiter in management decisions) but also with responsibility for stakeholder involvement in decision-making creates a new context in which the stakeholders could be told to 'go away and find their own agreed solution to allocation problems'. These solutions would be subject to certain constraints that the stakeholders would be aware of whilst the catchment or river basin authority would act as the final arbiter of the solution.

In France, the water law of 1992 requires that regulations on water use and water management be negotiated collectively and locally in each river sub-basin. An example of how a bargaining model might help to guide the negotiation process is provided by Leo Simon, Sophie Toyer and colleagues (Simon et al, 2003; Thoyer et al, 2001) for the Adour Basin, in the south-west of France.

The Adour Study

A 'many parties, many issues' bargaining model of stakeholder negotiations was developed which incorporates the interests of seven aggregate players, comprising three farmers, two environmental lobbies, the water manager and the taxpayer, and seven negotiation variables, including three individual irrigation quotas, the price of water and the sizes of three dams. The bargaining model was used to investigate the structure of the negotiating process and the effectiveness with which stakeholders can pursue their individual interests and the relevance of bargaining models as negotiation-support tools.

The formal structure of the multi-player, multi-issue game model, based on an extension to the two party game model originally derived by Rubenstein (Rubinstein, 1982), is given by Rausser and Simon (1991). The structure assumes: N players gather to negotiate over a given set of K policy variables x_k. Each player is characterized by a pre-defined payoff function (called the utility function) with respect to the negotiated variables. The negotiation is organized as a sequence of games with a finite number of bargaining rounds. At each round t, a proposer j among the N players is chosen randomly with a given access probability a_j and makes a proposal $X^j_t = (x^j_{1,t}, ..., x^j_{k,t} ..., x^j_{K,t})$ over the policy variables. All other players $i \neq j$ calculate the utility U^i they derive from this proposal and compare it with their reservation utility EU^i. A player's reservation utility is the utility he can expect from the following round $t+1$ and is defined as the sum of the player's utilities derived from each player's proposals (including himself) in the next round, weighted by their access probability:

$$EU^i = \Sigma^N_{j=1} a_j\, U_i\, (X^j_{t+1})$$

Players choose to move on to the next round when their reservation utility is higher than the utility derived from the proposer's offer. A compromise is reached when all players agree on a proposed set of policies, X. The game then ends.

A number of conclusions were drawn from the bargaining study: (i) farmer coalitions do better when the distribution of power among opponents is diffuse rather than concentrated, (ii) a coalition member can advance his own interests by ceding his own political power to another coalition member who is strategically better placed in the negotiations, (iii) the interests of the coalition as a whole will be advanced if its members cede access to a 'spokesman' representing their common interests.

The Schéma d'Aménagement et de Gestion des Eaux (SAGE) procedure for involving stakeholder involvement is still fairly new and the authors report that few SAGE outcomes have been officially ratified although many SAGE negotiations have been launched. They argue that there is a growing need for negotiation-support models which would: (i) help to identify the best negotiation structures, and (ii) accompany the negotiation process and help stakeholders to reach a stable compromise.

An Allocation Equity Thought Experiment

A 'thought experiment' based around negotiation theory, following the Rausser-Simon model, can perhaps illustrate how increased policy options (as identified in South Africa) might be used by negotiating stakeholders, under the 'threat' that the arbiter (the Catchment Management Authority) might impose a worse solution, to come up with a better solution for all parties.

A simple 'game' is considered for a hypothetical country which is experiencing similar allocation issues to those described for South Africa. For simplicity a game will be considered between only two players negotiating many issues. The players could be a representative of say, emerging enterprise (EE) farmers, who would be seeking to increase their allocation of irrigation water and commercial existing (CE) farmers who would recognize that in the interests of equity they would have to give up some of their allocation but would, nevertheless, be wishing as far as possible to retain it and the surety of their water rights.

If we were to assume that the catchment where these negotiations were taking place was already only just meeting the ecological reserve, that is there was no further allocatable water on offer, then the two players might be wanting to find a solution better than some 'expected' but undefined solution that might otherwise be imposed upon them by a Catchment Management Authority (CMA). This might be a minimum allocation to the EE farmers to satisfy equity considerations and an equal reduction in the allocation to the CE farmers.

This simple game with just two players has the ecological reserve allocation represented as a constraint. Multiplayer games could also be considered where the ecological constraint was replaced by a player negotiating for ecological flows and industry and supply representatives negotiating for their interests. For the moment let us consider that all of these are assumed within the constraint that there is no more allocatable water in the catchment. The game might then proceed as outlined below.

Round One

The EE farmers' representative puts forward a policy package including:

1 increased allocation of water to EE farmers (+5); and
2 reduced allocation to CE farmers (–5).

To illustrate how utility might change during the negotiations and to show how the process might lead to better outcomes, we will guess the utility to each group of farmers of the different policy interventions. Note that in a non-cooperative, Rausser-Simon type game, the players would not normally wish to disclose their utility evaluations. They would not necessarily need even to quantify utility, although by doing so it might help the players to better evaluate the different policy packages. For the sake of simplicity the utility of one unit of water is assumed here to be the same for each farmer group: 1 unit of water = 1 unit of utility (Table 7.3).

Round Two

The CE farmers' representative, acknowledging the need for a greater allocation to EE farmers and willing to accept some reduction in the allocation to CE farmers, accepts these components in the policy package. But the representative, believing that EE farmers can do something to improve efficiency

Table 7.3 *Thought experiment illustrating the use of negotiation theory for negotiating policy options including green water policy instruments, round one selections*

Round one – EE farmers' proposals						
Policy options, X	Select option	Utility EE, U^1	Utility CE, U^2	Green water management outcome	Blue water flows outcome	Flow change, volume units
X_1, Increase allocation of water to EE farmers	√	+5			Reduce catchment flow	−5
X_2, Reduce allocation to CE farmers	√	?5			Increase catchment flow	+5
X_3, Increase surety of licence to CE farmers from 3 to 10 years						
X_4, Remove alien invaders from land owned by CE farmers						
X_5, Expand EE area under dry land farming with a weed-free dry season						
Sum of utilities, U^i:	+5	−5		Net change in catchment outflow		0

of water use in the catchment, proposes a green water policy instrument which would reduce green water loss from the catchment by increasing the area of a land use which is likely to evaporate at a rate less than the indigenous baseline vegetation – dry land agriculture with a weed-free dry season:

1   Increased allocation of water to EE farmers (+2).
2   Reduced allocation to CE farmers (−1).
3   Expand EE area under dry land farming with a weed-free dry season.

The CE farmers' representative proposes a 2 unit increase in water to be allocated to EE farmers with a 1 unit reduction for CE farmers, with 1 unit released by increasing dry land area (Table 7.4).

Table 7.4 *Thought experiment illustrating the use of negotiation theory for negotiating policy options including green water policy instruments, round two selections*

Round two – CE farmers' proposals						
Policy options, X	Select option	Utility EE, U^1	Utility CE, U^2	Green water management outcome	Blue water flows outcome	Flow change, volume units
X_1, Increase allocation of water to EE farmers	√	+2			Reduce catchment flow	−2
X_2, Reduce allocation to CE farmers	√		−1		Increase catchment flow	+1
X_3, Increase surety of licence to CE farmers from 3 to 10 years						
X_4, Remove alien invaders from land owned by CE farmers						
X_5, Expand EE area under dry land farming with a weed-free dry season	√	−0.2		Reduce green water flow	Increase catchment flow	+1
Sum of utilities, U^i:	+1.8		−1	Net change in catchment outflow		0

Round Three

The EE farmers' representative agrees with the argument for making more efficient use of water in the catchment and accepts the proposed green water policy instrument which would aim to reduce green water loss from the catchment by increasing the area of dry land agriculture, although the extra work involved might represent a loss of 0.2 units utility. But, following the same argument, the EE farmers' representative proposes that the CE farmers also make water efficiency gains by removing alien invader trees from their lands. The policy package is now as follows:

1   Increased allocation of water to EE farmers (+4).
2   Reduced allocation to CE farmers (−2).
3   Expand EE area under dry land farming with a weed-free dry season.
4   Remove alien invaders from land owned by CE farmers.

Table 7.5 *Thought experiment illustrating the use of negotiation theory for negotiating policy options including green water policy instruments, round three selections*

Round three – EE farmers' proposals						
Policy options, X	Select option	Utility EE, U^1	Utility CE, U^2	Green water management outcome	Blue water flows outcome	Flow change, volume units
X_1, Increase allocation of water to EE farmers	√	+4			Reduce catchment flow	−4
X_2, Reduce allocation to CE farmers	√		−2		Increase catchment flow	+2
X_3, Increase surety of licence to CE farmers from 3 to 10 years						
X_4, Remove alien invaders from land owned by CE farmers	√		−0.2	Reduce green water flow	Increase catchment flow	+1
X_5, Expand EE area under dry land farming with a weed-free dry season	√	−0.2		Reduce green water flow	Increase catchment flow	+1
Sum of utilities, U^i :		+3.8	−2.2	Net change in catchment outflow		0

The representative also proposes a 4 unit increase in water to be allocated to EE farmers with a 2 unit reduction for CE farmers, with 1 unit released by increasing dry land area and 1 unit released by removing alien invaders (Table 7.5).

Round Four

The CE farmers' representative is willing to accept the policy package and the proposed reduction in water allocation and the estimated 0.2 unit loss in utility through having to manage alien invaders if he can obtain a longer-term guaranteed surety of the water allocation which will improve 'investor confidence' of the farmers and allow them to plan their irrigation infrastructure developments with a longer time horizon.

The CE farmers' representative proposes that the surety of the licence to CE farmers be increased from 3 to 10 years.

Table 7.6 *Thought experiment illustrating the use of negotiation theory for negotiating policy options including green water policy instruments, round four selections*

Round four – CE farmers' proposals						
Policy options, X	Select option	Utility EE, U^1	Utility CE, U^2	Green water management outcome	Blue water flows outcome	Flow change, volume units
X_1, Increase allocation of water to EE farmers	√	+4			Reduce catchment flow	–4
X_2, Reduce allocation to CE farmers	√		–2		Increase catchment flow	+2
X_3, Increase surety of licence to CE farmers from 3 to 10 years	√		+1		No change	0
X_4, Remove alien invaders from land owned by CE farmers	√		–0.2	Reduce green water flow	Increase catchment flow	+1
X_5, Expand EE area under dry land farming with a weed-free dry season	√	–0.2		Reduce green water flow	Increase catchment flow	+1
Sum of utilities, U^i:		+3.8	–1.2		Net change in catchment outflow	0

1   Increased allocation of water to EE farmers (+4).
2   Reduced allocation to CE farmers (–2).
3   Expand EE area under dry land farming with a weed-free dry season.
4   Remove alien invaders from land owned by CE farmers.
5   Increase surety of licence to CE farmers from 3 to 10 years.

The representative accepts the previous proposal for a 4 unit increase in water to be allocated to EE farmers with a 2 unit reduction for CE farmers, with 1 unit released by increasing dry land area and 1 unit released by removing alien invaders (Table 7.6.)

The representatives of the EE and CE farmers would therefore be able to put these proposals to the Catchment Management Agency. If the expectation of both parties might have been that in the absence of negotiations the CMA would have imposed a straight transfer anywhere in the range between 1.8 to 3.8 units from the CE farmers to the EE farmers, the negotiated outcome, also employing green water policy instruments, would have ensured a better outcome for both.

The incorporation of negotiation and games theory approaches have been shown to have benefit in other aspects of water management and international water cooperation (Dinar et al, 1986; Rogers, 1993) and they clearly have potential benefits for ILWRM. They not only provide a means for addressing what is becoming the classic problem of finding water allocation solutions that take into account irrigation (food), industry, water supply for humans and water for the environment, but they also provide a structure for involving stakeholders in debate and negotiations. They can also provide insights into the power relationships in negotiations, which may ensure more stable and harmonious agreements. Where it is possible to identify payoff utility functions for the different stakeholders, there is also the possibility of finding better solutions through the use of analytic and optimization procedures.

SOCIO-ECONOMIC METHODOLOGIES – EVALUATING DEVELOPMENT OPTIONS

The processes which determine how land use impacts on water resources are now becoming understood (see Chapters 1 and 2) and methods are now available for quantifying some of these impacts, particularly as they relate to forests (see Chapter 3). Methods have also been developed to attribute an economic value to water in its various uses and to land use in both its primary and secondary uses (see Chapter 4).

Management of land use and water resources requires this knowledge (and better knowledge in the future) of the interactions between land use and water resources, but it also requires methods through which this knowledge can be used so that the relative benefits of potential water resource developments or land-use changes can be assessed. These methods are required in local, regional and international contexts to assist the production of plans, guidelines, strategies and national and international policies and legislation. Increasingly, the 'secondary' uses of land and water, which can be grouped under conservation, amenity, recreation and environment (CARE), are assuming greater importance and these methods must be able to take these uses into account.

Socio-economic methodologies provide the necessary framework for evaluating and comparing different development options. These methodologies are being developed for specific land uses such as forests (Benson and Willis, 1991; Willis and Benson, 1989; Willis, 2002) and, more recently, for agricultural lands (Harvey and Willis, 1997). Socio-economic methodologies are also being developed (ERM and University of Newcastle upon Tyne, 1997) to assist the economic appraisal of the environmental costs and benefits of possible solutions for ameliorating low flows in rivers.

The concept of IWRM and ILWRM are relatively new to land use and water resource managers. These methodologies are even newer. It is important that these embryo evaluation frameworks, arguably crucial to the blue revolution, are fostered. They will need to be robust and defensible and they need to be understood by their practitioners so that they are not misapplied.

Use and Abuse of Socio-economic Methods

The English and Welsh Environment Agency (EA), the regulatory body, has a statutory duty to consider costs and benefits in exercising its powers (see Chapter 4). In collaboration with the Department of Environment, Transport and the Regions (DETR); the water companies regulator (Ofwat); and the water companies, it has developed a manual on approved methods of assessing the benefits of water schemes, known as the benefits manual (Foundation for Water Research, 1996).

The value, use and abuse of these socio-economic methodologies is well illustrated by their disposition in the conflict situation and inquiry which arose as a result of the application by Thames Water to abstract more groundwater at Axford in the environs of the River Kennet, a chalk stream in Wiltshire in the south of England. The stream is regarded as of high environmental quality, being both in a designated Area of Outstanding Natural Beauty and an SSSI; it is also valued by anglers as a trout river.

Thames Water applied to make permanent a temporary variation to its abstraction licence which had been in force for 15 years. The base licence entitled it to take up to $13,100 \text{ m}^3 \text{ d}^{-1}$) and the variation entitled it to take a further $7,400 \text{m}^3 \text{ d}^{-1}$ subject to a minimum flow of $61,400 \text{ m}^3 \text{ d}^{-1}$ being achieved in the river. The EA response was to impose a progressive increase in the minimum flow requirement which would have the effect of both cutting permitted abstractions at periods of low flows and reducing the base licensed volume.

Thames Water appealed on the grounds that the abstractions had a marginal effect on river flows and that recent changes in the river's ecology were due to drought, dredging of the river channel and management of water levels by anglers.

The appeal forced the EA into preparing a cost–benefit assessment, following the guidance of the benefits manual. The recommended cost–benefit analysis considers the public's 'willingness to pay' (WTP) for both 'use' benefits accrued from those using the river directly through activities such as angling and recreation, and 'non-use' benefits accrued from its aesthetic, cultural, conservation or legacy values, which can be realized without the need to visit the river. In retrospect, perhaps unwisely, the EA decided that a full WTP assessment involving extensive public opinion surveys would have been too costly and time consuming and it opted for a 'benefit transfers' approach which made use of previously collected WTP figures on other low-flow rivers such as the Darent in Kent. Using transferred WTP figures, the EA calculated the use value of the Kennet at £67,000 per year. Using this figure, with a discounting period of 30 years, the additional benefits of the river if Thames Water's abstractions were reduced, was calculated at a net present 'use' value of £0.4 million. The data from the Darent study showed that people up to 60km distant would pay an average of 32 pence per household per year per river to counter low flows. Again transferring these data to the Kennet, the EA multiplied these figures by the number of domestic water connections in Thames Water's supply area (three million) and, again discounting over 30 years, arrived at a net present 'non-use' value of £13.2 million. Thus the total calculated value of reducing abstractions was £13.6 million.

The 'non-use' values for the river were therefore set by the EA at a figure about 30 times the 'use' values. This high value comes about through the contentious use of the figure of three million water connections, as being appropriate for WTP calculations. Thames Water argued that its use was nonsensical as, had a smaller company with fewer connections been involved, the valuation would have been much less. They argued that the river was mainly a local issue and claimed only 100,000 people were affected. In the benefits manual it is recommended that where the outcome of a cost–benefit analysis may be dependent on the 'non-use' values, new fieldwork may be justified to improve confidence in the 'non-use' figures. The question of the size of population to consider in calculating 'non-use' values appears to be a fundamental problem in benefit assessment (END, 1998).

At the subsequent public inquiry the Environment Inspector overruled the EA and found in favour of Thames Water on this crucial question of how to calculate 'non-use' WTP. The inspector assigned the 'non-use' value at only £0.3 million. As Thames Water had calculated that the cost of replacing the abstractions with water from other sources would be £6.2 million, there was a substantial economic margin in favour of continuing with the groundwater abstractions. The Environment Secretary, in February 1998, endorsed the Inspector's findings and upheld Thames Water's appeal. The final outcome was a partial compromise as the inspector conceded that the Kennet's ecology was being harmed by low flows and ruled that the minimum river low flow should be raised from 61.4 to 90Ml.d^{-1}. Nevertheless, this was less than the 104Ml.d^{-1} sought by the EA.

The Axford inquiry highlights the present dilemma in the use of socio-economic methods for evaluating development options. Perhaps most seriously, misuse of these methods by the EA has brought their application into disrepute. The Darent study was not designed to yield transferable estimates. Even if it had been, considerable problems would remain in the calibration and aggregation over the relevant populations associated with the Kennet.

At present, methods for calculating transferable benefit estimates are in their infancy, although the study of low-flow rivers in the south-west of England (ERM and University of Newcastle upon Tyne, 1997) went some way towards generating transferable estimates for low-flow improvements. The production of robust, defensible and transferable methodologies for benefit evaluation to assist in the choice of development options remains a high priority for the blue revolution. Without these methodologies, a rational framework for setting development options in a form where production benefits can be compared against economic, ecological, equity and socio-economic considerations is lost to us.

SOFT SYSTEMS TOOLS

New developments in the field of operational research and management science have led to a number of new methodologies for dealing with unstructured situations that are intractable by 'hard' methods. These methods include problem structuring methods (PSMs) (Rosenhead, 1996), soft systems methodology (Omerod, 1996) and cognitive mapping. These methods, particularly the soft system methodology, can assist in the development of hydroinformatic and decision support systems by aiding the analysis of organizational activities and information flows and by facilitating the communication between system developers and users (Amezaga and O'Connell, 1998).

PSMs allow ill-defined situations involving humans to be structured to negotiate the way forward. These methods are currently being applied and are in fairly widespread use as management tools in some of the largest, multinational, commercial and marketing organizations. They may well have great relevance in the equally, if not more, complex field of land and water resource management.

Another approach, advocated by Simonovic and Bender (1996), is collaborative planning. To facilitate communication between people with different backgrounds, they have developed a collaborative planning support system (CPSS) which attempts to blend modern computer technologies with modelling and analysis tools in a user-friendly environment. The aim is to enhance the communication between proponents of resource development and those affected. This system can be considered as a module or component of a decision support system, but a module which specifically addresses stakeholder involvement and communication between stakeholders. Simonovic and Bender (ibid) describe the architecture of the module, which requires four components: the stakeholders, a list of 'grounded facts', a knowledge base and a potential list of evaluation criteria. The system operates by stakeholders supplying information to the module which describes their individual values or perception of important issues. From this process, the 'grounded facts' are generated and these are used to relate stakeholder values and issues to information useful for the assessment of trade-offs. Stakeholders can then supply their value information by selecting important features from the list of 'grounded facts'. Each stakeholder can maintain a list of selected facts and, collectively, can duplicate selections. This process indicates areas where there is agreement between stakeholders. The selected lists of 'grounded facts' are then 'translated' through a knowledge base to produce relevant multidisciplinary planning objectives which can then be evaluated using the predefined criteria. Simonovic and Bender (ibid) state that as trust can be a major concern among stakeholders, the knowledge base, which is usually composed of rules generated by experts who are often proponents of the development, is open to viewing and the source of the rules is made available. Simonovic and Bender (ibid) state that 'Communication is the key in this application. Common understanding and a potentially greater level of consensus is the desired result.'

Participatory Approaches

Principle Number Two of the Dublin conference report (see Chapter 4) states 'Water development and management should be based on a participatory approach, involving users, planners and policymakers at all levels'.

Whilst the participatory approach to water management and development was formalized relatively recently in the Dublin Statement in 1992, participatory approaches had been advocated, and participatory methodologies had been developed, much earlier by social and management scientists in governmental and non-governmental development organizations. Whilst the old mantra of the traditional water engineer may have been 'to meet all reasonable needs', the new mantra of the developmental social scientist is perhaps 'to meet all stakeholders and participate'. Participatory approaches (see Appendix 2) are undeniably a necessary component of the new approach to water management and a key component of the blue revolution. They are not, as zealous social scientists might sometimes suggest, a sufficient condition. There is a danger that participatory approaches are used as the 'stamp of approval' to justify prior conclusions and to deride perhaps perfectly sound solutions and results which have not been achieved through the full participatory process. It is not difficult to stage-manage 'participation' to provide the 'gloss' on decisions and approaches that are being sought by particular pressure groups. Nor is the participatory approach a substitute for the integrated or holistic approach. Interestingly, within the Dublin Statement the holistic approach is enshrined in Principle 1 whilst participation is embodied in Principle 2.

A particular danger is that sectors such as agriculture, forestry and environmental management might adopt the participatory process with religious zeal to foster their own sectoral ambitions, without considering the overall or integrated approach to land-use or water resource management.

The World Bank's Water Strategy (World Bank, 2004) also recognizes that participatory approaches, if taken too far, might undermine the legitimate authority of the state to make decisions and would effectively preclude the implementation of many infrastructure projects. In relation to the World Commission on Dams report (see Chapter 4) the view of the Bank is:

> *While there is agreement on the importance of the rights of affected and indigenous people, the World Bank believes that adoption of the World Commission on Dams principle of 'prior informed consent' amounts to a veto right that would undermine the fundamental right of the state to make decisions in the best interests of the community as a whole.*

And:

> *...while there is agreement on the importance of consultation and public acceptance, experience suggests that the multistage, negotiated approach to project preparation recommended by the World Commission on Dams is not practical and would virtually preclude the construction of any dam.*

The central issue is perhaps more to do with governance and the effectiveness of checks and controls within government systems than stakeholder participation per se. In the perhaps extreme example of Japan, there appear to be legitimate concerns from NGOs that Government-funded dams and infrastructure projects are being pursued to support the influential construction industry even though, in many cases, there is no obvious need for the structures.

Indigenous and Vernacular Knowledge

If stakeholder involvement in environmental, land and water management is to be more than tokenism by planning and decision-making authorities, efforts are required to both structure the consultative process and incorporate stakeholder knowledge:

> *Paradoxically, the planning ethos is open to all science, including 'vernacular' science or the 'common knowledge of ordinary folk'. Adaptive planning, like public response to hazards, requires options and experience; whilst the scientist may set up the valid options, it remains the experience of (and 'comfort' with) those options by the public which allow on-line adaptation of the plan to occur.* (Newson et al, 1999)

The incorporation of indigenous knowledge (IK) in development programmes dealing with natural resource management is discussed by Barr (1998). Although the incorporation of IK is now becoming more common and methodological research on the incorporation of IK within natural resources research is now being developed, Barr warns of the difficulties associated with linking overlapping spheres of knowledge between local people at one end of a spectrum, with the applied and basic sciences at the other, and with social scientists and anthropologists somewhere in the centre. He argues that, in theory, natural resources IK has much to offer in tackling natural resource management problems, but the practical realities of operating this type of interdisciplinary research are far from straightforward. Conflict, or at least disagreement, is recognized as a common feature of interdisciplinary research, especially where the disciplines are 'closely guarded cabals'. Barr suggests that computers may help bridge the paradigmatic differences between researchers and also provide the tools for the incorporation of IK. He cites the work of Walker and Sinclair (1998), in which computers have been used to develop cognitive maps of IK in agricultural and forestry systems, and work in the social sciences which has led to computer-assisted qualitative data analysis software, known as CAQDAS (Coffey et al,1996).

There may be other dangers in trying to incorporate IK. Barr and Gowing (1998), from experiences of participatory approaches for incorporating IK relating to floodplain management in Bangladesh, warn that the process can be easily 'captured' by locally influential people.

Lack of awareness of, and insensitivity towards, IK may have much graver dangers. Advocacy and the imposition by western scientists of ineffective agroforestry systems as a claimed means of increasing production in the developing world (see Chapter 2), counter to local traditions, has led to huge wastes in research and development funding and the suspicion and disbelief of local people (and some governments) in development efforts. Newson et al (1999) condemn 'unthinking westernism' for introducing the water closet into some semi-arid countries where it has become a symbol of social rank, although its widespread use would be inherently unsustainable, as another example of development going ahead contrary to local indigenous knowledge and experience.

INFORMATION TECHNOLOGY – HARD SYSTEMS TOOLS

Information technology tools are now being developed which can operate within or link with a 'soft systems' framework for assisting with the process of ILWRM, both for the development of national strategies and for the development and implementation of catchment plans. In earlier chapters it was shown how an understanding of the effects of land use, and land-use change, on water resources is one component of the knowledge base that is required to apply principles of IWRM. It was shown how models based on the 'limits' concepts have been applied for assessing forest impacts on water resources in both wet and dry climates of the world. Wet climate applications, where interception loss predominates, include the uplands of Scotland and the Otago catchments in the South Island of New Zealand. Dry climate applications include a study, reviewed in Chapter 6, of how land-use change in Malawi has altered the water balance of Lake Malawi and a regional study, extending the Malawi study, through the use of GIS technology to the Zambezi basin. Similar methodologies were also used to calculate the impacts of a proposed afforestation scheme for the Panama Canal watershed (see also Chapter 6). These land-use impact models and other models related to land use and water resources, including the economic, ecological, health and sanitation dimensions, can now be run on common databases through the use of decision support systems (DSS) and other GIS and model-linked tools. The use of these systems for advancing ILWRM– the blue revolution – is outlined below.

Decision Support Systems for ILWRM

Although a great deal of thought and effort underlies the development of the UNCED principles, and paramount importance is attached to them by governments and UN agencies, much less thought has been given to how these principles can actually be implemented. Agencies and organizations entrusted with the implementation of IWRM are largely at a loss when it comes to knowing how to put in place these procedures. This is a problem not only for the developing world, but also for the developed world where concepts such as stakeholder participation and demand management are still relatively new. Decision support systems have a role to play here in providing mechanisms not only for testing out the impacts of water resource management strategies on stakeholder interests – equity, environmental, ecological and socio-economic impacts – but can also assist water resource managers by providing a focusing framework for defining stakeholder issues and interrelationships.

The greatest strength of these systems is that they provide the means for integrating information from different disciplines: their greatest weakness is that their construction entails a degree of trust, cooperation and professional self-confidence from all the disciplines involved, which cannot necessarily be assumed at the outset and which may take considerable time and effort, through the development of a participatory approach, to establish. At the most fundamental level, DSSs can be of great value for ILWRM through allowing, perhaps for the first time, different data sets from the water resource disciplines (comprising, for example, surface water, groundwater and water quality) to be displayed together. The hydrologists, hydrogeologists and water chemists who collect these different data sets come from different professional backgrounds and do not necessarily have a tradition or ethos of working closely together; it is not uncommon to find their respective databases residing on different computer systems. Nor is it uncommon to find that these computers are in different buildings with little or no means of transferring or sharing data. With such a poor tradition of integration even among the closely related water resource disciplines, the task of integrating and soliciting cooperation among the wider disciplines that are involved (environmental science, ecology, socio-economics and health) presents the overriding challenge for DSS development. Ultimately, this will also determine if true integrated management of land and water resources can be achieved.

DSSs bring together different components of hydrologically related information technology within the new science of hydroinformatics (Abbott, 1991). They combine the capabilities of a database, GIS modelling systems and possibly optimization techniques and expert systems, all set within a graphical user interface (GUI).

Two 'milestone' publications (Jamieson, ed, 1996; O'Callaghan, 1996) described both the ethos and underlying philosophy of DSSs together with providing outline descriptions of the structure of some of these systems. The capabilities and limitations of regional hydrological models that are used in these systems had earlier been discussed by O'Connell (1995), and the means for integrating these models within DSSs, by Adams (1995). Two of these early systems, the WaterWare (Jamieson and Fedra, 1996) and the NELUP (O'Callaghan, 1995) systems are briefly described below to illustrate the basic concepts underlying the implementation of Decision Support Systems. The more recent EXCLAIM dissemination tool, which makes use of many DSS concepts, is also described.

The WaterWare DSS for Integrated River Basin Planning

A decision support system designed to meet the needs of the European water industry was developed using European Union funding under the EUREKA EU 487 programme. Three universities, a research institute and two commercial companies were involved in the development.

WaterWare Objectives

The system was designed to be capable of addressing a wide range of issues including:

- determining the limits of sustainable development;
- evaluating the impact of new environmental legislation;
- deciding what, where and when new resources should be developed;
- assessing the environmental impact of water-related development; and
- formulating strategies for river and groundwater pollution control schemes.

The system architecture is shown in Figure 7.5.

WaterWare Database and GIS

The database is able to hold data of a mixture of types, all of which are geo-referenced to a GIS. These include static or object-oriented data that are fixed in time and could include specifications, details and photographs of, for

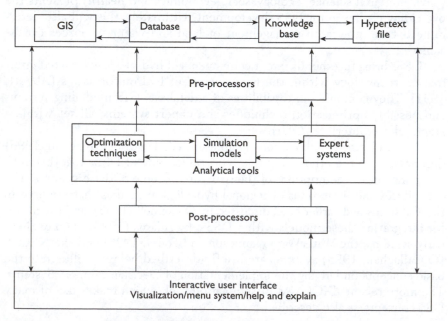

Figure 7.5 *WaterWare system architecture*

example, a treatment works or flow measurement station. Slowly changing data such as the treatment processes used or works configuration data are also accommodated, as are rapidly changing time series data such as daily flows or rainfall. Time series data can be displayed graphically in a number of ways and routines are available for statistical analysis of the data including calculation of the mean, standard deviation, cross-correlation coefficients and double mass curves.

The GIS contains all the spatial data on land use, elevation, geology, soil type, river and road networks in the appropriate raster or vector format. Options are available for specifying the sequence in which spatial files are overlaid and edited, and a zoom facility is also incorporated.

WaterWare Modelling Components

The standard WaterWare system has modelling components for groundwater and surface water pollution control, irrigation and domestic water demand forecasting, hydrological processes and water resource planning. For groundwater pollution control, a two-dimensional finite-difference model of flow and contaminant transport is incorporated to predict the movement of pollutants.

The decision support module comprises a three-stage process: an expert system to locate possible sites for scavenger boreholes, followed by an artificial neural network for assessing the performance of different combinations of boreholes, and finally, a generic algorithm for selecting the most cost-effective solution for reducing the pollution to a prescribed residual level.

For surface-water pollution control and for river restoration schemes, the DSS contains a one-dimensional stochastic river water quality model.

To achieve the lowest-cost solution for achieving a prescribed river water quality standard, a waste-load allocation module is configured to operate with heuristic search and linear programming algorithms to select the appropriate technologies for each effluent discharge. Alternatively, the module can be run to identify the most effective allocation for improving river quality for a fixed budget.

For water demand forecasting, either for irrigation or domestic supply purposes, the DSS incorporates an expert system shell. The FAO's CROPWAT model has been rewritten as a rule-based inference module within this shell to calculate irrigation demand requirements. All the data requirements are contained within the database, including GIS, topography, land use, soil type, rainfall and potential evaporation. The module, given fertilizer and water supply costs, is also able to calculate the economic returns from different combinations of crop and irrigation system (for example, surface, spray and drip).

The hydrological processes component contains a spatially aggregated daily rainfall/runoff model which is able to generate simulated flow records for unmonitored tributaries.

For more detailed modelling of the rainfall/runoff processes, the SHETRAN modelling system (Parkin et al, 2000) can also be used.

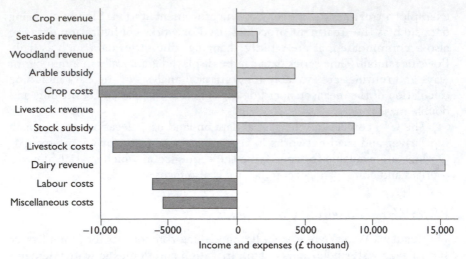

Figure 7.6 *Predicted income and expenses for the Tyne River Basin*

For water resource planning, a generic model was developed, operating on a daily time step, to simulate the balance between supply and demand and to indicate the frequency and extent of shortfalls. The model can be used to assess the water resource system and can be used with a screening model to minimize costs, both monetary and environmental, for the development of regional and national water plans.

The WaterWare system was first applied to the Thames Basin in southern England as a case study. Other applications include the Rio Lerma/Lake Chapala master plan in Mexico and water resource planning in the Occupied Palestinian Territories.

The NELUP Decision Support System

The joint Natural Environment Research and Economic and Social Research Councils' land-use programme, under which the NELUP DSS was developed, was an innovative programme designed to investigate the interactions between land use, water resources, economics and ecology. Whilst the WaterWare system is oriented more specifically towards the water industry for the planning and operation of water developments within river basins, the NELUP DSS is aimed at a higher level of land and water resource management which is more closely aligned with the wider objectives of ILWRM.

NELUP Design Objectives

This decision support system was designed to:

• integrate models covering economics, ecology and hydrology that describe the changes in the spatial pattern of land use and the impacts of these changes;

- integrate nationally available data sets which describe the biophysical and economic conditions within a river basin in a database; and
- create an interactive, user-friendly interface to the database and models to allow exploration of future land-use scenarios.

NELUP Database and GIS

To take into account both water resources, socio-economic and ecological issues related to land use requires extensive and compatible databases. In the NELUP DSS, spatial data are held within a raster GIS (GRASS) and non-spatial data are held within a relational database management system (ORACLE). The data sets include agricultural data, parish census data, farm business survey data, national vegetation data, digital river networks and river gauging records, but central and common to all the modelling routines are the four datasets comprising:

- digital elevation, derived from digitized contours of Ordnance Survey 1:50,000 maps (used for the definition of catchment boundaries and for the definition of land capability maps for the catchment level and farm level economics and for ecological models);
- land cover classified into 25 land cover types derived from Landsat imagery;
- soils data obtained from soil association maps and soil series parameter data which were provided by the Soil Survey of England and Wales; and
- meteorological data obtained from the Meteorological Office.

The Models

Three types of model are incorporated in the NELUP DSS: agro-economic, ecological and hydrological. These models can be used to investigate the characteristics of a region under its present land use and to evaluate how these characteristics will respond to specific land-use changes. A land-use change can be specified explicitly by direct intervention of the user of the DSS or implicitly as the result of economic policy shifts which encourages land owners to make changes in land use and land management.

The agro-economic linear programming models operate at two spatial scales, at the catchment scale and at the farm scale. The catchment-level model predicts the aggregated behaviour of a region by treating the area as a macro-farm. It is capable of taking into account the wide variation in agricultural activity that can exist across a region. Predicted land-use patterns can be disaggregated to a finer spatial resolution by categorizing the region according to its agricultural production potential. Given inputs of values for crop prices, agricultural subsidies, and costs of materials, the model will calculate changes in land-use patterns and income across the region, as, for example, in the Tyne River Basin (Figure 7.6).

The farm-level agro-economic model is similar in operation to the catchment-level model but it has the capability of investigating the potential

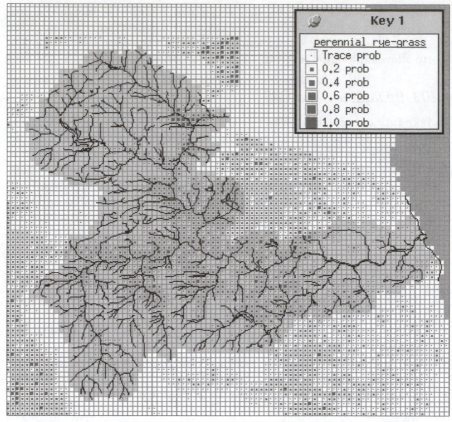

Figure 7.7 *Probability of perennial rye-grass in the Tyne River Basin*

response of a particular type of farm to changes in agricultural policy. Land-use change is modelled at the local rather than the regional scale.

Three types of ecological model (associative, vegetation environment management, and bird and mammal) are used to predict the distribution of various species within the landscape and how land use and environmental change will impact on these species distributions.

An associative model is used to predict the distribution of both plants and invertebrates by linking species distribution to their known occurrence in particular land cover types, through an ecological hierarchy comprising land cover, community and species. An example concerning perennial rye-grass in the Tyne River Basin is shown in Figure 7.7.

Variations in the distribution of species are predicted directly from a knowledge of the change in land cover.

A vegetation environment management model is used to indicate how changes in agricultural management, such as grazing pressure and fertilizer applications, will change species distributions. This model can also be linked to the farm-level economics model to predict the eventual impact of economic policy shifts on vegetation distribution and diversity.

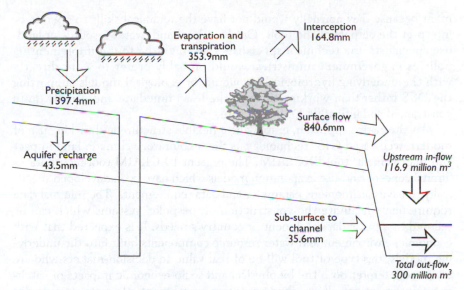

Figure 7.8 *Predicted components of the annual water balance for a sub-catchment of the Tyne*

A bird and mammal ecological model relates species distributions not just to individual land covers but, because these species are highly mobile, to the combination of land covers that they inhabit.

Two hydrological modelling systems are available in NELUP, the SHETRAN distributed, physically based system, which is also available in the WaterWare DSS, and the NUARNO system, which uses a spatially aggregated approach. In some respects the scales over which they would normally be applied are analogous to the scales used for the agro-economic models. NUARNO provides an overview of the catchment hydrology, whilst SHETRAN has the capability for analysing smaller scales in much greater detail.

Hydrological impacts are calculated by running the models with parameters relating to the existing land use to determine the existing hydrological regime (see example from the Tyne in Figure 7.8), and then running the models again with the new land-use scenario, determined either by the agro-economic or the ecological models.

Decision Support, Negotiation Support and the EXCLAIM Dissemination Tool

Decision support systems in support of ILWRM have been available since about 1996 but take-up has not been widespread. Perhaps part of the problem is that the tools have been developed without a clear understanding of potential user requirements and the necessary user skills. DSSs are not used by policymakers, donors or NGOs who have interests in land and water management because they normally would not have the technical skills to operate or interpret the outputs of the tools. On the other hand, water resource or land-use specialists, the technical specialists that might be found implementing policies in government ministries, would probably prefer to work directly with the underlying hydrological, economic or ecological models supporting the DSS rather than working through the less immediate and usually quite constrained and inflexible DSS structure.

An alternative approach, employing a flexible structure and making use of modern web-based GIS technology, is the 'exploratory climate, land impact and management' tool EXCLAIM. The present EXCLAIM tool incorporates 'limits' concept land-use evaporation models which have been developed specifically to have parsimonious parameter and data requirements. The minimal data requirements facilitate the construction of 'bespoke' systems which can be tailored to a particular catchment or country's needs. It is expected that with economic, environment and water resource components built into the underlying models, this type of tool will be of real value to decision-makers who are trying to interpret both the biophysical and socio-economic impacts of catchment interventions. Watershed managers, catchment planners or agencies responsible for planning developments, together with donor organizations, will have the tools to hand to assist with the implementation of the UNCED principles and meeting the Millennium Development Goals.

EXCLAIM shows how, using Falkenmark (2003) terminology, land-related interventions within a catchment affect the partition of rain falling on the catchment into blue water (liquid) flow and green water (vapour) flow out of the catchment.

EXCLAIM is currently being used as teaching tool, as a tool for negotiation support (NS) and as a means for disseminating knowledge of land and water interactions to policymakers.

The tool has been applied to demonstrate the impacts of catchment interventions, including changes in forest cover, irrigation and soil water conservation structures, in a range of countries including India, South Africa and Costa Rica. Where the appropriate socio-economic data is available the tool can also demonstrate how spatial changes in land use impact on job opportunities and economic production values.

A more recent development incorporates climatic variability. This allows the impacts of the land-use change scenarios to be investigated for not only an average rainfall year, but also, through the use of a slider, a range of rainfall years. The slider allows the selection of the driest to the wettest years in an historical record by moving the slider over the range of 5 to 95 percentile rain years. Although, so far, the tool has only been used to investigate scenarios using data on past climate records, it will also be quite feasible to replace these with data generated for a range of future climate change scenarios. This would allow the combined impacts of future climate and land-use changes to be explored in relation to effects on water flows, economics and people's livelihoods. The tool deals mainly with the impacts of catchment interventions on water quantity but the possibility exists for incorporating water quality issues also.

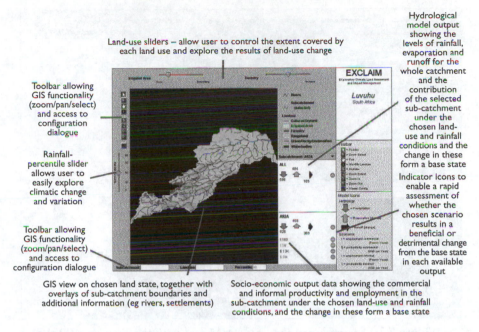

Land-use sliders – allow user to control the extent covered by each land use and explore the results of land-use change

Hydrological model output showing the levels of rainfall, evaporation and runoff for the whole catchment and the contribution of the selected sub-catchment under the chosen land-use and rainfall conditions and the change in these form a base state

Toolbar allowing GIS functionality (zoom/pan/select) and access to configuration dialogue

Rainfall-percentile slider allows user to easily explore climatic change and variation

Toolbar allowing GIS functionality (zoom/pan/select) and access to configuration dialogue

Indicator icons to enable a rapid assessment of whether the chosen scenario results in a beneficial or detrimental change from the base state in each available output

GIS view on chosen land state, together with overlays of sub-catchment boundaries and additional information (eg rivers, settlements)

Socio-economic output data showing the commercial and informal productivity and employment in the sub-catchment under the chosen land-use and rainfall conditions, and the change in these form a base state

Notes: Annotations show the use of climate and land-use sliders

Figure 7.9 *Screenshot of the EXploratory Climate Land Assessment and Impact Management (EXCLAIM) tool set up for the Luvuvhu catchment in South Africa*

The GIS-based tool was created using Java applet technology running in a web browser (James et al, 2005). An annotated screenshot of the tool, set up for the Luvuvhu catchment, part of the Limpopo river basin in South Africa, is shown in Figure 7.9. (The development version of the tool is available at http://www.needs.ncl.ac.uk/exclaim.)

An example of the output from the EXCLAIM tool for the Tengwe (A92a quaternary) catchment within the Luvuvhu, selected for the present land use, which represents the base data set of land uses from 1996, and for a median rainfall year, is shown in Figure 7.10.

A changed land-use scenario, selected by moving the forestry and irrigation sliders to expand the areas under these land uses, is shown in Figure 7.11. This scenario, with a change in land use but with the median climate, shows that the amount of runoff will be reduced, but not by more than 10 per cent. The display shows also how, using the socio-economic data associated with each land use following the approach of Olbrich and Hassan (1999), productivity and job opportunities will change with the change in land use.

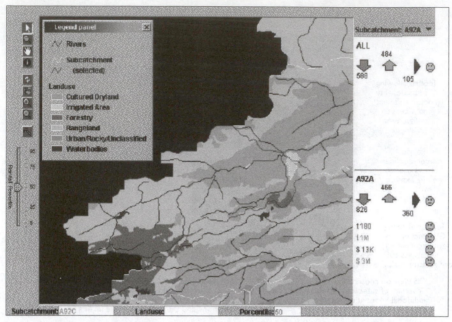

Figure 7.10 *Screenshot of the EXCLAIM tool with the Tengwe (A92a)
catchment selected for a present land-use and a median
rainfall climate scenario*

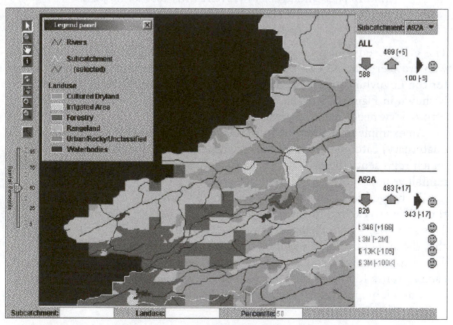

Figure 7.11 *Screenshot of the EXCLAIM tool with the Tengwe (A92a)
catchment selected for an increased forestry and irrigation scenario under
a median rainfall climate scenario*

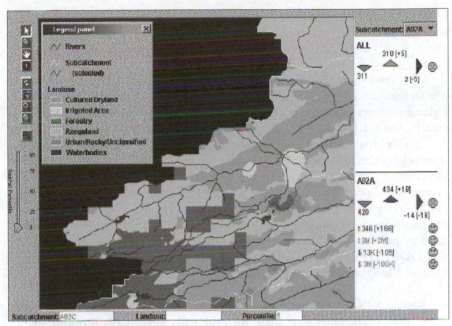

Note: 'Closure' conditions evidenced by negative flow – equivalent to negative water storage (soil, groundwater, surface water) over the year.

Figure 7.12 *Screenshot of the EXCLAIM tool with the Tengwe (A92a) catchment selected for an increased forestry and irrigation scenario and selected for a low (5 percentile) rainfall year, showing catchment 'closure'*

The impact of changing land use, together with a different climate scenario, is shown in Figure 7.12. Here the land-use change is the same as for Figure 7.11 but the climate slider has been moved to represent a dry year (5th percentile, i.e. once every 20 years it will be at least this dry). Here we see that the catchment would have been in a 'closure' condition, that is, there would have been no runoff out of the catchment for such a dry year. The negative flow would indicate a reduction in water storage within the catchment during the year, made up of changes in surface, soil and groundwater storage.

BRIDGING THE GAP BETWEEN POLICY AND RESEARCH COMMUNITIES

The argument was presented in Chapter 5 that the failure of many land and water policies to achieve the desired outcomes was often related to a mismatch between the public and scientific perceptions of the biophysical impacts of changing land use, that policies were more often based on 'land and water myths' than modern science. For ILWRM to succeed and for land and water policies to achieve positive outcomes, greater efforts are needed both to bridge the apparent gap between the policy and research communities and to ensure that recent research findings and policy developments in one country can be communicated and shared between policymakers in other countries.

The need to improve the links between researchers and policymakers is not an issue specific to ILWRM. The Global Development Network (GDN), a global network of research and policy institutes, has identified this as a cross-cutting issue affecting most aspects of national and regional development. The GDN, together with the Overseas Development Institute (ODI) are researching the links between research, policy and practice with the aim of developing simple tools for researchers and policymakers to help them promote pro-poor, evidence-based policies (GDN, 2004; Crewe and Young, 2002). They claim that whether research has been undertaken by academics or practitioners, research findings have often been ignored, distorted or underused by policymakers. Based on the results of a literature review, the GDN and ODI have developed a framework for understanding research policy linkages based on three hypotheses:

1   Research findings either (a) fit within the political and institutional limits of policymakers, and resonate with their ideological assumptions, or (b) sufficient pressure is exerted to challenge those limits.
2   Researchers and policymakers use appropriate networks, experts and chains of legitimacy for particular policy areas.
3   Research outputs are based on local involvement and credible evidence and are communicated via the most appropriate channels, style, format and timing.

Following the GDN-ODI Framework for improving policy linkages, a bridging research and policy (BRAP) network is now being set up as part of the 'Furthering Land and Water Policies – Improving Outcomes' (FAWPIO) project funded under DFID's Forestry Research Programme (FRP). This network aims to incorporate advocacy and promotion techniques and to disseminate new knowledge of the biophysical and socio-economic outcomes of land and water interventions that has been obtained from the FRPs cluster of projects dealing with forest and water issues. The network also aims to share research and policy experience through the partner countries engaged in this research. A number of mechanisms are proposed (Figure 7.13), including peer-to-peer networking of policymakers who are actively engaged in developing and implementing land and water policies in their own countries, the use of interactive workshops and the use of innovative media including e-fora and specialist policy- and water resource-focused journals such as *Land Use and Water Resources Research* (LUWRR) (www.luwrr.com hosted by Venus Internet).

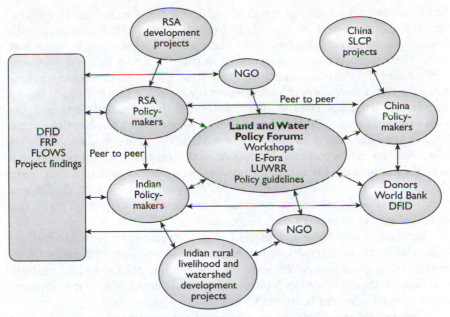

Figure 7.13 *The proposed Bridging Research and Policy Network that will be employed in the FAWPIO Programme to 'connect' findings from research and policy developments*

BLUE REVOLUTION – THE FUTURE

The ideals of ILWRM, the basis of the blue revolution, are now well developed, recognized and accepted. Within the last five years (since the first edition of *Blue Revolution* was published) there have also been major methodological advancements and innovative policy developments. Yet still, all too often, it appears that land and water policies in many parts of the world are still being driven by outdated myth-based assumptions about the value of certain courses of actions.

Research to Counter the Myths

Countering these land and water myths is proving a difficult task. Good science which is accepted by the science community, in the traditional form of peer-reviewed papers in reputable journals, remains a prerequisite. Unfortunately this science costs money, often big money, and a long time commitment. Getting better biophysical understanding of the interactions between different land uses (particularly different types of forest) on floods and low flows remains a priority, but the nature of the problem requires a combination of long-term measurement and modelling – both expensive exercises. The dangerous belief that soil water conservation and water retention structures, moving from the scale of a ditch to a field bund to a check dam, to a village tank and to a reservoir the size of the Kariba, are all necessarily benign technologies in terms of regulating flows or increasing infiltration is one that needs to be urgently addressed. These technologies come with a water resource cost. The cost is the almost inevitable increase in water lost from the catchment as evaporation resulting from the increase in water surface area and riparian area behind these structures. This downside is recognized by water development practitioners for big reservoirs but much less so for smaller structures. But the summed effect of the overenthusiastic installation of small structures distributed within a catchment can have the same impact as a large dam at the catchment outfall. The conceptualization of this issue and the means to measure, parameterize and model the processes in a way that is meaningful and helpful is urgently required. This would help development practitioners to better understand the causes of catchment water stress and catchment closure, allowing them to put in place the remedial actions to prevent such outcomes.

Similarly, a very major and interlinked issue requiring more research effort is in relation to the interactions between land use, soil water retention interventions and groundwater recharge; such research is needed to help address and reverse the catastrophic depletion of groundwater tables that is happening in countries such as India and China.

China might also allow an unprecedented opportunity for forwarding land and water research knowledge. The World's biggest experiment, the 31-million-hectare Sloping Land Conversion Programme in China together with the Natural Forest Protection Programme, which stipulated the protection of natural forests throughout the country (see Chapter 5), surely must present one of the best opportunities for really progressing our scientific understanding of the biophysical and socio-economic impacts associated with such changes in land use.

The need to plan land- and water-related developments to take account of climate variability and to allow adaptation to future climate change is another key area requiring urgent research effort.

Sharing Knowledge to Improve Outcomes

Perverse outcomes to land and water policies remain commonplace. Myth-based assumptions underlying policy may be one cause. Supposedly pro-poor policies which can be exploited by richer elites to the detriment of the poor (see Chapter 5) may be another. Government and donor organizations need to monitor better the programmes that they support to ensure that they are not partners to this deceit. But perhaps the greatest hope for ensuring improved outcomes from ILWRM developments is the sharing of knowledge and policy developments between countries, particularly where these countries have been able to show demonstrably better outcomes as a result of new methodologies and policies.

Swings of the Development Pendulum

Looking back, the pendulum of fashions in development has swung many times. In the 1970s the neo-Malthusian 'limits to growth' predictions of economic and environmental collapse resulting from unfettered population growth was a major concern of governments and development organizations. The belief in the new power of the mainframe computer for solving complex system problems heralded the reign of the technocrat. The 1980s saw many developed countries using overseas development funds as a way of boosting their own industries, particularly the civil engineering and defence industries in 'aid for trade' deals and the ascendancy of 'engineering-driven' agendas. The early 1990s saw (although the Club of Rome's environmental catastrophe predictions had largely been derided by then because they had not actually happened) the emergence of the environmental movement, culminating in the 1992 UNCED Earth Summit in Rio de Janeiro. This was the era of the environmentalists. The installation of the Labour Government in the UK in 1997 saw a new shift of the focus, taken up by many other countries, to poverty alleviation. The dusting down of previous sociologists' works and recasting of these as the 'livelihoods' approach, based on the pentagon of assets, heralded the era of the social scientist.

By the turn of the millennium, with the lack of much evidence to show that the livelihoods approach had fared any better than its predecessors in improving development outcomes, the new focus was on 'governance' – not that it was entirely obvious that the developed countries held the monopoly of the moral high ground on this issue. Counterviews to extreme environmentalist positions were also being voiced in books such as *The Skeptical Environmentalist* (Lomborg, 2001), with claims that many environmental problems were getting better not worse. The turn of the millennium also saw a renewed focus on poverty eradication as evidenced by the Millennium Development Goals (MDGs). The simplistic and implied assumption that each of these goals could be addressed independently is counter to the blue revolution recognition that, at least with regard to water-related developments, it is essential that a more integrated approach be used to avoid perverse outcomes. It is likely that a similarly integrated approach will be necessary to achieve the MDGs, an approach that recognizes that it will not always be easy to find win–win solutions to meeting the different goals and that there will inevitably have to be some hard decisions made in relation to trade-offs.

The early years of the 21st century see again the emergence of water-related engineering infrastructure projects as a new focus for development. 'We are back!' says the World Bank. Looking forward it is unlikely that any of these past concerns will go away. They are likely to reappear in one form or another. Engineering is back, and many believe that the Club of Rome's warnings (Meadows et al, 1972, 2005) of resource exploitation exceeding the 'limits' and 'overshooting' should not go unheeded. Although the modelling procedures and the assumptions underlying these warnings are not accepted by all parties and do not always follow most recent developments (one example of this is the 'old paradigm' assumption that forests necessarily have environmental and water resource benefits), it is clear that there are now examples in the world of unsustainable demands being put on some natural resource systems. The growing phenomenon of catchment closure, when little or no water flows out of a catchment, is one obvious example. The blue revolution would do well to take account of all the past swings of the pendulum and work towards putting in place science-based land and water management policies which are robust and defensible and which take account of many of these very real earlier concerns.

Appendix 1

IWRM and ILWRM Contact and Linking Organizations

- *The African Water Page* is now incorporated in the Water Page. The Water Page is an independent initiative dedicated to the promotion of sustainable water resources management and use. A particular emphasis is placed on the development, utilization and protection of water in Africa and other developing regions.
  WEBSITE: http://www.thewaterpage.com/index.htm
- *The American Heritage Rivers Initiative.* The American Heritage Rivers initiative was set up to help communities revitalize their rivers and riverbanks, through conserving historic buildings and natural habitats with a focus on history and heritage.
  WEBSITE: http://www.epa.gov/rivers/
- *CGIAR.* The Consultative Group on International Agriculture Research (CGIAR) is a consortium jointly supporting a system of 16 international agricultural research centres. The mission of the CGIAR is to contribute, through research, to the promotion of sustainable agriculture for food security in the developing countries. Four centres of particular interest to water-related issues are, the International Water Management Institute (IWMI) in Sri Lanka, the World Agroforestry Centre (ICRAF) in Kenya, the Centre for International Forestry Research (CIFOR) in Indonesia and the International Food Policy Research Institute (IFPRI) in Washington, USA.
  WEBSITE: http://www.cgiar.org/
- *CLUWRR.* The Centre for Land Use and Water Resources Research (CLUWRR) is the focus at the University of Newcastle upon Tyne for research into integrated land and water resource management. CLUWRR's mission is to both develop and apply methodologies and tools to support ILWRM at the local, regional, national and international scale.
  WEBSITE: http://www.cluwrr.ncl.ac.uk/
- *CSIRO Water Resources Division.* The Water Resources Division is a division of Australia's major government-supported national research organization, the Commonwealth Scientific and Industrial Research Organization (CSIRO) with centres in Canberra, Albury, Griffith, Adelaide and Perth.
  WEBSITE: http://www.csiro.au/

- *DFID.* The Department for International Development (DFID) of the British Government has, as its overall objective, the elimination of world poverty. It is committed to the development of efficient and well-regulated markets; access of poor people to land, resources and markets; safe drinking water and food security; the sustainable management of physical and natural resources; the efficient use of productive capacity; and the protection of the global environment.
  WEBSITE: http://www.dfid.gov.uk/
- *DHI Water & Environment.* DHI Water & Environment was formed in January 2000 by the merging of the Danish Hydraulic Institute (DHI) and VKI – Institute for the Water Environment. It is an independent, international consulting and research organization.
  WEBSITE: http://www.dhi.dk/AboutDHI/
- *DWAF.* The Department of Water Affairs and Forestry (DWAF) in South Africa is a world leader in applied water research and water management models.
  WEBSITE: http://www.dwaf.gov.za/
- *EA.* The English and Welsh Environment Agency (EA) is the largest environmental body in Europe. It is committed to achieving the objectives of integrated catchment management and development and is a key player in furthering the Government's sustainable development policies. It also has the responsibility for regulating water resources and for authorizing abstractions and effluent discharges.
  WEBSITE: http://www.environment-agency.gov.uk/
- *Environment and Heritage.* The goal of the Environment and Heritage Department of the government of Australia is to develop, in the national interest, a proper recognition of environmental, social and related economic values in government decision-making and activities.
  WEBSITE: http://www.environment.gov.au/
- *EPA.* The USA Environmental Protection Agency (EPA) is an independent agency created by Congress to protect public health and to safeguard and improve the natural environment – air, water and land. The EPA manages the American Heritage Rivers Initiative (see above).
  WEBSITE: http://www.epa.gov/
- *FAO.* The Food and Agriculture Organization of the United Nations (FAO) is much involved in land and water development worldwide, often with an inclination towards the agricultural use of water, but increasingly also on management issues.
  WEBSITE: http://www.fao.org/
- *GARNET.* The Global Applied Research Network (GARNET) is maintained by the Water Engineering and Development Centre (WEDC) (see below) as a mechanism for information exchange in the water supply and sanitation sector using low-cost, informal networks of researchers, practitioners and funders of research.
  WEBSITE: http://www.lboro.ac.uk/garnet/
- *Great Lakes Commission.* The aim of the Great Lakes Commission is to promote the orderly, integrated and comprehensive development, use and

conservation of the water resources of the Great Lakes Basin in the USA.
WEBSITE: http://www.glc.org/

- *GWP.* The Global Water Partnership (GWP) is an international network open to all involved in water resources management, including governments of developing as well as developed countries, UN agencies, multilateral banks, professional associations, research organizations, the private sector and NGOs. The objective of the GWP is to translate the Dublin–Rio principles into practice.
WEBSITE: http://www.gwpforum.org/

- *HR.* Hydraulics Research (HR) Wallingford is an independent organization specializing in civil engineering and environmental hydraulics and the problems of water management.
WEBSITE: http://www.hrwallingford.co.uk/

- *IAHS.* The International Association for Hydrological Science is an international non-governmental organization which deals with hydrology and water resources. It was established in 1922, incorporating the International Commission of Glaciers which had been set up in 1894, with the aim of bringing together hydrologists from all countries to promote the hydrological sciences.
WEBSITE: http://www.cig.ensmp.fr/~iahs/

- *IAWQ.* The International Association on Water Quality (IAWQ) is a professional membership association dedicated to the advancement of the science and practice of water pollution control and water quality management worldwide.
WEBSITE: http://www.iawq.org.uk/

- *ICID.* The International Commission on Irrigation and Drainage (ICID) is an international scientific and technical NGO dedicated to improving water and land management for the enhancement of the worldwide supply of food and fibre for all people. The objectives of ICID are to stimulate and promote the development and application of the arts; sciences; and techniques of engineering, agriculture, economics, ecology and social sciences in managing water and land resources for irrigation, drainage, flood control and river training, and for research in a more comprehensive manner adopting up-to-date techniques.
WEBSITE: http://www.icid.org/

- *ICOLD.* The International Commission on Large Dams is an international non-governmental organization which provides a forum for the exchange of knowledge and experience in dam engineering. ICOLD's aims are to ensure that dams are built safely, efficiently, economically, and without detrimental effects on the environment.
WEBSITE: http://www.icold-cigb.org

- *IH.* The Institute of Hydrology (IH), now part of the Centre for Ecology and Hydrology, investigates a combination of fundamental science and applied science to solve practical problems related to hydrology for government departments, international agencies and independent organizations.
WEBSITE: http://www.nwl.ac.uk/ih/

- *IIED.* The International Institute for Environment and Development (IIED) is an independent, non-profit organization promoting sustainable patterns of world development through collaborative research, policy studies, networking and knowledge dissemination, particularly with regard to global issues.
  WEBSITE: http://www.iied.org/
- *IPTRID.* The International Programme on Technology Research in Irrigation and Drainage (IPTRID) has been set up to enhance irrigation and drainage technology in developing countries. IPTRID is an independent multi-donor trust-fund programme hosted by FAO in its headquarters in Rome. It provides assistance to developing countries and development agencies for the formulation and implementation of sustainable agricultural water management strategies and programmes.
  WEBSITE: http://www.fao.org/iptrid/
- *IRC.* The International Water and Sanitation Centre (IRC) focuses on affordable technologies to provide clean water and adequate sanitation to poor people around the world. Working with partners in developing countries, IRC aims to disseminate knowledge and build capacity in partner organizations.
  WEBSITE: http://www.irc.nl/
- *IUCN.* The World Conservation Union was established in 1948 as the International Union for the Protection of Nature (IUPN) and became the International Union for the Conservation of Nature (IUCN) in 1956. Today it is a union of governments, government agencies and NGOs working at the field and policy levels, together with scientists and experts, to protect nature.
  WEBSITE: http://www.iucn.org/
- *IWMI.* The International Water Management Institute is a non-profit scientific research organization focusing on the sustainable use of water and land resources in agriculture and on the water needs of developing countries. IWMI works with partners to develop tools and methods to help the eradication of poverty through more effective management of their water and land resources.
  WEBSITE: http://www.iwmi.cgiar.org/
- *IWRA.* The International Water Resources Association (IWRA) has actively promoted, since its inception in 1972, the sustainable management of water resources around the world. IWRA seeks to improve water resource outcomes by improving our collective understanding of the physical, biological, chemical, institutional and socio-economic aspects of water.
  WEBSITE: http://www.iwra.siu.edu/
- *LUWRR.* Land Use and Water Resources Research is a web-based journal devoted to the water resource, ecological, economic, climate change, socio-economic, policy and sustainable development issues related to land use. A particular aim of the journal is to better connect science and policy so that management solutions can be found which take into account the competing demands for land uses which are productive; which sustain

peoples' livelihoods; which deliver conservation, amenity, recreation and environment/ecology (CARE) products; and which also provide water with the quality and quantity required for sustainable development.
WEBSITE: http://www.luwrr.com/

- *ODI.* The Overseas Development Institute (ODI) is an independent non-governmental centre for the study of development and humanitarian issues, and a forum for discussion of the problems facing developing countries.
  WEBSITE: http://www.odi.org.uk/

- *SEI.* The Stockholm Environment Institute (SEI) was established in 1989 as an independent foundation for the purpose of carrying out global and regional environmental research. The Institute is active in promoting international initiatives on environment and development issues.
  WEBSITE: http://www.sei.se/

- *SIWI.* The Stockholm International Water Institute (SIWI) is a policy think tank that contributes to international efforts to find solutions to the world's escalating water crisis. SIWI advocates future-oriented, knowledge-integrated water views in decision making, nationally and internationally, that lead to sustainable use of the world's water resources and sustainable development of societies. SIWI organizes the World Water Week in Stockholm and within it, the Stockholm Water Symposium.
  WEBSITE: http://www.siwi.org/

- *SustainAbility.* 'SustainAbility' is a strategic management consultancy and think tank dedicated to promoting the business case for sustainable development – satisfying the 'triple bottom line'.
  WEBSITE: http://www.sustainability.com/

- *UNDP.* The United Nations Development Programme (UNDP) is involved in water-related development activities worldwide. Capacity building, for example, in the field of water, is a major focal area.
  WEBSITE: http://www.undp.org/

- *UNEP.* The United Nations Environment Programme (UNEP) was established as the environmental 'conscience' of the UN system. Its mission is to provide leadership and encourage partnerships in caring for the environment by inspiring, informing and enabling nations and people to improve their quality of life without compromising that of future generations.
  WEBSITE: http://www.unep.ch/

- *WB.* The World Bank Group's mission is to fight poverty and improve the living standards of people in the developing world. It is a development bank which provides loans, policy advice, technical assistance and knowledge-sharing services to low- and middle-income countries to reduce poverty. In March 2000 the World Bank put in place a formal Water Resources Management Group (WRMG) which has an informative website.
  WEBSITE: http://lnweb18.worldbank.org/ESSD/ardext.nsf/18ByDocName/WaterResourcesManagement

- *WBCSD*. The World Business Council for Sustainable Development (WBCSD) aims to develop closer cooperation between business, government and all other organizations concerned with the environment and sustainable development.
  WEBSITE: http://www.wbcsd.org/
- *WEDC*. The Water Engineering and Development Centre (WEDC) at Loughborough University is a training and consultancy organization directed towards providing appropriate technologies for clean water and sanitation in the developing world.
  WEBSITE: http://wedc.lboro.ac.uk/
- *WRC(SA)*. The Water Research Commission (WRC) in South Africa does not undertake any research of its own, but it provides funding for research undertaken by institutions such as universities, government departments and industry. Furthermore, WRC monitors, directs and coordinates water research in South Africa and disseminates the findings. It is very well placed to assist in linking water research in South Africa with international initiatives. A comprehensive list of linkages on water in southern Africa is provided.
  WEBSITE: http://www.wrc.org.za/
- *WRSRL*. The Water Resource Systems Research Laboratory (WRSRL) is part of the School of Civil Engineering and Geoscience at the University of Newcastle upon Tyne. Its aim is to create and apply new technologies for planning and managing a sustainable water environment, integrating the latest methods in hydroinformatics, modelling and measurement. It carries out water-related research and training across the spectrum of strategic and applied research.
  WEBSITE: http://www.ncl.ac.uk/wrgi/wrsrl/
- *WSSCC*. The Water Supply and Sanitation Collaborative Council is a group of professionals from developing countries, external support agencies (ESAs), and non-governmental and research organizations all working in the water, sanitation and waste management sector. Its mission is to 'enhance collaboration among developing countries and ESAs so as to accelerate the achievement of sustainable water, sanitation and waste management services to all people, with special attention to the poor'.
  WEBSITE: http://www.wsscc.org/
- *WWC*. The World Water Council (WWC) is an international water policy think tank dedicated to strengthening the world water movement for an improved management of the world's water resources and water services.
  WEBSITE: http://www.worldwatercouncil.org/

Appendix 2

Glossary of Participatory Tools

This glossary is taken from the World Bank sourcebook on participatory approaches.

- *Access to resources.* A series of participatory exercises that allows development practitioners to collect information and raises awareness among beneficiaries about the ways in which access to resources varies according to gender and other important social variables. This user-friendly tool draws on the everyday experience of participants and is useful to men, women, trainers, project staff and field-workers.
- *Analysis of tasks.* A gender analysis tool that raises community awareness about the distribution of domestic, market and community activities according to gender and familiarizes planners with the degree of role flexibility that is associated with different tasks. Such information and awareness are necessary to prepare and execute development interventions that will benefit both men and women.
- *Focus-group meetings.* Relatively low-cost, semi-structured, small-group consultations (4 to 12 participants plus a facilitator) used to explore people's attitudes, feelings or preferences and to build consensus. Focus-group work is a compromise between participant observation, which is less controlled, lengthier and more in-depth, and pre-set interviews, which are not likely to attend to participants' own concerns.
- *Force field analysis.* A tool similar to 'Story With a Gap', force field analysis engages people in defining and classifying goals and making sustainable plans by working on thorough 'before and after' scenarios. Participants review the causes of problematic situations, consider the factors that influence the situations, think about solutions and create alternative plans to achieve solutions. The tools are based on diagrams or pictures, which minimize language and literacy differences and encourage creative thinking.
- *Health-seeking behaviour.* A culturally sensitive tool for the generation of data about health care and health-related activities. It produces qualitative data about the reasons behind certain practices as well as quantifiable information about beliefs and practices. This visual tool uses pictures to minimize language and literacy differences.

- *Logical Framework or LogFRAME.* A matrix that illustrates a summary of project design, emphasizing the results that are expected when a project is successfully completed. These results or outputs are presented in terms of objectively verifiable indicators. The logical framework approach to project planning, developed under that name by the USA Agency for International Development, has been adapted for use in participatory methods such as ZOPP and TeamUP. ZOPP, from the German term *zielo-rientierte projektplanung*, is a project planning and management method that encourages participatory planning and analysis throughout the project cycle. The TeamUP process assists stakeholders in planning and decision making, and encourages stakeholders to collaborate as an effective working group.
- *Mapping.* A generic term for gathering baseline data on a variety of indicators in pictorial form. This is an excellent starting point for participatory work because it gets people involved in creating a visual output that can be used immediately to bridge speech gaps and to generate lively discussion. Maps are useful as verification of secondary source information, as training and awareness raising tools, for comparison and for monitoring of change. Common types of maps include health maps, institutional maps (Venn diagrams) and resource maps.
- *Needs assessment.* A tool that draws out information about people's varied needs, raises participants' awareness of related issues, and provides a framework for prioritizing needs. This tool is an integral part of gender analysis, in developing an understanding of the particular needs of both men and women, and carrying out comparative analysis.
- *Participant observation.* A fieldwork technique used by anthropologists and sociologists to collect qualitative and quantitative data that leads to an in-depth understanding of people's practices, motivations and attitudes. Participant observation entails investigating the project background, studying the general characteristics of a beneficiary population, and living for an extended period among beneficiaries, during which interviews, observations and analyses are recorded and discussed.
- *Pocket charts.* Pocket charts are investigative tools that use pictures as stimuli to encourage people to assess and analyse a given situation. Through a 'voting' process, participants use the chart to draw attention to the complex elements of a development issue in an uncomplicated way. A major advantage of this tool is that it can be put together with whatever local materials are available.
- *Preference ranking.* This is also called direct matrix ranking, an exercise in which people identify what they do and do not value about a class of objects (for example, tree species or cooking fuels). Ranking allows participants to understand the reasons for local preferences and to see how values differ among local groups. Understanding preferences is critical for choosing appropriate and effective interventions.
- *Role playing.* Role playing enables people to creatively remove themselves from their usual roles and perspectives to allow them to understand choices and decisions made by other people with other responsibilities.

Ranging from a simple story with only a few characters to an elaborate street-theatre production, this tool can be used to acclimatize a research team to a project setting, train trainers, and encourage community discussions about a particular development intervention.

- *Seasonal diagrams or seasonal calendars.* These calendars show the major changes that affect a household, community or region within a year, such as those associated with climate, crops, labour availability and demand, livestock and prices. Such diagrams highlight the times of constraints and opportunity, which can be critical information for planning and implementation.

- *Secondary data review.* Also called desk review, this is an inexpensive, initial enquiry that provides necessary background information. Sources include academic theses and dissertations, annual reports, archival materials, census data, life histories, maps and project documents.

- *Semi-structured interviews.* These are also called conversational interviews and are partially structured by a flexible interview guide with a limited number of preset questions. This kind of guide ensures that the interview remains focused on the development issue at hand while allowing enough conversation so that participants can introduce and discuss relevant topics. These tools are a deliberate departure from survey-type interviews with lengthy, predetermined questionnaires.

- *Socio-cultural profiles.* Socio-cultural profiles are detailed descriptions of the social and cultural dimensions that in combination with technical, economic and environmental dimensions serve as a basis for design and preparation of policy and project work. Profiles include data about the type of communities, demographic characteristics, economy and livelihood, land tenure and natural resource control, social organization, factors affecting access to power and resources, conflict resolution mechanisms, and values and perceptions. Together with a participation plan, the socio-cultural profile helps ensure that proposed projects and policies are culturally and socially appropriate and potentially sustainable.

- *Surveys.* Surveys comprise sequences of focused, predetermined questions in a fixed order, often with predetermined, limited options for responses. Surveys can add value when they are used to identify development problems or objectives, narrow the focus or clarify the objectives of a project or policy, plan strategies for implementation, and monitor or evaluate participation. Among the survey instruments used in World Bank work are firm surveys, sentinel community surveillance, contingent valuation and priority surveys.

- *Tree diagrams.* Tree diagrams are multipurpose visual tools for narrowing and prioritizing problems, objectives or decisions. Information is organized into a tree-like diagram that includes information on the main issue, relevant factors, and influences and outcomes of these factors. Tree diagrams are used to guide design and evaluation systems, to uncover and analyse the underlying causes of a particular problem, or to rank and measure objectives in relation to one another.

- *Village meetings*. Village meetings have many uses in participatory development, including information sharing and group consultation, consensus building, prioritization and sequencing of interventions, and collaborative monitoring and evaluation. When multiple tools such as resource mapping, ranking and focus groups have been used, village meetings are important venues for launching activities, evaluating progress and gaining feedback on analysis.
- *Wealth ranking*. Wealth ranking is also known as well-being ranking or vulnerability analysis. It is a technique which allows for the rapid collection and analysis of specific data on social stratification at the community level. This visual tool minimizes literacy and language differences of participants. Participants are asked to consider factors such as ownership of, or rights to, productive assets; the lifecycle stage of members of the productive unit; relationship of the productive unit to locally powerful people; availability of labour; and indebtedness.
- *Workshops*. Workshops are structured group meetings at which a variety of key stakeholder groups, whose activities or influence affect a development issue or project, share knowledge and work toward a common vision. With the help of a workshop facilitator, participants undertake a series of activities designed to help them progress toward the development objective (such as consensus building, information sharing, prioritization of objectives and team building). In project as well as policy work, from pre-planning to evaluation stages, stakeholder workshops are used to initiate, establish and sustain collaboration.

References

Abbott, MB (1991) *Hydroinformatics: Information Technology and the Aquatic Environment*, Avebury Technical, Aldershot, England

Abbott, MB, Bathurst, JC, Cunge, JA, O'Connell, PE and Rasmussen, J (1986) 'An introduction to the European Hydrological System – System Hydrologique Européen', "SHE", 1: History and philosophy of a physically-based, distributed modelling system, *Journal of Hydrology*, 87, pp45–59

Adams, R (1995) 'The integration of a physically based hydrological model within a decision support system to model the hydrological impacts of land use change', *Scenario Studies for the Rural Environment*, Kluwer Academic Publishers, The Netherlands, pp209–214

Adams, B, Grimble, R, Shearer, TR, Kitching, R, Calow, R, Chen Dong Jie, Cui Xiao Dong and Yu Zhong Ming (1994) *Aquifer Overexploitation in the Hangu Region of Tianjin, People's Republic of China*, British Geological Survey, Nottingham

Allan, JA (1992) 'Fortunately there are substitutes for water: otherwise our hydropolitical futures would be impossible', Paper 2, in *Proceedings of the Conference on Priorities for Water Resources Allocation and Management*, Southampton, July 1992, Overseas Development Administration, London, pp13–26

Allan, JA (1996) 'Policy responses to the closure of water resources: regional and global issues', in Howsam, P and Carter, R (eds) *Water Policy: Allocation and Management in Practice*, Proceedings of the International Conference on Water Policy, Cranfield University, 23–24 September 1996, E & FN SPON, London, pp3–12

Allan, JA (2003) 'IWRM/IWRAM: a new sanctioned discourse?', Occasional Paper 50, SOAS Water Issues Study Group, School of Oriental and African Studies/King's College London, University of London

Allan, JA (2004) 'Water in the environment/socio-economic development discourse: sustainability, changing management paradigms and policy responses in a global context', SOAS Water Issues Study Group, School of Oriental and African Studies/King's College London, University of London, The University of Sheffield website, www.shef.ac.uk/uni/academic/N-Q/perc/resourcepol/papers/allan.pdf

Amezaga, JM and O'Connell, PE (1998) 'Unfolding the sociotechnical dimension of hydroinformatics: the role of problem structuring methods', in *Proceedings of the 3rd International Conference on Hydroinformatics*, Copenhagen, 24–26 August 1998, Balkema, Rotterdam, pp1193–1200

Anderson, HW, Hoover, MD and Reinhart, KG (1976) 'Forests and water: effects of forest management on floods, sedimentation, and water supply', General Technical Report PSW-18/1976, Berkeley, California: United States Department of Agriculture, Forest Service, Pacific Southwest Forest and Range Experiment Station

Arnell, NW (1996) *Global Warming, River Flows and Water Resources*, John Wiley & Sons Ltd, Chichester

Arnell, NW (2004) 'Climate change and global water resources: SRES emissions and socio-economic scenarios', *Global Environmental Change*, 14(1), pp31–52

Arthur, RAJ (1997) 'Water without limits', *Water and Environment*, pp16–19

Ashton, P, MacKay, H, Neal, M and Weaver, A (2002) *The Development of Strategic Investment Frameworks for the Environmental Governance Systems and Biodiversity Protection and Environmental Functioning Thrusts*, Report for the Water Research Commission, CSIR, Pretoria, CSIR Website: www.wrc.org.za/xcd/ WRC%20Environment%20XD%20strategy%20July%202003.PDF

Aylward, B (1998) *Beneficios y Costos De Oportunidad De La Conservación De Biodiversidad En El Corredor Biológico Panameño – Componente Atlántico*, Final Report to the Project on Rural Poverty and Natural Resources, Panamá: INRENARE/MIDA

Aylward, B (2002) *Report to the World Bank as Part of the Program for the Sustainable Management of the Rural Areas in the Panama Canal Watershed*, Aylward, Falls Church, VA

Aylward, B, Echeverria, J, Fernandez Gonzalez, AF, Porras, I, Allen, K and Mejias, R (1998) *Economic Incentives for Watershed Protection: A Case Study of Lake Arenal, Costa Rica*, Final report on a research project under the Program of Collaborative Research of Environment and Development, IIED, London

Baconguis, S (1980) 'Water balance, water use and maximum water storage of a dipterocarp forest watershed in San Lorenzo, Norzagaray, Bulacan, and Sylvatrop', *Philippines Forest Research Journal*, 2, pp73–98

Bands, DP, Bosch, JM, Lamb, AJ, Richardson, DM, Van Wilgen, BW, Van Wyk, DB and Versfeld, DB (1987) *Jonkershoek Forestry Research Centre Pamphlet 384*, Department of Environment Affairs, Pretoria, South Africa

Barr, JJF (1998) 'Use of indigenous knowledge by natural resources scientists: issues in theory and practice', Paper presented at the National Workshop on the State of Indigenous Knowledge in Bangladesh, Dhaka, 6–7 May, 1998

Barr, JJF and Gowing, JW (1998) 'Rice production in floodplains: issues for water management in Bangladesh', *Irrigation and Environment*, E & FN Spon, London

Bass, S, Dubois, O, Moura Costa, P, Pinard, M, Tipper, R and Wilson, C (2000) *Rural Livelihoods and Carbon Management*, International Institute for Environment and Development, IIED Natural Resource Issues Paper 1, IIED, London

Batchelor, CH (2005) Personal communication

Batchelor, CH, Rama Mohan Rao, MS and Manohar Rao, S (2003) 'Watershed development: a solution to water shortages in semi-arid India or part of the problem?' *Land Use & Water Resources Research*, 3, pp1–10

Batchelor, CH, Rama Mohan Rao, MS, Mukherjee, K and James, AJ (2001) 'Implementing watershed development and livelihood projects in semi-arid areas: experiences from the KAWAD Project', Paper presented at the DFID *Livelihoods and Water* Workshop, 31 October 2001, London

Bate, RN and Dubourg, WR (1994) 'A netback analysis of water irrigation demand in East Anglia', CSERGE Discussion Paper WM94, University College, London

Bates, CG and Henry, AJ (1928) 'Forest and stream-flow experiment at Wagon Wheel Gap, Colo.', Final Report on Completion of the Second Phase of the Experiment. Washington, DC, US Dept. of Agriculture, Weather Bureau, 1928, p79

Bell, JP (1976) *Neutron probe practice*, Institute of Hydrology, Report no 19, Institute of Hydrology, Wallingford, UK

Benson, JF and Willis, KG (1991) 'The demand for forests for recreation', *Forestry Expansion: A Study of Technical, Economic and Ecological Factors*, Forestry Commission, Edinburgh, Scotland

Berz, G (2000) 'Flood disasters: lessons from the past – worries for the future', *Proceedings of the Institute of Civil Engineers, Water and Marine Engineering*, 142 (March), pp3–8

Bhatia, R and Falkenmark, M (1992) 'Water resource policies and urban poor: innovative thinking and policy imperatives', paper presented to the Dublin International Conference on Water and the Environment, January 1992, Ireland

Blaikie, PM and Muldavin, JSS (2004) 'Upstream, downstream, China, India: the politics of environment in the Himalayan region', *Annals of the Association of American Geographers*, 94 (3), pp520–548

Blythe, EM, Dolman, AJ and Noilhan, J (1994) 'The effect of forest on mesoscale rainfall: an example from HAPEX-MOBILHY', *Journal of Applied Meteorology*, 33, pp445–454

Bonell, M (1993) 'Progress in the understanding of runoff generation dynamics in forests', *Journal of Hydrology*, 150, pp217–275

Bonell, M (1999) 'Tropical forest hydrology and the role of the UNESCO International Hydrology Programme: some personal observations' *Hydrology and Earth System Sciences*, 3, pp451-461]

Bonell, M and Gilmour, DA (1978) 'The development of overland flow in a tropical rainforest catchment', *Journal of Hydrology*, 39, pp365–382

Bosch, JM (1979) 'Treatment effects on annual and dry period streamflow at Cathedral Peak', *South African Forestry Journal*, 108, pp29–38

Bosch, JM and Hewlett, JD (1982) 'A review of catchment experiments to determine the effects of vegetation changes on water yield and evapotranspiration', *Journal of Hydrology*, 55, pp3–23

Bouten, W, Smart, PJF and De Water, E (1991) 'Microwave transmission, a new tool in forest hydrological research', *Journal of Hydrology*, 124, pp119–130

Boyd, C (1997) 'DFID White Paper – an ODI perspective', ODI website, www.oneworld.org/odi/

Brandt, J (1989) 'The size distribution of throughfall drops under vegetation canopies', *Catena*, 16, pp507–524

Brans, J, Vincke, P and Marescal, B (1986) 'How to select and how to rank projects: the PROMETHEE method', *European Journal of Operational Research*, 24, pp228–238

Brown, LR (1998) 'The Yangtze flood, the human hand, local and global', Worldwatch Institute website, www.worldwatch.org/alerts/pr98813.html

Bruijnzeel, LA (1990) *Hydrology of Moist Tropical Forests and Effects of Conversion: A State of Knowledge Review*, UNESCO International Hydrological Programme, Paris, France

Bruijnzeel, LA (2004) 'Hydrological functions of tropical trees: not seeing the soil for the trees?', *Agricultural, Ecosystems and Environment*, 104, pp185–228

Bruijnzeel, LA and Bremmer, CN (1989) *Highland–Lowland Interactions in the Ganges-Brahmaputra River Basin*, A review of published literature, ICIMOD Occasional Paper, no11

Calder, IR (1978) 'Transpiration observations from a spruce forest and comparison with predictions from an evaporation model', *Journal of Hydrology*, 38, pp33–47

Calder, IR (1986) 'The influence of land use on water yield in upland areas of the UK', *Journal of Hydrology*, 88, pp201–212

Calder, IR (1990) *Evaporation in the Uplands*, John Wiley & Sons Ltd, Chichester

Calder, IR (1991) 'Implications and assumptions in using the total counts and convection-dispersion equations for tracer flow measurements – with particular reference to transpiration measurements in trees', *Journal of Hydrology*, 125, pp149–158

Calder, IR (1992a) 'Hydrologic effects of land-use change' Chapter 13, in Maidment, DR (ed) *Handbook of Hydrology*, McGraw Hill

Calder, IR (1992b) 'A model of transpiration and growth of eucalyptus plantation in water-limited conditions', *Journal of Hydrology*, 130, pp1–15

Calder, IR (1992c) 'The hydrological impact of land use change (with special reference to afforestation and deforestation)', *Proceedings of the Conference on Priorities for Water Resources Allocation and Management*, Southampton, July 1992, Overseas Development Administration, London, pp91–101

Calder, IR (1996a) 'Water use by forests at the plot and catchment scale', *Commonwealth Forestry Review*, 75 (1), pp19–30

Calder, IR (1996b) 'Dependence of rainfall interception on drop size: 1. development of the two-layer stochastic model', *Journal of Hydrology*, 185, pp363–378

Calder, IR (1997) 'Capacity building support to the WRMS project', report prepared for the Government of Zimbabwe and the British Department for International Development, Ewelme, Wallingford, UK

Calder, IR (1998a) 'Review outline of water resource and land use issues', SWIM Paper 3, International Irrigation Management Institute, Colombo, Sri Lanka

Calder, IR (1998b) 'Water use by forests, limits and controls', *Tree Physiology*, 18, pp625–631

Calder, IR (1999) *The Blue Revolution: Land Use and Integrated Water Resources Management* (first edition), Earthscan Publications, London

Calder, IR (2000) 'Land use impacts on water resources', Background paper 1, FAO Electronic Workshop on Land-Water Linkages in Rural Watersheds, 18 September – 27 October 2000, FAO website, www.fao.org/ag/agl/watershed/

Calder, IR (2002) 'Forest valuation and water; the need to reconcile public and science perceptions', in Verweij, PA (ed) *Understanding and Capturing the Multiple Values of Tropical Forests*, Tropenbos Proceedings, Tropenbos International, Wageningen, pp49–62

Calder, IR (2003) 'Assessing the water use of short vegetation and forests: development of the Hydrological Land Use Change (HYLUC) model', *Water Resources Research*, 39 (11) p1318

Calder, IR (2004) 'Forests and water – closing the gap between public and science perceptions', *Water Science & Technology*, 49 (7) pp39–53

Calder, IR and Aylward, B (2005) 'Forest and floods: moving to an evidence-based approach to watershed and integrated flood management', *Water International*, (in press)

Calder, IR and Bastable, HGD (1995) 'Comments on the Malawi Government Water Resources Management Policy and Strategies', report to ODA, Institute of Hydrology, Wallingford, UK

Calder, IR, Batchelor, CH, Quibell, G, Gosain, A, Jewitt, G, Bosch, J, Large, A, Amezaga, A, Hope, R, James, P, Simpson, E, Garratt, J, Bailey, R and Kirby, C (2004) 'Global governance of water and the blue revolution – can we achieve better outcomes from land and water policies?' *Proceedings of the International Symposium: Global Governance of Water - Water and Human Security 8 September 2004*, UN House, Tokyo, Japan, Global Governance of Water website: http://park.itc.u-tokyo.ac.jp/ggwater/tia_project/intlmeet/sympo_8sept04e.html# programme

Calder, IR and Gosain, AK (2003) 'Inter-relating resource management issues within a DFID livelihoods framework where water and power management are a practical focus', *Proceedings of the KAWAD Conference on 'Watershed Development and Sustainable Livelihoods: Past Lessons and Future Strategies'*, 16 and 17 January 2003, Bangalore, Published by NR International, Kent, UK

Calder, IR, Hall, RL, Bastable, HG, Gunston, HM, Shela, O, Chirwa, A and Kafundu, R (1995) 'The impact of land use change on water resources in sub-Saharan Africa: a modelling study of Lake Malawi', *Journal of Hydrology*, 170, pp123–135

Calder, IR, Hall, RL and Prasanna, KT (1993) 'Hydrological impact of eucalyptus plantation in India', *Journal of Hydrology*, 150, pp635–648

Calder, IR, Hall, RL, Rosier, PTW, Bastable, HG and Prasanna, KT (1996) 'Dependence of rainfall interception on drop size: 2. experimental determination of the wetting functions and two-layer stochastic model parameters for five tropical tree species', *Journal of Hydrology*, 185, pp379–388

Calder, IR, Harding, RJ and Rosier, PTW (1983) 'An objective assessment of soil-moisture deficit models', *Journal of Hydrology*, 60, pp329–355

Calder, IR and Newson, MD (1979) 'Land use and upland water resources in Britain – a strategic look', *Water Resources Bulletin*, 16, pp1628–1639

Calder, IR and Newson, MD (1980) 'The effects of afforestation on water resources in Scotland: Land assessment in Scotland'. *Proceedings of the Royal Scottish Geographical Society, Edinburgh*, May 1979, Aberdeen University Press, Aberdeen, pp51–62

Calder, IR, Newson, MD and Walsh, PD (1982) 'The application of catchment, lysimeter and hydrometeorological studies of coniferous afforestation in Britain to land-use planning and water management', *Proceedings of the Symposium on Hydrological Research Basins*, Bern 1982, pp853–863

Calder, IR, Reid, I, Nisbet, T, Armstrong, A, Green, JC and Parkin G (2003b) 'Study of the potential impacts on water resources of proposed afforestation', DEFRA website: http://www.defra.gov.uk/environment/water/resources/research/

Calder, IR, Reid, I, Nisbet, T, Brainard, J and Walker, D (1999) 'UK water resources and planned lowland afforestation for community forests', *Proceedings of the 2nd Inter-Regional Conference on Environment-Water*, September 1–3, 1999, Lausanne, Switzerland

Calder, IR, Reid, I, Nisbet, T and Green, JC (2003a) 'Impact of lowland forests in England on water resources: application of the Hydrological Land Use Change (HYLUC) model', *Water Resources Research*, 39 (11), p1319

Calder, IR, Reid, I, Nisbet, T and Robinson, MR (1997b) 'Trees and Drought Project on Lowland England', Project proposal to the Department of the Environment, Institute of Hydrology & Loughborough University, UK

Calder, IR and Rosier, PTW (1976) 'The design of large plastic sheet net-rainfall gauges', *Journal of Hydrology*, 30, pp403–405

Calder, IR, Rosier, PTW, Prasanna, KT and Parameswarappa, S (1997a) 'Eucalyptus water use greater than rainfall input – a possible explanation from southern India', *Hydrology and Earth System Sciences*, 1(2), pp249–256

Calder, IR, Swaminath, MH, Kariyappa, GS, Srinivasalu, NV, Srinivasa Murthy, KV and Mumtaz, J (1992) 'Deuterium tracing for the estimation of transpiration from trees: 3. measurements of transpiration from eucalyptus plantation, India', *Journal of Hydrology*, 130, pp37–48

Calder, IR and Wright, IR (1986) 'Gamma-ray attenuation studies of interception from Sitka spruce: some evidence for an additional transport mechanism', *Water Resources Research*, 22, pp409–417

Calder, IR, Wright, IR and Murdiyarso, D (1986) 'A study of evaporation from tropical rainforest – West Java', *Journal of Hydrology*, 89, pp13–33

Calder, IR, Young, D and Sheffield, J (2001) 'Scoping study to indicate the direction and magnitude of the hydrological impacts resulting from land use change on the Panama Canal watershed' Report to the World Bank. Newcastle: Centre for Land Use and Water Resources Research, University of Newcastle upon Tyne

CAMP (2004) 'Catchment management and poverty', Final Technical Report to the DFID Forestry Research Programme, Newcastle: Centre for Land Use and Water Resources Research, University of Newcastle upon Tyne

Cannell, MGR, Mobbs, DC and Lawson, GJ (1998) 'Complementarity of light and water use in tropical agroforests; II, modelled theoretical tree production and potential crop yield in arid to humid climates', *Forest Ecology and Management*, 102, pp275–282

Carney, D (1998) 'Implementing the sustainable rural livelihoods approach', *Sustainable Rural Livelihoods: What contribution can we make?*, Papers presented at the Department for International Development's Natural Resources Advisers' Conference, DFID, London

CGIAR (2004) 'Alternatives to Slash-and-Burn', Programme website: www.asb.cgiar.org/txtonly/home.htm

Chapman, G (1948) 'Size of raindrops and their striking force at the soil surface in a red pine plantation', *Eos, Transactions American Geophysical Union*, 29, pp664–670

Chatterton, B and Chatterton, L (1996) 'Closing a water resource: some policy considerations', *Water Policy: Allocation and Management in Practice*, Proceedings of the International Conference on Water Policy, Cranfield University, 23–24 September, E & FN Spon, pp355–361

China Daily (2004) Article of 14 October 2004, reported in the China Ministry of Water website: www.mwr.gov.cn/english1/20041015/41358.asp

Chomitz, K and Kumari, K (1998) 'The domestic benefits of tropical forests: a critical review', *The World Bank Research Observer*, 13 (1), pp13–35

Chomitz, K and Thomas, TS (2003) 'Determinants of land use in Amazonia: A fine-scale spatial analysis' *American Journal of Agricultural Economics*, 85, pp1016–1028

City of New York (2004) 'New York City's Water Supply System, Watershed Protection', New York City website: www.ci.nyc.ny.us/html/dep/html/watershed.html

CJC Consulting (2003) 'Economic analysis of forestry policy in England', Final report for the Department for Environment, Food and Rural Affairs and H. M. Treasury, DEFRA website: http://statistics.defra.gov.uk/esg/evaluation/forestry/

Clayton, MH and Radcliffe, J (1996) *Sustainability, A Systems Approach*, Earthscan, London

Coffey, A, Holbrook, B and Atkinson, P (1996) 'Qualitative data analysis: technologies and representations', *Sociological Research Outline*, 1(1), website: www.socresonline.org.uk/socresonline/1/1/4.html

Cohen, Y, Fuchs, M and Green, GC (1981) 'Improvement of the heat pulse method for determining sap flow in trees', *Plant, Cell and Environment*, 4, pp391–397

Collinet, J, Monteny, B and Pouyaud, B (1984) 'Le milieu physique', *Recherche et Aménagement en Mileu Forestier Tropical H: le Projet Tai de Côte d'Ivoire*, Notes Techniques du MAB no 15, UNESCO, Paris, pp35–58

Collins, RO (1990) *The Waters of the Nile, Hydropolitics and the Jonglei Canal 1900–1988*, Clarendon Press, Oxford

Conway, G (1999) *The Doubly Green Revolution: Food for All in the 21st Century*, Cornell University Press, Cornell, NY

Conway, G and Toenniessen, G (1999) 'Feeding the world in the twenty-first century', *Nature*, 402, pp55–58

Conway, G and Toenniessen, G (2003) 'World hunger, feeding the world in the twenty-first century', *ScienceWeek* website: http://scienceweek.com/2003/sw030704-2.htm

Cooper, JD (1980) 'Measurement of water fluxes in unsaturated soil in Thetford Forest', Institute of Hydrology, report no 66, Wallingford, UK

Cooper, JD and Kinniburgh, DG (1993) 'Water resource implications of the proposed Greenwood Community Forest', project report, National Rivers Authority, UK

Courtney, FM (1978) Personal communication

Crabtree, JR (1997) 'The supply of public access to the countryside – a value for money and institutional analysis of incentive policies', *Environment and Planning*, 29, pp1465–1476

Crewe, E and Young, J (2002) 'Bridging research and policy: context, links and evidence', GDN and ODI, GDNET website: www.gdnet.org/rapnet/pdf/Bridging%20R&P%20WP.pdf

Dent, MC (2000) 'Strategic issues in modelling for integrated water resource management in Southern Africa', *Water SA*, 26, WRC website, www.wrc.org.za

DFID (1997) *White Paper on International Development*, Department for International Development, London

DID (1977) 'Sungai Lui representative basin report no 1 for 1971/72 to 1973/74', *Water Resources Publication*, 7, Drainage and Irrigation Department, Kuala Lumpur, Malaysia (cited by Bruijnzeel, 1990)

DID (1986) 'Sungai Tekam experimental basin', Transition Report July 1980 to June 1983, *Water Resources Publication*, 16, Drainage and Irrigation Department, Ministry of Agriculture, Kuala Lumpur, Malaysia (cited by Bruijnzeel, 1990)

Dietrich, WE, Windsor, DM and Dunne, T (1982) 'Geology, climate, and hydrology of Barro Colorado Island', *The Ecology of a Tropical Forest: Seasonal Rhythms and Long-term Changes*, Smithsonian Institution, Washington, DC, pp21–46

Dinar, A, Yaron, D and Kannai, Y (1986) 'Sharing regional cooperative gains from using effluent for irrigation', *Water Resources Research*, 22 (3), pp339–344

Dixon, JA, Scura, LF, Carpenter, R and Sherman, PB (1994) *Economic Analysis of Environmental Impacts*, Earthscan, London

DOE (1995) *Rural England: A Nation Committed to a Living Countryside*, Department of the Environment, The Stationery Office, London

DOE (1997) *Government Response to the Conclusions and Recommendations of the Environment Committee: 1st Report on Water Conservation and Supply*, Department of the Environment, The Stationery Office, London

DWAF (1996) *The Working for Water Programme*, Department of Water Affairs and Forestry, Cape Town, South Africa

DWAF (2003) 'Stream flow reduction allocations', DWAF website: www.dwaf.gov.za/sfra/default.asp

DWAF (2005) *Towards a Framework for Water Allocation in South Africa*, Department of Water Affairs and Forestry, South Africa

Dye, PJ (1996) 'Climate, forest and streamflow relationships in South African afforested catchments', *Commonwealth Forestry Review*, 75 (1), pp31–38

Dye, PJ and Poulter, AG (1995) 'A field demonstration of the effect on streamflow of clearing invasive pine and wattle trees from a riparian zone', *South African Forestry Journal*, 173, pp27–30

Dyer, AJ (1961) 'Measurements of evaporation and heat transfer in the lower atmosphere by an automatic eddy correlation technique', *Quarterly Journal of the Royal Meteorological Society*, 87, pp401–412

EEB (2004) 'EU water policy, making the water framework directive work', EEB website: www.eeb.org/activities/water/11-WFD-implementation-quality-a-snapshot-EEB-May2004.pdf

EEB and WWF (2004) '"Tips and tricks" for water framework directive implementation', EEB website: www.eeb.org/publication/general.htm

Elkington, J (1997) *Cannibals With Forks*, Capstone Publishing Ltd, Oxford, UK

END (1998) 'Water abstraction decision deals savage blow to cost-benefit analysis', Report 278, Environmental Data Services Ltd, London

Enters, T (1998) 'Methods for the economic assessment of the on- and off-site impacts of soil erosion', *Issues in Sustainable Land Management* no 2, International Board for Soil Research and Management, Bangkok

Enters, T (1999) 'Incentives as policy instruments – key concepts and definitions', in Sanders, DW, Huszar, PC, Sombatpanit, S and Enters, T (eds) *Incentives in Soil and Water Conservation – From Theory to Practice*, Science Publishers, Enfield, New Hampshire

Enters, T (2000) 'Financial assessment of land management alternatives: practical guidelines for data collection and calculations of costs and benefits', IBSRAM Global Tool Kit Series no 2, Bangkok: International Board for Soil Research and Management, Bangkok

Environment Agency (2001) 'Water resources for the future: a summary of the strategy for England and Wales' EA website: www.environment-agency.gov.uk

Environment Agency (2002) 'Managing water abstraction: the catchment abstraction management strategy process', EA website, www.environment-agency.gov.uk/cams

EPA (United States Environment Protection Agency) (1992) 'Nonpoint source news – notes', January–February 1992, Issue 18, Tesrene Institute, Alexandra, USA, EPA website: www.epa.gov/owow/info/NewsNotes/issue18/nps18con.html

ERM and University of Newcastle upon Tyne (1997) 'Economic appraisal of the environmental costs and benefits of potential solutions to alleviate low flows in rivers', report to the Environment Agency, Exeter, UK

ETFRN (2004) 'Vote for water', European Tropical Forest Research Network website: www.etfrn.org/etfrn/resource/frppub/prunings2004low.pdf

EUROPA (2000) 'The EU Water Framework Directive – integrated river basin management for Europe' EUROPA website, http://europa.eu.int/comm/environment/water/water-framework/indexen.html

Evans, RS and Nolan, J (1989) 'A groundwater management strategy for salinity mitigation in Victorian riverine plain, Australia', *Groundwater Management: Quantity and Quality*, Proceedings of the Benidorm symposium, October 1989 (IAHS publication no 188), pp487–499

Ewel, JJ (1986) 'Invasibility: lessons from south Florida', in Mooney, HA and Drake, JA (eds) *Ecology of Biological Invasions of North America and Hawaii*, Springer-Verlag, New York,

Fahey, BD and Jackson, R (1997) 'Hydrological impacts of converting native forests and grasslands to pine plantations, South Island, New Zealand', *Agricultural and Forest Meteorology*, 84, pp69–82

Fahey, BD and Rowe, LK (1992) 'Land-use impacts', in Mosley, MP (ed) *Waters of New Zealand*, New Zealand Hydrological Society, pp265–284

Fahey, BD and Watson, AJ (1991) 'Hydrological impacts of converting tussock grasslands to pine plantation, Otago, New Zealand', *Journal of Hydrology (NZ)*, 30, pp1–15

Fairhead, J and Leach, M (1996) *Misreading the African Landscape*, Cambridge University Press

Falkenmark, M (1989) 'The massive water scarcity now threatening Africa: why isn't it being addressed?' *Ambio*, 25 (3), p216

Falkenmark, M (1995) 'Coping with Water Scarcity under Rapid Population Growth', Conference of SADC Ministers, Pretoria 23–24 November 1995

Falkenmark, M (2003) 'Water cycle and people: water for feeding humanity', *Land Use and Water Resources Research*, 3, 3.1–3.4

Falkenmark, M and Rockstrom, J (2004) *Balancing Water for Humans and Nature, The New Approach in Ecohydrology*, Earthscan, London

FAO (2004) Aquastat home page, FAO website: www.fao.org/ag/agl/aglw/aquastat/main/index.stm

Finlayson, W (1998) *Effects of Deforestation and of Tree Planting on the Hydrology of the Upper Mahaweli Catchment*, Mahaweli Authority of Sri Lanka, ISBN 955 9185 02 0

Focan, A and Fripiat, JJ (1953) 'Une anné d'observation de l'humidité du sol à Yangambi', *Bulletin des Séances de l'Institut Royal Colonial Belge* 24, pp971–984

Ford, ED and Deans, JD (1978) 'The effects of canopy structure, stemflow, throughfall and interception loss in a young Sitka spruce plantation', *Journal of Applied Ecology*, 15, pp905–917

Forest Trends (2003) 'Developing markets and payments for forest ecosystem services', Forest Trends website: www.forest-trends.org/keytrends/pdf/techbriefs/7forestservices.pdf

Forestry Commission (2002) *Climate Change: Impacts on UK Forests*, Forestry Commission, Edinburgh

Forsyth, T (1998) 'Mountain myths revisited: integrating natural and social environmental science', *Mountain Research and Development*, 18 (2), pp107–116

Forsyth, T (2002) *Critical Political Ecology: The Politics of Environmental Science*, Routledge,

Foster SSD and Grey, DRC (1997) 'Groundwater resources: balancing perspectives on key issues affecting supply and demand', *Journal of the Institution of Water and Environmental Management*, 11 June, p193

Foundation for Water Research (1996) *Assessing the Benefits of Surface Water Quality Improvements*, FR/CL 0005, Marlow

Galay, V (1985) 'Hindu-Kush Himalayan erosion and sedimentation in relation to dams', Paper presented at the International Workshop on Watershed Management in the Hindu Kush-Himalayan Region, Chengdu, ICIMOD, Kathmandu, p26

Gardiner, J (1992) 'Integrated catchment planning and source control: a view from the NRA', Paper presented at the Conflo–92 Conference, Oxford University

Gash, JHC and Stewart, JB (1977) 'The evaporation from Thetford Forest during 1975', *Journal of Hydrology*, 35, pp385–396

Gash, JHC, Wright, IR and Lloyd, CR (1980) 'Comparative estimates of interception loss from coniferous forests in Great Britain', *Journal of Hydrology*, 48, pp89–105

GDN (2004) 'Bridging research and policy', GDN website: www.gdnet.org/rapnet/

Geerts, B (2002) 'On the effects of irrigation and urbanisation on the annual range of monthly-mean temperatures', *Theoretical & Applied Climatology*, 72, pp157–163

Giambelluca, TW, Fox, J, Yarnasarn, S, Onibutr, P and Nullet, MA (1999) 'Dry-season radiation balance of land covers replacing forest in northern Thailand', *Agricultural and Forest Meteorology* 95, pp53–65

Giambelluca, TW, Nullet, M, Ziegler, AD and Tran, L (2000) 'Latent and sensible energy flux over deforested land surfaces in the eastern Amazon and northern Thailand', *Singapore Journal of Tropical Geography*, 21, pp107–130

Giambelluca, TW, Tran, LT, Ziegler, AD, Menard, TP and Nullet, MA (1996) 'Soil-vegetation-atmosphere processes: simulation and field measurement for deforested sites in northern Thailand', *Journal of Geophysical Research (Atmospheres)*, 101, pp25867–25885

Gibbons, DC (1986) 'The economic value of water', Resources for the Future, Environmental Economics Series 027, The World Bank, Washington, DC, USA

Gilmour, DA (1977) 'Logging and the environment, with particular reference to soil and stream protection in tropical rainforest situations', *FAO Conservation Guide* no 1, FAO, Rome, pp223–235

Gleick, P (1996) 'Basic water requirement for human activities: meeting basic needs', *Water International*, 21, pp83–92

Gleick, P (2000) *The World's Water 2000–2001: The Biennial Report on Freshwater Resources*. Island Press, Washington, DC

Gosain, AK and Sandhya Rao, (2004) 'Impact of climate change on the water sector', in Shukla, PR et al (eds) *Climate Change and India – Vulnerability Assessment and Adaptation*, Universities Press, pp159–192

Gosain, AK, Sandhya Rao and Debajit Basuray (2003) 'Assessment of vulnerability assessment and adaptation for water sector', *Proceedings of the Workshop on Vulnerability Assessment and Adaptation due to Climate Change on Indian Water Resources*, Coastal Zones and Human Health, Ministry of Environment and Forests, New Delhi, India, June 27–28, pp17–24

Gosain AK and Tripathi CN (2003) 'Climate change and agriculture in India – a case study', in Dash, SK and Rao P (eds) *Assessment of Climate Change in India and Mitigation Policies*, WWF-India, pp29–38

Greenwood, EAN (1992) 'Deforestation, revegetation, water balance and climate: an optimistic path through the plausible, impracticable and the controversial', *Advances in Bioclimatol*, 1, pp89-154

Greenwood, EAN, Klein, L, Beresford, JD and Watson, GD (1985) 'Differences in annual evaporation between grazed pasture and *Eucalyptus* species in plantations on a saline farm catchment', *Journal of Hydrology*, 78, pp261–278

Grove, R (1995) *Green Imperialism: Colonial Expansion, Tropical Island Edens and the Origins of Environmentalism, 1660–1860*, Cambridge University Press, Cambridge

Haigh, MJ, Jansky, LB and Hellin, J (2004) 'Headwater deforestation: a challenge for environmental management', *Global Environmental Change*, 14, pp51–61

Hall, RL and Calder, IR (1993) 'Drop size modification by forest canopies – measurements using a disdrometer', *Journal of Geophysical Research*, 90, pp465–470

Hall, RL, Calder, IR, Gunawardena, ERN and Rosier, PTW (1996a) 'Dependence of rainfall interception on drop size: 3. implementation and comparative performance of the stochastic model using data from a tropical site in Sri Lanka', *Journal of Hydrology*, 185, pp389–407

Hall, RL, Allen, SJ, Rosier, PTW, Smith, DM, Hodnett, MG, Roberts, JM, Hopkins, R, Davies, HN, Kinniburgh, DG and Goody, DC (1996b) 'Hydrological effects of short rotation coppice', Institute of Hydrology report to the Energy Technology Support Unit, IH Wallingford, UK

Halvorson, AD and Reule, CA (1980) 'Alfalfa for hydrologic control of saline seeps', *Soil Science Society of America Journal*, 44, pp370–374

Hamilton, LS (1987) 'What are the impacts of deforestation in the Himalayas on the Ganges-Brahmaputra lowlands and delta?: Relations between assumptions and facts', *Mountain Research and Development*, 7, pp256–263

Hansen, J, Sato, M, Lacis, A, Reudy, R, Tegen, I and Mathews, E (1998) 'Climate forcings in the industrial era', *Proceedings of the National Academy of Science*, no95, pp12753–12758

Hardin, G (1968) 'The tragedy of the commons', *Science*, 162, pp1243–1248

Harding, RJ, Hall, RL, Neal, C, Roberts, JM, Rosier, PTW and Kinniburgh, DK (1992) 'Hydrological impacts of broadleaf woodlands: implications for water use and water quality', Institute of Hydrology, British Geological Survey Project Report 115/03/ST and 115/04/ST for the National Rivers Authority, Institute of Hydrology, Wallingford, UK

Harvey, DR, and Willis, K (1997) 'The social economic value of land', Research report to MAFF University of Newcastle upon Tyne, Newcastle upon Tyne

Hassan, R, Berns, J, Chapman, A, Smith, R, Scott, D and Ntsaba, M (1995) *Economic Policies and the Environment in South Africa: The Case of Water Resources in Mpumalanga*, Division of Forest Science & Technology, CSIR, Pretoria, South Africa

Hassan RM, Olbrich B and Crafford JG (2002) 'Measuring total economic benefits from water in plantation forestry: application of quasi I-O framework to the crocodile catchment in South Africa', *South African Forestry Journal*, 193, pp5–14

Hellin, J and Haigh, MJ (2002a) 'Better land husbandry in Honduras: towards the new paradigm in conserving soil, water and productivity', *Land Degradation and Development*, 13 (2), pp233–250

Hellin, J and Haigh, MJ (2002b) 'Impact of *Vetivaria zizanioides* (vetiver grass) live barriers on maize production in Honduras', in Wang, L, Wu, D, Xianing, T and Nie, J (eds) *Technology and Method of Soil and Water Conservation*, 12th International Soil Conservation Organization (ISCO) Conference, Proceedings, 3. Ministry of Water Resources, P.R. China, Beijing, pp277–281, SWCC website: www.swcc.org.cn/isco2002/index.htm

Hewlett, JD (1982) 'Forests and floods in light of recent investigations', *Proceedings of the Canadian Hydrology Symposium*, 1982 June 14–15, Fredericton, New Brunswick. Associate Committee on Hydrology, National Research Council of Canada, pp543–559

Hewlett, JD and Bosch, JM (1984) 'The dependence of storm flows on rainfall intensity and vegetal cover in South Africa', *Journal of Hydrology*, 75, pp365–381

Hewlett, JD and Helvey, JD (1970) 'Effects of forest clearfelling on the storm hydrograph', *Water Resources Research*, 6 (3), pp768–782

Hewlett, JD and Hibbert, AR (1967) 'Factors affecting the response of small watersheds to precipitation in humid areas', *International Symposium on Forest Hydrology*, Pergamon Press, Oxford, pp275–290

Hingston, FJ and Gailitis, V (1976) 'The geographic variation of salt precipitated over Western Australia', *Australian Journal of Soil Research*, 14, pp319–335

HMSO (1995) *Rural England – A Nation Committed to a Living Countryside*, HMSO

Hofer, T (1998a) 'Floods in Bangladesh: a highland-lowland interaction?' *Geographica Bernensia*, G 48, Switzerland: University of Berne, p171

Hofer, T (1998b) 'Do land use changes in the Himalayas affect downstream flooding?: Traditional understanding and new evidences', *Memoirs of the Geological Society of India*, 19, pp119–141

Hope, RA, Porras, IT and Miranda, M (2005) 'Can markets for environmental services contribute to poverty reduction: A livelihoods analysis from Arenal, Costa Rica', Report under the DFID Forestry Research Programme, (project no. R8174)

House of Commons Environment Committee (1996) *1st Report, Session 1996–97: Water Conservation and Supply*, The Stationery Office, London

Howell, P, Lock, M and Cobbs, S (1988) *The Jonglei Canal: Impact and Opportunity*, Cambridge University Press, Cambridge

Hsia, YJ and Koh, CC (1982) 'Water yield resulting from clearcutting a small hardwood basin in central Taiwan', *International Association of Hydrological Sciences Publication*, 140, pp215–220

Hudson, JA and Gilman, K (1993) 'Long-term variability in the water balances of the Plynlimon catchments', *Journal of Hydrology*, 143, pp355–380

Hummel, FC (1992) 'Aspects of forest recreation in Western Europe', *Forestry*, 65 (3), pp237–251

Huq, S (2002) 'Applying sustainable development criteria to CDM Projects: the PCF experience', PCFplus Report, Washington, DC

Huttel, C (1975) 'Recherches sur l'écosystème de la forêt subéquatoriale de basse Côte d'Ivoire: IV Estimation du bilan hydrique', *La Terre et la Vie* 29, pp192–202

ICOLD (2001) About the WCD Report 'Dams and development', ICOLD website: http://www.icold-cigb.org/final.htm

ICRAF (1994) *Annual Report*, International Centre for Research in Agroforestry, Nairobi, Kenya

ICRAF (2004) 'Rewarding the upland poor for environmental services', RUPES website: www.worldagroforestry.org/sea/Networks/RUPES/index.asp

Institute of Civil Engineers (2001) 'Learning to live with rivers', Final report of the Institution of Civil Engineer's Presidential Commission to review the technical aspects of flood risk management in England and Wales, UK Institute of Civil Engineers, November 2001

Institute of Hydrology (1994) *Amazonia: Forest, Pasture and Climate – Results from ABRACOS*, Institute of Hydrology, Wallingford, UK

Intercarib SA and Nathan Associates (1996a) *Análisis del Uso Actual y Potencial de los Recursos Naturales de la Región Interoceánica*, Volumen 1 de 2, Informe I, Panamá: Intercarib S.A. y Nathan Associates, Inc.

Intercarib SA and Nathan Associates (1996b) *Análisis del Uso Actual y Potencial de los Recursos Naturales de la Región Interoceánica*, Volumen 2 de 2, Informe I, Panamá: Intercarib S.A. y Nathan Associates, Inc.

IPCC (2000), 'IPCC, 2000: emissions scenarios', A Special Report of Working Group III of the Intergovernmental Panel on Climate Change, Cambridge University Press, Cambridge

IUCN (1998) 'The green accounting initiative', IUCN website: http://iucn.org/places/usa/gai-activitiespage.html

IUCN (2000) 'Vision for water and nature, a world strategy for conservation and sustainable management of water resources in the 21st Century', IUCN, Geneva, IUCN website: www.iucn.org/webfiles/doc/WWRP/Publications/Vision/VisionWaterNature.pdf

IUCN, UNEP and WWF (1991) *Caring for the Earth: A Strategy for Sustainable Living*, Earthscan, London

Ives, JD (2005) *Himalayan Perceptions: Environmental Change and the Well-being of Mountain Peoples*, Routledge, London and New York

Ives, JD and Messerli, B (1989) *The Himalayan Dilemma: Reconciling Development and Conservation*, Routledge, London

Ives, JD, Messerli, B and Jansky, L (2002) 'Mountain research in South-Central Asia: an overview of 25 years of UNU's mountain project', *Global Environmental Research*, 6(1), pp59–71

James, P, Garratt, J, Nash, E and Calder, IR (2005) 'Models, myths and maps: the development of web-based GIS tools for scenario testing and the simulation of water resource and socio-economic impacts of changing land-use', to be submitted to *Land Use and Water Resources Research*

Jamieson, DG (ed) (1996) 'Special issue: decision-support systems', *Journal of Hydrology*, 177

Jamieson, DG and Fedra, K (1996) 'The "WaterWare" decision-support system for river-basin planning: 1. conceptual design', *Journal of Hydrology*, 177, pp163–175

Jewitt, GPW, Horan, MJC, Meier, KB and Schulze, RE (2000) 'A hydro-economic assessment of the benefits of clearing alien vegetation from riparian zones in a South African catchment', In *Proceedings of the 7th British Hydrological Society Symposium*, University of Newcastle, Newcastle upon Tyne, Sep 6–8, 2000

Jin, Y and Liu, X (2000) 'Prospects of CDM for promoting sustainable development in China – accelerating foreign technology investment and technology transfer', Prepared for the Working Group on Trade and Environment, China Council for International Cooperation on Environment and Development

Johnson, RC (1995) 'Effects of upland afforestation on water resources: the Balquhidder experiment 1981–1991', report no 116, Institute of Hydrology, Wallingford, UK

Jones, JA and Grant, GE (1996) 'Peak flow responses to clear-cutting and roads in small and large basins, western Cascades, Oregon', *Water Resources Research*, 32, pp959–974

Kabat, P, Claussen, M, Dirmeyer, PA, Gash, JHC, Bravo de Guenni, L, Meybeck, M, Pielke, RS, Vörösmarty, CJ, Hutjes, RWA and Lütkemeier, S (eds) (2004) *Vegetation, Water, Humans and the Climate*, Springer-Verlag, Berlin, Heidleberg, New York

Kaimowitz, D (1998) 'Myths about forests and floods', Polex Newsletter December 7, 1998, CIFOR website: www.cifor.cgiar.org/

Kaimowitz, D (2000) 'Useful myths and intractable truths: the politics of the link between forests and water in Central America', UNESCO Workshop on Forest – Water – People in the Humid Tropics, Kuala Lumpur, Malaysia, July 31–August 4

Kaimowitz, D (2004) 'Forests and water: a policy perspective', *Journal of Forest Research*, 9 (4), pp289–291

Kerr, A (2001) *Dogs and Demons: the Fall of Modern Japan*, Penguin Books, London

Kilsby, CG, Ewen, J, Sloan, WT and O'Connell, PE (1998) 'Modelling the hydrological impacts of climate change at a range of scales', *Proceedings of the Second International Conference on Climate and Water*, Espoo, Finland, vol 3, pp1402–1411

King, N, Letsaolo, A and Rapholo, B (2003) 'Developing markets for watershed protection services and improved livelihoods in South Africa', CSIR and IIED discussion paper

Kirby, C, Newson, MD and Gilman, K (1991) 'Plynlimon research: the first two decades', report no 109, Institute of Hydrology, Wallingford, UK

Kline, JR, Martin, JR, Jordan, CF and Koranda, JJ (1970) 'Measurement of transpiration in tropical trees with tritiated water', *Ecology*, 51, pp1068–1073

Kuraji, K (2005) 'Green dam – a concept based on myths of the benefit of forest on water', submitted to the Headwater 2005 conference in Bergen, 20–23 June 2005

Kutcher, G, McGurk, S and Gunaratnam, J (1992) 'China: Yellow River Basin', Water investment planning study presented at a World Bank irrigation and drainage seminar (cited by Winpenny, 1996)

La Marche, J and Lettenmair, DP (2001) 'Effects of forest roads on flood flows in the Deschutes River, Washington', *Earth Surface Processes and Landforms*, 26, pp115–134

Landefeld, J and Carson, CS (1994) 'Integrated economic and environmental satellite accounts', *Survey of Current Business*, April, pp33–49

Landell-Mills, N and Porras, IT (2001) *Silver Bullet or Fool's Gold?: A Global Review of Markets for Forest Environmental Services and Their Impacts on the Poor*, Instruments for sustainable private sector forestry series, International Institute for Environment and Development, London

Langford, KJ (1976) 'Change in yield of water following a bushfire in a forest of *Eucalyptus regnans*', *Journal of Hydrology*, 29, pp87–114

Law, F (1956) 'The effect of afforestation upon the water yield of water catchment areas', *Journal of the British Waterworks Association*, 38, pp489–494

Leach, M and Mearns, R (1996) 'Environmental change and policy – challenging received wisdom in Africa', *The Lie of the Land*, Villiers Publication, London, pp1–33

Ledger, DC (1975) 'The water balance of an exceptionally wet catchment area in West Africa', *Journal of Hydrology*, 24, pp207–214

Le Maitre, DC, Van Wilgen, BW, Chapman, RA and McKelly, DH (1996) 'Invasive plants and water resources in the Western Cape Province, South Africa: modelling the consequences of a lack of management', *Journal of Applied Ecology*, 33, pp161–172

Leopoldo, PR, Franken, W, Matsui, E and Salati, E (1982a) 'Estimation of evapotranspiration of 'terra firme' Amazonian forest', *Acta Amazonica*, 12, pp23–28 (in Portuguese with English summary)

Leopoldo, PR, Franken, W and Salati, E (1982b) 'Water balance of a small catchment area in 'terra firme' Amazonian forest', *Acta Amazonica*, 12, pp333–337 (in Portuguese with English summary)

Leyton, L, Reynolds, ERC and Thompson, FB (1967) 'Rainfall interception in forest and moorland', *International Symposium on Forest Hydrology*, Pergamon Press, Oxford, pp163–168

Lill, WS van, Kruger, FJ and Van Wyk, DB (1980) 'The effects of afforestation with *Eucalyptus grandis* Hill ex Maiden and *Pinus patula* Schlecht et Cham on streamflow from experimental catchments at Mokobulaan, Transvaal', *Journal of Hydrology*, 48, pp107–118

Lomborg, B (2001) *The Skeptical Environmentalist*, Cambridge University Press

Loucks DP and Gladwell, JS (1999) *Sustainability Criteria for Water Resource Systems*, Cambridge University Press, Cambridge

Low, KS and Goh, GC (1972) 'The water balance of five catchments in Selangor, West Malaysia', *Journal of Tropical Geography*, 35, pp60–66

Lu, SY, Cheng, JD, and Brooks, KN (2001) 'Managing forests for watershed protection in Taiwan', *Forest Ecology and Management*, 143, pp77–85

Lull, HW and Reinhart, KG (1972) *Forests and Floods in the Eastern United States*, United States Department of Agriculture, Forest Service Research Paper NE-226

Luvall, JR and Murphy, CE (1982) 'Evaluation of the tritiated water method for measurement of transpiration in young *Pinus taeda*', *Forest Science*, 28, pp5–16

Macumber, P (1990) 'The salinity problem: the Murray', Murray-Darling Basin Commission, Canberra, Australia, pp111–125

Malcolm, CV (1990) 'Saltland agronomy in Western Australia – an overview', in *Revegetation of Saline Land*, Proceedings of a workshop held at the Institute for Irrigation and Salinity Research, Tatura, Victoria, Australia

Marshall, JS and Palmer, WM (1948) 'The distribution of raindrops with size', *Journal of Meteorology*, 5, pp165–166

Marston, R, Kleinman, J and Miller, M (1996) 'Geomorphic and forest cover controls on monsoon flooding, central Nepal Himalaya', *Mountain Research and Development*, 16 (3), pp257–264

Martens, J (2005) 'Report of the UN Millennium project', FES Briefing Paper February 2005, Global Policy Forum website: www.globalpolicy.org/socecon/un/2005/02martens.pdf

McCulloch, JSG and Robinson, M (1993) 'History of forest hydrology', *Journal of Hydrology*, 150, pp189–126

Meadows, DH, Meadows, DL, Randers, J and Behrens, WW (1972) *The Limits to Growth; A Report for the Club of Rome's Project on the Predicament of Mankind*, Universe Books, New York, USA

Meadows, DH, Randers, J and Meadows, DL (2005) *Limits to Growth: The 30-Year Update*, Earthscan, London

Meher-Homji, VM (1980) 'Repercussions of deforestation on precipitation in Western Karnataka, India', *Archiv fur Meerol Geophys Biokl*, Series 28B, pp385–400

Milburn, A (1997) 'The need for a blue revolution in the fresh water sector', *Proceedings of the First World Water Forum*, Elsevier, Marrakesh, Morocco, pp37–43

Miller, BJ (1994) 'Soil water regimes of the Glendhu Experimental Catchments', unpublished dissertation, Department of Geography, University of Otago, New Zealand

Ministry of Water Resources, China (2003) Panel of Academics from the Chinese Academy of Science suggestions in relation to the SLCP, website: http://shuizheng.chinawater.com.cn/zcyj/20030208/200302080026.asp

Mitchell, JK and Bubenzer, GD (1980) 'Soil loss estimation', in Kirkby, MJ and Morgan, RPC (eds) *Soil Erosion*, John Wiley & Sons, Chichester, USA, pp17–62

Moench, M, Dixit, A, Janakarajan, S, Rathore, MS and Mudrakartha, S (2003) *The Fluid Mosaic: Water Governance in the Context of Variability, Uncertainty and Change: A Synthesis Paper*, Published by Nepal Water Conservation Foundation, Kathmandu, Nepal and the Institute for Social and Environmental Transition, Boulder, Colorado, USA, website: http://idrinfo.idrc.ca/archive/corpdocs/118400/100361/FluidMosaic1.pdf

Molden, D (1997) 'Accounting for water use and productivity', SWIM Paper 1, International Irrigation Management Institute, Colombo, Sri Lanka

Monteith, JL (1965) 'Evaporation and environment', *Symposium of the Society for Experimental Biology*, 19, pp205–234

Morgan, RPC, Morgan, DDV and Finney, HJ (1984) 'A predictive model for the assessment of soil erosion risk', *Journal of Agricultural Engineering Research*, 30, pp245–253

Mosely, MP (1988) *Climate Change Impacts – The Water Industry*, CH 20, Ministry for the Environment, Wellington, New Zealand

Myers, N (1986) 'Environmental repercussions of deforestation in the Himalaya', *Journal of World Forest Resource Management*, 2, pp63–72

Nacario-Castro, E (1997) *When the Well Runs Dry: A Civil Initiative in Watershed Planning and Management in the Philippines*, Ramon Aboritiz Foundation Inc, Cebu, Philippines

Nanko, K, Hotta N and Suzuki M (2004) 'The influence of forest species and atmospheric phenomena on the throughfall raindrop size distribution', in Sidle, R, Tani, M, Abdul Rahim, N and Taddese, TA (eds) *Forests and Water in Warm, Humid Asia*, Proceedings of the IUFRO Forest Hydrology Workshop, Kota Kinabalu, Malaysia, pp81–83

New Scientist (1988) 'The Tree that Caused a Riot', 18 February 1988

New Scientist (2004) 'The great flood myth', June

Newson, MD (1990) 'Forestry and water "good practice" and UK catchment policy', *Land Use Policy*, 7 (1), pp53–58

Newson, MD (1991) 'Catchment control and planning: emerging patterns of definition, policy and legislation in UK water management', *Land Use Policy*, 9 (1), pp9–15

Newson, MD (1992a) *Land, Water and Development*, Routledge, London

Newson, MD (1992b) 'Land and water: convergence, divergence and progress in UK policy', *Land Use Policy*, 9 (2), pp111–121

Newson, MD (1997) *Land, Water and Development*, Routledge, London

Newson, MD, Gardiner, J and Slater, S (1999) 'River catchment planning', in Acreman M (ed) *Changing Hydrology of the UK*, Routledge, pp315–344

Nisbet, T (2002) 'Implications of climate change: soil and water', Chapter 5 in *Climate Change: Impacts on UK Forests*, Forestry Commission, Edinburgh

O'Callaghan, JR (1995) 'NELUP: an introduction', *Journal of Environmental Planning and Management*, 38 (1), pp5-20,

O'Callaghan, JR (1996) *Land Use: The Interaction of Economics, Ecology and Hydrology*, Chapman & Hall, London

O'Connell, PE (1995) 'Capabilities and limitations of regional hydrological models', *Scenario Studies for the Rural Environment*, Kluwer Academic Publishers, The Netherlands, pp143–156

Olbrich, BW and Hassan, R (1999) 'A comparison of the economic efficiency of water use of plantations, irrigated sugarcane and sub-tropical fruits', A case study of the Crocodile River catchment, Mpumalanga Province, Report no 666/1/99, Water Research Commission, Pretoria

Oldeman, LR, Hakkeling, RTA and Sombroek, WG (1991) Second revised edition, *World Map of the Status of Human-Induced Soil Degradation: An Explanatory Note*, International Soil Reference and Information Centre, Wageningen, The Netherlands

Olszyczka, B (1979) 'Gamma-ray determinations of surface water storage and stem water content for coniferous forests', PhD thesis, Department of Applied Physics, University of Strathclyde

Omerod, RJ (1996) 'Information systems strategy development at Sainsbury's', *Journal of Operational Research Society*, 46, 277-293.''

Ong, CK (1996) 'A framework for quantifying the various effects of tree-crop interactions', in Ong, CK and Huxley, P (eds) *Tree-Crop Interactions*, CAB International, Wallingford, UK, pp1–23

Ong, CK, Black, CR, Marshall, F and Corlett, JE (1996) 'Principles of resource capture and utilization of light and water', in Ong, CK and Huxley, P (eds) *Tree-Crop Interactions*, CAB International, Wallingford, UK, pp73–158

Ong, CK, Odango, JCW, Marshall, F and Black, CR (1991) 'Water use by trees and crops. Five hypotheses', *Agroforestry Today*, April–June, pp7–10

Pallett, J (ed) (1997) *Sharing Water in Southern Africa*, Desert Research Foundation of Namibia, Windhoek, Namibia

Panayotou, T and Hupe, K (1996) 'Environmental impacts of structural adjustment programmes: synthesis and recommendations', UNEP, Environmental Economics Series, paper no 21, Nairobi, Kenya

Parkin, G, Ewen, J and O'Connell, PE (1999) 'SHETRAN: A coupled surface/subsurface modelling system for 3D water flow and sediment and solute transport in river basins', *American Society of Civil Engineers Journal of Hydrologic Engineering*, 5, pp250–258

Paris21 (2004) 'Partnership in statistics for development in the 21st Century', Paris 21 website: www.paris21.org/betterworld/setting.htm

Pearce, AJ (1986) 'Erosion and sedimentation' (working paper) Environment and Policy Institute, Honolulu, Hawaii

Penman, HL (1948) 'Natural evaporation from open water, bare soil and grass', *Proceedings of the Royal Society of London*, Series A, 193, pp120–145

Penman, HL (1963) 'Vegetation and hydrology', Technical Communication 53, Commonwealth Bureau of Soils, Harpenden, UK

Pereira, HC (1989) *Policy and Practice in the Management of Tropical Watersheds*, Westview Press, Colorado, USA

Pereira, HC, McCulloch, JSG, Dagg, M, Kerfoot, O, Hosegood, PH and Pratt, MAC (1962) 'Hydrological effects of changes in land use in some E. African catchment areas', *East African Agricultural and Forestry Journal*, 27 (Special Issue)

Perrot-Maître, D and Davis, P (2001) 'Case studies of markets and innovative financial mechanisms for water services from forests', Forest Trends website: /www.forest-trends.org/resources/pdf/casesWSofF.pdf

Pimentel, D and Houser, J (1997) 'Water resources: agriculture, the environment, and society', *Bioscience*, 47, pp97–107

Pinchot, G (1905) 'A primer of forestry, part II – practical forestry', Bulletin 24, Part II Bureau of Forestry, US Department of Agriculture, Washington, DC

PMCC (1999) *Panama Canal Watershed Monitoring Project*. Final Report. Panama: US Agency for International Development, Autoridad Nacional del Ambiente, Smithsonian Tropical Research Institute.

Poels, R (1987) 'Soils, water and nutrients in a forest ecosystem in Surinam', PhD thesis, Agricultural University, Wageningen, The Netherlands (cited by Bruijnzeel, 1990)

Polex (2004) 'China imports the world's forests' (August 27, 2004), CIFOR website: www.cifor.cgiar.org/docs/ref/polex/english/2004/index.htm

Price, DJ, Calder, IR and Johnson, RC (1995) 'Modelling the effect of upland afforestation on water resources', report to the Scottish Office, Institute of Hydrology, Wallingford, UK

Raiffa, H (1982) *The Art and Science of Negotiation*, Cambridge, Mass., Belknap Press of Harvard University Press

Rama Mohan Rao, MS, Batchelor, CH, James, AJ, Nagaraja, R, Seeley, J and Butterworth, JA (2003) *Andhra Pradesh Rural Livelihoods Programme Water Audit Report*, APRLP, Rajendranagar, Hyderabad 500 030, India, NRI website: www.nri.org/WSS-IWRM/Reports/APRLPwra/APRLPwrafullA4.pdf

Ranganathan, R and de Wit, CT (1996) 'Mixed cropping of annuals and woody perennials: an analytical approach to productivity and management', in Ong, CK and Huxley, P (eds) *Tree-Crop Interactions*, CAB International, Wallingford, UK, pp25–49

Rao, MR, Sharma, M and Ong, CK (1990) 'A study of the potential of hedgerow intercropping in semiarid India using a two-way systematic design', *Agroforestry Systems* 11, pp243–258

Rausser, G and Simon, L (1991) 'A noncooperative model of collective decision making: a multilateral bargaining approach', Working Paper no 618, Department of Agricultural and Resource Economics, University of California, Berkeley, p50

Rees, JA, Williams, S, Atkins, JP, Hammond, CJ and Trotter, SD (1993) 'Economics of water resource management', R&D note 128, National Rivers Authority, Bristol, UK

Reid, I and Parkinson, RJ (1984) 'The nature of the tile-drain outfall hydrograph in heavy clay soils', *Jounal of Hydrology*, 72, pp289–305

Roberts, JM (1977) 'The use of "tree cutting" techniques in the study of the water relations of mature *Pinus sylvestris* (L): The technique and survey of the results', *Journal of Experimental Botany*, 28, pp751–767

Roberts, JM (1978) 'The use of the 'tree cutting' technique in the study of the water relations of Norway spruce (*Picea abies* (L) Karst)', *Journal of Experimental Botany*, 29, pp465–471

Roberts, JM, Rosier, PTW and Smith, DM (2001) 'Effects of afforestation on chalk groundwater resources', Centre for Ecology and Hydrology, Wallingford

Robertson, G (1996) 'Saline lands in Australia: extent and predicted trends', *Proceedings of the 4th National Conference and Workshop on the Productive Use and Rehabilitation of Saline Lands*, Promaco Conventions PTY Ltd, Australia

Robinson, M, Cognard-Plancq, AL, Cosandev, C, David, J, Durande, P, Fuhrer, HW, Hall, R, Hendriques, MO, Marc, V, McCarthy, R, McDonnell, M, Martini, C, Nisbet, T, O'Deag, P, Rodgers, M and Zollner, A (2003) 'Studies of the impact of forests on peak flows and baseflows: a European perspective', *Forest Ecology and Management*, 186 (1–3), pp85–97

Robinson, M and Dupeyrat, A (2005) 'Effects of commercial forest felling on streamflow regimes at Plynlimon, mid-Wales', Hydrological Processes, 19(6), pp1213–1226

Robinson, M, Moore, RE and Blackie, JR (1997) 'From moorland to forest: the Coalburn Catchment Experiment', Institute of Hydrology and Environment Agency Report, Institute of Hydrology, Wallingford, UK

Robinson, M and Newson, MD (1986) 'Comparison of forest and moorland hydrology in an upland area with peat soils', *International Peat Journal*, I, pp49–68

Robinson, M, Ryder, EL and Ward, RC (1985) 'Influence on streamflow of field drainage in a small agricultural catchment', *Agricultural Water Management*, 10, pp145–158

Roche, MA (1982) 'Evapotranspiration réelle de la forêt amazonienne en Guyane, Cahiers ORSTOM', *série Hydrologie*, 19, pp37–44

Rockstrom, J (2003) 'Water for food and nature in drought-prone tropics: vapour shift in rain-fed agriculture', *Philosophical Transactions Royal Society London B*, 358, pp1997–2009

Rogers, P (1993) 'The value of cooperation in resolving international river basin disputes', *Natural Resources Forum*, May, pp117–131

Rogers, P (1997) 'Integrating water resources management with economic and social development', Paper prepared for the United Nations Department of Economic and Social Affairs Expert Group Meeting, 1998, Harare

Rogers, P, Bhatia, R and Huber, A (1998) 'Water as a social and economic good: how to put the principle into practice', Technical Advisory Committee, Background Paper no 4, Stockholm, Global Water Partnership

Rojas, M and Aylward, B (2003) 'What are we learning from experiences with markets for environmental services in Costa Rica?', A review and critique of the literature, IIED, London

Rosenhead, J (1996) 'What's the problem? An introduction to problem structuring methods', *Interfaces*, 26 (6), pp117–131

Rosier, PTW (1987) Personal communication

Rowntree, PR (1988) 'Review of general circulation models as a basis for predicting the effects of vegetation change on climate', in Reynolds, ERC and Thompson, FB (eds) *Forests, Climate and Hydrology: Regional Impacts*, Kefford Press, UK, pp162–193

Rubinstein, A (1982) 'Perfect equilibrium in a bargaining model', *Econometrica*, 50, pp97–109

Rutter, AJ (1963) 'Studies in the water relations of *Pinus sylvestris* in plantation conditions: measurements of rainfall and interception', *Journal of Ecology*, 51, pp191–203

Rutter, AJ, Kershaw, KA, Robins, PC and Morton, AJ (1971) 'A predictive model of rainfall interception in forests: derivation of the model from observations in a plantation of Corsican pine', *Agricultural Meteorology*, 9, pp367–384

Saberwal, VK (1997) 'Science and the desiccationist discourse of the 20th Century', *Environment and History*, 3, pp309–343

Sampson, RN and Scholes, RJ (2000) 'Additional human-induced activities – article 3.4.' in *Land Use, Land Use Change and Forestry*, IPCC Special Report, Cambridge University Press, pp180–248

Sanderson, RA (1998) 'VIPER – vegetation investigation program for ESA research',

Users Guide and Reference Manual, Ministry of Agriculture, Fisheries and Food, Nobel House, London

Sanderson, RA and Rushton, SP (1995) 'VEMM: predicting the effects of agricultural management and environmental conditions on semi-natural vegetation', *Computers and Electronics in Agriculture*, 12, pp237–247

Scoones, I (1998) 'Sustainable rural livelihoods: a framework for analysis', working paper no 72, Institute of Development Studies, Brighton, UK

Scott, DF (1993) 'The hydrological effects of fire in South African mountain catchments', *Journal of Hydrology*, 150, pp409–432

Scott, DF and Lesch, W (1997) 'Streamflow responses to afforestation with *Eucalyptus grandis* and *Pinus patula* and to felling in the Mokobulaan experimental catchments, South Africa', *Journal of Hydrology*, 199, pp360–377

Scott, DF and Smith, RE (1997) 'Preliminary empirical models to predict reduction in total and low flows resulting from afforestation', *Water SA*, 23, pp135–140

Scudder, T (2005) *The Future of Large Dams: Dealing with Social, Environmental, Institutional and Political Costs*, Earthscan, London

Seaman, SR (2004) 'Crumbling foundations: Japan's public works policies and democracy in the1990s', PhD Dissertation, Duke University

Seckler, D (1996) 'The new era of water resources management', research report 1, International Irrigation Management Institute, Colombo

Shah, T (2005) *Groundwater and Human Development: Challenges and Opportunities in Livelihoods and Environment Water Science and Technology*, 51,8, pp27–37

Sherriff, J (1996) 'Water resources management in England and Wales', in Howsam, P and Carter, R (eds) *Water Policy: Allocation and Management in Practice*, Proceedings of the International Conference on Water Policy, Cranfield University, E & FN Spon, London, pp68–69

Shiklomanov, IA (1999) 'Climate change hydrology and water resources: the work of the IPCC, 1988–1994', in Van Dam, JC (ed) *Impacts of Climate Change and Climate Variability on Hydrological Regimes*, UNESCO International Hydrology Series, Cambridge University Press, Cambridge, pp8–20

Shuttleworth, WJ (1988) 'Evaporation from Amazonian rainforest', *Proceedings of the Royal Society London B*, 233, pp321–346

Sikka, AK, Samra, JS, Sharda, VN, Samraj, P and Lakshmanan, V (2003) 'Low flow and high flow response to converting natural grassland into bluegum (*Eucalyptus globulus*) in Nilgiris watersheds of south India', *Journal of Hydrology*, 270 (1–2), pp12–26

Sillitoe, P, Dixon, P and Barr, J (1998) 'Indigenous knowledge research on the floodplains of Bangladesh: the search for a methodology', *Grassroots Voice*, 1 (1)

Simmons, P, Poulter, D and Hall, NH (1991) 'Management of irrigation water in the Murray-Darling Basin', discussion paper 91.6, Australian Bureau of Agricultural and Resource Economics, Canberra

Simon, HA (1969) *The Sciences of the Artificial*, MIT Press, Cambridge

Simon, L, Goodhue, R, Rausser, GC, Thoyer, S, Morardet, S and Rio, P (2003) 'Structure and power in multilateral negotiations: an application to French Water Policy', Submitted to the Giannini Foundation of Agricultural Economics Monograph series, website: http://are.berkeley.edu/~simon/workingpapers/adour.pdf

Simonovic, SP and Bender, MJ (1996) 'Collaborative planning-support system: an approach for determining evaluation criteria', *Journal of Hydrology*, 177, pp237–251

SIWI-IWMI (2004) *Water – More Nutrition Per Drop*, Stockholm International Water Institute. Stockholm, SIWI website: www.siwi.org

Slater, S, Newson, MD and Marvin, SJ (1995) 'Land use planning and the water sector: a review of development plans and catchment management plans', *Town Planning Review*, 65 (4), pp375–397

Smith, EJ (1997) 'The balance between public water supply and environmental needs', *Journal of the Institution of Water and Environment Management*, 11 February, pp8–13

Sombroek, W (2001) 'Spatial and temporal patterns of Amazon rainfall: consequences for the planning of agricultural occupation and the protection of primary forests', *Ambio*, 30 (7), pp388–396

Stebbing, EP (1937) 'The threat of the Sahara', *Journal of the Royal African Society*, Extra Supplement, May, pp3–35

Stocking, M (1996) 'Soil erosion – breaking new ground', in Leach, M and Mearns, R (eds) *The Lie of the Land*, Villiers Publication, London, pp140–154

Stocking, M and Murnaghan, N (2001) *Field Assessment of Land Degradation*, Earthscan, London

Streeter, BA (1997) 'Tradable rights for water abstraction', *Journal of the Institution of Water and Environment Management*, 11, August, pp277–281

Sutcliffe, JV (1974) 'A hydrological study of the Southern Sudd region of the Upper Nile', *Hydrological Sciences Bulletin*, 19, pp237–255

Swanston, DN (1991) 'Natural processes', in Meehan, WR (ed) *Influences of Forest and Rangeland Management on Salmonid Fishes and Their Habitats*, Special Publication 19, American Fisheries Society, Bethesda, Maryland, pp139–179

Swift, J (1996) 'Desertification – narratives, winners and losers', in Leach, M and Mearns, R (eds) *The Lie of the Land*, Villiers Publication, London, pp140–154

Tañada, CR (1997) CUSW (A) *Mobilizing for Sustainable Water Resources*, The Asian Institute of Management, Eugenio López Foundation, Cebu

Taylor, A and Patrick, M (1987) 'Looking at water through different eyes – the Maori perspective', *Soil and Water*, 23,4, pp22–24

Taylor, CH and Pearce, AJ (1982) 'Storm runoff processes and sub-catchment characteristics in a New Zealand hill country catchment', *Earth Surface Processes and Landforms*, 7, pp439–447

Thoyer, S, Morardet, S, Rio, P, Simon, L, Goodhue, R and Rausser, G (2001) 'A bargaining model to simulate negotiations between water users', *Journal of Artificial Societies and Social Simulation*, 4 (2), JASS website, http://www.soc.surrey.ac.uk//JASSS/4/2/6.html

Tiffen, M, Mortimore, M and Gichuki, F (1994) *More People, Less Erosion*, John Wiley & Sons Ltd, Chichester

Times of India (2004) August 1st, 'Everybody loves farm suicides', *Times of India* website: http://timesofindia.indiatimes.com/articleshow/msid-798223,prtpage-1.cms

Tolentino, AS (1996) 'Legal and institutional aspects of groundwater development in the Philippines', in Howsam, P and Carter, R (eds) *Water Policy: Allocation and Management in Practice*, Proceedings of the International Conference on Water Policy, Cranfield University, E & FN Spon, London, pp283–289

Tuinder, BA den, Calder, IR, Helland-Hansen, E, Koziorowski, G, Murungweni, Z, Chidenga, E, Mujuru, L, Mutamiri, J and Bowen-Williams, H (1995) *Programme for the Development of a National Water Resources Management Strategy (WRMS) for Zimbabwe*, Ministry of Lands and Water Resources, Government of Zimbabwe

Turton, A R (1999) 'Water scarcity and social adaptive capacity: towards an understanding of the social dynamics of managing water scarcity in developing countries', MEWREW Occasional Paper 9, Water Issues Study Group, Department of Geography, SOAS University of London

UN (United Nations) (2000) Millennium Declaration, Resolution adopted by the General Assembly 55/2, New York, UN website: www.un.org/millennium/

UN (2001) 'Road map towards the implementation of the United Nations Millennium Declaration', New York, UN website: www.un.org/documents/ga/docs/56/a56326.pdf

UNCED (United Nations Conference on Environment and Development) (1992) 'Agenda 21 & the UNCED proceedings', *Proceedings of the UNCED Conference, Rio de Janeiro, Brazil*, 1992, UNCED, New York

UNDPCSD (United Nations Department for Policy Coordination and Sustainable Development) (1997) *Comprehensive Assessment of the Freshwater Resources of the World*, Commission on Sustainable Development, New York

UNDG (United Nations Development Group) (2003) 'Indicators for monitoring the millennium goals, development definitions, rationale, concepts and sources', United Nations, New York, Development Goals website: www.developmentgoals.org/Aboutthegoals.htm

UNDP (United Nations Development Programme) (2000) *Human Development Report, Human Rights and Human Development*, Oxford University Press

UNDP (2004) *Human Development Report*, UNDP website: http://hdr.undp.org/reports/global/2004/

UNESCO (United Nations Educational, Scientific and Cultural Organization) (2003) *United Nations World Development Report* UNESCO website: www.unesco.org/water/wwap/wwdr/

UNFCCC (United Nations Framework Convention on Climate Change) (2004) UNFCCC website: http://cdm.unfccc.int/

UNMP (United Nations Millennium Project) (2005) 'Investing in development: A practical plan to achieve the Millennium Development Goals', New York, UNMP website: www.unmillenniumproject.org

UNSCED (United Nations World Commission on Environment and Development) (1987) *Our Common Future*, Oxford University Press, New York

US Department of Agricultural Research Service (1961) 'A universal equation for predicting rainfall-erosion losses', USDA-ARS special report, pp22–26

USDA Forest Service (2000) *Forest Roads: A Synthesis of Scientific Information*, edited by Gucinski, H, Furniss, MF, Ziemer, RR and Brookes, MH, USDA Forest Service road management website: www.fs.fed.us/eng/road_mgt/documents.shtml

Van Lill, WS, Kruger, FJ and Van Wyk, DB (1980) 'The effects of afforestation with *Eucalyptus grandis* Hill ex Maiden and *Pinus patula* Schlecht. Et Cham. on streamflow from experimental catchments at Mokobulaan, Transvaal', *Journal of Hydrology*, 48, pp107–118

van Noordwijk, M, Chandler, FJC and Tomich, TP (2005) 'An introduction to the conceptual basis of RUPES', RUPES website: http://www.worldagroforestry.org/sea/Networks/RUPES/abs_13.htm

van Noordwijk, M, Lawson, G, Soumaré, A, Groot, JJR and Hairiah, K (1996) 'Root distribution of trees and crops: competition and/or complementarity', in Ong, CK and Huxley, P (eds) *Tree-crop Interactions*, CAB International, Wallingford, pp319–364

Versfeld, DB (1981) 'Overland flow on small plots at the Jonkershoek Forestry Research Station', *South African Forestry Journal*, 119, pp35-40

Versfeld, DB and Wilgen, BW van (1986) 'Impacts of woody aliens on ecosystem properties', in Macdonald, IAW, Kruger, FJ and Ferrar, AA (eds) *The Ecology and Control of Biological Invasions in South Africa*, Oxford University Press, Cape Town, South Africa, pp239–246

Walker, DH and Sinclair, FL (1998) 'Acquiring qualitative knowledge about complex agroecosystems; part 2: formal representation', *Agricultural Systems*, 56 (3), pp365–386

Walling, DE (1983) 'The sediment delivery problem', *Journal of Hydrology*, 65, pp209–237

Waugh, J (1992) 'Introduction: hydrology in New Zealand', in Mosley, MP (ed) *Waters of New Zealand*, New Zealand Hydrological Society, pp1–12

Index